ECONOCLASTS

Culture of Enterprise series

Previously published:

Human Goods, Economic Evils:
A Moral Approach to the Dismal Science
Edward Hadas

Third Ways:
How Bulgarian Greens, Swedish Housewives, and
Beer-Swilling Englishmen Created Family-Centered Economies—
and Why They Disappeared
Allan C. Carlson

A Path of Our Own:
An Andean Village and Tomorrow's Economy of Values
Adam K. Webb

ECONOCLASTS

*The Rebels Who Sparked the
Supply-Side Revolution and Restored
American Prosperity*

Brian Domitrovic

Wilmington, Delaware

The Culture of Enterprise series is supported by a grant from the John Templeton Foundation. *Econoclasts* was also supported by a grant from the Searle Freedom Trust. The Intercollegiate Studies Institute gratefully acknowledges this support.

Domitrovic, Brian.

    Econoclasts : the rebels who sparked the supply-side revolution and restored American prosperity / Brian Domitrovic.

        p. cm. —(Culture of enterprise series ; 3)
        Includes bibliographical references and index.

        ISBN 978-1-935191-25-4 (cloth : alk. paper)

        1. Supply-side economics—United States. 2. United States—Economic policy—20th century. 3. United States—Economic conditions—20th century. I. Title.

        HC106.8.D664   2009
        330.15'540973—dc22   2009019785

ISI Books
Intercollegiate Studies Institute
3901 Centerville Road
Wilmington, DE 19807-1938
www.isibooks.org

Manufactured in the United States of America

To Brother Robert Wilsbach, f.s.c.
pro Deo et Patria

Against all this, Youth, . . .
Youth with its insupportable sweetness,
Its fierce necessity,
Its sharp desire. . . .
—WILLA CATHER, *O Pioneers!*

CONTENTS

PART I

"A RECONSIDERATION OF THE TWENTIETH CENTURY"

1

THAT '70S FUNK

Two-thirds into the 1964 movie *Goldfinger*, in a scene set at a Kentucky stud farm, James Bond and the archvillain Auric Goldfinger discuss, as they sip mint juleps, Goldfinger's plan to invade Fort Knox. Bond, Goldfinger's prisoner at the moment, cannot see how the plan will succeed. "I've worked out a few statistics," he chides Goldfinger:

> Fifteen billion dollars in gold bullion weighs ten thousand, five hundred tons. Sixty men would take twelve days to load it onto two hundred trucks. Now, at the most, you're going to have two hours before the army, navy, air force, marines move in and make you put it back.
>
> GOLDFINGER: Who mentioned anything about removing it?
> *(Bond stops drinking. . . .)*
> GOLDFINGER: Is the julep tart enough for you?
> BOND: *(thinking)* You plan to break into the world's largest bank, but not to steal anything. Why?
> GOLDFINGER: Go on, Mister Bond.
> BOND: Mister Ling, the Red Chinese agent at the factory. He's a specialist in nuclear fission.—But of course!
> *(Goldfinger smiles back at him.)*
> BOND: His government's given you a bomb!

GOLDFINGER: I prefer to call it an atomic device. It's small, but particularly dirty.

BOND: Cobalt and iodine?

GOLDFINGER: Precisely.

BOND: Well, if you explode it in Fort Knox, the entire gold supply of the United States will be radioactive for . . . fifty-seven years!

GOLDFINGER: Fifty-eight, to be exact.

BOND: I apologize, Goldfinger. It's an inspired deal. They get what they want—economic chaos in the West—and the value of your gold increases many times.

GOLDFINGER: I conservatively estimate ten times.[1]

In the movie, the flaw in the plan is that Bond is able to woo Goldfinger's paramour, Pussy Galore, and with her help thwart the explosion—when there are 007 seconds left on the timer, of course.

In real life, the flaw would have been to suppose there was a need for it in the first place. In 1964, there would have been no reason whatsoever for a master criminal with a gold hoard to irradiate Fort Knox. One needed only a little foresight. For in due time, the desired effects would come about of their own accord.

Goldfinger wanted the value of his personal gold hoard to increase, "conservatively," by ten times. The price of gold was $35 per ounce in 1964. If Goldfinger had been able to wait ten years, he would have found gold at $175 per ounce. Had he sat tight for fifteen years, until 1979, he would have hit his target of $350 per ounce. Yet that ten-bagger of a price was a mere breather. Over the next year, 1979–80, gold more than doubled again, hitting the stratospheric mark of $800 per ounce. Goldfinger's estimate had been conservative, indeed. And no nuclear explosions needed.

Goldfinger's "Red Chinese" co-conspirators had wanted their bomb to cause economic chaos in the West. And that, too, came about in short order, especially in the United States.

From 1968 to 1982, the American stock market nearly collapsed, with the Dow Jones Industrial Average losing 70 percent of its real value. The "misery index," whereby the inflation and unemployment percentages are represented as real numbers and summed, blew through the historical trend of 6 to 8 early in the 1970s, plateaued in the double digits, then hit unlucky 21 in 1980. Interest rates also hit 21—no misprint, a 21 percent prime rate—in 1980. Big things that never were supposed to go bust declared default: New York City, most famously, and Chrysler, too.[2]

Those who tried to wait out the chaos by saving money were brutally punished. The greatest inflation since the Revolutionary War destroyed the value of funds in bank accounts, the stock market was in free fall, and municipal-bond issuers missed payments. The only thing to do was to stash cash in commodities. Because commodities originated in the geologic history of the planet, commodities had a guaranteed delimitation of supply and therefore could hold their value against inflation. Gold, oil, gas, land—everything in the commodities universe went up in the 1970s, as if everything in the earth had suddenly become impossibly scarce.

Internationally, a new, odd order dawned. Not only was the United States going through a time of troubles. So were its allies, the entire capitalist First World. The economies of Western Europe and Japan, which had expanded at high rates in the quarter century after World War II and owed so much of their success to trade with the United States, slowed down in the 1970s and began to approximate the grim conditions of the leading nation: minimal growth, inflation, unemployment. It was verification of the old saw: When the United States sneezes, the rest of the world catches a cold.

Yet the Soviet Union saw itself aggrandized as never before. This came as a shock, even to the Soviets. Before the 1970s, the USSR had had insuperable difficulties creating things of economic value, especially products for export. The Soviet economy was a few years from certain collapse when suddenly, in the 1970s, it was handed a new lease on life.[3]

The Soviet Union, by dint of its landmass, happened to harbor an inordinate stock of commodities. In the 1970s, because of the chaos in their own economies, the capitalist nations hauled all sorts of mining, drilling, and piping equipment into the USSR. This enabled the great commodity patrimony of North Asia—oil, gas, gold, metals—to be sold to external markets. People in the capitalist world were thereby unburdened of holding their own, rapidly devaluing currencies.[4]

The Soviets raked in a lot of cash—mainly dollars, for what that was worth. This allowed them to generously support Marxist movements in Latin America, Africa, Southeast Asia, and Afghanistan. Arab oil sheiks, too, saw their fortunes awake from the sleep of centuries; the price of petroleum followed gold in lockstep from 1973 to 1982.

It was a weird time, to say the least. It was particularly puzzling and dispiriting to Americans. The halcyon "postwar prosperity" that had characterized the years after 1945 seemed to be in terminal decline, a brilliant flash that had lasted for an unusually long spell and had given the illusion of permanence. It was hard to put a finger on what was going on. Sometime around 1970, everything started getting worse, economically, with every passing year.

Inflation had hitherto been rather unheard of. Now it reliably hit double-digit rates. Unemployment, theoretically a converse of inflation, and low since World War II, went up, too. Unemployment in tandem with inflation led to the popularization of a new word, "stagflation" (from stagnation plus inflation), which was on everyone's lips by the last days of disco. Entrepreneurial start-ups, the very stuff of the "American dream," passed from the scene; venture capital was waiting things out in commodities.

Then there was the government. Throughout the long 1970s, the federal government of the United States preoccupied itself with such things as fixing prices, pressuring labor unions not to take wage increases, begging shoppers to rein in their spending, mistaking nominal for real income in the tax code, adding regulations, running deficits, reneging on the pledge to exchange dollars for gold, and gobbling up an ever-increasing share of the gross national product (GNP). This was no ordinary downturn. It was not exactly the Great Depression, either. And it was hard to pin the blame on "business" for what was going on.

What *was* going on? Unsure, President Gerald Ford asked the nation in 1974 to "Whip Inflation Now." He also asked people to sign a pledge saying that they would refrain from new purchases, in the interest of holding down inflation. Five years later, with the same problems still raging, a memo to President Jimmy Carter proposed that America had gotten caught up in a "malaise," whatever that meant. In other words, leadership was befuddled. It had no answers.[5]

What Happened?
The most important fact about the economic funk of the 1970s, the stagflation decade, was that it stopped. For ten long years and then some, as stocks plummeted, inflation roared, unemployment climbed, municipalities defaulted, capital fled, and devalued dollars were shoved into the hands of Marxist despots and playboy oil sheiks, it was not necessarily reasonable to suppose that the new confounding reality would ever come to an end. After all, the last time the United States had experienced a protracted economic mess, the Great

Depression, it had taken the titanic event of World War II to bring about something like a reversion to the old status quo. Without some such unwanted catastrophe, would not the economic misfortunes of the 1970s endure forever?

It was only natural, therefore, that the battle cry that emerged was that of the 1976 movie *Network*: "I'm mad as hell, and I'm not going to take it anymore." Remarkably, a few people listened and took action. For come a certain juncture, and to virtually everyone's astonishment and pleasure, stagflation up and vanished from the scene.[6]

The economic history of the United States since World War II is one of the most stunning chapters in the modern history of nations. Easily the largest economy in the world in 1945—in that year accounting for fully half of world output—the United States, over the following sixty-two years, sustained a rate of growth unmatched in the annals of developed countries. The *trend* of United States growth from 1945 to 2007 was 3.3 percent per year. Developing countries—including Japan and those of Western Europe that had to climb out of the postwar rubble—exceeded this rate, often by large margins. But once the rapidly developing countries neared the output level, per capita, enjoyed in the United States, they could not sustain what the United States could. The U.S. rate of 3.3 percent per year is one and a half times the growth rate Japan and Western Europe have registered since 1982. This means that over the quarter century beginning in that year, America became fully one-third richer than the next richest economies, whereas a generation ago, these economies were at parity.[7]

This is a profoundly important fact. The unique ability of the United States to maintain a historic rate of economic growth over the long term is what has rendered this nation the world's lone "hyperpower," as the French are sometimes wont to say. The only other realistic aspirants to that status— China and India—will not see economic maturity for decades to come.

The exception to this trend was the stagflation decade: 1973–82. That was the only period since 1945 when the United States did not sustain a 3.3 percent rate of growth. Before and after this interregnum, there was the odd, mild recession or boom year, but the growth trend remained at that steady, historically high rate. Growth was 3.3 percent from 1945 to 1973, and it was 3.3 percent from 1982 to 2007. From 1973 to 1982, however, growth averaged 1.8 percent, essentially the rate that prevailed in the long semi-stasis that gripped Japan and Western Europe in the 1990s and the first decade of the twenty-first century.[8]

That the 1973–82 period proved to be an interregnum—as opposed to an augury of a new trend—is the most significant fact in the postwar economic history of the United States. It is also, from a geostrategic perspective, one of the most significant facts in the postwar history of world power relations.

Two pertinent questions immediately arise: What caused the stagflation decade, and what stopped it? The many florid answers to and contentious debates about these questions are too extensive to summarize. But one thing can be said for certain. Supply-side economics, which came into being in the midst of this period, made its raison d'être these two tasks: determining why the slowdown was occurring, and devising ways to stop it. As fortune—or was it ambition, shrewdness, and determination?—had it, the movement came to power and implemented policy immediately prior to the end of the interregnum.

Supply-side economics was the centerpiece of the most consequential revolution in economic policy since the New Deal: "Reaganomics," as it was for a brief period of time derisively known. Its policy prescription was to undertake tax cuts and to stabilize the means of exchange, that is to say, the dollar. The prima facie case that supply-side economics, implemented as it was in the early Reagan years, played a causative role in the most significant development in American—arguably world—economic history of recent times is so strong that if we were not curious about it, we would be intellectually negligent.

Our curiosity will be met by curiosities. For supply-side economics was by all accounts a renegade, maverick movement driven largely by figures removed from or hostile to the economic establishments in academia, Washington, journalism, and business. In the early 1970s, all of two academic economists could be counted in the movement. The rest of the first "supply-siders" comprised a subterranean crew of journalists, congressional staffers, and business forecasters, many of whom were unknown to the others, and virtually all of whom were under forty years of age. That these people assigned themselves the task of solving the nation's economic problems, seized the policy initiative, and were present at the reestablishment of postwar prosperity is a fascinating story. And it is almost completely unknown.

It is a story that we must know, however, if we are to understand the foundation of the summit of prosperity and geopolitical significance that America has occupied until very recently, and from which America appears to be stepping away in the current financial crisis. It is a story that has inspired a great many places around the globe to emulation, as countries yearning for First World development, from China to Lithuania, have shown by enlisting those who were the young supply-side heroes of the 1970s and 1980s as policy advisors. And it is a story that has not been properly told, because supply-side economics has attracted a philistine opposition jealous of its accomplishments and bent on misrepresenting its record.

Wall Street Journeys

That '70s Show nostalgia aside, the 1970s were failing years, years of the worst long-term economic performance in all of American history exclusive of the Great Depression. This funk had commensurate effects on the nation's psyche. It was no accident that during this time Bill Gates could get his company out of the garage only by signing a contract with IBM. If you did not have a lifeline to the biggest, richest, most established companies, like IBM, you could forget about raising capital. With marginal income-tax rates upwards of 70 percent, there was no such thing as venture capital. And then, despite this advantage, the IBMs of the world engaged in mass layoffs. Was America facing an apocalypse?

Books said yes. Paul Ehrlich's *Population Bomb* (1968) and William and Paul Paddock's *Famine 1975!* (1967) initiated one of the trendiest genres of the stagflation era's nonfiction: the economic alarm. Both of these books (which were discussed incessantly in the 1970s) predicted worldwide famine, including in the United States, within a few years. A more understated entry in the genre became the decade's alarmist book par excellence: *Limits to Growth* (1972), the report of a concerned group of academics and businesspeople who called themselves "The Club of Rome." *Limits* contended that resources were running out as population expanded, that the abundant postwar prosperity was proving to be a mirage, and that the world would have to get used to dramatically lower living standards.[9]

Scholars validated the basic points. Christopher Lasch, in *The Culture of Narcissism* (1979), made the eminently reasonable observation that high and certain inflation was causing harm to the psyche and habits of Americans. Inflation made people spend now, forgo saving, and despair about preparing for the future. For Lasch, inflation prompted a new kind of inwardness, a "narcissism," about getting one's due now—essentially the same conclusion that prompted Tom Wolfe to call the 1970s the "Me Decade." Lester Thurow, in an immensely discussed book of 1980, *The Zero-Sum Society,* made a similar point in arguing that the nation now felt that no solution to stagflation could be concocted without some constituency in the nation losing in a very big way.

The 1970s are also justly known for end-of-all-things movies: *Airport, The Swarm, Soylent Green, King Kong,* and *Network.* Yet Americans are a plucky people, and they are particularly fond of their prosperity. They were not going to be led like lambs to the slaughter into impoverishment, idleness, and mediocrity, no matter the economic conditions and the counsel from intellectuals. So in the 1970s, there were also David-versus-Goliath cultural megahits that brought emotional sustenance and a new reservoir of resolve to the nation, above all the movie *Star Wars* (1977) and the book *Watership Down* (1972).

On Wall Street, the 1970s began with misplaced enthusiasm. The market went up 50 percent from 1970 to 1972, with the Dow peaking over 1,000 in early 1973, a level not breached again for a decade. It was the era of the "Nifty Fifty" stocks, of big companies—especially McDonald's and Polaroid—that seemed able to predict the next consumer fad. The surge in the market attracted new, young investment talent to Wall Street. Soon, however, stocks went into their long hibernation, even declining once inflation was accounted for. Many of the young traders and brokers who had come to Wall Street in the heady days of the late 1960s and early 1970s drifted away to other pursuits (including a successful stockbroker named Martha Stewart).

The people who remained on Wall Street after 1973 necessarily were determined to stick things out. It was much harder for the young than for the old. Wall Streeters who had begun their careers in the 1940s, '50s, or even '60s had already piled up fortunes and could satisfy themselves with hedging in the 1970s. Aspiring traders and brokers, in contrast, had no fortunes to hedge. They had come to Wall Street to make money, and now the economic horizon seemed to be permanently bleak. However much profit could conceivably be made playing gold, oil, commodities, currencies, and short sales, it paled in comparison to how much could be made in the context of a general economic boom, the kind that the nation had enjoyed for a full generation after World War II.

This particular condition gave rise to the first supply-side activists. It was not accidental that the torchbearers of the supply-side revolution would, almost to a person, be young and under forty (and sometimes under thirty). The prospect of permanent stagflation greatly frustrated the young and ambitious. It was one thing for the representatives of "old money" to intone about the necessity of adjusting to "diminished expectations," a standard 1970s catchphrase. It was quite another for an unmade young person impatient for worldly success to concede to that adjustment.

The venue where supply-side economics first took shape, where gathered the first revolutionaries who would stage the quixotic and ultimately successful quest against stagflation, was a restaurant in lower Manhattan in the shadow of the American Stock Exchange. The Amex was New York's junior stock exchange, and in 1974, Michael 1 was a rookery for Wall Street's junior varsity. The restaurant (now gone) drew a crowd of "Wall Street wannabes," the "financial world's young and maybe rising." Young brokers and traders would congregate there, settle into "tufted leather armchairs [and] lean back with a drink or pitch forward into a porterhouse," fire up their imaginations, and "virtually see the deals of future years"—all this in the words of supply-side economics' first impresario, Robert L. Bartley, the editorial-page editor of the *Wall Street Journal.* In 1974, he turned thirty-seven.[10]

Bartley, who had taken an executive post at the *Journal* two years earlier, began to notice that a number of young people on Wall Street, as well as a few people in the academic and governmental economics establishments, were impatient with the new talk about "diminished expectations." The new idiom seemed to be a rationalization for not diagnosing and solving problems and getting on with the business of success. Curious, Bartley started to corral some of these skeptics for discussions, and they held their gatherings over martinis and steaks at Michael 1.

The Wall Streeters came and talked, but soon everyone kept quiet and listened to two surpassingly interesting men, both academics. Robert A. Mundell, forty-two, was an economics professor who had just come to Columbia; he was accompanied by his friend from his days at the University of Chicago, the thirty-four-year-old Arthur B. Laffer. Mundell was something to behold. He had long hair worn below his shoulders, yet he was half again the age of any living hippie. Not only was he curious to look at; he was also hard to listen to. One of the reasons silence fell when Mundell spoke at Michael 1 was that you could barely tell what he was saying. He talked in a low slur, glided over syllables, sprinkled in wry remarks, and had a Canadian accent to boot. Future opponents of supply-side economics would say that these characteristics merely testified to Mundell's rumored alcoholism.[11]

Laffer was clean-cut, a little pudgy, and had the wide smile and flair of a showman. After he became famous during the 1978 California tax revolt, reporters would interview him at his spread near Los Angeles while exotic birds came and perched on his shoulder. In 1985, Peggy Noonan, a doe-eyed presidential speechwriter, met Laffer at the White House as he was telling a dirty joke. She supposed he was "an advance man."[12]

At Michael 1, the good buddies Mundell and Laffer were prodded to share their ideas by the man who had brought them there—not Bartley, but Bartley's employee at the *Journal* editorial page, Jude Wanniski. In 1972, Bartley had tried to make his first hire a young George Will, but Will had turned him down. So Bartley had taken a flier on another green Washington reporter, Wanniski, who was then thirty-six. Wanniski had come from Las Vegas, and he looked it, with his hot rods, black shirts with white ties, and showgirl wife. Wanniski loved books, big ideas, and interviewing people. He knew nothing about economics. In 1971, while working for a political circular in Washington, he got to know Laffer, who was serving on President Nixon's budget staff while completing his Ph.D. Laffer told Wanniski about his Chicago friend Mundell, and in the midst of the 1974 stagflation, Wanniski often connected with the pair in New York. The gatherings at Michael 1 began.

When Wanniski began prompting Mundell and Laffer, this is what they said. They said that the stagflation crisis was certainly not the fault of business, capitalism, or "the system," as many supposed. Rather, the stagflation crisis had originated with government. Stagflation had come about because of two large governmental intrusions into the economy. First, the government had taken to destabilizing the means of exchange—the dollar—by printing it with abandon. This was the origin of inflation. Second, the government had jacked up tax rates, particularly on income that people earned as they got richer. This brought about disincentives to work and poisoned the well of capital formation. Unemployment was the necessary result.

The solution to the problem was clear: stabilize the dollar and cut taxes. Instantly—and Mundell felt it would be instantly—inflation would disappear and productive employment would soar. The diagnosis and solution were both clear and simple. The logic, evidence, and proof that underlay them were complex and the product of intensive research and reflection. Mundell and Laffer held sway at Michael 1 for good reason: what they had to say was penetrating and impressive, the stuff of experts.

Mundell was already an imposing figure in academic economics. He had written papers in the early 1960s, before he was thirty, about currencies and exchange rates that charted entirely new ground. Everyone soon realized that this work would one day win him the Nobel Prize (and it did, in 1999). Laffer was his most dedicated, brilliant, and opportunistic pupil. Together, they offered a plan for escaping the stagflation crisis for good. Nobody called it "supply-side economics" at the time. The best Wanniski could do for a name was "The Mundell-Laffer Hypothesis."[13]

Despite Mundell's scholarly eminence, and despite Laffer's high position in the federal government, the two found it rough going whenever they tried to convince the lions of economics of their views on stagflation. Beginning in the years of the Kennedy administration, Mundell found his advice to the Federal Reserve—keep it simple and stabilize the price level—attacked by high-ranking insiders at the Fed and at the International Monetary Fund. When in 1971 he gave a lecture in Italy that fully predicted the economic woes of the coming decade and offered a clear path of escape, the lecture and its offprint went uncited and ignored by everyone except those in the nascent supply-side demimonde.[14]

As for Laffer, he had been sucker-punched by the dean of American economics, Paul Samuelson of MIT, in a blow that might have ruined other careers. Laffer (working for Nixon) made some bold Mundellian predictions in 1971 about the American economy that in due time were borne out perfectly. But before Laffer could be vindicated by history, Samuelson took to the rostrum at the University of Chicago economics department to give a talk that ridiculed Laffer's forecast and mocked the man's name: "Why They Are Laughing at Laffer" was the title of the talk. As Martin Anderson, a former Samuelson student, observed years later:

> Samuelson's lecture, especially its title, was cruel and reckless, and could cripple and destroy the intellectual reputation of a young scholar. And it was an uneven match. . . . Samuelson's brilliant mind and knack for razor sharp analysis was hidden behind a homely face. His small, pointed ears gave him an extraterrestrial look. . . . He was small, and he was mean. But what he did to Laffer that day in Chicago, even by academic standards of morality, was an extraordinary example of intellectual bullying.[15]

Merciless criticism followed supply-side economics wherever it went. This was so not only in its years of ascendancy during the Reagan administration, when such criticism could be laughed off, but from the very beginning, when the embryo of supply-side economics could have been snuffed out of existence

once and for all. It is not difficult to imagine why those who occupied prominent establishment positions were quick to ignore Mundell's insights or to try
to sabotage Laffer's career. Mundell and Laffer were telling the state's paladins
of economics to stop doing what they were doing—indeed, to stop doing things
in general. Mundell's advice to the Federal Reserve was to abandon its mis-
conception that the bank could do anything useful in the economy outside of
maintaining a stable price level. If it felt it could help out the employment situation, smooth out booms and busts, or provide "fairness" lacking in the private
banking sector, it was wrong on all counts. Any deviation from maintaining
stable prices would cause problems (specifically inflation and an international
currency crisis) of the greatest magnitude. Mundell's advice to the Fed was to
aspire to be as good as the gold standard of yore, when the fixed price of the
yellow metal kept consumer prices steady (and when growth boomed). Fed
policy should be so transparent in this regard that one should say of it what
Mundell once said of the gold standard: "So simple a monkey could run it."[16]

The problem, by the 1960s and 1970s, was that central banking had attracted
not low-wattage brains, not humanoids or monkeys, but some of the most cre-
dentialed and proud economics Ph.D.s in the world. It was hard for such men to
believe that monetary policy should be so transparent and simple that anyone
could supervise it, that it only required watching the most obvious statistic—the
price index—and increasing the dollar supply when it went down and doing the
reverse when it went up. Central banking had become one of the highest callings
in the economics universe, the top of the heap, with Fed chairmen in particular
"elevated in prestige beyond all reason," as Robert D. Novak once lamented.[17]

John F. Kennedy disliked his own Fed, but he did plenty to encourage the
idea that top government servants were incredible intellects, people whose
rare and special talents were needed in order for the country to function at
a sophisticated, late-industrial level. On his death, his wife, Jacqueline, only
magnified this impression by referring to the departed administration as
"Camelot." Mundell rejected such romanticism when he informed the Federal
Reserve that its mission was workmanlike, the stuff of technicians. That the
Federal Reserve was in no position to take Mundell's advice became clear
in 1978, when Congress passed the Humphrey-Hawkins Act. The new law
implied that the Federal Reserve had the responsibility of seeing to it that the
nation had full employment.[18]

As for the government's masters of taxation, Mundell and Laffer essentially told them, too, to simplify in the extreme. Taxes, high and complicated

in the stagflation era, should be low and simple, and they should stay that way. As Laffer never tired of repeating, "The more you tax something, the less you get of it." In the 1970s, income derived from work was being taxed at a particularly acute rate. So was entrepreneurialism (in the form of a capital-gains tax that in many cases, incredibly, exceeded 100 percent). The inevitable result was that fewer people chose to work, or to undertake new ventures that would create jobs—a perfect recipe for unemployment.

Mundell and Laffer knew that taxation was a political issue, the knottiest perhaps there was. In the 1960s and 1970s, academic economists had been dignifying progressively high taxes, calling them "stabilizing" and such, but the Michael 1 contingent knew that the problem lay with Congress. The tax code was a series of unrelated, unrecognizable addenda that was primarily the result of decades of deal-cutting. The code had not swallowed the economy whole before the 1970s only because inflation had been low. Once inflation hit, new statutes were required for taxes not to be raised automatically and stratospherically.[19]

Here the culprit was "bracket creep." The brutal logic is as follows. If the federal tax rate at $10,000 of income rises from 33 percent to 50 percent, everyone making $10,000 whose income keeps up with inflation will see his tax rates rise accordingly. If there is 100 percent inflation over a decade, and one's salary increases from $10,000 to $20,000, one has seen no real gain in income. But there is a shocking change in the tax bill. Instead of paying a third of the same real income in taxes, one pays a third on the first half of income, and half on the next. Bracket creep thus became the great scourge of the taxpayer in the stagflation years. As Mundell once observed, "No wonder the stock market hated inflation!"[20]

In order for taxes not automatically to be raised in the inflationary 1970s (as they were in point of fact), statutes had to be changed. Academic suasion and the counsel of experts, even if forthcoming, were likely to have little effect in this regard. True Washington operators, acting in the innards of Congress, were needed in order to push through tax-reform legislation. Fortuitously, just as the Michael 1 dinners were becoming regular in the mid-1970s, a group of tenacious congressional staffers dedicated to bringing about major tax reductions was independently congealing in Washington.

The main figure in this group was Norman B. Ture, an old Washington hand who had served on the staff of the Joint Economic Committee of Congress (JEC) and worked on the huge JFK tax-cut bills of the 1960s. In the late

1960s and early 1970s, Ture had continued to preach the necessity of cutting taxes and arresting bracket creep. His message finally gained some traction in 1974, when a young congressman named Jack Kemp, only recently retired from a rather distinguished career in professional football, introduced a bill calling for tax cuts. The bill was reworked by staffers, particularly Paul Craig Roberts (then thirty-five), who would in time become as synonymous with supply-side economics as Mundell and Laffer.

Initially, the fight for tax reduction and against bracket creep was made only by members of Congress at a far remove from leadership—Kemp, of Buffalo, New York; Marjorie Holt of Maryland; John Rousselot of California; William A. Steiger of Wisconsin; and Senators Orrin Hatch (class of 1977) of Utah and William Roth of Delaware. There was scant support from the White House. At no moment in the 1970s did a president propose a real lowering of tax rates. The only genuine tax cut presidentially signed into law during the decade was the capital-gains reduction portion of the Revenue Act of 1978, and President Carter hated having to sign that bill.

Nonetheless, the backbenchers, their staffs, and a large contingent from the JEC soldiered away at tax-cut bills. In time, powerful members became converts to the cause. The crucial moment came in early 1980, when Lloyd Bentsen, the Democratic senator from Texas who was widely regarded as a leading presidential or vice-presidential candidate, made himself the lead signatory on a JEC report urging tax cuts.

Even so, President Carter fatefully refused to call for tax cuts as part of his reelection campaign, even with both the misery index and the prime lending rate heading toward 21. This left the tax-cut cause, championed by a senior Senate Democrat, to be taken up by Carter's Republican challenger. Ronald Reagan endorsed the revised form of Kemp's 1974 bill (now called Kemp-Roth) and won the election resoundingly. The supply-side 1980s were soon under way. Reagan cut taxes, the Fed tightened money, and the quarter century after 1982 saw growth back on the high line that had held before the '70s. Postwar prosperity had not been a mirage after all.

Paradigm Shift

The term "supply-side economics" originally was a term of mild derision. It was coined by an opponent, economist Herbert Stein, father of the comic actor Ben Stein (who makes fun of supply-side economics in *Ferris Bueller's Day Off*). An advisor to Presidents Nixon and Ford, and a Republican worried about budget deficits, Herbert Stein was the first to speak of "supply-side fiscalists." He did so in a 1976 remark to a group of established Washington economists in which he referred, bemusedly, to the upstart staffers behind the Kemp bill. Word about the remark got to Wanniski, and he liked it. He tweaked the term, making "supply-side fiscalists" "supply-side economics," and by 1980 everyone in the movement was using the latter term to describe their views. In the meantime, the New York and Washington supply-siders had discovered each other and begun coordinating strategy. The *Wall Street Journal* popularized the movement's ideas, and in 1978 Paul Craig Roberts replaced Wanniski at the *Journal.*[21]

"Supply-side economics" was an apt term. It captured the essence of the Mundell-Laffer hypothesis as well as of the congressional tax-cut movement. Both sought to make it easier to work and produce and thereby end stagflation.

Inflation was by its very nature an inducement not to work and produce, but to consume and demand, to spend one's dollars before they devalued. By the late 1970s, this truth had become obvious to many observers, including noneconomists such as Christopher Lasch. If inflation were conquered, people would once again seek to gain income through work and investment, because in the context of stable prices, income holds its value. Yet this work and investment would be for naught if new income were then confiscated by taxes. Hence, a monetary policy aimed at maintaining stable prices, coupled with a tax policy aimed at stimulating personal initiative, was necessary in order to cure stagflation. Together, such policies would increase what was produced—that is, "supply"—in the economy.

The term "supply-side economics" implies an obverse, "demand-side economics." And this label, too, was apt. Demand-side economics, or "Keynesianism" (after the British economist John Maynard Keynes, in his Great Depression phase), holds that modern economic problems stem from people not spending enough money. In consumerist America, this always has been a bizarre premise. Nonetheless, Keynesianism dominated American economic thought in the 1960s and 1970s. In the Keynesian teaching, inflation is tolerable because it means that people are out there spending money vigorously, demanding, pushing up prices in the name of growth. Taxes, in turn, take money from people who might save it rather than spend it, and then give that money to the one entity that will assuredly spend it: government.

Oddly enough, the greatest Keynesian of the postwar era was Richard Nixon. "I am now a Keynesian in economics," he told the *New York Times* in 1971 as he prepared to devalue the dollar. Stagflation had been gathering implicitly in the demand-side policies of the late 1960s, but it was Nixon who charged ahead with the finishing touches. When he devalued the dollar (that is, when he removed its link to gold in August 1971), Nixon knew that inflation would likely ensue. But inflation can be a good thing, under Keynesian logic, because it solves unemployment, and unemployment had been creeping upward since the late 1960s. Moreover, Nixon had a trick that would keep inflation bottled up: price controls. He saw before him the best of both worlds. He would have low unemployment as a result of inflationary pressures, and low inflation because of price controls.[22]

Nixon's wild Keynesian gambit gave the nation exactly what one of Nixon's own budget lieutenants, Laffer, had predicted: "runaway inflation in the United States." The price controls were a failure. They discouraged businesses from supplying and hence employing workers, and prices eluded the controls anyway, shooting up significantly. Stagflation soon arrived. Nixon's successors, Ford and Carter, failed to grasp what was going on. Both tried to salvage the hopeless system of price controls, both refused to address bracket creep in the tax code, and both were helpless in the face of the falling dollar.[23]

There will be much to say about the justice of using the term "Keynesianism" as a proxy for the policy mind-set that became discredited with the great stagflation. Surely, Keynes (who died in 1946) would have been appalled at a great many things undertaken in his name in the 1970s. Keynes was a great changer of his own mind, ready to admit mistakes and reformulate his own theories from scratch if they proved faulty in practice. In this regard, Keynes compares favorably with Einstein. As Keynes famously once said after an opponent accused him of equivocation: "When the facts change, I change my mind. What do you do, sir?"[24]

Moreover, Keynes loved to solve problems. Over his long career, the Western economies provided plenty of them—the currency and supply crises of the Great War, the roaring chaos of the 1920s, the Great Depression, the domestic penury (in Britain) that accompanied World War II. At every great economic juncture, Keynes modified his previous views to account for changed conditions. This is one reason that his collected writings run for thirty volumes. It is fanciful to imagine that Keynes would have tolerated the "Keynesian" lassitude toward stagflation that formed the inertia against which supply-side economics strove mightily to apply momentum.

A question that has long dogged the economics profession, stocked as it has always been with big brains, is why in heaven's name it could not heal itself in the 1970s and cure stagflation forthwith. Why was it necessary for a crew of subterranean revolutionaries, the supply-siders, some of whom lacked rudimentary economics credentials, to come on the scene, fight all sorts of intransigence, and capture a rising political figure's imagination for the health of the American economy to be restored? Could not mainstream economics have righted the ship?

Academic economics, for its part, fully realized in the 1970s that it bore responsibility both for creating stagflation and for being slow with a solution. During the stagflation years, academic economics said, in effect, that it would figure out a solution, but it needed time—a lot of time. There were new, un-Keynesian paradigm shifts under way in the universities, including monetarism and "rational choice theory," but it remained unclear precisely how these innovations should influence policy. Economics, like most academic disciplines, is a deliberative thing, its intellectual revolutions passing through stages of theory, proof, recommendations, implementations, and reflections, with years of real experience gobbled up in the meantime. If a pressing problem requires a new kind of solution, academic economics by nature will not be able immediately to furnish it.[25]

The dean of the profession, the man universally regarded as the voice of academic economics in the 1970s, Robert E. Lucas of the University of Chicago, confided all this to his colleagues in a remarkable statement in 1978:

> In the present decade, the U.S. economy has undergone its first major depression since the 1930s, to the accompaniment of inflation rates in excess of 10 percent per annum. . . . These events did not arise from a reactionary reversion to "classical" principles of tight money and balanced budgets. On the contrary, they were accompanied by massive government budget deficits and high rates of monetary expansion, policies which, although bearing an admitted risk of inflation, promised according to modern Keynesian doctrine rapid real growth and low rates of unemployment.
>
> That these predictions were wildly incorrect and that the doctrine on which they were based is fundamentally flawed are now simple matters of fact, involving no novelties in economic theory. The task now facing contemporary students of the business cycle is to sort through the wreckage, determining which features of that remarkable

intellectual event called the Keynesian Revolution can be salvaged and put to good use and which others must be discarded. Though it is far from clear what the outcome of this process will be, it is already evident that it will necessarily involve the reopening of basic issues in monetary economics which have been viewed since the thirties as "closed" and the reevaluation of every aspect of the institutional framework within which monetary and fiscal policy is formulated in the advanced countries.

In other words, academic economics had enabled stagflation. Everything must now be rethought—the discipline needed a revolution.[26]

Unfortunately, by 1978 the nation's patience was already wearing thin. Prices had increased 87 percent in a decade, the misery index was pushing 15, savings in bank accounts and the stock market were being viciously denuded by inflation, and the tax code remained oblivious to all that was going on. The nation had no time to wait for the definitive solutions of economic scholarship, which might not come until Keynes's famous long term, the one in which "we are all dead."

In the Great Depression the nation had endured its one extended bout with penury. From 1933 on, however, President Franklin D. Roosevelt gave the inescapable impression that he was trying with the utmost strenuousness to solve the problem. Though unemployment never went below 14 percent in the 1930s, the nation was confident that under FDR serious things were being done to get the nation moving again. During the great stagflation of the 1970s, leadership responded in a very different manner. Economists pleaded guilty and asked for more time. Politicians, including three presidents, either offered discredited solutions or suggested that the nation get used to the new reality. Thus, it was only natural that America responded enthusiastically to the supply-side renegades who exuded confidence and regarded the problem as eminently solvable.[27]

Today, at a generation's remove from the implementation of supply-side policy in the early Reagan years, one thing is certain: *The economic results that supply-side economics foresaw at the time did in fact come to pass.* From 1982 until 2007, growth was at exactly the mark set in the halcyon post–World War II period. The Big Five of macroeconomic statistics—gross domestic product (GDP), GDP per capita, inflation, unemployment, and interest rates—were on the same, prosperous level between 1982 and 2007 as they had been in the pre-stagflation postwar period. This is not to say that supply-side economics was solely responsible for the restoration of the American economy to its historical (and historic) trend. Supply-siders did not start the businesses, introduce the technologies, or develop the markets that impelled the post-1982 boom. What they did do, however, was to instruct the government precisely how to get out of the way of an economy full of potential.

The Toreador and the Bull

In academic economics today, the causes of the second postwar boom have become a hot topic. If one historical explanation has gained precedence in the academic domain, it is that deriving from the "New Growth Theory" of Stanford economic theorist Paul Romer. Romer has argued, convincingly, that the remarkable technological advances of the past generation, coupled with equally remarkable ideas about how to make use of these advances in products and the marketplace, are responsible for the new long boom. The New Growth Theory does not give primacy of place to changes in macroeconomic management, and for good reason: the revolution in technology, products, and markets of the last quarter century occurred because of the economic activity of millions of creative persons—not because of the actions of officials at the Federal Reserve or Treasury. Microsoft, Apple, Intel, Dell, Google, Wal-Mart, Home Depot, McCaw Cellular, Starbucks, Goldman Sachs, Federal Express—such corporate big dogs of the 1980s, 1990s, and 2000s have compelling, even epic, success stories.[28]

The impact of supply-side economics remains somewhat unrecognized for another reason, too. Supply-side economics was never meant to be a sustained policy requiring annual recalibration and reapplication. In this it differed markedly from Keynesianism. Rather, the purpose of supply-side economics was to solve one problem: the great stagflation. Establishing a high trend line of American growth was the furthest thing from the supply-siders' minds in the 1970s, because that trend line already had been definitively established by history. The matter at hand was *re*establishing the trend line. Once that discrete matter was dealt with, the supply-siders would allow the economy to achieve its healthy potential.

A metaphor from Spanish bullfighting can perhaps illustrate the point. A toreador can bring a muscular, energetic bull to a full stop simply by lowering a sash in front of its face. With the lifting of the sash, the bull surges forward for as long as it desires. So it was with the American economy. Bursting with potential in the 1970s, a potential inherent in the nation's inherited entrepreneurial knack and enhanced by a technological revolution of historic dimensions, the American economy found itself held in place by a master wielding a sash. The master was the government, the sash a destabilized means of exchange and a punitive tax system. Come a certain juncture, the sash was lifted, the bull surged, and the lore since has been of the energy, dynamism, and insatiability of the bull.

Such is as it should be, perhaps. But the story of how the prodigious American economy was once shackled and then became free is of renewed and crucial importance in the context of the contemporary global financial crisis. As a new presidential administration implements demand-side policies discredited only a little more than a generation ago, the insights of supply-side economics take on fresh significance. Fortunately, on the one hand, supply-side doctrines are now to be found scattered throughout the toolbox of present-day economics. As Bruce Bartlett, one of the supply-side congressional staffers in the 1970s, has successfully argued, supply-side economics has deeply affected standard economic teachings about incentives, taxes, monetary policy, and growth. Furthermore, five figures associated with supply-side economics have become Nobel laureates. (The academic prince of supply-side economics, Mundell, won the prize in 1999. The other laureates are Robert Lucas, whose respect for supply-side economics intensified greatly after the nation's economic performance in the 1980s; Lucas's student Edward Prescott; the pioneer of the "public choice" school of economics, James Buchanan; and Milton Friedman, who endorsed supply-side economics heartily as a Reagan advisor in the 1980s.)[29]

On the other hand, there remains the strange matter of supply-side economics' opposition. Originally, in the 1970s, such opposition as there was tended to be Olympian and condescending. With the passing of the decades, which seemed to vindicate so comprehensively everything the supply-siders had argued for, the opposition has become lowbrow, vengeful, and desperate.

The first sharp jab at supply-side economics, once it became a serious political force, came from George H. W. Bush, who notoriously commented on the 1980 campaign trail that his rival Ronald Reagan endorsed "voodoo economics." The implication was that the numbers did not add up. The "voodoo economics" charge was a political loser for Bush, but the epithet lived on. During the Reagan presidency (1981–89) it was constantly invoked in discussions of "Reaganomics." More recently, the tone of anti-supply-side economics invective has come to make Bush's attack seem positively genteel. Here is a sampling of the ire recently leveled against supply-side economics:

PAUL KRUGMAN: "Biologist Richard Dawkins has argued famously that ideas spread from mind to mind much as viruses spread from host to host. . . . Supply-side economics, then, is like one of those African viruses that, however often it may be eradicated from the settled areas, is always out there in the bush, waiting for new victims."

JONATHAN CHAIT, of the *New Republic*: "The [*Wall Street*] *Journal* is perhaps most famous for helping to transform supply-side economics from a crank doctrine ridiculed by mainstream economists and rejected by Washington policymakers into a crank doctrine ridiculed by mainstream economists yet embraced by Washington policymakers."

MICHAEL KINSLEY, of *Slate*: "The classic Republican phony theory is, of course, supply-side economics . . . , based more on theory than evidence."

DAILY KOS: "The Greatest Lie ever told the last thirty some odd years is the theory of supply-side economics."

From various blogs:

"Supply-side economics has become the triumph of faith over evidence."

"When you think Supply-Side Economists you need to think Mob Lawyers and not honest participants in an economic debate."

"Long-term fiscal responsibility does not reduce long-term growth even if the Laugher [*sic*] Curve nitwits . . . keep saying it does."

"Isn't Prescott an actual supply-side economist? This is like being an Intelligent Design biologist. It can't be ignorance; it's got to be dishonesty."

The Prescott referred to in the last comment is Edward Prescott, the 2004 economics Nobelist.[30]

At least until the economic crisis of 2008–9, such mean-spirited opposition to supply-side economics, which is almost solely a product of the punditry and blogosphere, had not had a great deal of practical effect. Reagan's tax and monetary revolution was the consensus on which the nation predicated its long prosperous march for a quarter century. Internationally, supply-side economics became tremendously popular and successful. Perhaps the greatest effect the criticism had was in the realm of recollection. The history of supply-side economics is generally misunderstood when not unknown, and not only in blogs, but within journalism and scholarship as well. It certainly has never been told with the weight of archival sources brought to bear; hence the present book.

Academic historians harbor a mistaken assumption that they have actually performed scholarship on supply-side economics. As a current textbook written by college professors and covering American history since 1945 puts it:

> Although historians' evaluations of Reagan . . . have softened over time, . . . their views of Reaganomics have remained almost uniformly unfavorable. . . . Where disagreements have emerged, they have been modest, ranging from how great a drag on the economy the Reagan deficits and accumulating debt were, to how much Reagan's tax cuts contributed to the growth in inequality. . . . Few of the countless fond recollections of Reagan's presidency after his death in 2004 even mentioned the supply-side economics with which Reagan was so closely associated, so overwhelming is the evidence for this doctrine's failure to achieve the goals its advocates proclaimed.

We should not be misled by such comments. For historians, as historians, have said approximately *nothing* about the history of supply-side economics.[31]

History distinguishes itself from the other disciplines by its special method, pioneered by Herodotus: it reads the sources that are contemporaneous and pertinent to the event in question. There are *primary* sources, those left by witnesses that testify to the event in question; *secondary* sources, or "secondary literature," works of historical narrative and analysis that historians compose on the basis of primary sources; and *tertiary* sources, summaries of the secondary literature. It is debatable whether there is even one single work of secondary literature in academic history concerning supply-side economics. There does not appear to be one scholarly book or article, in the discipline of history, on the topic of supply-side economics that has called on and analyzed the relevant complement of primary sources. Not one.[32]

This is not to say that historians have refrained from making remarks and passing judgment on supply-side economics. The tertiary literature is full of such stuff. As in the above excerpt, textbooks written by historians have all sorts of things to say about supply-side economics. So too do the essayistic monographs (a subset of tertiary literature), which historians write as they strive to give impressions of an era on the basis of selective, largely nonarchival evidence.[33]

The very existence of all the tertiary literature on the subject of supply-side economics does not accord with the usual practice of the discipline of history. According to the usual practice, historians first endeavor to command the source base as they struggle to compose works of secondary literature. Once a significant complement of secondary literature is produced, tertiary literature arises to synthesize it. In the case of supply-side economics, there is tertiary literature in the absence of secondary literature. This means that there are historians who speak and write, at times volubly, about supply-side economics despite the nonexistence of scholarship founded on primary sources.[34]

What, then, is the basis of historians' commentaries on supply-side economics? Opinion, mostly. Historians may have interesting opinions about many things—particularly things having to do with history—but until they practice their disciplinary specialty and read the pertinent sources, their opinions are not informed as historians' opinions can and should be. The great Swiss historian Jacob Burckhardt put it this way to his students: "You must know how to read"—sources, that is. We may have to offer a prefatory emendation to Burckhardt in the case of historians and supply-side economics: "The first task of historians is to recognize that they are obliged to read sources."[35]

Perhaps these points would be not so piquant if the sources pertaining to the history of supply-side economics in archives and libraries were not so vast and rich. Arthur Laffer's curriculum vitae runs for forty-four pages. Robert Mundell's includes hundreds of entries. Yet virtually none of the written work of these two founders of supply-side economics has appeared as evidence in historical scholarship. Historians have left undisturbed the publicly available archival collections of Robert Bartley, Jude Wanniski, Jack Kemp, William A. Steiger, and Reagan's Treasury Department. Historians have left largely unconsulted the incredibly detailed and revelatory memoirs of Bartley and

Paul Craig Roberts, as well as the run of *Wall Street Journal* editorials from the 1970s through the Reagan years. The early history of supply-side economics is now half a century into the past. It is high time for history to be true to its responsibilities and to consider in a methodologically serious way the momentous phenomenon that was supply-side economics.

Another reason that supply-side economics is important is that it proved one of the most consequential political forces in the United States' third century. Not only did the implementation of supply-side economics under Reagan coincide with a restoration of America's prosperity and premier geopolitical position. It also attended the greatest domestic political realignment of recent history: the reestablishment of the Republican Party as a national, indeed populist, political force in all branches and levels of government. It did not have to be that way. Democrats advocated supply-side economics until Reagan endorsed it. Had they stuck to their original position, perhaps the realignment would not have occurred.

Finally, there are practical consequences to letting supply-side economics go unchronicled and thereby misunderstood. The financial and economic crisis that has gripped the country in 2008 and 2009 happened after half a decade's worth of loose money from the Federal Reserve and under the prospect of a tax increase. Public officials (and others) have been quick to compare the crisis with that of the 1930s. Strangely, they have not thought to make comparisons closer in time: to the colossal 1974–75 or 1980–81 stagflation recessions, for example. But then, there are no histories of these latter crises, and in particular no histories of what solved them.

The nasty swoon of the financial markets and the hesitation of the economy as a whole during this crisis mean that economic actors are looking to the political process for clues about what the future holds. That future may well be determined by how well we understand the supply-side attainments of three decades ago.

2

1913

The founders [of the Federal Reserve] did not intend to create either a central bank or a powerful institution; had they been able to foresee the future accurately, they might not have acted.

    —ALLAN H. MELTZER, *A History of the Federal Reserve, Vol. 1: 1913–1951*

One of Professor Mundell's most outstanding qualities is his ability to delve into the past to foretell the future.

    —BERNARDO PAÚL, foreword to Robert Mundell's "International Monetary Dilemma," 1979

At one point during the December 1999 Nobel Prize award banquet in Stockholm, Robert Mundell was asked to say a few words. He obliged, but he could not resist also bursting into song. He was the award banquet honoree, and he had given a stunning formal address two days before. Enough of the monotone of the spoken lecture; it was time to belt out "My Way," as made famous by Frank Sinatra. There was no karaoke machine, let alone a band, to make straight the irregularities of the singer. And while drink had served wondrously to lubricate the voice of the Chairman of the Board, the same could not be said for Mundell.[1]

Those attending the award banquet who knew him—Robert Bartley, for example—were aware that Mundell liked to cut loose. What were those 1970s dinners at Michael 1, after all, but a series of very nice nights out on the town? As for academic conferences, Mundell had long before grown tired of the tedious things; so he had decided to host them himself, and in a way that would ensure swell times. In 1969, as a hedge against inflation, Mundell had bought an old palazzo in Siena. There people would come and talk economics, while taking care to eat, drink, and be merry in ways that Italian Renaissance men and women would have approved.[2]

But Mundell was belting out "My Way" that Nobel night in Stockholm not only because he liked to cut loose, or because he patronized all things Canadian, the lyricist of "My Way" being Ontario's own Paul Anka. Mundell was singing an ode to his own career.

What Mundell had done his way, of course, was to champion supply-side economics. The static he had received from his fellow professors had been easy enough to take—Mundell had been first among these equals since the 1960s. When he had first fully elaborated the supply-side solution of tax cuts coupled with stable money—at a 1971 talk in Italy—he was about to win a Guggenheim, the fellowship reserved for the fixed stars of the intellectual firmament. As for the pundits, when they belittled supply-side economics in their increasingly trashy way, they always seemed to make sure to avoid casting much criticism in Mundell's direction. The scribbling opponents of supply-side economics viscerally understood that Mundell was too formidable an intellect to take on directly. Better to go after the lesser figures.[3]

In any case, Mundell was determined to keep swimming against the current. In his formal Nobel address, he had revealed that he was striving to do more than merely revolutionize economics. He was now interested in revolutionizing history as well.

Mundell gave his address the rather immodest title of "A Reconsideration of the Twentieth Century." The title was apposite. For Mundell proposed to be the first to identify certain things that had given the century its distinctiveness—a distinctiveness that had taken the form of depression, totalitarianism, war, and genocide on the one hand, and bouts of freedom and prosperity on the other. Few outside of Mundell's own circle, including professional historians, had encountered such an interpretation before. The address would prove daring, original, ambitious—and plausible. "I will argue," said Mundell, "that many of the political changes in the century have been caused by little-understood perturbations in the international monetary system, while these in turn have been a consequence of the rise of the

United States and mistakes of its financial arm, the Federal Reserve System." "Had the price of gold been raised in the late 1920s," Mundell continued with characteristic boldness, "or, alternatively, had the major central banks pursued policies of price stability instead of adhering to the gold standard, there would have been no Great Depression, no Nazi revolution, and no World War II."[4]

The first step in determining what supply-side economics was is to comprehend its perspective on history. As its opponents never recognized, supply-side economics was not merely a reassertion of classical economics; it was also, self-consciously, a response to the changed conditions of the twentieth century. Supply-side economics had a theory of history as much as it had a theory of money and economic behavior. Indeed, supply-side economics had a theory of why it itself was necessary to prosperity in the twentieth century, whereas before it had not been.

Mundell's Nobel address is the greatest statement of supply-side economics' historical vision. The address must be the first source consulted in any attempt to chronicle the history of supply-side economics and account for its existence. This source, moreover, helps to reveal the way that, over the years, Mundell inspired others in the supply-side movement. These other thinkers developed variations on his historical themes and fleshed out explanations of why the twentieth century had developed as it did. And the greatest of Mundell's historical themes—the central point of his address—was that the twentieth century had begun in 1913.

A Dubious Debut

For all one hears about, say, 1914, 1929, 1945, 1968, 1989, and 2001, 1913 may well be the most important year in modern American—if not modern world—history. In 1913, the last three major reforms of the Progressive era were enacted: the direct election of senators; the federal income tax (both of these by constitutional amendment); and the Federal Reserve System of central banking. Today, the direct election of senators is a footnote to history. The income tax and the Federal Reserve, however, have shaped life as we have known it in the century since 1913. One thing is certain: there would have been no supply-side economics without the changes of 1913. For restraining the institutions created that year—the income tax and the Federal Reserve—is the essence of supply-side thinking.

"The international gold standard at the beginning of the twentieth cen-

tury operated smoothly to facilitate trade, payments, and capital movements,"
recalled Mundell in his Nobel address.

> Balance of payments were kept in equilibrium at fixed exchange rates
> by an adjustment mechanism that had a high degree of automaticity.
> The world price level may have been subject to long-term trends but
> annual inflation or deflation rates were low, tended to cancel out, and
> preserve the value of money in the long run. The system gave the
> world a high degree of monetary integration and stability.
>   International monetary systems, however, are not static. They
> have to be consistent and evolve with the power configuration of the
> world economy. Gold, silver, and bimetallic monetary standards had
> prospered best in a decentralized world where adjustment policies
> were automatic. But in the decades leading up to World War I, the
> central banks of the great powers had emerged as oligopolists in the
> system. The efficiency and stability of the gold standard came to be
> increasingly dependent on the discretionary policies of a few signifi-
> cant central banks. This tendency was magnified by an order of mag-
> nitude with the creation of the Federal Reserve System in the United
> States in 1913. The Federal Reserve Board, which ran the system,
> centralized the money power of an economy that had become three
> times larger than either of its nearest rivals, Britain and Germany.
> The story of the gold standard therefore became increasingly the
> story of the Federal Reserve System.[5]

Mundell's argument here and elsewhere in "A Reconsideration of the
Twentieth Century" will require a good deal of explication. In preparing to
embark upon this task, it is useful to review the rather innocuous history of
the creation of the Federal Reserve and the income tax.

The Federal Reserve System and the income tax would never have come
into existence had America not prospered so expansively in the years preceding 1913. From 1870 to 1913, the American economy grew at the breakneck rate
of 3.9 percent yearly. This rate of growth attracted and was in part propelled
by tens of millions of immigrants, made the United States the richest country
in the world by any measure, and resulted in there being quite a few very rich
people—including billionaires J. P. Morgan and John D. Rockefeller.[6]

The latter portion of this period, the fifteen years or so before 1913, was the Progressive era, when legislators, journalists, and activists often going by the name of "muckrakers" strove to temper the "excesses" of the dazzling industrial age through law and moral suasion. The legislative successes of the Progressives include the establishment of national parks, food safety standards, and antitrust regulation.

These reforms sought to restrain the activities of large businesses—businesses that might over-log the West, or pass off bad food as good, or overcharge for goods and services because they had a monopoly. These reforms did not target rich individuals per se. That would be the task of the 1913 reforms. What might their unhelpful habits be? Sitting on one's money, not putting it to productive use, blowing it on finery, manipulating the markets.

Theodore Roosevelt addressed this topic in his "Man in the Arena" speech of 1910. Given at the Sorbonne in Paris, it is perhaps the most famous speech ever made by a former president. Roosevelt acknowledged that civilization generally benefited from its rich inhabitants. Among the rich were to be found those, as Roosevelt put it, with the "money touch," people whose knack for monetary matters was so great that they were indispensable not only to business, but also to government, as it sought to fulfill its role of economic supervisor. And yet there were also the idle, spendthrift, and avaricious rich. As Roosevelt said:

> But the man who, having far surpassed the limit of providing for the wants, both of body and mind, of himself and of those depending on him, then piles up a great fortune, for the acquisition or retention of which he returns no corresponding benefit to the nation as a whole, should himself be made to feel that, so far from being desirable, he is an unworthy, citizen of the community; that he is neither admired nor envied; that his right-thinking fellow countrymen put him low in the scale of citizenship, and leave him to be consoled by the admiration of those whose level of purpose is even lower than his own.[7]

Something had to be done, Roosevelt argued, to get all the rich to fulfill their noblesse oblige. He suggested that suasion and shame might be sufficient. The acts on the table for 1913 would take things a step further by enshrining the allegedly needed correctives in law.

Given the incredibly consequential effects of the Federal Reserve and the income tax, one can be forgiven for supposing that there was drama associated with their birth. There was little. Many among the American rich had themselves militated for the income tax (previously adopted temporarily, such as during the Civil War), just to get the muckrakers off their backs. It was widely held at the time that the tax would compel the rich to "give back" (today's catchphrase) to the society that had rewarded them so much. Nevertheless, the original income tax was tiny. It did not begin until income hit around $60,000 in today's dollars, and the maximum rate was all of 7 percent. It traveled the arduous route of the constitutional amendment process with only token opposition.[8]

Somewhat more controversy was associated with the creation of the Federal Reserve, but this had all occurred back in 1907. In that year, one of the serial stock market panics that happened every ten years or so once again required that J. P. Morgan be called on to bail the markets out. Morgan was disinclined to do so. Nonetheless, in October 1907, as the crash deepened, Morgan found himself beseeched at every turn by failing competitors. One of them, on being brushed off by Morgan, shot himself in despair. Morgan finally relented and decided to assure the markets that he would start lending and buying.[9]

As Ron Chernow deliciously narrates in his incomparable *House of Morgan,* once Morgan started his interventions in October 1907, he also started dropping hints that he wanted to be rewarded for his white knight's role. To be specific, Morgan wanted the depressed stock of a company named Tennessee Coal & Iron. This company's market value, in the crash conditions of October 1907, was $45 million. John Moody, of bond-rating fame, calculated the stake to have an economic value in the neighborhood of $1 billion. That is to say, Morgan, aside from pumping money into the markets generally, also wished to be allowed to buy a company at no premium to its crash price—a price that would skyrocket once Morgan resettled the markets. It amounted to his exorbitant fee for services rendered.

Morgan got Tennessee Coal & Iron, and the episode left observers wondering if there could not be some other, less expensive and less groveling way to guarantee market credit during crashes. Could not the government be authorized to perform the role of white knight, and for free? A bill was introduced in Congress that became the seed of the Federal Reserve Act of 1913. Morgan, for his part, was behind the reform. He had tired of his visible role as financial market savior. He wished to make money as privately as possible, and he thought a Federal Reserve System that could supply the markets with money on demand could both be controlled by the House of Morgan and provide public relations cover for it. By 1913, there was nary opposition to the creation of the Fed. Its supporters included all constituents of the ideological rainbow: Morgan, Wall Street, the Progressives, the Populists (who had been hammering away at the "New York money trust" for decades), the Congress, and President Woodrow Wilson.

Naturally, no one knew that the greatest monetary crisis of modern history—dating back at least to the sixteenth century—would occur within the year. When World War I broke out in 1914 (with the United States neutral), the role of the Federal Reserve was suddenly transmogrified into something entirely different from—indeed, entirely alien to—the quaint, domestic, savior-of-the-markets-and-the-farmers role that had been imagined by its Progressive creators. Huge new responsibilities in the realm of international monetary affairs fell to it. It is hard to imagine that had the Federal Reserve Act been delayed by even one year, until December 1914, it would have passed without dedicated attention to the role thrust upon any large neutral nation's central bank by a world war. The Federal Reserve created in 1913 came upon the world scene in 1914 as a rookie, as, in Mundell's words, "the new boy on the block."

The overriding new responsibility that came to the Federal Reserve with the advent of the war was management of the international gold standard. Here it is necessary to offer a small tutorial on the gold standard—the "barbarous relic," as Keynes said of it in 1923, and on which Mundell has long been economics' greatest expert.[10]

During the high period of the "second industrial revolution," as it is known in economic history, 1873–1914, many countries throughout the world at most times guaranteed their paper currencies in specific quantities of gold. The economics behind this system, rather fully elaborated by David Hume in the eighteenth century, were formidable. If a country produced more currency than it could back up in gold, its prices would rise; people would perceive what was going on and redeem their devaluing paper currency for gold. The gold would still have exchange value, because it could be redeemed for any number of other paper currencies that were still solid. Therefore, countries issuing currency took extra care to maintain gold reserves appropriate to their currency float. If they did not, their currencies would be vacated and it would become impossible to participate in international commerce.

This was one aspect of one of the central characteristics of the gold standard—its "automaticity," the economics parlance that Mundell used in the Nobel address. It was virtually automatic that a currency issuer would be immediately punished for overprinting. Because of this automaticity, such practices rarely occurred.

Automaticity also refers to another aspect of the gold standard, its capacity to manage the ebbs and flows of imports, exports, and exchange and interest rates. Under a gold standard, when countries run trade deficits, with imports exceeding exports, net exporting countries will naturally receive more of net importers' currencies than importers will receive of exporters' currencies. Exporting countries will redeem the extra currency in importers' gold and convert the gold into their own currencies. "Automatically," an importer's currency becomes an exporter's, with the importers keeping the goods. So exporters trade, knowing that the foreign paper money they get is good paper money, as good as their own.

Importers will in turn find themselves with less gold and thus will have to cut paper supply. There will be a scarcity of money in importing countries, interest rates will rise, and more foreign capital will be attracted. Soon the system will return to balance, with an equal exchange of goods and services.

In terms of settling international accounts, the system worked so well through 1914 that scarcely anyone thought to notice it when the Federal Reserve statutes were being drawn up. The concerns surrounding the creation of the Fed were entirely domestic. The only discernible international issue at stake in the run-up to the 1913 Federal Reserve Act was a vague concern that the United States was "late"—it was one of the last major countries to set up a central bank in this period.[11]

The domestic orientation of the Federal Reserve was starkly illustrated in its structure. There were to be twelve Federal Reserve banks, theoretically equal, dispersed geographically around the country, including banks at such prairie strongholds as Kansas City, Dallas, St. Louis, and Minneapolis. This system was supposed to keep the Fed's ear close to the concerns of the farmers, invariably cash-strapped and in favor of a higher dollar-to-gold ratio.

Events of 1914 forced upon the Federal Reserve a question no one had thought to ask before: What if a great part of the world's gold migrated to the United States? For this was the specific crisis occasioned by the Great War. The belligerents, once they realized it would be a long war, began to make provisions for loans and exports from the United States, which remained neutral and thus economically productive. This naturally caused significant amounts of gold to flow to the United States, both as collateral for the loans and as payment for the imports. The "automatic" return of gold to the belligerents would occur only if they themselves soon became exporters of goods or importers of capital. But these things are unthinkable in countries engaged in a protracted, resource-devouring war. Thus, when gold came to the United States after 1914, it parked there.

The situation was magnified after August 1914, when the belligerents, in desperation, decided to go off the gold standard. The pressures of war finance simply became too much to bear. Britain, France, Germany, Austria-Hungary, Russia, and the Ottoman Empire—each country concluded that it could not be constrained in its struggle to procure equipment and pay soldiers by tying its domestic currency to gold. These countries further reasoned, correctly, that going off gold would not occasion a run on their currencies. For one thing, there were few foreign holders of their currencies, outside of creditors from the United States, who could flee from them. For another, domestic holders of currencies could be persuaded to keep holding through appeals to patriotism. There would be riotous domestic inflation, but that could be chalked up to the "sacrifices" demanded of the home front in a time of war.

When the parties at war went off the gold standard, even more gold migrated to the United States, by far the largest country where gold still retained its exchange function. The Federal Reserve faced a difficult decision. In the space of a few years, the nation's gold stock had doubled. Should it monetize the new gold? Should it issue new dollars commensurate to the increase in gold stock?[12]

Simplicity suggested yes. If the Federal Reserve supplied more dollars equal to the increase in gold, the exchange price of gold ($20.67 at the time) did not need to be altered. If, on the other hand, the Fed did not issue new dollars, then either the new gold would have to be "sterilized" (designated as not to be used for monetary purposes) and essentially rendered worthless, or the dollar price of gold would have to be lowered. "Maintaining the price of gold" was long a battle cry of the classical gold standard days before 1914, and the rookie Fed decided to increase the U.S. dollar float, by a factor of about two.[13]

For Mundell, this was the decision that put the twentieth century on its course. It was the decision that brought about that indelible characteristic of the twentieth century, inflation, along with its twin, unemployment; the decision that made the United States the financial arbiter of the world, for good or ill; the decision that prompted governments around the world to new feats of imagination about what their currency values (and hence their terms of trade) should be; and ultimately, the decision that called forth innovative new solutions to the problems it caused—including supply-side economics. Without this decision, Mundell believed, there would have been "no Great Depression, no Nazi revolution, and no World War II."

Whence the Roaring '20s?

It would take two-thirds of a century, Mundell said in his address, for the implications of this decision—the Federal Reserve's doubling of the dollar float during the period of U.S. neutrality in World War I—to be fully recognized. He credited several contemporary economists, including Ludwig von Mises of Austria, for perceiving key aspects of the problem at the time. But the institution that mattered was oblivious. To have recognized the dangers of its own decision would have taken remarkably keen understanding on the part of the Federal Reserve, and it wasn't yet up to the task.[14]

The immediate effects of the decision came quickly. For the first time in peace, the United States experienced acute price inflation. U.S. prices went up 13 percent in 1916, 18 percent in 1917, 20 percent in 1918, and 15 percent in 1919—an astonishing 83 percent increase in four years, a rate to which even the worst four years of the 1970s could not aspire. By way of comparison, the inflation rate in the United States in the generation prior to the Fed's creation, the high period of the industrial revolution, 1879–1914, was 0.6 percent per annum.[15]

The inflation of 1916–19 was no doubt abetted by American entry into the war in 1917. Not only was the United States monetary float far ahead of any historical norm, the nation was now diverting a key resource of supply, the young men of its workforce, to the front as soldiers. Much more money was chasing fewer goods. Business became confused as never before, wage rates stagnated, and when the war ended, the soldiers came home to jobs with pittance salaries. It was the nation's first stagflation episode. The terrible strikes of 1919, of the Boston police force, of steelworkers across the country, widely attributed to "foreign agitators," were a function of the stickiness of wage rates in the face of an 83 percent increase in consumer prices over four years.

By the end of 1919, the Federal Reserve had decided to take action. In Mundell's view, that action befitted the Fed's rookie status. "Instability continued," Mundell said in the Nobel address, when "the Federal Reserve engineered a dramatic deflation in the recession of 1920–21, bringing the dollar (and gold) price level 60 percent of the way back toward the prewar equilibrium."

Frightened by the strikes and inflation of 1919, the Federal Reserve jacked up interest rates and courted austerity. Austerity came, and hard. Inflation turned negative in 1920–1921. Unemployment jumped to 12 percent—a rate possibly higher than in any previous depression in America's industrial history.[16]

It was a confusing, difficult time. With all the new dollars flooding the economy from 1914 to 1919, businesses had become accustomed to higher prices for their products. The collapse of prices left businesses with little incentive to produce. Moreover, the principal means by which the Federal Reserve constrained the money supply, raising interest rates, implied that even if businesses wanted to produce in the context of falling prices, the cost of capital would be exorbitant. "There was a natural, if regrettable tendency," wrote Milton Friedman and Anna Schwartz of Federal Reserve behavior during this episode, "to wait too long before stepping on the brake, as it were, then to step on the brake too hard, then, when that did not bring monetary expansion to a halt very shortly, to step on the brake yet again."[17]

Warren Harding, elected in 1920, inherited the task of fixing things. Harding is nearly always ranked as one of the worst presidents in American history in surveys on the subject. This is a testament to the severe economic illiteracy of the historians and pundits who take part in such surveys. Harding's administration (along with moves by the Federal Reserve) largely solved the most difficult problem that the American economy had ever faced in peacetime. Indeed, had the solution undertaken under Harding's auspices been applied in 1929–30, it is likely that the Great Depression would have been averted.

Harding took little interest in policy, but in one of the greatest acts of delegation in the history of the presidency, he chose Pittsburgh banker extraordinaire Andrew Mellon as his secretary of the treasury and assigned him with addressing the task of fixing the economy. Mellon succeeded brilliantly. He had been dubious about the Federal Reserve tightening of 1920–21, tightening that had effectively sterilized more than half of the post-1914 gold (Mundell's calculation was 60 percent). Mellon, himself one of the great creditors of the industrial age, knew that in difficult times the economy—particularly the banking system and business borrowers—must be kept afloat. Most certainly, the functioning agents of the economy were not to be kept at bay because of some preordained dollar-to-gold ratio. From his post at Treasury in the early 1920s, Mellon urged the Federal Reserve to concede the existing price level, lower rates from austerity levels, and let the economy take as much money as was consistent with stable prices.[18]

Next, Mellon ensured that, given the lifting of austerity, there would be economic return to new investment, sales, and employment. That is to say, Mellon proposed, sponsored, and got through Congress a series of tax cuts. These cuts brought the top marginal rate down from 73 percent to 25 percent, brought the bottom rate down to 1 percent, and increased the minimum income subjected to tax by about 50 percent. Tax cuts along with currency stabilization, what Mundell would call the "policy mix," achieved two things. It enabled the dollar to hold its value, and it guaranteed that people had dollars. (Under austerity, the dollar putatively has value, but its scarcity is so great that nobody can take advantage of it.) In addition, after 1921, the Federal Reserve—in a crucial move not reprised later, at the onset of the Great Depression—followed Mellon's cue and made price stability its overriding goal. For the "seven fat years" of 1922–29, the Federal Reserve would use the real signals of the economy to tell it how many dollars to produce.[19]

Richard K. Vedder and Lowell E. Gallaway, the definitive experts on unemployment in the twentieth century, have written that

> the seven years from the autumn of 1922 to the autumn of 1929 were arguably the brightest period in the economic history of the United States. Virtually all the measures of economic well-being suggested that the economy had reached new heights in terms of prosperity and the achievement of improvements in human welfare. Real gross national product increased every year, consumer prices were stable . . . , real wages rose as a consequence of productivity advance, stock prices tripled. . . . It was in the twenties that Americans bought their first car, their first radio, made their first long-distance telephone call, took their first out-of-state vacation.

In other words, once Mellon's recommendations were applied and the Federal Reserve committed itself to a discipline of price stability, the Roaring '20s ensued.[20]

Supply-side economics was born with the actions of Mellon and the Fed in the face of the first great stagflation. The essence of supply-side economics lies in using the two levers of governmental economic leverage for the specific uses at which they are most adept. Monetary policy is capable of maintaining the price level. Tax policy is capable of spurring growth. The "policy mix" of stable money plus tax cuts is the secret to escaping stagflation. Achieving both aspects of the policy mix at once—immensely difficult to achieve in practice, given the cumbersome machinery of constitutional government—will solve the problem immediately, with no "austerity" or "trade-offs" thrown into the bargain.[21]

In contrast, when monetary and tax policies aim at things to which they are ill-suited, the results show it. Monetary policy that seeks to boost growth, the chimera of the 1970s and putatively the norm for the Federal Reserve since the 1978 Humphrey-Hawkins statute, will only create growth eaten away and hobbled by inflation. Tax increases meant to stave off inflation will produce a governmental displacement of the real economy and hence fewer jobs. The policy mix done wrong produces stagflation. The solution to the policy mix done wrong is the policy mix done right.

The debts that supply-side economics owes to classical economics, particularly to such eighteenth- and nineteenth-century theorists as Hume, Adam Smith, Jean-Baptiste Say, David Ricardo, and Alfred Marshall, must not obscure the fact that supply-side economics can exist only in the world created by 1913. Without institutions like the Federal Reserve that can make large, sustained mistakes in monetary policy, and without an income tax that can significantly reduce the operating room of the private economy, there can be no policy levers for supply-side economics to manipulate. Had there been no Federal Reserve, it would not have been possible to gain control of it and stabilize money after 1921. Had there been no income tax, it would not have been possible to cut rates to overcome the austerity effects of tight money. Supply-side economics arose after 1913 because its raison d'être was 1913.

A word here must be said about income tax rates after 1913. Rates went up astronomically once the United States started arming and then entered the war in 1917. From the 1913 ceiling of 7 percent, the top rates ballooned all the way to 77 percent in 1918. In addition, taxes began to be levied at $1,000 instead of $3,000 of income (roughly $20,000 versus $60,000 in today's dollars). The increase in rates along with the broadening of the base represented a departure from the implicit consensus that had brought about the Sixteenth Amendment in 1913, a consensus that the rich should be tempered—not the upper and middle classes soaked—by taxes.[22]

The high tax rates of the late 1910s unquestionably contributed to stagflation. They introduced bracket creep, enabled the tax-code conflation of nominal with real gains in income, depressed capital formation, and pushed employment costs higher—all issues reprised in the 1970s. After his success in 1921, Mellon turned to contemplating the new enormities involved with the income tax, a tax that in theory, given the open-ended nature of the Sixteenth Amendment, was limitless. He published his thoughts in a book of 1924, one of the most remarkable treatises ever penned by a sitting public official. The book was called *Taxation: The People's Business*. Passages of this book come as close as anything produced in the 1970s and 1980s to specifying the essence of supply-side economics. An example:

> The history of taxation shows that taxes which are inherently exces-
> sive are not paid. The high rates inevitably put pressure upon the
> taxpayer to withdraw his capital from productive business and invest
> it in tax-exempt securities or to find other lawful methods of avoid-
> ing the realization of taxable income. The result is that the sources
> of taxation are drying up; wealth is failing to carry its share of the
> tax burden; and capital is being diverted into channels which yield
> neither revenue to the government nor profit to the people.

For Mellon, the income tax had become an instrument that ensured that the resources of the rich would not be put to productive use—precisely the oppo-site of what Roosevelt had envisioned at the Sorbonne in 1910. Mellon's deter-mined efforts at Treasury led to further rate cuts in 1924 and 1926, and the Roaring '20s were thereby perpetuated.[23]

The Faulty Return to Gold

World War I devastated Europe. The continent's economies did not recover after the armistice of November 1918 nor after the peace treaty of the follow-ing spring. The war had eliminated nine million young men (and maimed millions of others) and laid waste to regions of considerable size, greatly reducing productive capacity. Russia had it the worst. Economic production in that country in 1920 was down 85 percent from the 1913 level, and a famine in that year and the next killed five million people. Russia was a special case, however. It was the revolutionist Lenin's policy that the country's economy be entirely denuded, so that it would be impossible for well-equipped conspira-cies to rise up against the Bolshevik regime.[24]

As for the rest of Europe, it took until 1927 for the production levels of 1914 to be equaled. France was the fastest grower of the slow lot, with Britain lagging behind, and Germany far behind. This only magnified the difference in relative size between the European economies and that of the United States. European economies were at 1914 par in 1927, whereas from 1914 to 1927, the economy of the United States grew by two-thirds.[25]

Robert Mundell has often been misidentified as a "gold bug"—as an archaic defender of "the gold standard" or, something he particularly bristles at hearing, of "a single world currency." In truth, he has long contended that the classical gold standard justly died because of the large relative size, by 1913, of the United States economy in comparison to any other national economy. As Mundell observed in his Nobel address, in 1913 the American economy was already three times larger than any other (second place belonged to Germany). And with the massive differential in growth rates from 1914 to 1927, this difference was greatly magnified. Now, if one country is tremendously large and influential in the world economy, it alone has the capacity to break the gold standard. This is not so when there are several countries at the top, all of the same relative size (Britain, Germany, and the United States were roughly the same size in 1890). In this case, if one country overprints currency, its currency will be shunned because there are others to resort to. In contrast, when there is one country far bigger than any others, its currency will not be abandoned for overprinting misbehavior, because the economy of that country is simply too large not to do considerable business with and its currency too omnipresent to avoid.[26]

In "A Reconsideration of the Twentieth Century," Mundell recalled that "World War I made gold unstable."

> The instability began when deficit spending pushed the European belligerents off the gold standard, and gold came to the United States, where the newly created Federal Reserve System monetized it, doubling the dollar price level and halving the real value of gold. The instability continued when, after the war, the Federal Reserve engineered a dramatic deflation in the recession of 1920–1921, bringing the dollar (and gold) price level 60 percent of the way back toward the prewar equilibrium, a level at which the Federal Reserve kept it until 1929.
>
> It was in this milieu that the rest of the world, led by Germany, Britain, and France, returned to the gold standard. The problem was that, with world (dollar) prices still 40 percent above their prewar equilibrium, the real value of gold reserves and supplies was propor-

tionately smaller. At the same time, monetary gold was badly distributed, with half of it in the United States. . . . In the face of this situation would not the increased demand for gold brought about by a return to the gold standard bring on a deflation?[27]

For Mundell, gold was an unstable reference point for currencies in the 1920s because of two factors: the recent actions of the Federal Reserve and the great relative size of the U.S. economy. The master of the dollar had printed so such money in connection with the large inflows of gold during World War I that the price level of goods and services exploded by something on the order of 100 percent. Even after the dramatic Fed tightening of 1920–21, prices were still 40 percent higher than before.

All this made the implicit dollar price of gold far higher, perhaps half again as high, as the explicit rate ($20.67 per ounce). This encouraged speculation and brought about scarcities in gold. Many people reasoned that eventually the United States would have to concede that the dollar price of gold should be officially raised by something like 50 percent, to $30 or $35 an ounce. It paid to be a holder of gold, not currency, and to wait things out.

If the United States had been a small country, and as a small country had undervalued gold in its own currency, it would have mattered very little. Gold would not have been hoarded worldwide, because a small country does not have the credibility to monetize a great part of the world's gold at a new, higher price. Yet the United States entered the 1920s several times larger than any other national economy. Differential growth rates would soon make that gap even greater. And through it all, it was widely believed that the U.S. might reprice gold upward. It was this specific uncertainty about the dollar price of gold, for Mundell, that haunted the international economy in the 1920s and set the stage for the calamities that brought about the Great Depression.

There were four conceivable options available to European currency masters as they sought to reestablish their issues in the wake of World War I. First, they could fix to gold (at the prewar or whatever parity) and deal with the exchange-rate blow that might come with a dollar devaluation. Second, they could fix to gold and devalue commensurately with the United States, should the United States choose that path. Third, they could make their currencies "flexible," not fixed to anything and priced solely by the marketplace. Fourth, they could fix to something other than gold, perhaps to a basket of commodities or some other functional proxy for the price level, or to the dollar.

As economics has come to realize over the decades—largely because of Mundell's prizewinning research of the 1960s—the only tenable option was the fourth. The first two options involved using gold in the 1920s as a monetary standard. That was ill-advised in the changed environment. Keynes understood this, in 1923 aptly calling the gold standard a "barbarous relic." Mundell has long insisted that he himself is the best expositor of the reasoning behind Keynes's famous turn of phrase:

> The post-war system "gold standard" differed from that before 1914. Keynes had pointed out in his *Tract on Monetary Reform* that "the gold standard had already become a barbarous relic," one of the most misquoted and misunderstood lines in the history of economics! Keynes meant by this that the gold standard had come to depend on the policies of two or three central banks. He might just as well have said one central bank, the Federal Reserve System. The Federal Reserve System made the gold standard impossible. With the U.S. economy in the 1920s five times larger than its nearest competitor, and the Federal Reserve by far the most important central bank in the world, the future of the gold standard for the rest of the 20th century rested with the Federal Reserve. For the next half century, the key price in the world was the dollar price of gold relative to the dollar price of commodities.

For Mundell, the essential thing to do in the changed circumstances was for the Federal Reserve to target price stability. This could be done by whatever useful means availed itself as a good measure of prices, from a basket of commodities to an index of consumer prices.[28]

Option three, "flexibility," was a mirage. Having sampled the draught of overprinting during the war, European governments had eliminated any real possibility of a system of "flexible" exchange rates for their currencies. European governments simply did not have the credibility for markets to value their currencies "fairly." The markets would always bet against these currencies in the expectation of more printing. To counteract this, the European currency issuers conceivably could have amassed prodigious reserves of currencies not their own (especially dollars), as well as gold, to be used to buy their own currencies in the open market so as to shore up their prices against shorts and negative speculation.

But whence were these reserves to materialize? Gold was being hoarded worldwide, when not simply parked with the United States' central bank. Dollars, for their part, were uncollectable; it was Europe that owed the United States dollars from all the World War I debt, not the other way around. Flexibility was unworkable.

That left a simple commitment to price stability as the only real option. Interestingly, this was what the United States pursued from 1922 to 1929. The Federal Reserve conceded the inflation since 1914 (partially drawn down by the 1920–21 austerity) and aimed to keep prices of goods and services where they were, at the new level, for the future. The new Fed discipline worked: consumer prices in the United States moved all of 1.8 percent cumulatively between 1922 and 1929.[29]

A path was now "open to avoid the deflation [and depression] of the 1930s," claimed Mundell. Namely, this was "to give up the idea of returning to the gold standard, and living with a system in which the world price level was more or less managed by the Federal Reserve System." With the Federal Reserve deciding, after 1921, to ignore the international speculation in gold and to target domestic price stability, all that was required in addition was for the European nations to fix their currencies to the stable dollar. "But no European country," Mundell continued, "was willing to concede that position of leadership to a new and untried central bank of a country that, however dominant, was not even a member of the League of Nations." So European countries strove to get their currencies back on gold. This was a type of heroism, and superciliousness, that the world could have done without.[30]

At a 1922 monetary conference, the major European countries agreed to aim at making their currencies convertible to gold, perhaps even at pre-1914 rates. The goal was pursued through 1929, though there were riotous exceptions. Notoriously, the non-gold-backed German currency collapsed in value. German prices increased by a factor of 1.4 trillion in 1923–24—Exhibit A in any discussion of hyperinflation. Yet in general, the European currencies achieved a functional fix to gold in the latter part of the '20s.[31]

The '20s were not roaring in Europe, but after 1925 there was a decided uptick in production and prosperity on the continent, particularly in Germany and France. How did the Europeans back their currencies in gold in this period, given that they had already surrendered so much gold to the United States, that they had printed currency with abandon since 1914, and that such gold as could be bought on the marketplace was dear and scarce?

In a word, fudge factors. There were two. The first was the development of a proxy to gold—dollars, or, even more secondarily, access to dollars. Since the ratio of gold to the dollar was never disturbed in the U.S., the logic ran, the dollar is "as good as gold" at the pre-1914 level. Dollars held in reserves were the equivalent to gold held in reserves, in that the U.S. was good to honor an exchange request for an ounce of gold on presentation of $20.67. The increased demand for dollars for currency reserves on the part of the weaker (that is to say, European) countries meant that creative means had to be used to get dollars to Europe. Chief among these came to be bailouts like the Dawes and Young Plans of the latter portion of the 1920s, whereby the United States provided huge dollar credits to Europe.

The second fudge factor was a general agreement among all involved not to ask for gold redemptions too insistently from any currency producer. Indeed, there came to be a sort of gentleman's agreement whereby only the dollar and the pound sterling were to be understood as truly convertible to gold. Even in these cases, however, it was generally expected that redemptions of currencies into pounds or dollars and subsequent demands for gold would be kept at a minimum so as to enable sustainability.[32]

This procedure had its flaws—though it was successfully reprised under the currency arrangements made at Bretton Woods in 1944—and it did fail in the hour of acute pressure. Yet the procedure was not in theory unworkable. Mundell strenuously defended the gropings toward international currency stability of the 1920s against such critics as Jacques Rueff, who argued that the '20s were fated to collapse into chaos and poverty. All that was needed, for Mundell, was a commitment to currency stability. If the U.S. had kept dollars stable (vis-à-vis consumer prices or commodities or whatever), and the other nations had effectively fixed to the dollar, there would have been price stability and easiness of trade. Business would have boomed, employment would have surged, incomes would have risen, and loans would have been paid off. Indeed, this essentially happened worldwide in the several years before 1929.[33]

Yes, the United States had underpriced gold, an underpricing that encouraged redemptions of dollars (and pounds) into gold and the hoarding of capital. Yet this too could have been solved merely by the U.S.'s raising the dollar's redemption price of gold, an action eventually taken in 1934, when it was too late. Had the Fed recognized that its policy of price stability from 1922 to 1929 was the right one, and had the United States (or someone), in a diplomatic feat for the ages, convinced the world that a permanent rate of exchange to the U.S.

dollar under such Fed discipline was the right policy, the Roaring '20s would have been extended indefinitely in both time and place.

It is of more than historical interest that after World War II, when the United States was in an even stronger position to dictate terms to the world, these are the very terms that it chose. Not coincidentally, in that later period, a multinational boom ensued and lasted for decades. In 1944, history would be learned from, and the world would not be condemned to repeat it. But as for 1929 and the brave newness that it would usher in, Mundell only could offer his lamentation that had "the price of gold been raised in the late 1920s, or, alternatively, had the major central banks pursued policies of price stability instead of adhering to the gold standard, there would have been no Great Depression, no Nazi revolution, and no World War II." We are now in a position to explain this remarkable claim.

The Crash

The stock market crash of 1929 occurred only for manic traders. If one bought stocks in January 1929, one's portfolio was in the black in April 1930. One had to do something like buy in August 1929 (when most brokers were on vacation), or buy high on margin, to have had any reason to jump out the window in October 1929. In itself, the crash was not much of an event, however lurid certain personal stories of October 1929 may have been. Still, the crash has long been cited as a "cause" of the Great Depression.[34]

Supply-siders have weighed in with their views. For Mundell, Paul Craig Roberts, Robert Bartley, and Jude Wanniski, the crash most certainly did play a role in causing the Depression, but only because it occasioned unnecessary reactions that themselves were responsible for the incredible eleven-year downturn. Mundell specified his view in the Nobel address:

> For decades economists have wrestled with the problem of what caused the deflation and depression of the 1930s. The massive literature on the subject has brought on more heat than light. One source of controversy has been whether the depression was caused by a shift of aggregate demand or a fall in the money supply. Surely the answer is both! But none of the theories—monetarist or Keynesian—would have been able to predict the fall in the money supply or aggregate demand in advance. They were rooted in short-run closed-economy models which could not pick up the gold standard effects during

and after World War I. By contrast, the theory that the deflation was caused by the return to the gold standard was not only predictable, but was actually, as we have noted above, predicted.

The gold exchange standard was already on the ropes with the onset of deflation. It moved into its crisis phase with the failure, in the spring of 1931, of the Viennese Creditanstalt—the biggest bank in Central Europe—bringing into play a chain reaction that spread to Germany, where it was met by deflationary monetary policies and a reimposition of controls, and to Britain, where, on September 21, 1931, the pound was taken off gold. Several countries, however, had preceded Britain in going off gold: Australia, Brazil, Chile, New Zealand, Paraguay, Peru, Uruguay, and Venezuela, while Austria, Canada, Germany, and Hungary had imposed controls. A large number of other countries followed Britain off gold.

Meanwhile, the United States hung onto the gold standard for dear life. After making much of its sensible shift to a monetary policy that sets as its goal price stability rather than maintenance of the gold standard, it reverted back to the latter at the very time it mattered most, in the early 1930s.

Instead of pumping liquidity into the system, it chose to defend the gold standard. Hard on the heels of the British departure from gold, in October 1931, the Federal Reserve raised the rediscount rate in two steps from 1½ to 3½ percent, dragging the economy deeper into the mire of deflation and depression and aggravating the banking crisis. As we have seen, wholesale prices fell 35 percent between 1929 and 1933.[35]

For Mundell, the Great Depression got under way for a specific set of reasons. After 1929, with the stock market dip and fears of what we today would call a recession, there soon came to be, worldwide, a large demand for valid currency. With an economic downturn probably imminent, people wished to hold money that would keep its value in case there were unemployment and such—money that would get one through a "rainy day."[36]

In practice, this meant significant claims on the part of currency holders for pounds sterling and dollars. Under the loose, informal rules of the 1920s, British and American currencies could be redeemed for quantities of gold at the generous pre-1914 parity. Therefore, for example, a holder of French francs worried about a rainy day could immediately get lots of gold by exchanging the francs for sterling or dollars and turning around and demanding gold for these currencies.

This sort of thing had rarely happened before 1929 because everyone knew that there really was not enough gold to cover big redemption demands and that such behavior would ruin the arrangement. Moreover, in the last years of the '20s, times were booming. You wanted to be in an investible medium, currencies, not a safe haven, gold. But the onset of troubling times can lead people to break the rules, especially informal and implicit ones, and this is what happened.[37]

Technically, the French started it. After the stock market dip of 1929, the French economy stayed relatively buoyant. Yet as gold flowed into the country, the Bank of France refused to monetize it with new francs. Gold, scarce as it was through the 1920s, was now getting sterilized in France. If monetary authorities thought it prudent to hoard gold, inevitably individuals would follow suit.[38]

It would not be correct, however, to "blame" the French for ruining the strange modus operandi of the post–World War I currency system, because the United States essentially copied France's playbook. In the face of the new pressures after 1929, the United States defended its gold hoard by sterilization instead of by raising its price.

In short, the United States forgot the lessons of its World War I mistake. The U.S. failed to realize that back in 1914–17 it had reduced the value of all its gold when it monetized the new gold that had flowed in from the belligerents. In those years, it had increased monetary gold without increasing economic production at the same rate; indeed, the ratio of gold to production was twice as high after 1919 as before 1914. The price of gold should have reflected this. It did not—the conversion ratio was kept at $20.67.

Furthermore, in the wake of 1929 the United States failed to realize that its 1919–21 policy, when the Fed de-monetized 60 percent of the World War I gold in a desperate attempt to undo the original mistake, was folly. Not only had this action left gold 40 percent undervalued throughout the 1920s, it had also created an immense depression that was solved only when the whole thing was dropped in favor of price stability. As the 1929 crisis hit, there were two possible courses of action for the Fed. There could be a replay of the horrendous 1919–21 experience and a reduction of the money supply so that the remaining 40 percent of World War I gold would be sterilized; or, much more simply, the dollar redemption price of gold could be raised by 40 percent.[39]

As Mundell has said innumerable times, the problem of 1929 was resolvable. In his Nobel address, he made the obvious point that a gold standard is meant to maintain a given price level. In the early 1930s, as monetary authorities strove to defend the 1914 values of currencies in gold, prices were brought back to the 1914 level, the interim having been an inflationary period. There was deflation, currencies appreciated, and it became wise to hold money, rather than use it. What should have occurred, on the part of all major currency issuers, particularly the United States, was an immediate repricing of gold upward. This would have both stemmed the conversion demands for gold and encouraged people to use money for investments or spending, rather than hoard it.[40]

Yet in the face of demand for pounds and dollars, the British and the Americans took the curious and intransigent step of refusing to supply any more. It might be said that had they supplied more pounds and dollars, there would have been still greater demands for redemptions in gold, gold that did not exist. In any case, if currencies are going to be demanded and not supplied, the economic consequence necessarily will be deflation.

The British showed the Americans the way. After 1929, the British simply complied with the old sterling parity to gold—a parity that had been made ludicrous by the post-1914 overprinting—in the face of all the new demands for gold. Soon they nearly ran out of gold. So the British suspended convertibility in 1931.

The massive conversions of French francs and other currencies to sterling and sterling to gold in this period, 1929–31, meant that the money supply in Britain and those countries whose currencies were being converted to sterling dropped dramatically, far more than any drop in economic production. Deflation started to materialize, and with deflation came disincentives to spend and to borrow, making the environment for business sales and expansion bleak. The recession initially on the minds of those who had moved to redeem currencies for sterling and then gold was in fact materializing—precisely because of the actions of the currency redeemers themselves.

The American reaction was both more severe and more significant. As in Britain, foreign currency redemptions for dollars increased, as did domestic requests for redemptions. In the face of this new demand for the dollar, the Federal Reserve raised interest rates—by a factor of one and a third. This was tantamount to restricting access to dollars at the very moment that there was a surge in demand for them. The Fed feared that the Grim Reaper that was clearly drawing nigh on Britain—the exhaustion of the U.K.'s gold supply—would soon turn to stalk the United States, unless it took preventive action. This action could have been raising the price of gold, by 40 percent or whatever the prudent proportion might have been. But the Federal Reserve chose instead to restrict the pool of dollars.[41]

Inevitably, therefore, deflation also materialized in the dollar zone, the United States and those countries redeeming into dollars and gold. This was a far bigger zone than anything having to do with the pound sterling. Now deflation visited a great part of the world, including the United States. Deflation brought on an unwillingness to spend and borrow, with commensurate effects on business production and the inevitable result of unemployment.

The actions taken by Britain and the United States—and particularly the United States, on account of its size and its dramatic tightening of the dollar in the face of sharp demand—constituted the ill-advised "defense of gold" that Mundell lamented. These actions had not at all been a defense of the gold standard, he argued, but rather of a very poor misunderstanding of it.

The point of the old gold standard had been to ensure stable prices and trade as well as capital flows to places that promised returns. In the early 1930s, "defending gold" had transmogrified into something that meant engineering a historic deflation and the flight of capital out of currencies and thus out of investments. Keynes called the gold standard a "barbarous relic" in 1923 for a reason. Acting as if it still existed in its old form would bring about calamity.[42]

The die of the Great Depression was cast by 1931. With everyone raiding his bank account to get currency to convert to gold before the gold ran out, and with the Federal Reserve remaining imperious by making access to new dollars difficult, the bank failures came. Deposits vanished, and the Fed refused to play the lender-of-last-resort role that J. P. Morgan had perfected. As Mundell said in his address, "The banking crisis was now in full swing. Failures had soared from an average of about 500 per year in the 1920s, to 1,350 in 1930, 2,293 in 1931, and 1,453 in 1932."[43]

"The deflation of the 1930s has to be seen," Mundell reflected, "not as a unique 'crisis of capitalism,' as the Marxists were prone to say, but as a continuation of a pattern that had appeared with considerable predictability before—whenever countries shift onto or return to a monetary standard." Conceivably, the problem still could have been solved in the early 1930s. After all, uncannily similar conditions had existed just ten years before. In 1921, the Fed had dropped the austerity policy that had resulted in double-digit unemployment and committed itself to keeping the money supply at a level where prices were stable. At Treasury, Mellon had engineered tax cuts. In tandem, these moves had ensured that money that was worth something was out there in the economy. The Roaring '20s testified to the validity of this "policy mix." Was such a solution not in the offing after 1931? Mundell spoke the bitter truth:

> Monetary deflation was transformed into depression by fiscal shocks. The Smoot-Hawley tariff, which led to retaliation abroad, was the first: between 1929 and 1933 imports fell by 30 percent and, significantly, exports fell even more, by almost 40 percent. On June 6, 1932, the Democratic Congress passed, and President Herbert Hoover signed, in a fit of balanced-budget mania, one of its most ill-advised acts, the Revenue Act of 1932, a bill which provided the largest percentage tax increase ever enacted in American peacetime history. Unemployment rose to a high of 24.9 percent of the labor force in 1933, and GDP fell by 57 percent at current prices and 22 percent in real terms.[44]

The tariff applied the coup de grace to the international banking system. With the world's creditor, the United States, now blocking sales of foreign goods in the United States, it became impossible for foreign debtors to accumulate dollars to meet payments. The loans would have to be written down. Biggest were the Dawes and Young loans to Germany, loans which had both successfully reinvigorated the German economy after 1925 and greatly increased the dependency of the German economy on the American market. So Germany too was staring at 25 percent unemployment in 1932, the year that Hitler made his bid for power.

As for the tax hike, oddly enough it was done under Mellon's auspices. The federal government was actually worried about defaulting on its bonds. About the only thing that can be said about American economic performance in the early 1930s was that the federal government did not, in fact, default. The price paid for this achievement may well have been the remainder of the 1930s and the first half of the 1940s.

Given deflation, a lack of access to foreign markets, and a confiscatory tax code, the Great Depression became an immovable object. Deflation meant that consumers chose to hoard appreciating money rather than spend it, ruining the outlook for business sales. Business could not find recourse in international trade, because that had collapsed with the tariffs. When income and profits could be gained in this environment, they were largely siphoned off to government via taxation. It was a recipe for economic stasis, and that is what the nation got. GDP growth per capita in the United States for the decade 1929–39 was about a perfect zero.[45]

Furthermore, and more portentously, the nations of the world were no longer interdependent economically. They were no longer knit together in patterns of currency redemptions and trade. It became every country for itself. The United States was largely satisfied with its lot—it was a huge country with vast resources. But smaller countries that lacked resources, above all Germany and Japan, were not satisfied with their lots. Aggressive warfare was there to foretell.

This historical vision, hewn precisely by Mundell in Stockholm in 1999, was often in the thoughts of the supply-siders as they confronted the difficulties of the 1970s and early 1980s. In that later period, the institutions of 1913 were once again showing signs of running amok. Must the world collapse again, to paraphrase Mundell, into "depression, revolution, and war"? This question, in various forms, haunted the supply-siders as they sought to capture intellectual leadership as well as the helm of policy during the '70s funk. If and when they arrived "in the arena," they were sure they would do what Mellon and the Fed had done the first time, in the early '20s—and what had been done in 1944 at Bretton Woods.

3

A HOTEL IN NEW HAMPSHIRE

[T]he quarter century of this regime [of Bretton Woods] was exemplary
in its stability, growth, and economic development, perhaps unmatched
at any time outside an imperium, such as the Roman Empire.
—ROBERT MUNDELL, *Wall Street Journal,* September 30, 1981

In 1937, the worldwide, eight-year-long depression seemingly as intractable
as ever, a Viennese economist by the name of Ludwig von Mises put his
finger on what certain nations had finally decided to do about it. He published
his thoughts in a brief article given the piteous German title *"Autarkie—der
Weg ins Elend: Internationale Arbeitsteilung ist Grundlage der europäischen Kultur."* In
English, this is "Autarky—the Road to Poverty: The International Division of
Labor Is the Basis of the European Way of Life."[1]

Autarky is an ancient economic concept. Named by the Greeks, it means
complete economic self-sufficiency. An autarkic country is one that does not
engage in foreign trade. It manufactures itse lf everything that it uses and
consumes. No autarkic country has ever been prosperous. In the Middle Ages,
European political entities averaged about one hundred square miles in size, if
not less (today's Liechtenstein is a residue of this order). If the tiny statelets of
medieval Europe strove to be autarkic, it meant a subsistence existence at best.
Even a glimpse of prosperity required trading with one's neighbors.[2]

With the rise of larger political entities, of nation-states, after Isabella's establishment of Spain in 1492, autarky continued to prove a route to poverty. After its "Siglo de Oro" of international ambition, which ended around 1600, Spain was the only European nation of the time to fix its gaze inward. Spain's exclusive preoccupation with itself and its remote imperial acquisitions led to a long experience with unprofitability that lasted until the death of Franco in 1975. Alternatively, from the seventeenth through the nineteenth century, Britain, Holland, France, and to some degree even Poland rode international trade to unprecedented heights of prosperity. In the years before 1914, Japan, Germany, Argentina, the United States, and (haltingly) Russia and Austria also caught the trade bug. Each of these nations in turn realized its highest growth rates in history.

Openness to trade helped form the essence of what it meant to be European, Mises proposed in his 1937 article. It would be one of the last appeals Mises was able to make to his fellow Austrians, with Hitler's *Anschluss* looming. The Nazis promised Austria that they would remove the country from the international economy—and that was supposed to be a good thing. Mises begged to differ, saying that cosmopolitanism and trade had always been the secret to Austrian success. The Nazi takeover came in 1938.

Mises fled, his house and papers ransacked by the Gestapo shortly thereafter. He became a refugee, in 1940 finally gaining entrance to the United States, where he planted himself for good. Mises made it his mission to give warning to his adopted nation. In a remarkable series of essays and in his book *Omnipotent Government* (1944), Mises strove to inform an American readership what the Axis aggressors were militating for. The Germans and Japanese, Mises said, wished to achieve national economic self-sufficiency, or autarky. He argued that each of these two nations had realized, after the collapse of the exchange-rate system in the early 1930s, that international trade had become too unreliable. If you wanted to prosper, you had to go it alone.[3]

The problem was that no one was equipped to do so. Certain countries mistakenly thought they were so equipped, and they remained optimistic in their isolationism. The United States thought it had all the prerequisites of prosperity between its shores, including a mind-boggling supply of diverse natural resources and citizens with a penchant for work and a "can-do" spirit. The New Deal, for Mises, represented the United States' own autarkic effort; it meant to solve the Great Depression by going it alone. Government was to get everyone employed within the country, producing exclusively for each other, and without business skimming off the top.

The USSR also thought that its size would allow it to go it alone and prosper. Hard work, a novel and insistent ideology (communism), and the marshaling of native resources under "five-year plans" would bring about superabundance of both food and manufactures.

The aspirations of the United States and the Soviet Union in the 1930s would prove delusional. In the United States, pre-Depression prosperity remained unachievable throughout the '30s, with unemployment never dropping below 14 percent and starvation remaining a constant threat. In the Soviet Union, fifteen million died in famines caused by the Five-Year Plans and the purges necessary to cover up the fiascos.[4]

Germany and Japan, however, were different. They never suffered from the delusions of the United States and the Soviet Union that prosperity was possible under the conditions of autarky such as they existed in the 1930s. They knew that they were medium-sized nations without enough resources to supply their economies. Japan believed, and not incorrectly, that it would starve if forced into conditions of autarky on its home islands. A Germany nurtured on the pseudo-Darwinian warnings of *Mein Kampf* harbored similar fears.

For economic reasons, therefore, aggressive warfare became an attractive option. Japan and Germany would aspire to seize territory. Japan would take Manchuria, followed by parts of China, so as to feed and equip itself without having to rely on trade with the West. Germany would acquire resource-rich *Lebensraum* to its east. If there were home populations in these regions with a prior claim to their resources, these populations would face expulsion, slavery, or liquidation.

As Mises wrote in the early 1940s, in America:

> It is therefore of no use to tell the aggressors, as the pacifists do: Do not fight. . . . These aggressors are convinced that victory pays. The Japanese argue: If we conquer Australia and make it consequently possible for 20 million Japanese to settle down in Australia, we will raise wage rates and standards of living for all Japanese, both for the emigrants and for those staying at home. . . . In our age of economic nationalism the only method to prevent war is armaments. Watch your borders day and night!

Any Allied peace that was to follow this war, Mises held, must be sure to hold high the principles of international economic cooperation, of trade, and of the stability of the means of exchange. Mises favorably quoted the Atlantic Charter, the Allied blueprint for postwar peace devised in the dark hour of 1941: "The governments of the United States and of the United Kingdom . . . will endeavor . . . to further the enjoyment by all States, great or small, victor or vanquished, of access on equal terms, to the trade and to the raw materials of the world which are needed for their economic prosperity."[5]

The pope saw things the same way. Approvingly, the secular Mises quoted Pius XII's Christmas message of 1941: "Within the limits of a new order founded on moral principles, there is no place for that cold and calculating egoism which tends to hoard the economic resources and materials destined for the use of all to such an extent that the nations less favored by nature are not permitted access to them."

Mises, Pius, and the Atlantic Charter had an improbable vision for the future in view of the Nazi and Fascist domination of the Continent, which had been completed by the close of 1941. Yet this vision was destined to win. International trade and the exchange of resources and goods would become the hallmarks of "postwar prosperity"—the great run of economic success that would last a quarter century, from the late 1940s until the early 1970s, in all regions of the world that had endured the Great Depression and World War II, exclusive of those subject to communism.

Ludwig von Mises, fifty-nine in 1940, could not get a job in the U.S. when he arrived as a refugee that year. He had already written most of the work that would make him widely known as one of the century's greatest economic thinkers. But he was a "conservative," dubious of the New Deal and insistent on gold. The University of California jumped at the chance to pretend that it was offering him a job, so as to ensure Mises an entrance visa to the United States. But the offer was a phony all the way, meant only to keep Mises, a Jew, out of Hitler's clutches. Mises spent the early 1940s looking for a full-time position.[6]

Mises began to publish a string of books with Yale University Press, to write for the *New York Times* and other organs, to consult for the Republican Party, and to mentor Henry Hazlitt, the greatest economic commentator of the century. In his consulting for the Republicans in the election year of 1944, Mises insisted that the party drop its historical commitment to trade protectionism and fantasies of autarky.

Mises also told the party that "there is no other means . . . to improve the general standard of living than to increase the quantity and to improve the quality of products. This can be effected only by increasing the amount of capital available." He took off the table the obvious but false solution to this problem: "A sound and stable currency is a prerequisite of economic prosperity. An increase in the quantity of money in circulation and credit expansion . . . [will] result in depression."[7]

Expand capital and stabilize the currency—in his memorandum to the Republican Party platform committee of 1944, Mises became the first economic theoretician to state the objectives of what three decades later would go by the name "supply-side economics." Mises did not have a means for attaining these apparently contradictory objectives at once, but he was musing in that direction. Such means would in time become apparent, both to policymakers disinclined to supervise a "Carthaginian peace" after the war's end in 1945, and to a Canadian who at that point was yet a boy.[8]

The Mount Washington Hotel

Robert Mundell turned eight in 1940. He lived in the village of his birth, a tiny, one-room-schoolhouse outrider of Kingston, Ontario. Kingston, a town of several thousand inhabitants at the time, could have been bigger than it was. It stands at the confluence of the Great Lakes with the St. Lawrence River. At virtually every other geographical juncture of the Great Lakes–St. Lawrence Seaway system, there sits a massive city—Chicago, Detroit, Buffalo, Toronto, Montreal. Charming Kingston looks large only in comparison to its opposite number on the American shore, Cape Vincent, New York, which even today claims a population of only 750.

As an adult, Mundell would recall that small observations he had made during his boyhood in and around Kingston had led to his interest in economics. Farms covered the hundred miles or so north of Kingston, before the land gave way to the moose- and mosquito-infected forests of the Algonquin. The Kingston hinterlands were then, as now, devoted to dairy farming. While working as a teen in a cheese factory, Mundell noticed how the farmers behaved when they brought their goods to market. They were fastidious about small margins of price, quantity, and rates of exchange. It was an observation that would stick with Mundell and cause him to think.[9]

In the summer of 1944, when Mundell was eleven, there would occur at a clutch of ski resorts in northern New Hamsphire, some two hundred miles distant, perhaps the greatest diplomatic gathering of the twentieth century, a gathering now clearly of greater positive consequence than Versailles. The gathering became known by its location: Bretton Woods.

During World War II, as the fighting and atrocities got worse, the United States contemplated abandoning its pledge in the Atlantic Charter not to sow a Carthaginian peace. The plan that has forever been associated with the name of Henry Morgenthau, Franklin D. Roosevelt's secretary of the treasury, suggested in 1944 that a defeated Germany be reduced to a strictly agricultural state under Allied watchfulness. Under the "Morgenthau Plan," the Germans were not to rebuild after the war, but rather to de-build, to the extent that Allied bombing had not done the job for them.[10]

As for the rest of the world, it was to be integrated into a functional economic system—the elusive goal of the 1920s. Morgenthau's deputy, Harry Dexter White, was charged with figuring out how. He was to be assisted by Britain's John Maynard Keynes. Specifically, the two men were to come up with a system of currency exchange for the postwar world that would respect the realities of the broken gold standard and be superior to what had prevailed since 1919. White and Keynes basically agreed on what should be done, with the final plan favoring White's views where there were differences of opinion. FDR and Winston Churchill recommended that their plan be implemented.[11]

Ironically, White was one of the most determined and highly positioned espionage agents that the Soviet Union was ever able to hire in the United States. And yet if anyone "saved capitalism" in the aftermath of the Depression and war, it was White.[12]

The features of the "bilateral agreement" between the United States and Britain were as follows. The participating countries' currencies would trade to the dollar at fixed rates of exchange, the rates to be determined by a board and changeable if they proved unpropitious. The dollar, in turn, would be convertible to participating countries' central banks at $35 per ounce of gold. This was the dollar price of gold that FDR had set in 1934, finally correcting the dollar overproduction of the 1910s, but far too late at that point to save the banking system or to prevent the international drive to autarky.

In order to help countries function under the plan, the agreement envisioned two new institutions, which would soon be called the International Monetary Fund (IMF) and the World Bank. The IMF would assist those countries whose currencies were fixed to the dollar when there were temporary problems maintaining the fixed rate of exchange. The World Bank would assist those countries whose currencies were not yet fixed to the dollar.

The plan clearly recognized what had become the unspeakable truth in the 1920s: the United States possessed virtually all the world's gold. If currencies were to be fixed to gold, their central banks had to have it. Central banks did not have gold in the '20s, but their currencies were fixed to it anyway. Savvy investors got out of currencies—that is, from business enterprises— and into gold, expecting a price spike. Given the evacuation from enterprise, the Depression ensued, and a few profiteers walked off with fortunes.

In the 1930s, as European and Asian nations went to war, the world's monetary gold once again migrated to America. This time it was sterilized. Any subsequent international gold standard would have to recognize these facts. And indeed, under the bilateral agreement of 1944, currencies would be fixed to the entity that was legitimately backed in gold, the dollar. There would be no flight from enterprise because all currencies were on the same footing, and the mooring was the dollar at a correct ratio to gold.

The United States and Britain urged countries around the globe, including some still under Axis occupation, such as China, to come to the United States to discuss and ratify the arrangement. Forty-five countries sent representatives. The meeting site was the Mount Washington Hotel, the shambling 1902 edifice in the Bretton Woods region of New Hampshire that is now a National Historic Landmark. The forty-five nations sent so many advisors, adjutants, translators, and hangers-on along with the official representatives that the massive hotel, and every hotel nearby, was stuffed with attendees. Regular guests had to be shooed away. By any measure, the conference was an organizational mess. But the plan was ratified largely intact, and it was no mess at all.

Shortly after the war ended in 1945 and their plan began to be put into practice, White and Keynes died. Both men had suffered acute stress from the conference, its run-up, and its aftermath. White also may have worried that his treason would be discovered. It is not unreasonable to conjecture that had he lived to see the congressional career of Richard Nixon, he would have been found guilty of espionage and sent to prison, if not executed.

The Soviets were at Bretton Woods, where they obtained all sorts of information about White's plan and its background and assumptions. Ironically, they likely found White's espionage to be deeply depressing. For White, though a traitor, was a strangely honest man. He wanted to see capitalism succeed—and communism along with it. He enthusiastically offered the Soviets the opportunity to make the ruble convertible to the dollar and hence to gold. Doing so would make the Soviets able to trade anywhere in the world— and give them direct access to America's gold. Would that not be grand?[13]

The Soviets slinked away from the conference saying no thanks, and thereafter forbade their satellites from joining the Bretton Woods arrangement. Surely, the Soviets reasoned that joining Bretton Woods would mean they must refrain from overprinting the ruble, lest the IMF investigate and the country become a trade pariah. But overprinting had been a Leninist stock-in-trade since the earliest days of the revolution. Overprinting not only ruins the market economy in preparation for communism, as Lenin argued; it also comes in handy when pretending to pay your troops and operatives. The Soviet Union, with an empire gained in World War II, knew that it was going to have to buy a lot of peaceableness among its new client peoples. To take away one of its prime, if fraudulent, means of doing so was unthinkable.

That is to say, what Harry Dexter White effectively did in his espionage for the Soviet Union was to expose its economy as a house of cards. Here was the Soviet Union, which had employed desperate means to acquire gold over the past twenty-five years (melting down the Russian Orthodox Church's monstrances, selling the czar's art to Mellon, conning the Spanish Republicans out of their hoard), walking away from direct access to the mother lode, the gold reserves of the United States.

It was a moment of truth, and no one at the time saw it. White had inadvertently gotten the Soviets to demonstrate that they had no faith in their own economy. He had, in his naïveté, gotten the Soviets in a game of chicken with the United States: Did they really want free access to American gold, the only price being a legitimate currency on their part? In turning their back on Bretton Woods, the Soviets gave their answer.

Postwar Prosperity

Supply-side economics arose in the 1970s because Bretton Woods had both succeeded spectacularly and collapsed ignominiously. There can be no mistake that in the high years of the Bretton Woods system, roughly 1950–70, the world economy accomplished incredible feats. European and Japanese growth was sustained at a nearly 7 percent rate, and the United States (which had started at a higher basis) enjoyed long booms at over 4 percent. These are historic figures. Nor can one fail to notice that after 1971—when the dollar was disassociated from gold and fixed exchange rates ended—growth collapsed and stagflation became endemic.

In the 1970s (and this was one of the hottest topics at Michael 1), debates raged over how good Bretton Woods had been. The supply-side consensus was that it had been very good indeed, lacking only a little fine-tuning. Robert Bartley, for one, felt that restoring the Bretton Woods order, with certain improvements, should essentially be the final goal of supply-side economics.[14]

Mundell spoke approvingly of Bretton Woods in his Nobel address, distinguishing it from the interwar "bungled return" to gold. "The new system," he said, "differed greatly from the old gold standard. For one thing, the role of the United States in the system was asymmetric. . . . The dollar was the only currency tied to gold." Furthermore, "another difference of the new system from the old was that not even the United States was on anything that could be called a full gold standard. The dollar was no longer in the old sense 'anchored' to gold; it was rather that the world price level, and therefore the real price of gold, was heavily influenced by the United States. Gold had become a passenger in the system."[15]

Here Mundell effectively said that at Bretton Woods, nations realized what Keynes had wanted them to realize at Versailles: that the "full gold standard" had become a "barbarous relic" on account of the disproportionate size and power of the United States. Gold would be stable only if the United States did not overprint currency and thus kept it stable.

Clearly, the United States dictated terms at Bretton Woods. Countries either accepted a fixed rate to the dollar or were faced with the sure prospect of everyone shunning and dumping their currency. There was only one country that, relatively successfully, declined the Bretton Woods fixed rate of exchange to the dollar in favor of market pricing of its currency. This, oddly enough, was Mundell's own Canada.[16]

Bretton Woods also foreclosed another avenue of "flexibility," one that "Keynesianism" would soon determine to be a matter of national sovereignty. Countries could not deficit spend. In *The General Theory of Employment, Interest, and Money* (1936), Keynes had insisted on deficit spending. But the key question was whether it was to be financed through domestic saving or central bank purchases with new—that is, newly printed—money. (International financing of budget deficits was off the table in the era of autarky.) The thrust of the *General Theory* was invariably toward overcoming the constraints that the domestic savings rate places on the economy. Therefore, Keynesianism, as it grew out of the germ of the *General Theory*, advocated the right, if not the duty, of central banks to buy their government's debt with newly created money.[17]

Under Bretton Woods, this policy would produce an untenable consequence. If countries printed extra money, they would be able to claim an inordinate share of dollars and hence the United States' gold. Alerts would go off, the IMF would be brought in, and a plan would be set up to wind down the deficit spending.

Yet what if a country had good reason to deficit spend—for example, as in the *General Theory,* to mop up unemployment, or to fight a just war? The IMF would have to be convinced. It could buy the debt (or the extra currency supplied for the debt) and sterilize it, bringing back to par claims on the dollar and gold. That was the rub—the IMF would have to be convinced. And the IMF was a functionary of the United States. The United States controlled the Bretton Woods system, showing the high prerogatives of strength. If the United States chose not to support another currency's fix to the dollar, this currency would die as an international means of exchange. Countries would have to be on their best behavior, in theory, so that the United States would not isolate their currencies by ending support for the fix to the dollar. And conceivably, the United States could construe "best behavior" to mean acquiescence to the American geopolitical vision.

But no matter what, the United States had to ensure that gold sold for $35 per ounce in the open market. If gold prevailed at a higher price in the market, central banks would logically seek to redeem currency for dollars and gold so as to make a profit on selling the gold privately. Furthermore, Bretton Woods sowed the seeds of its own destruction in a clause that permitted countries to fix independently to gold. Perhaps the deal was not so asymmetric after all.

Here is where the United States failed to comprehend exactly what it had pledged at Bretton Woods. The United States never fully realized its own responsibilities—above all, not to overproduce the dollar so as to make the $35 price of gold untenable. For if it did overproduce, perhaps by means of the Fed's purchase of federal debt, the world would become flush with dollars, and people would expect a price spike in gold. It would be the 1920s all over again.

The American economy took a curious route during the first several years after 1945. Policymakers wanted to avoid a recurrence of the domestic experience of the 1930s, whatever the international monetary implications. However, for the three years following 1944, the economy shrunk by 13 percent. Accompanying this was not deflation, as in the 1930s, but the reverse. Inflation exploded. Price controls set during the war were lifted, and from 1945 to 1948 the consumer price index shot up 34 percent, a stunning total for a three-year period and exceeded in peacetime only by the worst years of the long 1970s. Following World War II, the United States traded depression for an acute period of stagflation. Actually, it was "shrinkflation," in that the economy was contracting as prices surged.

The 34 percent depreciation of the dollar by 1948 was sufficient to erase any excess gold that the United States had been hoarding since the 1930s, when it was sterilizing the gold coming in from trade with European belligerents. During the war, the United States started unsterilizing the gold—that is, printing money in the absence of gains in the real economy. After 1948, if inflation was to occur at all in the American economy, markets would push gold above \$35 and jeopardize Bretton Woods.[18]

Shrinkflation was a puzzling experience. It confounded the president, Harry Truman. And yet shrinkflation did play into the government's hands in one way. It enabled the national debt to be cut down.

In 1945, the federal debt was simply massive. At 110 percent of GDP, it was two and a half times as big as it was in January 2009, before the stimulus bill was passed. Most of the debt had been taken on to pay for the New Deal and the war. By 1955, the debt had been halved to 55 percent of GDP. Several things helped to bring this about. First, inflation reduced the value of the debt by a third. Second, progressive taxation ensured that wages that kept up with inflation were taxed at ever higher rates—bracket creep, as it would be called in the 1970s. There were twenty-four rate brackets in the income-tax code as of 1946, and if an earner's income appreciated with inflation, a disproportionate part of the gain went to the government because of the new high rate at which the gain was taxed. The patriotic bond-buyers of World War II found that they were holding wasting assets. If they tried to compensate by making more money, they got bigger tax bills.

Something had to give for the economy not to fall into depression again. Republicans, a majority once again in Congress in 1948, passed a tax cut and overrode Truman's veto. This marked the end of the shrinkage and arrested inflation. Growth for the six years following 1947 was 4.6 percent per annum and proved the death knell of the Depression. Prices stopped increasing in 1948 and 1949, though they burped higher, by 12 percent, in 1950–51.[19]

The reason that the inflation of 1945–47 and 1950–51 did not ruin Bretton Woods immediately is that the dollar price of gold, \$35 per ounce, was probably a little high to begin with. Because of the deflation of the 1930s, the \$35 price was more appropriate to the 1920s. By printing to get out of debt in the 1940s, the United States "caught up" to the price of gold, to which it had committed first in 1934 and again in 1944.

Mundell summarized these developments as follows:

World War II brought a repetition of the monetary imbalances of
World War I. The devaluation of the dollar and gathering war clouds
in Europe made the dollar a safe haven and the recipient of gold to
pay for war goods. The United States sterilized the gold imports and
imposed price controls. It was therefore able to run deficits without
going off gold. Because gold was still "overvalued" in this era of "dollar shortage," interest rates remained incredibly low. . . .

   At the end of the war, the U.S. price level doubled as a result of
the end of price control, the unleashing of pent-up demand, and the
expansionary monetary policies of the Federal Reserve System that
continued to support the bond market. The postwar inflation halved
the real value of the public debt, increased tax revenues as a result of
"bracket creep" in the steeply progressive income-tax system (which
rose to 92.5 percent), halved the real value of gold, and eliminated its
overvaluation. After further inflation during the Korean War and the
onset of steady "secular" inflation, gold became undervalued.[20]

For Mundell, the first bout of inflation, immediately after the war, was not
sufficient to jeopardize Bretton Woods, but rather ratified its pricing of gold.
But the second, smaller bout in the 1950s was sufficient to make people—that
is to say, foreign central banks—wonder whether they would not be better off
holding gold than dollars.

   Inflation in the 1950s was low—not effectively zero, as in the great days
of the international gold standard, 1870–1914, but the lowest in the era of the
Federal Reserve. Consumer prices from 1951 to 1955 increased an infinitesi-
mal 1.1 percent, and for the remainder of the decade at about 2 percent per
year. This approximation of dollar-price stability was sufficient to make for
stable prices for anyone who chose to fix to the dollar. Yet this fixing took a
little time. The countries of the world that had committed to Bretton Woods
spent the late 1940s and early 1950s setting up central banking and tax and
spending norms that would be consistent with the looming requirements.
Some were successful earlier than others.[21]

   West Germany, relieved of the Morgenthau Plan by the Cold War, effectively had a stable currency by 1948. The West German reforms of the late
1940s, reforms that freed the markets and fixed the currency, were akin to the

United States' supply-side reforms of the 1980s. The British were the ditherers. Britain's Labour government was intent on nationalizing wide swaths of industry, health care, and the universities. This required deficit "flexibility" incompatible with Bretton Woods.

By the early 1950s, most major countries were ready for Bretton Woods, though some did not formally subject themselves to IMF discipline until the late 1950s, not least because doing so meant not taking Marshall Plan money. In any event, the Bretton Woods system was in place by the early 1950s, whether de jure or de facto.

The resulting national growth rates were stunning. New terms were added to the lexicon, such as the German mouthful *Wirtschaftswunder,* or "economic miracle." Japan and West Germany especially, those former autarky-seekers, were the star performers. Debates still rage about the causes of postwar prosperity, but there is general agreement that the vaunted Marshall Plan was but secondarily responsible for the postwar boom abroad. The $13 billion in recovery aid that the United States supplied Europe in the several years after 1947 would have been useless had the United States continued to devalue the dollar, which it did not. And the enterprises seeded by Marshall Plan capital would have faced a poor business climate had the means of exchange been subject to chaotic shifts in the 1950s.[22]

As for the United States, its domestic economy finally boomed. The 1929 peak of the stock market was finally breached in 1954, en route to a trebling of the indexes in the 1950s. Sustained high growth, low unemployment, low inflation, and sound money—the kind of economic performance that had enabled the nation to come into its own in the decades before 1914—were finally restored. The guarantee, under Bretton Woods, to foreign central banks of $35 gold was not incidental. It ensured that there would not be too many dollars chasing goods, even in the home market. Everything was on track.

Enfant Terrible

At war's end in 1945, Robert Mundell's father retired from his post as a sergeant at arms in the Canadian military. The family moved from Kingston (home to Canada's war college) to British Columbia. There, Robert finished high school and enrolled at the University of British Columbia in Vancouver.

Mundell wished not to be a financial strain on his parents, whose pension was being rudely devalued by the postwar inflation. So he took on an assortment of jobs. He delivered papers and groceries and made sausages. He worked at logging camps, peat bogs, and sawmills. He kept house and washed dishes. He babysat. He joined the reserve army.[23]

At university, Mundell studied economics and Slavonic studies. His choice of majors revealed his rootedness. Throughout the first six decades of the twentieth century, western Canada was a favorite destination for Eastern European and Russian immigrants. Kingston had spurred young Robert to think about economics, and British Columbia the Slavs.

Mundell crossed the nearby border in 1953 to enroll in an economics program at the University of Washington in Seattle. There, Mundell recollected fifty years later, "I had my first real brush with macroeconomics, mathematical economics, and international trade." After a short while, "I had come to the conclusion that I was destined to be a really good economist, so I decided to study at the best possible place even if I had to borrow the money." In 1954, he left Washington for the Massachusetts Institute of Technology (on a scholarship), where he was to complete doctoral exams with lions of the field, including Charles Kindleberger and Paul Samuelson.[24]

Mundell was by no means a mathematics savant, such as might be necessary to survive the rigors of MIT. He later admitted, "I never told anyone that when I began graduate work, I had zero knowledge of even rudimentary calculus." At MIT, Mundell learned math quickly. He got so good at geometry that he soon became known as the greatest composer of graphs in economics. Still, Mundell retained his ability to describe theories and arguments in words, as opposed to equations. Indeed, his 1961 article "A Theory of Optimum Currency Areas," one of the most influential articles in modern economics, consisted of eight pages of simple, direct prose.[25]

In 1955, Mundell took a fellowship at the London School of Economics, where he began writing his MIT dissertation. In England, Mundell got to know additional luminaries in economics, the most important of whom was Harry Johnson, a Canadian who was nine years Mundell's senior. Johnson was beginning to reassess Keynesianism, which would become his life's great work and eventually identify him as one of Keynes's most formidable critics. Johnson had tired of all the talk that Keynes had "changed everything" with the *General Theory* and began to suggest that counterrevolutions have greater intellectual merit than revolutions. In the 1960s, Johnson and Mundell would be colleagues on the University of Chicago faculty, where Johnson would make his mark as the adjudicator of Keynesianism and monetarism.[26]

Mundell finished his dissertation in 1956 and spent the next few years at various stops: Chicago, his alma mater the University of British Columbia, Stanford, and an international studies center in Italy. In a fateful move, in the fall of 1961, he returned to the United States to do a stint at the research department of the IMF. On his first assignment, he caused a tempest. The reverberations have continued to this day.

The American economy had slowed in the latter years of the 1950s and the early 1960s. There was a recession in 1953, then in 1957, then in 1960. Republican Dwight D. Eisenhower had managed to preside over three recessions in just eight years. The reasons were not so mysterious. The great run of postwar growth had taken place in 1947–53, when GDP shot up by 4.6 percent yearly. This growth had been buoyed by actions like the 1948 tax cut and the federal government's commitment to retire the debt. The latter ensured that new deficits would not be financed by fiat money from the Fed. Inflation dropped to nil in 1949. It was a de facto supply-side policy mix.[27]

When the first Eisenhower recession hit, in 1953, Republicans (who controlled Congress) insisted on a tax cut. Eisenhower rejected these calls, even with the top rate effectively at 90 percent. Republicans lost Congress the next year, and tax cuts were retired as an issue. Growth in the eight Eisenhower years was thus 2.4 percent yearly, 48 percent off the pace set by his predecessor Truman. Given the prodigious 1.7-percent-per-annum population growth of 1953–61, the Eisenhower record on growth is the worst of all postwar presidents. Indeed, the impression that there was a period of "Eisenhower prosperity" is one of the most recalcitrant myths in American economic history. It wasn't until Eisenhower was *out* of office that there was a real boom. In the 1950s, the man in the gray flannel suit was a victim of slow economic growth.

Hence the piquant themes of the 1960 presidential election: economic sluggishness and its apparent geopolitical consequence, the "missile gap" with the Soviet Union. The Democratic candidate, John F. Kennedy, made "Get this country moving again" his mantra against the Republican Nixon, who as the sitting vice president was saddled with the burden of incumbency. When Kennedy took office in early 1961, one of his highest priorities was to fix the growth problem.

Among the advisors Kennedy brought to Washington were top, broadly Keynesian economists from around the nation, including Walter Heller from the University of Minnesota and James Tobin (a future Nobelist) from Yale.

Paul Samuelson, Mundell's graduate advisor, was also "constantly consulted" by these members of the Council of Economic Advisors (CEA).[28]

Keynesian economics—that is, the economics derived from the *General Theory*—had a clear policy solution to the problem of slow growth. Above all, aggregate demand was to be increased. The central matter addressed in the *General Theory* is the strange propensity of modern capitalist economies to supply more than consumers wish to demand. Keynes thought, in the 1930s, that business innovates more rapidly than consumer preferences change. "Equilibrium," where supply and demand meet, is elusive under Keynesianism, because supply tends to exceed demand.

Given this predicament, the Keynesian prescription is to introduce an agency from outside the market to lift demand to the level of supply. This agency is government. Government can take action that ensures that what is supplied is bought. If such action is not taken, supply will contract to the low level of demand, businesses will close, and the most unpleasant and politically portentous of all economic problems will result: unemployment.

To today's casual observer, it is odd to encounter an economic theory that insists that the consumer's preference is not to buy. Our world of malls, online shopping, credit cards, "black Fridays," and home equity loans seems strongly to imply the opposite. It must be remembered that Keynes wrote the *General Theory* during the thick of the Great Depression, when indeed consumers were not buying. It made *sense* for consumers not to buy. Currencies were steadily gaining in value in the face of deflation, so deferring purchases made one richer. That the *General Theory* came to be a policy manual for economies undergoing not deflation but inflation was one of the singular ironies of the 1960s and 1970s.

The classic Keynesian policy action in the face of slow growth is to boost demand by means of government spending, lower taxes, or both—in a word, through deficits. Government spending is a component of demand as a whole, "aggregate demand." If aggregate demand is low and unemployment is looming, the government component can be increased to bring aggregate demand to the par of supply. Reduced taxes, for their part, enable individuals to devote more of their income to demand.

The only danger from the Keynesian stimulus of demand through deficits is increased inflation. New demand brought about by government spending and lower taxes could overshoot supply, supply which had trended down because of slack demand, and cause a rise in prices—an unpleasant development, but not as severe as unemployment.

Hence there arose, just in time for JFK, a solution to the inflationary problem. This solution to the Keynesian "solution," known as the "neoclassical synthesis," was inspired by the work of Samuelson and Tobin. Supply and employment were to be supported by expansionary monetary policy from the Federal Reserve. Excess demand that showed up as inflation on account of the cheap money was to be monitored by the federal government and countered with taxation. The Fed was to keep money loose, and the United States was to run a budget surplus. In time, the special mechanism of the neoclassical synthesis, taxation to mop up excess dollars supplied by the Fed, would go by the name "fiscal drag."[29]

Keynesian and "neoclassical" verities swirled around the Kennedy White House and Congress as Washington contemplated what to do to boost growth in 1961 and 1962. Policymakers found the slow growth rate to be the paramount problem. The American obligation under Bretton Woods to ensure the $35 price of gold was of secondary importance.[30]

As Mundell noted in his Nobel address, in the early 1960s four options were offered to stimulate the economy. As for the first two options, "Keynesians, led by Leon Keyserling [Truman's CEA chair], pushed for easy money and an increase in government spending. . . . The Council of Economic Advisors, following the Samuelson-Tobin 'neoclassical synthesis,' advocated low interest rates to spur growth and a budget surplus to siphon off excess liquidity and prevent inflation."[31]

Both of these approaches envisioned loose monetary policy, with fiscal policy—or government tax and spending policy—being the variable. The two further alternatives were for monetary policy to be tight—a restriction on new money from the Fed—with fiscal policy again the variable. Option three, Mundell observed, was picked up by the U.S. Chamber of Commerce (he should have said the Republican Party, for the chamber would soon change its tune). It called for tight money and balanced budgets—the counsel of the status quo and vaunted Republican "prudence." Nobody contemplated the fourth alternative, tight money and expansive fiscal policy, until Mundell brought it up.

This was the tempest that Mundell created in 1961. When Mundell arrived at the IMF in the fall of that year, stimulus packages were the topic du jour. Mundell's supervisor, the economist Jacques Polak, asked his new, twenty-eight-year-old researcher to weigh in with his thoughts. Mundell replied that he had already written several articles on precisely this subject.

Polak countered that "not enough people have got the message." It had to be done one more time, bluntly.[32]

Mundell took to his task with gusto, consolidating the arguments of several of his previous articles and completing his paper within a week. A colleague asked Mundell what he thought of what he had written, and Mundell had a moment of faux self-deprecation that would come back to haunt him. He could not get Italy, where he had been living for two years, out of his mind. He quoted Bizet composing *Carmen*: "If it's trash they want, I'll give it to them."[33]

This "trash" was a paper titled "The Appropriate Use of Monetary and Fiscal Policy for Internal and External Stability," eight pages in length, with just one graph and no equations. The paper, an IMF Departmental Memorandum of November 8, 1961, was (as a matter of protocol) forwarded to the member governments of the organization. After some in-house wrangling, the paper was also published, with a crucial footnote change, the following March in the *IMF Staff Papers*.[34]

Mundell had indeed gone over the same ground before. In previous work, he had shown that the appropriate policy toward slow growth was tight money and loose fiscal policy—perhaps lower taxes. He remembered the very moment when he had begun to realize that this was the correct "policy mix." It was at Stanford in 1958, shortly before the birth of his first son. One day when he was at his desk, drawing graphs and doing calculations, he had an "Aha!" moment. He recalled: "I was so taken with [my new] idea—elated might be a better word—that I put pencil and paper down, to prolong the enjoyment of the suspense about what would, with a little more work, unfold."[35]

The realization that Mundell had begun to have in 1958, and that burst upon Washington in 1961, may be summarized as follows. Monetary tightening produces a rise in the rate of interest. A rise in the rate of interest attracts foreign capital. Tax cuts bring about domestic expansion and a reduction in unemployment. Domestic expansion does not, however, produce inflation. For inflation, by definition, is absent if capital is flowing into the country. Capital inflows are a sign that the currency is not depreciating, as under inflation, but appreciating. With the Mundell policy mix, you get an inflation-free boom.

The key was that the economy under consideration be a member of the world economy. In an autarkic country, a rise in the rate of interest would attract money away from domestic consumption toward savings, depressing economic activity. The tax cut would offset this by enabling more money for consumption. But the net effect on output would be zero, and the problem of sluggishness would remain unaddressed.

Mundell summarized his position with these words: "Monetary policy ought to be aimed at external objectives and fiscal policy at internal objectives, and . . . failure to follow this prescription can make the disequilibrium situation worse than before the policy changes were introduced." Each policy instrument should have one target and one target only; fiscal policy ought to aim at domestic growth, and monetary policy at currency stability. Mundell called this narrowing of purposes "effective market classification."[36]

Mundell offered not only to get the economy moving again, but to do so while maintaining the value of the dollar. To minds nurtured on Keynesianism and the neoclassical synthesis, Mundell was speaking in contradictions.

As Mundell later recalled, his paper "created quite a fuss. All kinds of objections were made: It was 'contrary to U.S. policy,' it would have a 'bad influence on developing countries,' there was 'no difference between monetary and fiscal policy,' the 'use of monetary and fiscal policy in opposite directions would cancel out,' and so on." Then the "Federal Reserve Board of Governors . . . mounted an attack on [the] paper. Herbert Furth [and a colleague] wrote a sharp critique." Furth was senior advisor to the policymaking body of the Federal Reserve; his was an important mind that had to be changed if Mundell's new policy mix was to be adopted in practice.[37]

Furth's critique was typical in that its objections had to do with practical mechanics rather than any analytical flaw. Furth wrote (in 1964) that "the U.S. constitutional system does not favor a flexible fiscal policy"—a fair point, and one that would be rued during the 1981–82 recession as the nation waited for tax cuts to phase in while money remained tight. He noted that the relationship between monetary policy and interest rates was indirect, "probably rather indeterminate." Summing up practical objections such as these, rather than giving a disproof of Mundell's geometry, Furth recommended that "it would be rash to abandon the use of monetary and fiscal policy for domestic purposes, and even more so to rely on monetary policy alone to correct a [foreign] payments imbalance."[38]

Academic debates over Mundell's suggestions continued through the mid-1960s. Mundell eagerly weighed in with further papers, contesting objections and expanding his argument. In the meantime, Kennedy and the Fed went ahead and unconsciously adopted Mundell's advice and implemented the policy mix, to remarkable effects in the economy.[39]

Mundell's Vision Prevails

Mundell made a mistake in his recollections (including in the Nobel address) when he said that the neoclassical synthesis of loose money and budget surpluses was the policy mix advocated by Kennedy's Council of Economic Advisors. That was indeed the policy urged by the authors of the neoclassical synthesis, Samuelson and Tobin, in the years prior to Tobin's ascendency to the CEA in 1961 and Samuelson's addition to the Kennedy economic transition team in late 1960. But it was not, ultimately, either the mix that the CEA advocated or the policy implemented under Kennedy.

The first economic report of Kennedy's CEA, in March 1961, discussed the possibility of using loose money and high taxes but fell short of advocating that policy. Indeed, the wording in the CEA report was horrendously unclear, even by economics standards: "The revenue-raising power of the . . . Federal tax system can . . . indirectly increase incentives for private investment by facilitating a policy of relative monetary ease." More noticeable in the report were the numerous suggestions of tax cuts. Typically, the word "temporary" qualified the report's mention of tax cuts, business and personal, but such talk was indubitably there. The report, following Kennedy's own public rhetoric, indicated that if economic performance did not quickly improve, tax cuts would be likely. "A further program of economic recovery might consider . . . income-tax cuts, [which] provide a fast method of enlarging the private income stream and speeding recovery."[40]

As for monetary policy, the report called for lower long-term interest rates—the rates that apply to borrowers funding investments such as houses and business plant and equipment—and higher short-term rates. The logic here was that low long-term rates would stimulate supply and employment in the economy. There would be no offsetting flight from the dollar, however, because cash would be attracted to short-term instruments bearing high rates. That is, there would be no pressure on gold at $35 an ounce, because short-term rates would ensure that cash would be kept in dollars, as opposed to foreign currencies with claims on dollars and hence the gold stock.[41]

This policy of low long-term and high short-term interest rates went by a name inspired by the smash pop music hit (and dance) of 1960, Chubby Checker's "The Twist." "Operation Twist" would enable the Federal Reserve to stimulate the economy while maintaining "external stability"—the goal of Mundell's policy mix. But it would do it all through the instrument of monetary policy. Mundell thought the Twist risible.[42]

Despite the urgency to "get this country moving again," Kennedy did little by way of implementing economic policy in his first year in office. Growth stayed at the old Eisenhower rate. Yet prices crept up, introducing the possibility that the U.S. might have to devalue the dollar, a prospect Kennedy dreaded. Kennedy tried voluntary price controls, but these failed spectacularly when U.S. Steel double-crossed him in April 1962 by reneging on an agreement. This episode gave rise to one of the most colorful of JFK's lines, one often cited by Robert Bartley (then a cub reporter): "My father always told me that all businessmen were sons of bitches."[43]

As Bartley recalled, businessmen started wearing buttons saying "S.O.B. Club" as the Dow industrials declined some 28 percent in the spring and summer of 1962. Kennedy relented with a "take a businessman to lunch" campaign, suggested personal rate cuts, and finally implemented one of the primary suggestions of the 1962 CEA report: business-tax cuts, particularly on investment and depreciated equipment. He then used his January 1963 State of the Union address to call for personal-tax cuts. These came early the following year, under Lyndon Johnson. The February 1964 tax cut was a legislative memorial to Kennedy. It dropped personal-tax rates from a stratospheric 91 percent to 70 percent at the top of the scale, and from 20 percent to 14 percent at the bottom.[44]

Kennedy's tax cuts certainly did not represent the actualization of the neoclassical synthesis, or even the CEA's revision of it. To be sure, Kennedy's CEA had strongly recommended, in 1961 and early 1962, the kind of business-tax cuts that came in summer 1962. But the CEA also made it clear that it would advocate personal cuts only as a last resort, and on the condition that such cuts were small, temporary, and revocable. Therefore, the JFK tax cuts, for businesses in 1962 and personal income in 1964, were consistent with the policy recommendation that Mundell had made when he came to the IMF in 1961.

So why did Kennedy make the moves? Through the first year and a half of his administration, as the CEA kept talking about the Twist, business allowances, and "stand-by" tax cuts on the personal side, Kennedy bided his time. But with the stock market implosion of summer 1962, the administration started getting it from all sides. A CEA memo reported in July of a visit with its European counterparts: "At its June . . . meeting, the EPC [an economic policy board] agreed that the U.S. needs to have more expansionary fiscal policy to . . . maintain economic recovery; at the same time, the U.S. must be prepared to use tighter monetary policy to prevent deterioration of its balance of payments." As for policy specifics, the Europeans counseled that in

choosing between "increasing government expenditures" and "reducing taxation," "the growth needs of the U.S. economy, and the need to strengthen the
confidence of investors, should be taken into account."[45]

To make the tax-cut point clear, the CEA memo went on to observe that
the European committee "noted that the U.S. Administration has already
announced that it will submit to Congress this summer an income-tax reform
measure together with proposals for income-tax reductions to become effective in January 1963."[46]

It is not unreasonable to assume that European economic policymakers,
such as those making the above recommendation, had read or heard about
Mundell's *IMF Staff Papers* article of three months before, an article which
came with summaries in Spanish and French, as well as the Departmental
Memorandum of the previous November on which it was based, a memorandum sent to all member governments.

The gentle suasion of the Europeans toward the Kennedy administration found a tough counterpart in the American business community. Walter
Heller, the CEA chair, allowed in the summer of 1962 that it was time for the
administration to ask, "Where did we go wrong?" He knew that among private forecasters, the "more optimistic . . . expect a continued upward creep in
GNP for a few quarters before an absolute decline begins." Heller and other
administration officials consulted Kennedy's despised businessmen and got a
clear recommendation: cut marginal tax rates considerably.[47]

The CEA was willing to depart from the neoclassical synthesis to a small
degree. In 1962, Heller was prepared to trim income-tax rates by 4 percent,
taking the top rate from 91 percent to 87 percent, with commensurate, temporary cuts in the other brackets. The business representatives consulted by the
administration insisted on more. Ford Motor's economist said that a 10 percent,
across-the-board cut in rates was necessary, and the cut had to be permanent.
Heller chose to interpret permanent as meaning "between one-and-a-half and
two years." The Chamber of Commerce shot the moon with its recommendation: a permanent cut in the top rate to 65 percent. The CEA shook it off. Yet
a year and a half later, a top rate of 70 percent was law. Perhaps the 5 percent
difference was meant to stave off the impression that the avatars of the neoclassical synthesis had capitulated to the S.O.B. Club.[48]

Explicitly, there was no "supply-side economics" in the early 1960s. Perhaps there did not need to be. Perhaps the logic of the sequence of the Kennedy
tax cuts amounted to a revision of the neoclassical synthesis, itself a revision of

Keynesianism. Business tax cuts would come first, in order to give suppliers a head start on producing. But there would be no personal-tax increases to stave off demand before the new product came on line, as in the neoclassical synthesis. Rather, two years later, cuts in the personal rates would enable the new products to be bought. There would be no inflation (according to this logic) because new demand was not introduced into the system until well after the stimulus to the productive process had been initiated.[49]

The Federal Reserve, for its part, unconsciously adopted Mundell's policy mix and the recommendation of the Europeans. The Fed more than tripled the abnormally low (1.17 percent) federal funds rate of July 1961 over the following four years. The policy mix came to exist de facto, and the results were stunning. Yearly GDP growth from 1961 to 1968 was 5.1 percent, the kind of number usually reserved for developing dragons, not mature economies expected to be capital exporters. Unemployment dived, and inflation only inched up, from 1 percent in 1961 to all of 1.6 percent in 1965. Federal revenues grew by more than 50 percent from 1962 to 1968.

It was the last great boom of "postwar prosperity" before the 1970s, when nearly everyone came to think of such periods as gone forever. Perhaps Mundell technically had nothing to do with it; then again, perhaps he did. At any rate, it was clear that Mundell had scored an intellectual coup. He rode his success to a professorship at the University of Chicago, easily the greatest economics department in the world. If there was not a general acknowledgment that of all the policy options on offer in 1961, Mundell's was the closest to what had been implemented—and to spectacular practical results—there certainly was a general acknowledgment that Mundell's model was revolutionizing economics.

Shortly after Mundell composed his paper in 1961, Jacques Polak's associate, Marcus Fleming, returned to the Washington office of the IMF. He had been working along similar lines as Mundell (possibly having read Mundell's earlier essays) and published his findings the following year. Soon the "trash" that Mundell had drawn up in the fall of 1961 was cited widely as the *locus classicus* of the newly christened "Mundell-Fleming model," whereby international capital flows are a significant determinant of national economic performance, along with fiscal and monetary policy. Behind the model was the iron logic of effective market classification, which urged that fiscal and monetary policy instruments each be used only for one thing—specifically, the one thing at which they are most adept.[50]

The Mundell-Fleming model is often called, simply, the "open-economy model" or the "open-economy macro-model." This is on account of its reminder that in the Bretton Woods world, money can be readily converted into different currencies. There is no such thing as "management" of a national economy by means of fiscal and monetary policy, which after all is the upshot of Keynesianism. Capital flows, which are beyond the control of national managers, have their function, too.

That the Mundell-Fleming model remains to this day a fecund commonplace of economics, a starting point in macroeconomic considerations of the whole world, is one of the most uncontroversial things one could think to say about economics as it is practiced in its advanced form. Or, as the American Economic Association put it succinctly in 1997: "Even today, modern interpretations of [the Mundell-Fleming model] remain the primary workhorse for international economic policy analysis."[51]

Yet when Mundell's policy mix came to be advocated by journalists and congressional staffers in the 1970s, it was met with charges of amateurism and superficiality. Even after Mundell won the Nobel in 1999, commentators strove to disassociate it from supply-side economics. David Warsh, of the Economic Principals blog, wrote, falsely, that "Mundell . . . had all but dropped out of economics by 1978. . . . He returned in the late 1990s to accept a Nobel Prize for the work he had done in the 1950s." Even Robert Barro, a friend of supply-side economics who surely knew better, wrote in *BusinessWeek* in 1999 that "whatever the merits of supply-side economics . . . —and I would say there are many—these ideas had nothing to do with the work that resulted in a Nobel prize."[52]

The bitter truth that the gainsayers of supply-side economics could never face was that the foundation of the maverick movement of the 1970s had been laid in the center of academic and theoretical economics shortly before that movement became an urgent necessity in the stagflation period. This fact would become a matter of great misrepresentation, prevarication, and turf protection on the part of supply-side's detractors, complicating our ability to understand and appreciate supply-side economics—let alone economics in general—to this day.

The Mundell-Fleming model was intense, intellectual stuff. Who really understood it, and who stood to gain and lose on account of its theoretical power and practical results? Mundell revealed some of the stakes involved in his policy revolution when he observed, at a remove of some forty years,

"At first it wasn't popular. This was to be expected because it recommended a complete reversal of the prevailing policy mix. The Samuelson-Tobin neo-classical synthesis might have had some merits in a closed economy, but it was completely indefensible in an open economy on fixed exchange rates."[53]

The contribution of the Mundell-Fleming model to historical understanding was that it indicated what had been gained by the Allied victory in World War II and consolidated by Bretton Woods. In the cooperative world won by the war and defined by Harry Dexter White's plan, money was free to move wherever it wished within the dollar-anchored system. This compelled all nations to keep the value of their currencies stable and to seek to expand their economies through other measures, such as tax-code reform and the elimination of trade barriers.

There could be no quibbling with the results. The Bretton Woods boom—which lasted for a quarter century—showed the world what could have been after Versailles. For this reason, the 1970s were a decade merely of stagflation and funk—rather than world war. Yet the collapse of Bretton Woods seemed to portend the end of all things just the same.

4

BITTER FRUITS

Who would complain if the world economy in the next fifteen years were
as prosperous as the last fifteen?
—ROBERT MUNDELL, addressing Congress, July 28, 1965

In the 1970s, the United States led the world to the brink of economic
collapse without ever knowing it. It simply didn't understand what it was
doing.
—ROBERT L. BARTLEY, *The Seven Fat Years*

At the end of his revolutionary article titled "The Appropriate Use of
Monetary and Fiscal Policy for Internal and External Stability," Robert
Mundell offered a simple rule of thumb. An instrument of economic policy
should do one thing and one thing only. If you want to do more than one thing,
have as many instruments for the purpose. Monetary policy is best at control-
ling the flows of the dollar, tax policy best at affecting the level of economic
activity. Combine the two, and *voilà*: a policy mix to reverse the conditions
that gave Kennedy the nod over Nixon in the election of 1960.

Business taxes were cut in 1962 and personal taxes in 1964; at the same
time, the Fed raised interest rates. In these years, Mundell's research rever-
berated in important economic and policy circles. Yet the twenty-nine-year-
old Canadian was by no means the éminence grise behind the actions that

resulted in 1960s prosperity (as the neoclassical-synthesis people strove to be). As Mundell recollected after the fact, he basically lucked out. He elaborated the successful policy mix, but probably without influencing it a great deal. He was a kid, after all, a bureaucracy staffer, no less. "Fortunately for the United States (and me), President Kennedy reversed the policy mix to that of tax cuts to spur growth in combination with tight money to protect the balance of payments," wrote Mundell. "The result was the longest expansion ever (up to that time) in the history of the U.S. economy, unmatched until the Reagan expansion of the 1980s."[1]

In 1965, a year after the passage of the personal rate cut, the whole thing began to unravel. Lyndon Johnson had shoved the tax cut to the front of the congressional schedule in late 1963, so as to be able to sign into law a fitting memorial to the fallen Kennedy. But then it came time for Johnson's own agenda. This would be an ambitious program of government spending—first for the "Great Society," and then for "that bitch" (LBJ's term, needless to say): the Vietnam war.

Mundell had dismissed in a footnote, in his "Appropriate Use" article of 1962, the idea of using government spending as a fiscal tool to target domestic growth. He preferred tax cuts. Mundell would have to say this much more noticeably than in a footnote as time wore on, because government spending—coupled with tax *increases* intended to help government revenue catch up—was about to become all the rage.

From 1962 to 1965, federal outlays increased by 10.7 percent total, or 3.4 percent a year. Taking inflation into account, real outlays increased 2 percent annually over these three years. These are small numbers. From 1965 to 1969, in contrast, federal outlays increased by 55 percent total, or 11 percent per year—7 percent annually, in real terms. These are large numbers.

In 1967, Johnson asked Congress for a tax increase. Real federal revenues would surge 33 percent from 1962 to 1968, a 4.8 percent yearly raise on top of the cost of living. In the world of work, this is to do very well indeed. But to the shopaholic LBJ, financing as he was both the Great Society and Vietnam, still more was desired. The tax increases he sought would come in 1968 and 1969, quite a package of them: a 10 percent income-tax surcharge; the minimum tax; a reduction in the capital-gains exclusion; and supercharged bracket creep. These would prove fully sufficient to usher the nation into the 1970s. But before all that, LBJ had tried another stratagem, which was to get the Fed to foot his bills.[2]

William McChesney Martin, the chairman of the Federal Reserve since 1951, was the one Johnson had to convince. Initially, things did not look promising. When Martin's Fed raised an interest rate in 1965, Johnson took Martin aside—"to the woodshed"—to explain to him why the Fed needed to do what the president wanted. Martin's Fed must have been intimidated, because for the remainder of Johnson's term as president the federal funds rate barely cleared the accelerating inflation rate.[3]

Economist-cum-historian Allan H. Meltzer has lifted the veil over the Fed's behavior in the 1960s in his magisterial work on the history of the Federal Reserve. Meltzer uncovered an astonishing fact about Martin: his Fed, against all assumptions to the contrary, had virtually nothing to do with keeping a lid on money growth in the years 1951–65, the eminent period of stable prices in the United States during the postwar period. Meltzer discovered that Martin truly believed that the Federal Reserve was "independent within the government," that is to say, an executor of the wishes of the government. "Independence within government meant, to Martin," Meltzer wrote, "that the Federal Reserve had to help finance budget deficits. Congress and the Executive set the budget. The Federal Reserve was the agent of Congress. He believed it could not fail to finance the deficit without greatly increasing interest rates. In the 1950s and early 1960s, financing deficits was not a persistent problem. After 1965, the problem became persistent."[4]

This discovery is arresting because it means that in the high period of Bretton Woods, in the 1950s and early 1960s, the Federal Reserve did not commit itself to maintaining prices, and thus a stable price of gold, which was the anchor of the world economy and the guarantor of world trade. Rather, independent commitments on the parts of Congress and the president to keep budget deficits (and hence monetary expansion) under control underlay the stability of prices in this period. In light of this revelation, fiscal hawks such as President Eisenhower and Wilbur Mills (chairman of the House Ways and Means Committee) must be reevaluated by historians in a new and more appreciative fashion.[5]

At any rate, once the LBJ spending ramped up in 1966, cruising at a 7 percent real increase per year, the Federal Reserve obliged it. Real interest rates stayed low while the Fed made sure that there was no "liquidity crisis" as new federal debt looked for bidders on the open market. And new federal debt there was. The budget deficit had fallen from 1962 to 1965, from the small peak of $7.1 billion in 1962 to the tiny total of $1.4 billion in 1965. From 1966 to 1968, the deficit went to $4 billion, then $9 billion, then $25 billion. And these deficits mushroomed, it must be remembered, in the face of historic real increases in federal revenue.[6]

All this is to say that the dollar supply increased dramatically as the private economy was displaced by government. It was a perfect recipe for inflation— more currency and fewer goods—and it made a fair bid to become stagflation. The 1 percent inflation rate of the first half of the 1960s gave way to a one-point increase every year starting with 1965, with the consumer price index hitting 6.2 percent in 1969. The unemployment rate held steady at below 4 percent, but that was both supported by a ravenous military draft and fated not to last.

Exorbitant Privilege

This time, the world got angry. During the United States' previous serious bout with inflation, in the seven or so years after World War II, the world was in no condition to complain about American overprinting. Everyone was horribly penurious. Making nice with the United States was the overriding order of the day.

Not so in the late 1960s. Countries made stronger by the postwar boom were getting weary with the United States for exporting inflation to the rest of the world. Given fixed exchange rates, any inflation in the United States immediately made itself felt in the rest of the Bretton Woods order. What made it particularly galling was that the process was entirely a one-way affair. No other country could overprint and see its inflation ripple throughout the world. Foreign overprinting simply produced spurious claims on the dollar and hence on the United States' gold, claims that the IMF was charged with policing and bringing to an end.

France was the first to react in the wake of the LBJ inflation. The French had particular cause to be touchy. In 1958, as it prepared for war to keep its Algerian colony, France ran deficits and thus incurred IMF inquisitiveness. There was a mild financial crisis, and the country had to figure out how to pay for the war while warding off the IMF. Within four years, France would let Algeria go. But not before it had crossed many minds that the Bretton Woods order was a constraint on national sovereignty—and especially on the conduct of foreign policy.[7]

Furthermore, the United States did not play by its own rules. It started running a war in 1965 and seemed pleased to increase the dollar float as an expedient. The IMF was unconcerned, because it cared about *claims* on dollars, not about more dollars per se. It appeared that the United States could produce currency to underwrite whatever domestic or foreign policy venture caught its fancy. It all seemed to testify to the "exorbitant privilege" enjoyed by the United States under Bretton Woods, French president Charles de Gaulle was heard to say. He had a point.[8]

De Gaulle had found an advisor in a wizened veteran of the currency adventures of the 1920s, a redoubtable economist and policymaker named Jacques Rueff. In the 1960s, Rueff devoted himself to imploring the United States to be true to its obligation to the rest of the world. That obligation was to keep prices stable—specifically, to keep the dollar convertible to gold at a set rate.

The mechanism that "guaranteed" world price stability was the dollar's convertibility to gold at $35 an ounce. Overprinting on the part of the United States, the theory went, would prompt an increase in the market price of gold. Foreign central banks would seek to redeem more of their own currency in dollars, and for those dollars get underpriced gold from the United States at $35. Foreign central banks would then turn around and sell the gold on the market for the higher price, making a nice profit. Meanwhile, the U.S. gold stock would be depleted, jeopardizing the whole system. This, indeed, was the unwelcome prospect that Kennedy had contemplated before the Mundellian policy mix started to be implemented in 1962.

By 1965, the problem was that the United States had also learned how to finesse the system. It had devised all sorts of expedients to get around the limitation of the $35 price. There was, of course, Operation Twist. The central lyric of a sequel to Chubby Checker's tune was "Let's twist again like we did last summer / Let's twist again like we did last year." So too did Operation Twist resuscitate itself after its first appearance in the 1961 economic report. It emerged again in 1965 as the United States sought to staunch the outflow of overprinted dollars to foreign central banks by raising short-term rates and keeping long-term rates low. "Let's twist again like we did last year," indeed.[9]

The Twist was not the half of it. By the latter 1960s, the United States had availed itself of an assortment of stratagems to keep the extra dollars it was printing out of foreign hands. It limited capital exports. It issued bonds indexed against a potential dollar devaluation. It made soldiers stationed in Europe spend their pay on base. It urged allies to buy arms in the United States. It suggested agreements whereby foreign central banks would play along and choose not to seek redemptions in dollars and then gold. And it zeroed in on that vehicle of currency crisis, the vacationer taking dollars abroad and spending them. In what surely must tally as one of the most hapless statements of the modern presidency, Lyndon Johnson asked for this sacrifice on January 1, 1968: "I am asking the American people to defer for the next two years all nonessential travel outside the Western Hemisphere."[10]

These games drove Rueff mad. Even if, somehow, on account of the Twist and other expedients, the U.S. gold stock was not pressured by foreign claims in the face of the overproduction of the dollar, the world still had to digest the resultant unwelcome price inflation. The United States ran "a deficit without tears," Rueff said, although he meant that the tears were monopolized by foreigners who absorbed American inflation whether they wanted it or not. Interviewed by the *Economist*, Rueff recalled a metaphor that explained what it meant for the United States to issue dollars while providing that they not be used as dollars: "You know the story of the monk who wanted to eat meat on Friday; he said to the rabbit, 'I baptize you a carp.'"[11]

Rueff prompted de Gaulle to be the first foreign leader to go public with a clear admonition to the United States to not overproduce the dollar. In a February 1965 press conference, de Gaulle strongly urged the implementation of an international gold standard that all nations, the United States included, would respect. Rueff's own position was that the United States had so overproduced the dollar that it would have to raise the redemption price for an ounce of gold to $100.[12]

Such a devaluation of the dollar would have been even more dramatic than that undertaken by Franklin Roosevelt in the depths of the Great Depression. Rueff felt that the unraveling of Bretton Woods was sure to result in a similar catastrophe, just as the 1920s gave way to the 1930s. He may have been maudlin to a fault. His collected writings on the dollar crisis of the 1960s bore the moralistic title *The Monetary Sin of the West*. He was, all too appropriately, a member of the Académie française, his chair previously occupied by the lyricist Jean Cocteau. The epigram to *Monetary Sin* was a plaint:

> There is tragedy in the world because
> men contrive, out of nothings, tragedies
> that are totally unnecessary—which means
> that men are frivolous.

But maudlin or not, Rueff successfully rallied the world to insist that the United States keep its responsibilities under Bretton Woods or scrap the system outright. And he prompted de Gaulle to start asking the United States for gold in exchange for France's accumulated dollars.[13]

Through 1968, France kept it up, requiring gold for its dollars. The United States had to do something. LBJ seems to have seriously believed that a tax increase would help solve the problem. In his New Year's statement of January 1968, Johnson identified his "anti-inflation tax" (a 10 percent income-tax surcharge) as the primary weapon he would use to defend the dollar. The logic was that by raising taxes and bringing the budget into balance (achieved in 1969), the Federal Reserve would not need to monetize the $25 billion budget deficit. There would be fewer dollars, less inflation, less inflation panic, and hence smaller claims on gold.[14]

In addition to the tax increase, the vacationers' moratorium, and all the rest, Johnson also took aim at business. He announced that he wanted to "restrain direct investment abroad" by U.S. businesses. The numbers he ventured were arresting: He spoke of "invoking my authority . . . to establish a mandatory program" whereby business investment in the developed world would be limited to 65 percent of the total of previous years. And any investment made under this restraint would have to be vetted by the Commerce Department. Again, the logic was that fewer dollars going abroad, this time via investors, would mean smaller foreign claims on the U.S. gold stock.[15]

It was astounding stuff for the president of the United States to tell business that some of its most lucrative investment and profit opportunities were being foreclosed. The "developed countries" Johnson referred to in his statement were Japan and those of Western Europe, then growing at hyperbolic rates of 6 percent or more per year. Here was American business being told that whatever meager investment it was to be allowed in these regions would have to pass the muster of Commerce bureaucrats.

The final plank in Johnson's platform to shore up the dollar was government spending. He pledged "an intensified five-year, $200 million Commerce Department program to promote the sale of American goods overseas." He also offered another $500 million in export financing. What LBJ was taking away with one hand he was trying to give back with the other. Government would cast a wary eye on investment opportunities in the developed world, opportunities that business identified of its own accord. Yet government would also seek to encourage sales in that same developed world, sales that business had not sought to make on its own. And all roads passed through Commerce.[16]

The Dow Jones Industrial Average first hit the mythical threshold of 1,000 in 1966. The Dow touched 1,000 again in 1968. It then waited a full sixteen years, until 1982, to breach that level permanently. But the index did not merely tread water in the interim. It actually collapsed in the period, because the price level trebled and gains were unindexed and assessed at high tax rates. Robert Bartley once took aim at the "old saw that the stock market predicted nine of the past five recessions." "[I]t has always been my view," he wrote in 2000, "that in the other four Washington got the message and mended its ways in time." One of those times was the action taken by Kennedy in the summer of 1962.[17]

Fiddling with price controls to fix inflation as the gold-dollar ratio teetered, JFK had found himself burned by U.S. Steel. A few months later, Kennedy reversed course, dug deep into the 1961 economic report, found the nugget that recommended tax cuts, and committed himself to them. The stock market had been sending signals all the while, declining 28 percent while Kennedy gathered his thoughts. If the market was predicting a recession, it got it spectacularly wrong. The great 1960s boom was about to get under way.

The market's vexation from 1966 to 1968 got precisely the opposite response from LBJ. Instead of offering a plan for removing governmental constraints on the real economy, the president put forward a wide-ranging program of governmental intervention. As a proxy for real, private-sector business activity, the market indexes had no reasonable course but to evince skepticism.

No die was cast for good in 1968. Policy mistakes can almost always be reversed. But two things were necessary for the year not to be fateful, at least in terms of allowing the 1970s not to fester as the malaise and stagflation decade. There had to be policy intelligence and understanding, and there had to be resolve in composing and administering an antidote. As it happened, Robert Mundell found audiences especially cool in the wake of that year.

Mundell Shifts

Mundell watched the policy-mix implosion of the latter 1960s with increasing incredulity. For a time, he moved from the IMF to the Brookings Institution, where he joined others in pondering the great macroeconomic question of the day: What to do with faltering Bretton Woods?

Mundell soon adopted the view that Bretton Woods did not have to be saved, but rather wound down and replaced with something else. His view did not defy the expectations of Bretton Woods at its founding. In 1944, the world wanted a reliable gold standard, and only the United States had gold in any quantity. In the future, after a period of general economic growth and the buildup of dollar reserves, foreign currency issuers could reclaim their proper apportionment of gold and fix their currencies to it independently. In this regard, Bretton Woods included a clause that permitted countries to fix to gold on their own.

In testimony to Congress and in articles written between 1965 and 1969, Mundell diagnosed what was happening and what needed to be done, given the conditions that had developed because of LBJ's flailing attempts to salvage the system. Mundell accepted the premises of the "Triffin dilemma," titled after a Belgian economist of that name, that under Bretton Woods countries had an inordinate incentive to accumulate dollar reserves. Dollar reserves enabled a country to ward off the IMF, in that a country could use reserve dollars to buy up its own currency on the foreign exchanges, to prevent the currency's exchange rate to the dollar from sinking. Because the prospect of IMF intervention was so scary, according to the Triffin dilemma, the United States was naturally invited to supply more dollars, far beyond its gold stock.

Mundell proposed a reform that consisted of a renewed version of his 1962 policy mix. The Federal Reserve should target price stability, and fiscal policy, the growth of the domestic economy. If foreigners wanted to scoop up dollars for their own investment and reserve currency needs, the Federal Reserve would have to supply them, because otherwise domestic prices in the United States would *fall* as dollars were removed from the American economy by foreigners. The Triffin dilemma would be eluded despite the accommodation of foreign interest in the dollar, because these extra dollars, indeed all dollars, would not be convertible to gold. The anchor of the new system would be not gold anymore, but the policy intelligence and benevolence of the United States. "Under the dollar standard the U.S. monetary system would, as it does now, create a certain amount of money each year," Mundell explained. "Part of this would be acquired by Americans and part by foreigners. . . . [That is,] the United States sells some of its currency abroad and that enables it to acquire real resources . . . in return. [This process] gives it an access to real resources that other countries do not have[,] . . . called an 'exorbitant privilege' by General de Gaulle." "It would be more correct to call it," Mundell went on to say, "a great advantage conferred on the United States." Furthermore, "If there is a dominant country . . . , that country can and should govern its policies according to the needs of internal stability, and smaller countries should adjust to it. There is no more socially useful service a very large country like the U.S. can perform for the entire world than to preserve price stability and full employment for itself."[18]

With such remarks, Mundell essentially predicted the budget deficits of the 1980s. When finally the United States showed resolve in reestablishing the value of the dollar in the early 1980s, foreigners wanted it in scads. Yet the American economy also had a ravenous appetite for new money at that time, given a resurgent growth rate. So emerged into its season in the sun the instrument by which foreigners most prefer to take their dollars: the thirty-year Treasury "long" bond, by which budget deficits are financed.

But 1968 was a long way from 1983. Mundell realized, in the late 1960s, that his proposals were more than a little dreamy. The intelligence and benevolence of the United States, as was only too clear, were not at all to be counted on, and Mundell knew that the lacuna in his system was a reliable anchor. Gold would no longer suffice because of the Triffin dilemma. In time, Mundell would finally hit on a means to force the United States to conduct enlightened policy—a rival reserve currency. His musings in this regard would earn him the nickname, richly deserved, of the "godfather of the euro." (The second stage of supply-side economics, which continues in full blush today, has concerned itself with reformulating the world monetary system by means of guaranteeing the dollar along the lines of what Mundell had first sketched in the 1960s.)

But first came the initial stage of supply-side economics. LBJ's expedients to stop dollar outflow did nothing to break the momentum of the run on gold. In March 1968, the gold position of the United States became untenable. Somehow, the United States got its major partners to agree to an unlikely compromise. The United States would no longer strive to ensure the $35 market price of gold and—the unlikely part—foreign central banks could continue to claim from the United States, for $35, an ounce of gold, so long as they agreed not to turn around and sell it.

The compromise may have had a prayer if the United States had then committed itself to ensuring that the dollar held its value—by, for example, letting the private economy run its course. But Johnson's policies aimed at the opposite. One of the remarkable things about the expedients that the federal government concocted to save Bretton Woods in the run-up to 1968 is that they were all kept in place, even expanded upon, despite the fact that the reason they were introduced—maintaining a dollar link to gold—was dropped unceremoniously in 1968. LBJ's "inflation tax" soon morphed into all the other tax increases of 1968–69. Commerce spending on phantom export opportunities remained in place. Capital controls abroad would soon be joined by price controls at home. The real economy was getting boxed into a corner in the name of Bretton Woods, and Bretton Woods was over.

Chicago

In 1965, Mundell accepted an offer to become a full professor in the department of economics at the University of Chicago. There he joined perhaps the greatest constellation of economic minds ever assembled. Chicago was rivaled only by the Edinburgh of Smith and Hume in the eighteenth century, the School of Salamanca in the sixteenth, or the various universes of Marshall, Jevons, Walras, Menger, Keynes, and Mises in the fin de siècle.

The *paterfamilias* of the Chicago group was Frank Knight, who aside from bringing accounting into the twentieth century—the practical positive effects of which can probably be measured in the trillions of dollars—was also one of the more important intellectual historians of his era. His student and later fellow faculty member, Milton Friedman, would eclipse Keynes as the greatest economist of the twentieth century. Other figures filled out the firmament of the discipline: Harry Johnson, Mundell's peer in international economics; F. A. Hayek, the Mises disciple who transformed philosophy as well as economics; and a slew of others, all future Nobelists, including George Stigler, Ronald Coase, Gary Becker, and Merton Miller. Then there were the graduate students, headlined by Robert E. Lucas. It was obvious that Mundell, thirty-two at the time of his appointment, was a rising star who belonged among this group. Indeed, very soon he became a prospect for the Nobel Prize in economics, which started in 1969.[19]

The collapse of Bretton Woods invigorated the field of international macroeconomics like nothing else, even Versailles. It is a paradoxical truth that great economists emerge exactly when economies start to function poorly. When economies do well, particularly stupendously well, great economists are rather superfluous and hence are not generally to be found. An example is the United States during the nineteenth century.

Something was breaking in the late 1960s, however, and economists had to be called on to suggest a fix. The great rising economic theory of the day, indelibly associated with Chicago and especially Milton Friedman, was the

theory recently christened "monetarism." If not inordinately complex, monetarism is immensely profound as an intellectual construct and as a policy.
There will be much said about monetarism in subsequent chapters, particularly concerning the functional alliance between it and supply-side economics during the Reagan years. At this juncture, it is fair to summarize Milton
Friedman's monetarism this way: economies succeed if monetary policy is
gotten right, and they struggle if monetary policy is gotten wrong. Mundell
was by no means a monetarist, in that he felt, following his notion of "effective
market classification," that monetary policy was good for one thing and one
thing only, stabilizing the value of the currency. Fiscal policy, tax cuts in particular, were also required to move a national economy out of a sluggishness
brought about, perhaps, by misguided monetary policy.[20]

Monetarism's founder and oracle, Friedman, was also passionate about
one other thing. He insisted on flexible exchange rates, exchange rates among
national currencies set daily by the market. Friedman's view was that fixed
rates were an unwarranted intrusion on the pricing authority of the market.
Surely the market knew best how much a dollar should trade for in marks, yen,
or lire. A fixed rate of exchange set at a governmental convention, such as at
Bretton Woods, struck Friedman as an absurdity.[21]

Mundell and Friedman got into holy, and altogether friendly, battles in the
seminar rooms. Friedman was earnest and gracious, and Mundell loved to play
provocateur. Mundell's former student, Rudiger Dornbusch, recalled that

> every so often there was a gladiator event, a workshop where for
> some reason faculty from different areas got together and got at each
> other. Mundell vs. Friedman were special events. Friedman obviously
> admired the sheer creativity of Mundell but would not let him get
> by; sparks would fly. Mundell recognized Friedman as an icon but
> understood that he could play the bad boy with success. I remember
> the unspeakable from Mundell: "Milton, the trouble with you is you
> lack common sense." Both won the argument; we could not choose.
> But even so, each had their cohort and the cohort would imitate the
> master in style and speech and mannerisms.

For Friedman's epigones, this meant wearing ill-fitting sack suits and
looking a little geeky. For Mundell's, this meant having a "continental appearance and demeanor," as Dornbusch remembered. Mundell favored turtlenecks

and such appurtenances of European bohemia. But he also was to be seen in the kind of vertical-striped, buttoned-down sport shirts that the Kingston Trio had last worn around 1960, though they were offered a brief reprise a few years later by the Beach Boys. (Mundell's haircut was Brian Wilson's.) Mundell puffed on a pipe, which in the late 1960s still made young men look interesting.[22]

"And then there was the day," Dornbusch recalled in 2001, "when Mundell presented to a full-full house his new theory of the policy mix—monetary policy for price stability, fiscal policy for supply-side growth. Suffice it to say that this was a very noisy afternoon." "It failed to convince," Dornbusch said on another occasion. Of course, this was not actually a new theory. Mundell had been invited to join the senior faculty at Chicago in the first place because of his work advocating this policy mix. The *IMF Staff Papers* brouhaha was already years in the past when this noisy afternoon in Chicago took place.[23]

The "open economy macro-model" inaugurated by Mundell and Fleming had in fact already begun to revolutionize economics. But not everyone saw the same lessons in it as Mundell. The main implication of the model concerned capital flows. In the Keynesian conception of closed domestic economies, raised interest rates simply take money away from consumption in favor of saving. Yet in an open international economy, raised interest rates in one country may result in increased money in that country's economy, without any decrease in the money devoted to demand. This may occur because the economy is open to "flows" from the rest of the world.

The conclusion commonly drawn from the Mundell-Fleming model is that typical economic stabilization measures, such as those of Keynesianism, are not so effective, indeed that national economic management is difficult to achieve. The model implies a "leaky bucket," a phrase coined by LBJ's CEA chairman, Arthur Okun. Loose money might help reduce a nation's unemployment, but at the expense of capital flight, which itself is a cause of unemployment. Budget deficits financed by the central bank might stimulate a country's economy, but at the prospect of inflation, and therefore again at the cost of capital flight and unemployment. Countries could try to goose their economies through monetary and fiscal measures, but they had to be aware that the resultant leaks of capital abroad could defeat their purpose.[24]

Supply-side economics in the 1970s and '80s would intensify this argument, saying that the process is not so much "leaky" as "thermodynamic," and holding that raised rates of return brought about by enlightened monetary policy along with tax cuts may attract foreign capital in enormous quantities. And if such capital does arrive, both supply and demand are enhanced. For foreign capital flows enable domestic earners to do whatever they wish with their money, to save or to spend it. They may indeed spend it, given that the new savings opportunities created by higher returns could be substantially gobbled up by the foreign flows.[25]

Monetarists at Chicago and elsewhere, including Friedman, Allan Meltzer, and Paul Volcker, came to insist that tax cuts and sound money are very good things, but that they are not apt instruments of stabilization policy during a crisis. Flexible monetary policy and the adjustment of exchange rates are better at ending a crisis, with tax cuts and monetary stability affecting the long term. In contrast, supply-side economics would argue that not only are monetary stability and low taxes good things in the long run; the best route out of economic crisis, particularly of the stagflation kind, is to tighten money and cut taxes.[26]

All these debates about stabilization and tax cuts and capital flows would roar in the 1980s. But in the late 1960s, debate was a luxury, because a crisis was in fact under way. It became imperative not merely to figure out what to do, but to do what was figured out. Otherwise moves would be made out of desperation. This is what happened. The dollar standard backed into in March 1968, when member countries agreed with the United States not to truck in gold on the open market, was not so much a policy as yet another expedient. A dollar standard could have worked, but it had to be a *sound* dollar. Without a gold guarantee, what was to enforce the dollar's soundness?

The short answer was the Federal Reserve. But it was immediately co-opted by the new president, Richard Nixon. In 1969, Nixon appointed one of his own economic advisors, Arthur F. Burns, as chairman of the Fed. Burns had been Eisenhower's CEA chairman and had known and gotten along with Nixon for years. The new Burns Fed kept money loose, just as in Martin's last five years.

The reason was to stave off unemployment. Nixon made it clear to aides, and surely to Burns, that his administration was to prefer inflation to unemployment, as if there were a trade-off between the two. As Nixon said to his own CEA chairman, Paul McCracken, in 1969: "I don't go along with the idea that sees us as heroes on inflation but villains on unemployment." Thus, the inflation that had stirred in the mid-'60s continued domestically and spread via fixed rates to the linked countries. Clearly, the dollar standard was in its death throes.[27]

Sensing a future of runaway prices, Mundell made an investment. In 1969, he put down $10,000 for a broken-down castle in Siena, Italy, that dated from the time of St. Francis of Assisi. He reasoned (correctly) that real property would appreciate disproportionately in an age of inflation. He called the place "Santa Colomba" and soon "Palazzo Mundell."[28]

St. Sebastian

It turned out that Mundell was a little too cool and mellow, perhaps too "continental," for Chicago, and in 1971 he decided to make his future elsewhere. He applied for and won the top fellowship in American academe, the Guggenheim. The month before he left the Chicago faculty, he gave a statement of his policy-mix views one more time, at a conference on global inflation held in Bologna, Italy, in April 1971. In attendance were virtually all the world's top macroeconomists, including Jacques Rueff. There, Mundell made the case, once again, for tightened money and lowered taxes. After a few sessions, the attendees stopped talking about all other matters. Everybody ganged up on Mundell, from his old boss Marcus Fleming to Harvard's Gottfried Haberler to Brookings's Walter Salant. Rueff knew something big was going on and was frustrated at having to keep relatively quiet. (He wished his English were better.) By the end of the conference, Mundell had garnered a new nickname—St. Sebastian, because he was taking so many arrows.[29]

The arrows generally had to do with the impossibility of the policy mix. Tight money shrinks the economy, lower taxes expand it—a zero-sum result. Tax cuts expand the economy but loose money only results in inflation. Was Mundell picking favorites? "Why should an expansionary monetary policy have more effect on prices than an increased budget deficit has?" asked Fleming. "I feel that Bob still hasn't answered [this] perfectly reasonable question." Haberler (a relative by marriage of the policy mix's old critic Herbert Furth) pressed the issue. He said that Mundell was right in adducing the recent history of tax cuts, such as that of 1948. "It turned out that the tax cut was the right thing to do—though for very different reasons from those that Bob mentioned." Haberler also wondered whether Mundell was not being magical in insisting that "flows" from abroad would break the contradiction of tight money and tax cuts. Mundell finally became testy with Haberler, saying he was "parroting" his arguments.[30]

Yet it eventually became clear that this Sebastian was no martyr. The conference closed, and Mundell remained very much alive and well. None of the arrows had really stuck. As British economist Lionel Robbins said, "I am in a muddle about Bob's proposition. In the end, I nearly always agree with him." Fritz Machlup of Princeton: "As usual, Mundell has put a puzzle before us. I am trying to solve it." Mundell not only had weathered the attacks. He also had shown that his arguments were so viable that the top minds in academic economics had to think seriously about becoming reoriented toward them.[31]

Surely it was frustrating to Mundell that the conference participants still treated his policy mix as a novelty. A decade had passed since Mundell first created a sensation at the IMF, and the doctrine had been roundly vindicated in practice since 1962. One of the conference participants, Fritz Machlup, an occasional arrow-slinger himself, arranged for Mundell's major remarks to be reprinted in his Princeton department's journal, *Essays in International Finance*. Mundell obliged, his article appearing one month later, in May. The piece, fated to be one of the most consequential in the modern history of economic literature, would be overlooked in academic forums. Yet today it stands as the founding statement of the supply-side revolution that faced down the 1970s.[32]

Events began to come to a head as spring turned to summer in 1971. After 1968, the nations fixed to the dollar had started playing a little trick on the United States. They started asking for redemptions in gold for their dollars at $35 per ounce. They had agreed not to trade that gold on the open market, where prices were higher. But they surely reasoned, correctly, that the United States would not sit idly by while its gold stock was reduced to nil. The United States would be forced to renegotiate the system or end it entirely. Then, countries would be free to sell the gold they had accumulated for dollars on the open market for an amount well above the $35 price. It was a game of chicken, and the United States deserved to be made to play it.[33]

"The Dollar and the Policy Mix: 1971," the title of Mundell's Princeton article, is not the cheeriest entry in the Mundell oeuvre. Typically, Mundell's work exudes the disposition of its author: extroverted, playful, incisive, wry; in a word, fun. But there is anger in "The Dollar and the Policy Mix," and that anger effectively announced that, in the future, Mundell would be taking his case to the public.[34]

The distended supply of the dollar in the late 1960s and the tax increases and new regulations thought to counteract it presaged a recession in 1969–70. It would be of the dreaded double-dip variety, where quarterly decreases in gross national product are initially overcome, only to have another down quarter before a return to growth. Unemployment, which had held at under 4 percent through the monetary ease of the late 1960s, went to 5 percent and then 6 percent in 1970 and 1971. Inflation, in the 1 percent range through the period of the JFK tax cuts, moved beyond 5 percent by the late 1960s and stayed there through the recession.

"The idea that monetary acceleration necessarily increases employment," Mundell wrote in "The Dollar and the Policy Mix," "is one of those tired clichés that have . . . , by repetition, become elevated into a dogma and end up doing more harm than good." He went on: "The theoretical basis for the cliché is certainly not well founded in economic theory. . . . Nevertheless, the idea remains rooted in the psyche of part of the public, especially governmental officials, and part of the economics profession. . . . In the United States in 1970, the money supply expanded at a rate [upwards] of 12 per cent, but unemployment jumped from 4 per cent to 6 per cent while prices continued to rise at . . . 5 per cent. This occurrence alone should wake people up."[35]

Here Mundell was taking aim at the so-called Phillips curve, a warhorse of armchair economic analysis throughout the 1970s but annihilated in academic economics as early as 1971. The Phillips curve held that there was an inverse relationship between inflation and unemployment. It therefore implied that policy tools which could induce or restrain inflation would be effective in doing the opposite to unemployment. The original research underlying the Phillips curve was obscure, but Paul Samuelson had written positively about it in 1960 and provided it with received-truth status.[36]

Knives sharpened. Friedman, Edmund Phelps, and then Robert Lucas laid into the logic and evidence of the Phillips curve in the late 1960s and early 1970s. All three of these economists' Nobel Prize citations referred to their work on the Phillips curve. Yet it is odd that multiple Nobels would be given for the defeat of a doctrine that had collapsed on first pass. This is testament to the resiliency of the Phillips curve in policy circles and of the colloquialism born of its reception: "overheating." Lucas said it best in his Nobel address: he realized that the Phillips curve was wrong when he put on the same plot the unemployment and inflation rates of the United States from the postwar quarter century. The graph was a hash.[37]

Mundell was angry in 1971 because obvious lessons from recent macroeconomics were being paid no heed in Washington. He implied that the responsibility for this state of affairs partly lay with monetarism, in that monetarism argued that monetary policy largely determined the economy: if you get the money supply right, monetarism seemed to counsel, all the hard work in getting the economy to hum will be done. Monetarism represented a grave temptation to Washington policymakers bent on acquiring quick and comprehensive means of control over the economy.

Mundell put it in italics: "*The United States [does] not have inflation immune tax structures.*" "If a country has a progressive-tax system," he wrote, "an increase in the price level increases the real value of taxes and . . . reduces real aggregate demand. This means that *an increase in the money supply* combined with a proportionate increase in [wages] *reduces* employment. The longer inflation goes on without an adjustment of taxes the more it reduces actual output below potential output." There was no trade-off at all between inflation and unemployment. Rather, given tax rates that increase with income, the relationship is direct: inflation *causes* unemployment. Inflation removes income from savers and spenders, gives it to government, and thereby reduces the size of the real economy. By 1971, American policy had brought about a Phillips curve that was a line shooting up. Higher inflation brought with it higher unemployment.[38]

The harms that the nation incurred in bringing this predicament upon itself were serious. "The 1968 tax increase," Mundell wrote, "was a colossal blunder. . . . For, while money [was] expanding at a [high] rate . . . , the tax increase in 1968 interposed a barrier to real expansion, causing the inflation rate to accelerate rather than decline. The tax increase cut into real expansion and increased inflation." He rued the "*actual policy mix* [of] fiscal tightness combined with an excessive monetary expansion. We got a depression without stopping the inflation." For all the expedients LBJ had put in place to pay for guns and butter, Mundell offered this accounting: "The 1969–71 recession was an economic catastrophe which cost more in wasted resources than the cumulative economic cost of the war in Asia, more than the entire GNP of 800 million Chinese." Alas, the nation could have had it all. But only if it had pursued the "*correct policy mix* [of] a reduction in the rate of monetary expansion . . . combined with a tax reduction. This would have stopped the inflation rate without causing a depression. . . . A whole year's growth . . . was lost."[39]

So what to do in 1971? Mundell argued that the solution endorsed by monetarism was both false and objectionable. This was the "*recession method*" (Mundell's italics), whereby the Federal Reserve would withhold or suck money out of the economy in order to bring prices back to par. There would have to be increased unemployment, but such were the costs of recovering from a monetary policy that had been too loose. This "solution" made Mundell furious:

> The economic cost of the recession method is $96 billion [in May 1971]. This bloodletting is probably the minimum bill for getting inflation to 2 percent a year by the method adopted. . . . Spread over two years, $96 billion is greater than the annual GNP of most countries in the world. It is a fantastic cost that, if it is accepted, would undermine the entire philosophy of monetary management. If indeed the cost of reducing the inflation rate . . . were put to the American people as a bill for $96 billion, or almost $500 per person . . . , the public might prefer to put up with the inflation.

Mundell laid into the "economic generals," the "prima donnas of economic academe," and an "economics profession" that was "far from guiltless" in engineering the mess and now proposed the wrong medicine. Then he articulated his own plan.[40]

This was the same plan that he had offered Jacques Polak at the IMF in 1961, the same plan that underlay the Mundell-Fleming model, the same plan that in several years would form the nucleus of supply-side economics. "The correct policy mix," Mundell wrote, "is based on *fiscal ease* to get more production out of the economy, in combination with *monetary restraint* to stop inflation. The increased momentum of the economy provided by the stimulus of a tax cut will cause sufficient demand for credit to permit real monetary expansion at higher interest rates."[41]

Mundell took care to specify several things about his views that apparently kept getting overlooked. First, by "fiscal ease," he meant tax cuts, not new government spending. Aside from providing for more demand, tax cuts also "increase profits and raise the return to capital." That is, tax cuts spur new investment as well as boost the consumer. Second, by "monetary restraint" Mundell did not mean starving the economy of money. Proper monetary restraint might even involve a significant increase in the money supply. If tax cuts raise rates of investment return as well as encourage more consumer spending, the demand for dollars may require the Fed to provide more money than it had during the inflationary period meant to be brought to an end. And yet inflation would go down as new money arrived to support growth, as opposed to the price level. As Mundell put it, "Growth of *real* output raises

real money demand and thus abets the absorption of real monetary expansion
into the economy without inflation."[42]

Mundell dwelled on these points for a reason: the masters of American
economic policy, let alone the commentators on the sidelines, were oblivious, if not hostile, to them. Through the early 1980s, supply-side economics
had to battle two great dragons. The first was the (false) Keynesian insistence
that tax cuts are inflationary. The second dragon—monetarism—had more
impressive intellectual credentials. Monetarism had a high opinion of its own
potencies. If poor monetary policy is practiced, in the canons of monetarism,
the mistakes can be cured only by good monetary policy. But as the cure is
administered, some time may pass. Thus, as inflation brought about by mistakenly loose monetary policy is removed by monetary policy that is correctly
tight, a recession occurs. The intensely severe 1981–82 recession, the worst
since the Great Depression, was a function of a power play between supply-
siders and monetarists over the degree of monetary restraint necessary to end
inflation, given a program of tax cuts.

"The Dollar and the Policy Mix: 1971" encapsulated all the major tenets
of the supply-side movement that would coalesce over the next several years.
It diagnosed the problem of modern sluggishness as deriving from the mis-
use of the institutions of 1913—that is, the Federal Reserve and the income
tax. It identified the specific origins of stagflation in the interaction between
inflation and the progressive tax code. And it established (by reiteration) the
supply-side method of dealing with economic crisis: currency stabilization
plus tax cuts.

Mundell's paper conferred one more essential characteristic on the
nascent supply-side movement. It insisted that economic growth is a natural
and permanent condition, something that stops only by being interrupted by
an outside agency, specifically government. Supply-side economics' unfailing
orientation toward growth would be the chief reason it was attractive not only
to the young men and women of Wall Street, Congress, and journalism who
rallied to its banner as growth flagged in the 1970s, but to Ronald Reagan as he
sought the presidency in 1980. And yet the orientation toward growth was also
a chief reason that supply-side economics would be held in suspicion by its
critics, critics who felt that after the era of postwar prosperity, growth should
be subordinated to the goal of more evenly distributing wealth.

Unfortunately, at the time it was published, Mundell's Princeton article
had no chance of affecting policy. The decade 1971–81 could not have vio-

lated Mundell's recommendations more rudely. The money engines would be gunned, and taxes raised, as never before—by stealth, and through bracket creep. The stagflation that gripped the nation (and world), in time making the inflation, unemployment, and growth rates of 1971 seem positively quaint, would appear increasingly difficult to resolve, even as Mundell's paper sat on library shelves unread.

In short order after that May, the crisis reached its conclusion. In one of the most fateful moves of the modern presidency, Nixon took the dollar off gold on August 15, 1971. Foreign central banks were now assured that the United States would not redeem the dollars that they had been accumulating for gold, at $35 or any other price. The anchor of the Bretton Woods system was now officially gone. For a time, countries still strove to fix to the dollar, in the vain hope that the United States would keep it stable.[43]

Nixon opted for an expedient to make that happen: price controls. New bureaucracies in Commerce and elsewhere would monitor prices of all sorts of goods and services in major industries and threaten to punish producers if specified price bands were breached. Soon, unions came under pressure not to seek wage increases, so that employers could still make a profit given the controls.[44]

Controls opened up promising new business opportunities for Washington lobbyists. Exemptions from controls could lead to profit gushers and an unlevel playing field. Big business stood to gain over small business, in that lobbying takes money, contacts, and experience. Robert Bartley began ruminating on these matters and realized that one acute effect of controls was to diminish entrepreneurialism. His work in this area would win him the Pulitzer Prize.[45]

Price controls were an artificial device through and through, meant to paper over Federal Reserve overprinting in the absence of a dollar link to gold. Even if controls could in fact keep inflation at bay, it would have to be at the expense of output, innovation, and wage growth. In a word, the price was stagnation. Given that new government bureaucracies had to be created to interpose themselves into business (and labor) decision-making, the net effect would inevitably be negative.

Nixon's Fed gunned the monetary engines prior to the 1972 election, this despite Nixon's keeping Milton Friedman around the White House to give a patina of respectability to his economic policy. Controls nearly collapsed under the pressure. The threat remained that they would return with a vengeance if business and labor acted unreasonably. The year 1973 threatened to be the great juncture, the year postwar prosperity indubitably ended.[46]

A curious incident occurred within the Nixon economic team in early 1971. At the Bureau of the Budget (then being reconstituted as the Office of Management and Budget), a staffer, working with a colleague, made a bold prediction about the year's gross national product. The staffer—chief economist at OMB at the age of thirty—was Arthur B. Laffer, on leave from a faculty post at the University of Chicago and still fulfilling his requirements for the Stanford Ph.D. He and his colleague David Ranson shocked the economics profession by predicting a GNP number far higher than the consensus forecast. Laffer said that the 1971 GNP would come in at $1.065 trillion, about $20 billion higher than the consensus forecast.[47]

In economics circles, everyone started mentioning that number, "1065," usually to ridicule it. Not only was it excessively "optimistic" (although all Laffer had done was to say that high inflation would be reflected in nominal GNP), but Laffer and Ranson had used only a small number of variables in preparing their forecast. Not only was it likely to be proven wrong, but it was also arrived at through methodologically superficial means. Later in the year, newly minted Nobelist Paul Samuelson crowned all the crowing with his "Why They Are Laughing at Laffer" talk at Laffer's own Chicago.[48]

In 1976, the revised GNP numbers showed that Laffer's forecast had hit the 1971 number on the dot. Furthermore, in the coming years stagflation would embarrass all the received ways of doing economic forecasting. *Fortune* asked whether anyone cared to notice that Laffer had been proven correct a half decade later. Laffer, meanwhile, had become too busy to care. He had become consumed with the task of teaching the nation what it had done wrong in economic policy, where it was headed if it failed to change course, and the sure way it could extricate itself from its bizarre predicament.[49]

In the great transition year of 1973, Laffer began writing occasionally for the *Wall Street Journal*. His second contribution to the editorial page, in January 1974, was called "The Bitter Fruits of Devaluation." It was an intriguing piece. It began: "Inflation is plaguing not only the housewife but also the economics profession. Over the past year, . . . consumer prices rose at a rate of nearly 9 percent. Conventional economic views did not predict and cannot explain increases of this magnitude." Laffer went on to assert that the agent of change was Nixon's taking the dollar off gold—"devaluation." Yet Laffer believed that "the mystery of the current bout of inflation is readily solvable."[50]

At Bologna, and in "The Dollar and the Policy Mix: 1971," Mundell had made a similar observation. He had written: "There are no economic costs to a balance-of-payments policy that can be escaped by avoiding its discipline, unless one sees the answer in more American inflation masquerading as expansion." "There are no economic costs"—another way, perhaps, of saying "free lunch," the most notorious epithet in the sayings of economics, an epithet hurled at supply-side economics repeatedly in the face of its 1980s successes. Whatever Mundell and Laffer were getting at in the early 1970s, as the great stagflation rose to its feet, the only people who were really interested in listening made up the clutch of drinkers and diners at Michael 1.[51]

Part II

Demimondes

5

MICHAEL 1

Since about 1974, the recuperative powers of this great nation have been
at work.
—ROBERT L. BARTLEY, commencement address, Iowa State University, 1981

In 1971, as his prediction of that year's GNP created a squall in Washington, Arthur Laffer befriended a journalist who called him on the phone about it. Jude Wanniski was a reporter for the *National Observer*, a political circular operated by Dow Jones, publisher of the *Wall Street Journal*. Wanniski had called Laffer because the "1065" GNP forecast had become a common topic of discussion among Washington newshounds. The two struck up a friendship. Wanniski liked that this potentate of the Office of Management and Budget indulged his basic questions about economics. "Stupid questions," Wanniski would later recall. Such as: "What's the law of supply and demand?"[1]

Wanniski was not the only one interested in brushing up on his economics. It was becoming something of a national pastime. For in the early 1970s, the economy began to fail badly, and people wanted answers. Economists were nearly as confused as everyone else. They were thrown a lifeline in October 1973, when the Organization of Petroleum Exporting Countries (OPEC) signaled that it would triple the price of oil. The "oil shock" would soon become most economists' convenient catchall explanation for the raging inflation, recessions, and stock-market plunge that characterized the economy in the late Nixon and Ford-Carter eras. But in reality, the inflation crisis was in full swing before the OPEC shock of late 1973. OPEC moved to raise prices precisely because the currency instability emanating from the United States was already troubling the world. In the twelve months before the OPEC announcement, consumer prices in the United States increased by 8 percent, breaking out of the 5 percent range established in Nixon's first term, a rate that itself was quadruple the historical norm.[2]

The inflation of 1973—of that year prior to October—caused as many problems as anything that was to come from Arabia. During 1973, prices shot up acutely—housing, furnishings, apparel, medical care, tobacco. And to crown it off, there was one great commodity, of greater importance even than oil to daily life, whose price rose the most in 1973, transfixing the nation in disbelief. That commodity was food, which suffered 15 percent inflation that year. Food became the first major commodity to burst out of the 5 percent inflation band and goad the general index up to unseen levels, a leadership role later assumed by oil, gas, and various metals naturally delimited in supply. The inflation laggard in 1973 was transportation (the price of which increased 3 percent), making it logically impossible that rising "energy" costs were responsible for inflation at the grocery store.[3]

Eggs went up 49 percent in 1972–73, pacing the category of poultry, meats, and fish, which rose 25 percent as a group. Yet in the face of these huge increases, supplies were literally destroyed. On the evening news, a nation aghast saw workers at a Texas farm drown forty thousand chicks because poultry prices nevertheless were not going to be high enough to recoup costs. In April there was a more or less effective one-week national boycott of meat, organized by housewives at wit's end over big markups.[4]

It took the events of October 1973—OPEC, the Oakland A's World Series victory, and the Watergate "Saturday Night Massacre"—for the food crisis to be supplanted as the most talked-about national story. The OPEC shock in particular took the nation's mind off the bizarre inflation saga of 1973. Nixon had spent the year striving to "control" and then "freeze" food prices, which led to ever more desperate price increases and the withholding and destruction of supply. Finally, a very old and very reliable explanation for the food crisis emerged: the weather. It was El Niño's fault.[5]

The overall price level was primed to go up another 11 percent at an annual rate through May 1974 when nascent supply-siders first convened to talk about what the deuce was going on. Inexplicable food crises, after all, are not the stuff of major, developed countries, especially ones ornamented by economists. In the meantime, the main economic metric started to teeter and then fall: the GDP growth rate peaked for the long term in 1973.

Quarterly GDP growth entered into its most degenerating two-year period since the Great Depression. Over a seven-quarter period from 1973 to 1975, GDP went down five times, which meant that there was at least one recession and possibly another in the period, making for a double dip, as in 1969–70. In early 1975, GDP was still 3 percent off the 1973 mark, an enduring contraction the likes of which had been completely unknown during the quarter century of postwar prosperity. And in the recession years of 1974 and 1975, consumer prices somehow increased at World War I rates—11 percent and 9 percent, respectively. At the end of 1975, the economy was only marginally bigger than it had been in 1973, and prices were 25 percent higher.

For a while, it looked like the stock market would not hold. In 1973–74, the indexes fell halfway to zero before snapping back somewhat in 1975. The Dow industrials stabilized at about 850, 15 percent below the 1966 peak. There had been 66 percent inflation in the interim, however, meaning that if you had been holding the whole while, you were getting killed. Then there was unemployment: it surged to 9 percent in 1975, easily the highest level since the Depression, a rate that was one-quarter higher than during any postwar recession.

In the midst of this bewildering mess, people began to recall an apt statistic created back in the '60s by LBJ's CEA chair, Arthur Okun. Almost as a joke, Okun had mimicked the weather service's combining of heat and humidity in a "discomfort index." Okun summed the unemployment and inflation rates to form an "economic discomfort index." In Okun's day it had been at 6 or 7, but in 1975 it hit an unthinkable 18. This wasn't mere discomfort, so someone recast the metric as the "misery index." For his part, Paul Samuelson, who had forgotten about Laffer, chipped in by resurrecting another dormant and previously inapplicable term. This was the inelegant portmanteau, the contradiction in terms, the impossibility that became the great dread word of the 1970s: "stagflation."[6]

Impresario

Jude Wanniski had come to Washington in 1962 after stints at papers in places like Anchorage and Las Vegas to work as a "newshound" (said Bartley) and "street-fighter" (said another colleague) for the *National Observer.* When he met Laffer in 1971, Wanniski knew nothing about economics, but he was already a veteran journalist.[7]

Wanniski had grown up in Brooklyn. His father had been a miner until Jude's birth in Pottsville, Pennsylvania, in 1936, moving the family to New York City the next year to take a job as an apartment super. Jude developed intellectual interests and a love of reading as a teenager, when he also flirted with Marxism. His grandfather (also a miner) and his father tugged him in different directions. The grandfather had him read Marx; his father, a union man, insisted on being "100 percent American."[8]

On enrolling at Brooklyn College, Jude chose to major in natural sciences. But like the Dodgers, he felt the pull of California. After a year, he left Brooklyn for UCLA, where he studied political science and received a master's in journalism. He cottoned to a certain style of outrageousness characteristic of the West Coast. Thus did he arrive to the *National Observer,* in 1962, in a Buick Riviera convertible and lamé outfit, with a leggy Vegas showgirl (his wife) riding shotgun.

The *National Observer* editor who hired him had been trolling the nation for new talent and had found Wanniski at a paper in Las Vegas. He remained proud of his hire, even as Wanniski was never able to crack the social circuit of the high Washington reporters. The veterans on the *Observer* staff were snooty toward him and made him the target of practical jokes. Wanniski looked like he was from deepest Eastern Europe—Ukraine, Lithuania, or Poland. He was dark and swarthy, a son of the working class, and he wore black, of all things, in the 1960s. In one office prank, his mates told him that the man in the next room (who was actually soon to be the CEO of Dow Jones) was a bewildered visitor from Latin America. Wanniski invited Warren Phillips out for a drink to show him the ropes, and everybody busted a gut.

Nobody doubted that Wanniski was a diligent, crack reporter. His beat was in service of a page-two column about congressional gossip, and in that space Wanniski displayed a talent for spotting up-and-coming members. (This talent soon went to his head, for against all evidence to the contrary, he claimed, in 1980, to have made Jack Kemp into a political force by rewriting his tax bill. This claim would begin the long alienation from many of the supply-siders that Wanniski would endure until his death in 2005.)[9]

What really impressed his editors at the *National Observer,* and what led to his move to the *Wall Street Journal* in 1973, was that Wanniski was inquisitive about ideas. When he started asking Laffer those stupid questions in 1971, Wanniski seems to have had the presentiment that he was about to embark upon a major intellectual journey, the law of supply and demand beginning a quest that would lead to his own maturation as an intellectual—and perhaps to some great boon for the nation and society at large. The United States would be in need of such a boon, because, as Laffer had told him after the close of the gold window in August 1971, "it is not going to be as much fun to be an American anymore."[10]

Wanniski kept conversing with Laffer through the high-inflation periods of 1972, 1973, and 1974. At Laffer's behest, he attended a summit on inflation featuring leading economists, Mundell included, convened by the American Enterprise Institute (AEI) in May 1974. AEI was one of the conservative think tanks that began to flourish in Washington in the 1970s and 1980s (others included the Cato Institute and the Heritage Foundation). It did a great deal to extend academic and policy research into areas untouched by scholars stuck in the establishmentarian rut. Former Bill Clinton advisor Sidney Blumenthal and others have argued that the formation of these think tanks was essentially an admission on the part of conservatives that their ideas were mere adjuncts to political ideology, that they lacked the heft necessary to pass muster in the usual scholarly venues. The claim is wild, particularly in view of the proceedings of that most extraordinary conference of May 1974.[11]

The neoclassical synthesis and other vaunted macroeconomic paradigms of the 1960s—which had produced the Twist and other fancy expedients—seemed entirely clueless by 1974. Something had gone badly wrong in macroeconomic thinking, and it was time for a new seriousness. Now the main hegemon was monetarism, which, despite Friedman's frequent contact with Nixon and Burns, threatened to escape the current crisis unscathed. Monetarists were successfully arguing that the White House and Fed had not taken their advice. Indeed, in 1973, prominent monetarist Allan Meltzer and a colleague started the Shadow Open Market Committee. Twice a year, this group of twelve eminent monetarists would discuss recent Fed and White House economic moves and issue a statement saying what the government should have done, according to sound principles.[12]

At the AEI conference, the old defenders of controls and expedients were manifestly chastened. Gottfried Haberler, the Harvard professor whom Mundell had suggested was partially responsible for the criticism of his *IMF Staff Papers* piece back in 1962, and with whom Mundell had recently had that sharp exchange at Bologna, conceded that his preference for continued controls on wages and prices seemed rather irrelevant. It was medicine-taking time, and the monetarists were going to be the ones stout enough to show the way. Meltzer was supported by others in arguing for a restriction in the growth of the money supply, government spending cuts sufficient to fund a budget surplus, and no Federal Reserve intervention in support of the exchange rate of the dollar. Business and spending constituencies might howl under the pressure, but inflation would be wrung out, and the nation would be prepared to start again from scratch.[13]

For his part, Mundell virtually dismissed the current crisis. He said that it was not so portentous, that it could come to an end forthwith. He established that inflation was an international problem and had next to nothing to do with higher oil prices being "forced" upon the world. He provided a table showing commodities that had risen in price as much as or more than oil in recent years, among them cotton, rice, and wheat, with sugar beating oil's price increase by a factor of three. Next to this was a table of national money creation over the same period, showing increases of great magnitudes. Since the United States in particular had given up on mooring the dollar to gold in any credible way in the 1960s, and since the convention up to that point had been for the world's currencies to be priced in relation to dollars, this was the result: "Confidence in currencies in general declined and a shift out of money and financial assets commenced. A worldwide 'scarcity' of land and . . . raw materials . . . emerged. [Soon] the prices of metals, foods and minerals more than doubled. Shortages of beef, sugar and grains appeared, but gold and oil led to the most dramatic 'crises' and received the most attention from the public." Note Mundell's scare quotes.[14]

Print too much money, and you get higher prices—prices so high that people inordinately want real goods (especially commodities) as opposed to currencies, in expectation of future devaluations. The commodities "crisis" was a money crisis. Priority must be placed on solving that: "The only effective anti-inflation policy is one that few countries have tried: tighter money." And then this prediction, fully borne out in the 1980s: "If inflation is brought under control, the increase in the price of oil may not be maintained any more than the increase in the price of gold."[15]

As for the increase in the price of oil that the world had already endured, Mundell dismissed talk that any such "shock" could push the world (or the United States) into a depression. The big nations' economic cooperation organization, the OECD, had just made such a prediction, and Mundell ridiculed it. "Oil revenues will flow back into international capital markets not much more slowly than they are accumulated and will be available for financing expansion elsewhere."[16]

The question that Mundell left dangling was whether these oil dollars in prodigious quantities, soon headed for Western banks and investment accounts, would be put to productive use. About this he was not so sure. For the investment environment in the West was no longer benign, on account of taxation. Mundell mused for a while on the stock market. Many issues appeared to be "grossly undervalued." "Presumably equity should be a viable hedge against inflation since it represents a claim on real output and assets which should go up with the general level of prices." Yet how undervalued really was the market, Mundell asked himself, given that gains in stock prices that merely kept up with inflation were understood by the unindexed tax code to be taxable? If stocks appreciated yearly by 8 percent—the rate of inflation—holders would have no real gain. But on selling, they would have to declare the 8 percent on their returns and pay taxes on it—upwards of 50 percent in the federal code, 70 percent on dividends. Why, in this environment, would investors make an investment in stocks, or any vehicle whose inflation appreciation would appear to the tax code as a real gain?[17]

Mundell did not come out and say it, but he heavily implied it: Cut taxes, and all the oil money going to Arabia will finance real investment and expansion in the West. Keep taxes progressive and unindexed for inflation, and that oil money will simply sit in bank accounts, prop up consumer prices, and eventually find creative outlets in things like flier loans to lesser-developed countries. The United States, as the dominant economy, possessed the key. It could opt for real increases in production and wealth or for inflation alone. All it had to do was stabilize the dollar and cut taxes to get the former. If it stayed the course, it would continue to get the latter.[18]

Wanniski spoke with Mundell for the first time at the AEI conference. It marked the beginning of a friendship that would last for the remaining three decades of Wanniski's life. Wanniski, Mundell, and Laffer (who also gave a paper at the conference) agreed to get together for a discussion, and the result was a Wanniski profile of the two economists, which appeared a few weeks later on the *Journal* opinion page. The three promised to meet thereafter whenever Laffer was in New York, where Mundell was taking a professorship at Columbia. (He remains there today, holding the school's highest academic rank: University Professor.)[19]

The meeting of Wanniski, Laffer, and Mundell after the AEI conference was the germ of the Michael 1 gatherings that would transpire over the next two years. Those gatherings, which would include Robert Bartley and members of his circle, would be run by Wanniski, who was now conversant in economics, particularly the new economics of Nobelist-in-waiting Mundell. In December 1974, with the exception of the earlier profile, Wanniski made his *Journal* economics debut. He wrote about what he had learned from Mundell during the past few months. Mundell went over the copy so that its economics was clear and sound. With the title "It's Time to Cut Taxes," this piece introduced supply-side economics to the medium—the *Journal* opinion page—that would, in time, convey supply-side economics to the center of power.[20]

"It's Time to Cut Taxes" provided an overview of Mundell's prescription for addressing modern sluggishness, the prescription Mundell had been repeating since 1961. No one in international macroeconomics would have learned anything new by reading Wanniski's piece, aside from Mundell's specific recommendation of a $30 billion tax cut in 1975. Indeed, the piece quoted a number of economists who indicated their familiarity with Mundell's views. One of them, Keynes biographer Roy Harrod, said that Mundell was one of the "greatest economists in the world."

The piece was adroitly written—Wanniski was a gifted writer, particularly gifted with the virtue of conciseness. Yet it was not much more than a patchwork of Mundell's conference statements from the past several years. "It's Time to Cut Taxes" did not indicate that its source material was at that point getting rather antique. If it had, readers would have been made aware—and perhaps angry—that Mundell's advice had not been taken throughout the duration of the stagflation, which had been in bloom since the 1969–70 recession. The article echoed "The Dollar and the Policy Mix: 1971": "The level of U.S. taxes has become a drag on economic growth in the United States. . . . The national economy is being choked by taxes—asphyxiated." And: "To stop inflation, you need more goods, not less."

Wanniski summarized the Mundellian solution: cut taxes to sharpen "incentive to produce"; use monetary policy to shrink the dollar supply and the tax cut to ensure that people continue to have scarcer and thus more valuable dollars; observe as foreign capital is attracted to the country in the face of a tax cut, ameliorating the effect of tight money. "It's Time to Cut Taxes" was a perfectly capable summary of the argument that Mundell had been making in the universe of international macroeconomics since 1961.

Two Continents

This point is of more than incidental interest, given what Wanniski did the very week that "It's Time to Cut Taxes" appeared in the *Wall Street Journal* in December 1974. A few days before the article appeared, Wanniski presided over a meeting that would become the single most famous incident in the history of supply-side economics: the sketching of the "Laffer curve" on a paper cocktail napkin at the Two Continents restaurant in Washington, D.C. The napkin incident would somehow come to represent, among casual observers as well as critics, both the founding moment of supply-side economics and a metaphor for its theoretical superficiality.

The napkin story is not well sourced. We do know that Wanniski had superlative contacts in Washington, which to date had entirely been in the realm of politics. He knew particularly well President Ford's chief of staff, Donald H. Rumsfeld, and Rumsfeld's deputy, Richard Cheney. When Ford entered office in August 1974, stagflation was roaring. Ford had no idea what to do about the economy, and Wanniski sensed it. He quickly told Rumsfeld that he had a secret policy initiative that could shore up the Republican side in the November congressional elections. Rumsfeld, ever busy, delayed meeting Wanniski until after the election, in which the Republicans took one of the great drubbings of all time. For years afterward, Wanniski maintained (with some plausibility) that the midterm vote of 1974 had been a referendum not so much on Watergate as on the economy.[21]

At any rate, Rumsfeld dispatched Cheney to meet Wanniski and Laffer that December at the Two Continents, which was across the street from Treasury. Rumsfeld had known Laffer from his stint in Nixon's OMB and had a high opinion of him. He even told Wanniski that he thought Laffer was "a genius." Apparently Rumsfeld was going to take to the president any reasonable suggestion that Wanniski and Laffer related to Cheney. Their problem was simply to get the message across.[22]

Ford had been considering a "tax cut" whereby rebate checks would be mailed out to taxpayers, perhaps in the amount of $100, a one-time deal. He was reluctant to cut tax rates because the revenue loss would be indeterminate, permanent, and possibly large. Laffer kept insisting, at the Two Continents, that this was not so, that a cut in tax rates would perhaps bring in *more* revenue. He whipped out a pen, took a paper napkin from the bar, and drew a graph of a "McDonald's arch lying on its side" (Bartley's description), with tax rates the vertical and revenues the horizontal axis. If tax rates were so high that they cleared the farthest reach in the arch's bulge, cutting them would produce more revenue. The idea was that as taxes become exorbitant, people stop trying to earn income.[23]

The meeting had no effect. The Ford administration soon mailed out rebate checks. At the time, nobody knew about or had heard of the Laffer curve. That would not come until four years later, when Wanniski made the Laffer curve the centerpiece of his best-selling book, *The Way the World Works.* Laffer himself would become chagrined by the whole thing, not recalling the incident precisely and worrying that he might have defaced the lovely cloth napkins that he remembered as de rigueur at the Two Continents.[24]

There will be more on the napkin incident later, but the essential point is that the Laffer curve was presented to two persons in December 1974. "It's Time to Cut Taxes" was presented to two million (the readership of the *Journal*) the very same week. "It's Time to Cut Taxes" not only spoke of the academic vetting of the supply-side argument. It also took time to address the revenue issue. As for the academic vetting, Wanniski's article correctly got across the fact that Mundell was a phenomenon in international economics. As for government revenue, the article carefully laid out the Mundellian position, making two central points.

The first was that while tax cuts reduce government revenue, they also reduce expenditures. By increasing incentives to produce, tax cuts bring people off the unemployment rolls and hence lessen the jobless benefits paid by the government. Wanniski showed that given the automatic tax increases of bracket creep, incentives decline, supply grows short, and unemployment and thus government obligations go up. "If taxes are not cut now," Wanniski wrote, "government deficits might even exceed the amount implied by a tax cut." This is an essential line, for it indicates that Wanniski, in December 1974, within days of the napkin sketch, recognized that tax cuts implied, along with spending reductions, revenue losses. Perhaps not great revenue losses, perhaps revenue losses less than would result from permitting bracket creep to continue unabated, but revenue losses all the same.

The second point was that the financing of a deficit caused by tax cuts would be not only easy, but economically benign. To fail to grasp this point is, indeed, to fail to grasp a central doctrine of supply-side economics. In the original Mundell-Fleming model of the early 1960s, the driving idea was that improved returns in a country, as brought about by tight money and tax cuts, so attract foreign investment that the country becomes cash flush. This was the reason Mundell was confident in asserting, in 1971, that there were "no economic costs" to addressing balance-of-payments problems in this way.

In "It's Time to Cut Taxes," Wanniski wrote that Mundell "disagrees with both the Keynesians and the classical economists on the ... effects of a tax cut." And then quoting Mundell: "Keynesians only look at the effect on demand. ... They neglect the financing side. ... The classical economists are only concerned about the 'crowding-out' effect," by which, Wanniski continued, Mundell "means the effect of deficit financing on the private capital market [where] government financing [requirements] crowd out private borrowing that would otherwise go into capital expansion."

Wanniski sketched Mundell's views further: "The finance required for the tax cut would be less than what would be needed if the recession is allowed. ... Mundell believes the size of the credit pool would automatically expand as the prospect of real economic growth engendered by the tax cut allows a recovery of real savings." And, Wanniski noted, "the tax cut will draw money from abroad."

The record from Wanniski, the impresario of the Two Continents meeting that gave us the Laffer curve on a napkin, was abundantly clear in December 1974. Wanniski understood that tax cuts might cause revenue losses. He also believed, after Mundell, that deficits arising from these losses would be easily financed, given the new excitement for dollar-denominated assets that would result from tight money and tax cuts.

On the latter point, Wanniski argued, following the Mundell-Fleming model, that both domestic investors waiting inflation out in commodities and foreigners looking for a strong dollar would flock to American financial instruments if Mundell's "policy mix" were implemented. The deficit would be financed along with any number of new capital projects. All this was not only stated in the Mundell oeuvre. It was also roundly summarized by Wanniski, and checked by Mundell, the very week that Laffer put pen to napkin.

Clearly, Laffer drew his curve because Dick Cheney was having trouble following the conversation. This is verified by the Wanniski-Cheney correspondence that took place over the next several years, in which Wanniski kept outdoing himself, in long letters, trying to explain Mundell's and Laffer's arguments. At one point, Wanniski's letters to Cheney got so schoolmarmish that Robert Bartley had to tell Cheney not to be put off by them. Cheney still had trouble getting it. As he ran for a House seat in 1978, Cheney wrote Wanniski,

"I'm spreading the word on Kemp-Roth [the across-the-board marginal tax cut]. You guys better know what you're talking about."[25]

Laffer did not have to write on a napkin to communicate effectively with William E. Simon, Ford's treasury secretary and a more important policy-maker than Cheney, an assistant to the chief of staff. Two weeks before the Two Continents meeting, Laffer, whose advice Simon asked for regularly, sent Simon a three-thousand-word document titled "Economic Reform Program." Laffer's paper elaborated the strategy of tightening money to stabilize prices and cutting marginal taxes to sponsor growth. It was the policy mix as cure for stagflation. As Laffer explained to Simon, in "the enclosed program . . . I have tried to capture fully my own views as to what must or should be done to halt inflation, thwart the recession and preserve the gains once obtained." Laffer also sent Mundell's AEI paper to Simon.[26]

All this is to say: to view the Laffer curve napkin as the formal statement of supply-side economics as of December 1974, with increasing government revenues as the primary objective, is to mangle the historical record.

Mundell, for his part, had dealt with the question of deficits time and again since he had first proposed his model. At the Bologna conference that yielded "The Dollar and the Policy Mix," the question of deficits had prompted Mundell to get testy with Gottfried Haberler. Haberler thought deficits inflationary not because of any increase in "demand," but because the Federal Reserve characteristically printed money to finance them. Mundell countered that in his model, the Federal Reserve would ignore the deficits and keep one objective—price stability—in mind. Therefore, deficits would not be inflationary and yet would be financed, probably by foreign flows. Given the demise of inflation, the whole world would rush to dollar-denominated assets, in particular U.S. Treasury bonds. At Michael 1, when Bartley asked Mundell who would pay for tax cuts, Mundell responded: "The Saudis will finance that."[27]

In the wake of "It's Time to Cut Taxes," Wanniski devoted himself to elaborating the supply-side argument. He published a much-expanded version of "It's Time to Cut Taxes" in Irving Kristol's journal, the *Public Interest*. That article, which appeared in spring 1975 as "The Mundell-Laffer Hypothesis," showed that Wanniski had absorbed the arguments made by both professors. It is as excellent and beautifully written a summary of Mundell's and Laffer's economics as has ever appeared. Wanniski's opening lines, canvassing the economic policy fiascoes of the previous several years, captured the grim comedy that official economic policy had become:

The United States has been passing through an economic nightmare. It seems like just the other day—and it was—that American economists of the first rank spoke confidently of "fine tuning" the economy to assure a predetermined rate of economic growth within acceptable bounds of inflation and unemployment. . . .

Obviously, the profession has been experiencing an intellectual crisis. Over a six-year period, . . . Nixon shot into the twitching patient every antibody the economic doctors of Cambridge and Chicago prepared. And always the vital signs declined. Money was tightened and money was eased. Mr. Nixon became a Keynesian and a "full-employment" budget was installed. Deficits were run on purpose and deficits were run by accident. The Phillips curve, a wondrous device . . . , was enshrined in the textbooks. . . . The dollar was devalued again, then floated. Wages and prices were controlled . . . , and a jawbone was brandished. At the end of all these exertions, many are beginning to wonder whether the patient was sicker than had been thought or whether the medicine has been making him sicker than he was.[28]

The Education of Robert Bartley

For a little while after he started at the *Journal* in 1973, Wanniski spent a lot of time—"immoderate time," says one commentator—with his superior, Robert Bartley. As they were both living in temporary quarters, Wanniski and Bartley had dinner together regularly and took long walks in lower Manhattan. They got used to having extended, even philosophical, conversations about the news and trends of the day. They became close friends, even intellectual partners. In the fall of 1974, this meant, among other things, that Wanniski was telling Bartley all he was learning from Mundell and Laffer, and he was changing Bartley's mind.[29]

Two years earlier, at the age of thirty-five, Bartley had been named editor of the *Journal*'s editorial page. The first move Bartley made in December 1972 was to take Wanniski from the *National Observer*. He had hoped to lure the young Princeton political theorist George Will, but Will turned him down in favor of a congressional staff job.[30]

Bartley had moved up the ranks since joining the *Journal* in 1962, after taking a bachelor's degree in journalism at Iowa State and a master's in political science at Wisconsin. Bartley had grown up in Iowa State's university town, Ames. His father was on the faculty, a professor of veterinary science. The

Bartley family was comfortably middle class, but the son's upbringing was austere. Indeed, there was something austere about Bartley's way of thinking, as well as his manner. The conciseness of his writing made Wanniski look voluble, and Bartley was reticent to a fault. Colleagues were used to his saying absolutely nothing in places like the elevator, but they did not mistake his reticence for mental inertness.[31]

Bartley was a small man who was not particularly athletic (though like everyone else in the 1970s, he played tennis). He wore thick glasses and simple clothes and was very convincing when he told people that he had been a high school debater. He was inveterately midwestern. He had been born on Columbus Day (1937), had married his high-school sweetheart, had a deceptively sharp sense of humor, and was suspicious of the Ivy League. At times, he confided that Ivy Leaguers had always seemed to him too ready to accommodate their ways of thinking to contemporary trends. Their ambition often made them blinkered, intellectually. Midwesterners, on the other hand, were more private and hence better prepared to think through hard issues and to buck trends. Even so, he hired plenty of Ivy Leaguers for the *Journal,* particularly Dartmouth grads.[32]

Bartley was also deeply patriotic, and what bothered him most about the 1970s was that political and opinion leaders accepted the prospect of "diminished expectations"—slower growth, a more confined role for the United States in the world, resignation in the face of troubling social and cultural indicators. As Bartley reflected on his retirement in 2002, he had always insisted that "problems have solutions." Bartley had supply-side economics in mind, but he could also have meant the Cold War and the overcoming of the cultural and spiritual paralysis that "the '60s" and Watergate had imposed on the nation. He fought on all these fronts in the opinion pages of the *Journal.* Of all the major figures in this book, Bartley is the only one with significant accomplishments outside the realm of supply-side economics.[33]

Bartley was assigned to *Journal* bureaus in Philadelphia and Chicago in the early 1960s, and he soon started impressing people. After two years of writing news stories, he was sent to New York and assigned to the editorial page, where he continued to break news in opinion pieces. (Bartley would continue this practice as editor, giving rise to his remark that "journalistically, my proudest boast is that I've run the only editorial page in the country that actually sells newspapers.") As the 1960s worsened, Bartley hardened into a Vietnam hawk and an opponent of the counterculture, the

Democratic convention of 1968 being a watershed moment for him, as it was for many others.[34]

After his appointment to the top of the editorial page in December 1972, Bartley at first mainly wrote about politics. He almost never wrote about economics. That was largely the province of older staff, such as the former editor, Vermont Royster, and the house monetarist, Lindley H. Clark. The economics of the *Wall Street Journal* during Bartley's first several years as editor was distinctly establishmentarian. Sound money, prudent business management, balanced budgets, no gimmicks—these were the themes of the page, which closely aligned with Mundell's characterization of the Chamber of Commerce in the early 1960s. The *Journal* riotously disagreed with Nixon on his dollar devaluations and price controls, but by no means would it tolerate a budget deficit. And it exhibited no particular interest in the promise of entrepreneurial start-ups.

These were Robert Bartley's views, too, in the early 1970s. He did not come around to the Mundell policy mix until 1975 or 1976. The sticking point was deficits. But there was one thing, from early on, that Bartley would not tolerate: acquiescence to slow growth.

Bartley was a dedicated reader, and just as Wanniski was becoming transfixed by Mundell and Laffer, Bartley was following one of the raging academic debates of the day. This was the clash of the titans of the Harvard philosophy department, John Rawls and Robert Nozick. Rawls's *Theory of Justice*, published in 1971, argued that it would be most just if no one could press advantages of any kind over anyone else. According to Rawls, policy that reduces inequality, even at the expense of general prosperity, is policy that is just. Nozick, a libertarian, countered in *Anarchy, State, and Utopia* (1974) that one's own advantages are so knit up with one's own identity, one's own self, that to deprive persons the opportunity of pressing advantages would be to deprive persons of their very nature. Justice must be something that respects human differences.

Bartley did not at all become a Nozickian, but he found Rawls especially objectionable. He could not tolerate the idea that prosperity might be deliberately diminished in the name of some other good. He wrote a Rawlsian professor at Harvard whom he had gotten to know in early 1976, "I have been pondering your off-hand remark that the Rawls criteria may not provide enough equality to satisfy you. I very much doubt you actually believe that. Would you really require a lower standard of living among the least advantaged in the interest of promoting equality by reducing other living standards even more?" The professor wrote back with an exceptionally long letter—the kind that busy journalists do not have the time to luxuriate over—saying that he hoped the electorate could be made to see that reducing prosperity as a means of redressing inequality was a good thing. Bartley's concise reply: "I think the chief difference between us is that you would be willing to increase accumulation if you could find some way to do so without increasing inequality, where I would be willing to reduce inequalities if I could find some way to do so without reducing accumulation."[35]

Bartley hated the strand of opinion that held that the economic crisis might be a good thing for America. Maybe America could learn to be responsible, to do with less, to think about more important things, such arguments ran. The prime representative of views of this sort, to Bartley, was Jimmy Carter. When Carter, as president, asked America to rethink its consumerist priorities, particularly regarding its energy use, in a way that was the "moral equivalent of war," Bartley attacked him mercilessly. The *Journal* editorial page repeatedly referred to this suggestion by its acronym, "MEOW."[36]

Thus, in the mid-1970s, Bartley was desperately seeking a way for America to climb out of its economic funk. Even before Wanniski started imploring Bartley to become a convert to the Mundell-Laffer side, Bartley had concluded that the highest priority of governmental policy had to be the restoration of economic growth. He realized that stagflation had given the opponents of American growth (whom he suspected of having been nurtured on 1960s anti-Americanism) the platform they needed to try to convince the electorate that growth was not such a good thing after all. Bartley even feared that big business might seek to cut a deal with the opponents of growth, in hopes of retaining certain privileges and a permanent lease on life. Big business, thought Bartley, was no more interested in American dynamism than were John Rawls's disciples. If anything, Bartley suspected, big business would rather tamp down dynamism to ensure its own perpetuation. Best to keep the pressure on, he felt, by ensuring competition from new entrants.[37]

A 1992 society column for the *New York Observer* said that Bartley was "not the first scholarship boy to have his entire life turned topsy-turvy by a well-meant invitation to dinner at the Ivy Club or the Porcellian or the Union Club, and to have silently resolved, on the spot, amidst gleaming plate and sparkling crystal, to do and say whatever it may take to be invited back, preferably with regularity." This gets things exactly wrong. As Bartley's 1980 Pulitzer (for "Down with Big Business") was sufficient to indicate, Bartley

came alive in the 1970s because he sensed that establishments were starting to cut deals with stagflation. They needed to be shaken up in favor of
the grand American tradition of entrepreneurial growth. In Bartley's memoir,
The Seven Fat Years, he identified three heroes of the victory over 1970s funk,
three iconic figures behind so many of the new businesses that in the 1980s
led America's economic resurgence: "college dropouts, breakaway engineers
and illegal immigrants."[38]

Wall Street Wannabes

The long walks that Wanniski took with Bartley in time led to get-togethers
with Mundell and Laffer. These were the gatherings at Michael 1, the brass-
and terracotta-festooned place in Manhattan's Financial District. The group
met about once a month, on Monday evenings at six, from late 1974 through
early 1976.[39]

There were seven regulars: Mundell, Laffer, Wanniski, and Bartley, plus
Charles Parker, Lew Lehrman, and Jeffrey Bell. They were joined from time
to time by an assortment of others, including young Wall Streeters, *Journal*
staffers, and the odd Washingtonian. Parker was in investments and picked
up the bill, Bell was a conservative political activist recently returned from
Vietnam, and Lehrman was an exceedingly successful drugstore entrepreneur
who was a year younger than Bartley. After a while, Lehrman began to host
the meetings at his Lehrman Institute on the Upper East Side.[40]

The little group made quite clear its firm rejection of teetotalism. Mundell
was famous for his drinking, and the others simply tried to keep up. The preferred cocktail was a dry martini. All this was typical of the period. As Robert
Novak recalled business habits back then, "Alcohol was a way of life. . . . A
Nixon subcabinet officer as my guest . . . on one occasion downed three double
bourbons on the rocks before lunch and sipped a single bourbon during the
meal, telling me nothing unintended in the process. I considered as a wimp the
rare news source who would order campari and soda or kir. I cannot remember
anyone ordering iced tea."[41]

Perhaps because of his alcohol intake, Mundell was hard to understand—
aurally, hard to understand. He talked in "an old man's voice," according to
one journalist, swallowing syllables in a pleasant, slow-moving rasp. In 1975,
he had also taken to wearing hair past his shoulders. But his weird voice and
unusual appearance notwithstanding, Mundell's thoughts moved a mile a minute. It took intense concentration on the part of a listener to follow Mundell's

every point. Here is where Laffer played a crucial role, especially for Bartley. Laffer had known Mundell since the 1960s, when they were both at Chicago, and he could elaborate his points perfectly. As Wanniski put it, "There is no joint Mundell-Laffer paper. Mundell, the prime mover, writes the theory. Laffer, more the empiricist, provides the data support, contributing slices of theoretical inspiration along the way." Inspired by the Mundell-Fleming model, Laffer had written mainly on international capital flows. His book on short-term private capital flows was published in 1975, in the heyday of the Michael 1 meetings. His research had cast serious doubts on the plausibility of such things as the Twist. At AEI in 1974, Laffer had shown that even inflation behaves like capital, moving from country to country almost instantaneously, calling into question the very idea of national economic policy.[42]

The Michael 1 dinners mattered to the participants in various ways. Mundell and Laffer got a ready and potentially influential audience. Lehrman found people who were willing to give ear to his intellectual interests in economics. Bell was inspired to pursue a political career. Parker would bring supply-side ideas into the world of investment research. But from the standpoint of history, by far the most important thing the dinners did was to change Bartley's thinking. The Michael 1 dinners made him a supply-sider, and by so doing, they made the *Wall Street Journal*—the nation's largest newspaper by circulation—the vehicle through which the nation would come to be introduced and accustomed to, if not always converted to, supply-side economics.

Wanniski played the emcee at Michael 1, making sure that the professors stayed on track and told the visitors from the real world what they needed to hear. This was an important role. Mundell could be a rambler. He was famous for answering questions with questions. In later years, in the age of e-mail, when Bartley would need a quick clarification from Mundell explaining a tic in the international currency system, Mundell would respond first with some stanzas from Pope and then relate his point through allegory. No wonder Wanniski was so necessary.[43]

What Bartley learned at Michael 1 may be boiled down to four main points. First, he learned that the Federal Reserve did not necessarily control monetary policy. Laffer drew a little box, perhaps on a napkin, representing the main target of Federal Reserve exertions, the stock of money measured by a statistic called "M1." M1 was essentially the balances of individual bank accounts in the United States. Laffer then drew all sorts of other boxes representing worldwide stashes of dollars. Not least were the oil and currency reserve dollars held in bank accounts around the globe, tremendous magnitudes of dollars by 1975. Laffer told Bartley that should investment returns improve in the United States, foreign dollars would rush into the country, offsetting any liquidity effect of a tight money policy that the Federal Reserve might wish to initiate.

Bartley began to get it. If the Fed stuck only to pursuing a moderate monetary policy, other means could be found for enhancing growth. This led Bartley to reject monetarism, which implied that monetary policy was the key both to the price level and to domestic expansion. If the price level got out of control, the correction necessarily involved a monetary contraction that undermined growth and produced "austerity." That is why for monetarism, the great sin was for the Fed to let the price level get out of control. Because then it would have to starve the economy. But would the economy really have to be starved, Bartley began to wonder, if there existed an offsetting policy tool, perhaps in the form of tax cuts?

As Bartley recalled, "another Mundell aphorism" at Michael 1 was that "for every policy goal, you need a policy lever." This was the second thing Bartley learned at Michael 1. And so did Bartley reveal that he had been green in 1975. Mundell had been repeating this formulation in prominent academic forums since the early 1960s, and the inaugural Nobel Prize in economics had gone to Jan Tinbergen in 1969 for conceiving of the general concept. Yet that was the point of the Michael 1 gatherings: to acquaint the editorial-page editor of the most significant business newspaper in the nation with the specifics of "effective market classification." This was Mundell's solution to inflationary stagnation, the solution implemented blindly from 1962 to 1964, but not since.[44]

With the Mundell-Laffer hypothesis and effective market classification, Bartley now saw, the Fed had to do just its one job and not worry about austerity. If during the great inflation of the 1970s, as Mundell had said at AEI, the Fed constrained the production of dollars, the tax code could step in to ensure that production and growth prospects were unaffected, indeed enhanced. As Laffer instructed Bartley, this was to be done not through rebate checks, but by lowering marginal tax rates. Lower tax rates at the margin mean that extra production is taxed less—a recipe for growth. Lower marginal rates create "incentives"—the term that really lies at the heart of supply-side economics, not the "Laffer curve."

Third, Bartley learned that the new economics of Mundell and his protégés had some unsettled questions. Mundell knew that the Fed had to focus solely on discipline, but what discipline? And what was to be the role of gold? These questions led to disagreements at the restaurant. Mundell was impressed with the monetary policy of the Roaring '20s, when the Federal Reserve concerned itself not with the overall stock of dollars or gold but with the domestic price level. While this may have led to a "gold shortage," the economy still posted a run of noninflationary 4 percent–plus growth that ended only when the Fed abandoned its policy. Lehrman, on the other hand, was more of a hard-money man, indeed an avowed disciple of Jacques Rueff.

Fourth, Bartley learned that all this was not wild new theory, but extrapolations from the classical tradition of economics. As Laffer told Bartley, "Say's law. . . . That's what you believe in." Say's law is one of the most un-Rawlsian doctrines in the annals of the Enlightenment. Say (a French theorist of Napoleonic vintage) had said that new production in free markets is by definition noninflationary. If cognizant actors, pursuing advantages, choose to produce new goods and these goods are sold, then necessarily the price of all other goods goes down. The price level remains the same, but the economy gets bigger. In other words, the possibility of noninflationary growth had been long enshrined in economic theory.[45]

Thus was Bartley tutored at Michael 1 during the Ford recessions. Yet by early 1976, his editorials at the *Journal*, by his own admission, were still firmly within the tradition of the Republican Party. The sticking point was budget deficits. Bartley could not conceive of trading a tax cut, however beneficial, for a deficit. He had to have guarantees of spending cuts, too, meaning no deficits.

Amid the confusions of the Ford years, "Keynesians," as they were invariably called, argued that deficit spending was the key to emerging out of the recession. Bartley loathed the idea of making common cause with Keynesians by giving in to deficits, a move that Mundell and Laffer seemed to imply would make sense. In fact, Bartley joined Ford's treasury secretary, William Simon (himself soon a convert to supply-side economics), in using the term "crowding out" to argue against deficits on any grounds. Their argument was that if the government borrowed to finance a deficit, there would be less money in the credit markets to support growth, especially if there was tight money from the Fed. Mundell and Wanniski had already challenged this view, but Bartley remained unmoved. He knew that to get spending cuts from the massive Democratic majority in Congress was impossible, so in the name of preventing deficits and attendant crowding out, he argued that the line must be held on taxes.[46]

In the meantime, the editorial page Bartley had inherited in 1972 was going through a wrenching process of soul-searching as the stagflation solidified. Being generally allied with conservative Republicanism was obviously no longer sufficient, as the Republicans seemed as bereft of ideas as everyone else. A board of contributors to the page was formed in 1976 and stacked with establishmentarian voices, including three former CEA chairs, one of whom was Walter Heller. Heller, Herbert Stein, and Paul McCracken were clear on one thing—namely, that received economic wisdom had become woefully inadequate. Despite his fealties to the "crowding out" theory, Bartley came to realize that another repackaging of Keynesianism, even if done "responsibly" by Republicans and conservatives, was not going to solve the problems that bedeviled the nation's economy in the mid-1970s.[47]

It was not Mundell, Laffer, or Wanniski who brought Bartley around to the absolute necessity of tax cuts. Rather, it was a business economist named Alan Reynolds, a contributor to the libertarian magazine *Reason* and to William F. Buckley's *National Review*. Reynolds was Bartley's junior by five years. Their correspondence in 1975 and 1976 finally converted Bartley. Reynolds had been writing in *National Review* that the positive "incentive" and "reflow" (government revenue) effects of a marginal tax cut could be considerable. Bartley wanted an ironclad promise that these effects would be so large that a deficit would not emerge. As late as April 1976, Bartley wrote Reynolds, "As for the question of marginal tax rates[,] I believe that to come out with government revenue unchanged, the incentive effects of the tax reduction would have to be implausibly high."[48]

Reynolds strove to explain that Bartley was missing the point. There were various ways to structure a tax cut. All efforts should be focused on finding the policy that provided for the most incentives in the real economy, and then implementing that policy. As Bartley seemed to grasp, it was not important to lower average tax rates, the total amount of tax an individual pays divided by income. Rather, it was imperative to lower marginal tax rates, tax percentages on the next increment of income earned, so that new initiative—new supply, the stuff of growth—would result. The main point that Reynolds was at pains to make was this: do not scotch a good, marginal tax cut because of "reflow" inadequacies. That would be to miss an excellent opportunity to power the economy ahead.

Reynolds believed that thinking about tax and spending cuts in aggregate was too general—too macroeconomic, too Keynesian. Reynolds believed (with most conservatives) that all government spending beyond a certain low minimum was equally inert, if not counterproductive, as an economic force. But tax cuts greatly varied in their economic effects. A rebate, as Bartley also believed, was akin to an expenditure: nil or counterproductive in its economic effects. Indexing the code for inflation or cutting marginal rates, however, promised a different outcome. These moves foretold changes in the ways people organized their economic activity, and the outcome would be growth.

Reynolds implored Bartley to recognize that to insist on "paying for" tax cuts with spending cuts was to ignore the vast differences there were among *kinds* of tax cuts. A better strategy would be to encourage making tax cuts a top priority and not necessarily linked to restraint on the spending side. "It would have been better," Reynolds wrote to Bartley in the wake of the Ford rebate, "to concentrate on the specific design of the cut." "It makes a difference which taxes are cut," he said to Bartley on another occasion.[49]

Bartley finally went over to the other side in 1976. Perhaps Bartley was a little skeptical of Wanniski's advocacy of marginal tax cuts, given that Wanniski was entirely new to economics and had a weakness for enthusiasms. Perhaps Bartley thought Mundell a little weird, Laffer a little inexperienced. But Michael 1 brought Bartley to the brink of conversion, and Alan Reynolds pushed him over. On the opinion page of the *Journal,* Bartley moved to put marginal tax cuts on the table as nonnegotiable.

James Baker, Reagan's chief of staff and treasury secretary, who was dubious about tax cuts in the 1980s, took to that same opinion page in 2001 to say that he was now a "reformed drunk" about tax cuts. If in the 1980s he had excelled at coming up with every rationalization in the world for going slow on tax cuts, Baker wrote, he now believed that tax cuts were entirely necessary. All responsibility for deficits must be borne by spending. Baker was following in Bartley's footsteps. For by the time Bartley wrote an editorial titled "Keynes Is Dead" in January 1977, after all those martinis at Michael 1, he too had become a reformed drunk.[50]

6

THE HILL

We are not the victims of sinister or uncontrollable forces, but of wrong-headed policies and leaders who are doing a poor job.
—SENATOR LLOYD BENTSEN, Texas Democrat, 1974

Supply-side economics won its spurs in the congressional policy process. The story of how it prevailed on analytical and political grounds contradicts its image as an extreme and risky policy, fostered on a beguiled public and president by a few voodoo magicians.
—PAUL CRAIG ROBERTS, *The Supply-Side Revolution*

Alan Reynolds not only persuaded Robert Bartley to become a tax cutter. He also was courier of the label that Bartley would identify with for the rest of his life: supply-sider. In spring 1976, Reynolds attended a symposium for Washington-area economists at a resort in Virginia called the Homestead. The symposium was hosted by James Buchanan of Virginia Tech. Buchanan was then working on the economics of budget deficits. In a few years, he would embark on a theoretical study of the Laffer curve, work that would make the curve one of the basic tools of academic macroeconomics. In 1986, Buchanan would win the Nobel Prize.[1]

At the symposium, AEI economist Herbert Stein referred briefly to a new theory making noise in Washington. This was the theory propounded by the "supply-side fiscalists." Among economists, he winked, its adherents numbered "maybe two." He was perhaps referring to Laffer and Wanniski, whose mission as frequent visitors to the nation's capital was to make converts to the Mundell-Laffer hypothesis among political officeholders.[2]

As a battle standard, "the Mundell-Laffer hypothesis" was never going to do. Wanniski knew that. The term was clumsy; it sounded as if it came out of a science lab. Then Reynolds called. He related to Wanniski Stein's condescending remarks about the "supply-side fiscalists." Wanniski thought it over and realized that there was potential in the name. The muse struck. Wanniski would call his movement "supply-side economics."[3]

Herb Stein was a Republican and by all accounts a conservative. He was a stalwart at AEI. He had been chairman of the Nixon Council of Economic Advisors. He was a member of the new *Wall Street Journal* Board of Contributors, writing regular columns meant to counterbalance those of another board member, the Keynesian Walter Heller, formerly of Camelot. But Stein had been involved in orchestrating Nixon's gimmicks as the dollar was delinked from gold. He was one of the officials who had repaired to Camp David with the president in mid-August 1971 to prepare the announcement of the close of the gold window and the advent of the "New Economic Policy" (the allusion to Lenin was missed) of wage and price controls. As Robert Bartley was fond of saying, it was fitting that they had all departed for Camp David on Friday the Thirteenth.[4]

Thus, Stein had been compromised by his time in the Nixon White House, and he exited government service in 1974 unsure of what kind of economic wisdom to dispense. He turned to humor, including self-deprecation. His columns in the *Journal* made light of everything, including how, at home, he and his wife would marvel at the prevalence of confusing economic counsel. What were all the old economists, including himself, supposed to say, now that they had been in power and the result was stagflation? Stein would title a memoir, alluding to the oft-heard razz against economists, *On the Other Hand. . . .*[5]

In early 1976, the double-dip recession imperceptibly over, Stein was in a mood to discount every economic doctrine, especially an upstart movement with "maybe two" supporters. Even so, his term, supply-side fiscalism, was largely apt. Traditionally, "fiscalism" was the view that boosting demand via tax cuts or spending increases (as opposed to by loose money) was the best way to address sluggishness. Yet here were fiscalists—they wanted to cut taxes—who sought to increase not demand but supply, via incentives. Stein's term, however, failed to capture the other half of the Mundell policy mix: tight money, which brings in international dollars for capital expansion at home.

Stein exaggerated, of course, in saying that there existed only two supply-side fiscalists. As Reynolds apprised Bartley, another economist at the Homestead seemed to agree with them. This was William Niskanen, chief economist of Ford Motor. At the conference, Reynolds told Bartley, Niskanen had said that an "increase in the marginal tax rate should be expected to reduce hours worked, the formation and maintenance of human and physical capital, the relative employment in more onerous occupations . . . , the relative employment and investment subject to . . . monitoring by the tax authorities, and the relative employment and investment in the taxing jurisdiction."

"Stein was wrong," Reynolds concluded. "There are a lot more than two economists who buy this line."[6]

Indeed, in March 1976, there were something like two *hundred* persons advocating supply-side fiscalism. Not all were economists, but all were in a position to address the stagflation conundrum. Among economists, there were Mundell, Laffer, Niskanen, and Reynolds. Buchanan can be counted, too, given that he was primed to do a great deal to give academic legitimacy to supply-side economics, particularly the Laffer curve. Among economically minded journalists, there was Wanniski, and by that time also Bartley. There were also the other Michael 1 attendees, five to ten in number.

There were further dozens on Capitol Hill. Even the veterans of Michael 1 were only dimly aware that in early 1976, a cadre of tax cutters was congealing in the legislative branch among certain junior members of Congress, their staffs, and their consultants. The major figures included Senators Lloyd Bentsen and William V. Roth, as well as Orrin Hatch, who would win a Senate seat later that year; Marjorie Holt, John Rousselot, and Jack Kemp in the House; staffers on the House Budget and Joint Economic Committee (JEC) of Congress, including especially Paul Craig Roberts and Stephen J. Entin; and JEC-veteran-turned-consultant Norman B. Ture.

Indeed, as Stein spoke, a bill laden with supply-side provisions was gaining ground in the House. The Jobs Creation Act, introduced under another name in December 1974, called for a menu of tax cuts so that the nation's economic production would be increased and inflation tamed. On March 15, 1976, Jack Kemp, the bill's sponsor in the House, announced that he had 106 cosponsors.[7]

It was the theoretical work of Norman Ture—another Chicago economist—that had given Kemp's bill its intellectual inspiration and burnished its provisions. If Ture was not one of Stein's "maybe two" supply-side fiscalists, the oversight is inexplicable. For by 1976, Ture had been pushing Capitol Hill in a supply-side direction for two decades.

In 1977, Ture published a book that summarized the economic theory he had been assembling since the 1950s, the theory now at the brink of being put into practice with the Kemp bill. *The Effects of Tax Policy on Capital Formation* was a black-letter book, at first glance something only an accountant could love (the Financial Executives Research Foundation had commissioned it). But beneath the accountant-speak, the book packed a wallop. Ture could just have easily titled it "Fifteen Ways to Cut Business Taxes and Have the Economy Grow, Inflation Defeated, Employment Rebound, and Tax Revenues Surge." The work represented a precise link between the Kennedy tax-cut movement of the early 1960s and the rising supply-side movement of the 1970s.[8]

Ture

Ture (pronounced "tour-RAY"), born in 1923 in Ohio, became one of Milton Friedman's first graduate students at Chicago in 1947. He took the doctorate and went on to jobs at the state and federal level before settling into a staff economist's position on the JEC in 1954. In Washington, Ture got to know Representative Wilbur Mills, who in 1957 became chairman of the House Ways and Means Committee.

Before the recession of 1957, Ture had been a Keynesian. In the 1950s, Ture had believed, notwithstanding his Chicago training, that the manipulation of aggregates—the money supply and the total level of taxes and spending—was the important thing to concentrate on in order to bring about high growth, high employment, and stable prices. By the end of the sluggishness of 1957–62, Ture had changed his mind. He came to believe that what needed to be done, in pursuit of the same objectives, was to remove governmental impediments to profit-seeking. Above all, the way must be cleared for businesses to foresee profits when they make investments.[9]

As the spate of sluggishness extended beyond 1957, more members of Congress (Kennedy included), along with their staffs, began to ponder how to get the country moving again (as in Kennedy's 1960 election catchphrase). Mills, in consultation with Ture, came to desire a tax action that would boost growth and yet not result in a significant budget deficit. Paying little heed to the tax-increase counsel of the neoclassical synthesis, Mills focused on tax cuts.[10]

As the early economic reports of Kennedy's CEA had argued, the nation was more prone to spend than produce, so production had to be attended to above all. The CEA first contemplated both business-tax cuts and low long-term interest rates. But the Federal Reserve foreclosed the latter option by raising interest rates. Therefore, the stimulus had to be business-tax cuts. JFK and his CEA dithered for a while. Alarm bells went off in the stock market in early 1962. Mills, assisted by Ture, encouraged Kennedy to implement the business-tax cuts, which he finally did, and the boom ensued. In the offing, Mills and Ture also pressed Kennedy to cut personal rates, which eventually came in 1964 under Lyndon Johnson.[11]

Mills was sure he got his bills in the Revenue Acts of 1962 and 1964. He believed, correctly, that growth, employment, and tax revenues would all surge after the tax cuts passed, and that this robustness would buoy the dollar. Mills moved on to other things after 1964 (such as the creation of Medicare), but Ture did not. He became absorbed with the issues raised by the acts, particularly the stimulation of economic growth.

The Revenue Act of 1962 cut business taxes in two basic ways. Businesses could claim some expenditures for new equipment against their taxes, and their "depreciation" schedules were shortened and reorganized on more friendly terms. Depreciation refers to the way that businesses deduct the purchase of equipment used by their workers against yearly income subject to taxation. Depreciation recognizes that purchases of equipment can be both infrequent and expensive. When a business buys a machine for workers to use, the hope is that the machine will last a long time and make good on the large amount of money sunk into it when it was bought.[12]

At tax time, it is often not economical for a firm to claim the entire cost of an equipment purchase in the year in which the purchase was made. This is because the purchase price might be so large that it exceeds the amount of profit, or taxable income, that the firm has that year. Therefore, a firm will claim a portion of the purchase price every year in which the equipment helps to generate profits until the entire price is used up—that is, until the purchase is depreciated.

Furthermore, from the perspective of the government, equipment retains value to its owner until it is fully "used up"—and even then it can be disposed of as scrap. Equipment always has value. It can be sold. Therefore, the government strives to ensure, through the treatment of depreciation in the tax code, that only that part of equipment that "wastes away" can be deducted.

Otherwise, the government would effectively be buying equipment that business can sell for a profit.

By rights, depreciation is a term of art, an issue entirely within the precincts of accounting. A nettlesome aspect is that the most economical sort of depreciation varies from business to business. It is unlikely that the IRS is going to set a standard that applies well to all capital-intensive businesses in the United States. Accountants do that best on a case-by-case basis. In deference to this reality, the 1962 act both shortened standard depreciation schedules and gave businesses flexibility to devise their own schedules. If audited, companies would be permitted to make their case before the IRS.

Ture studied the Revenue Act of 1962's provisions on depreciation with particular intensity. His study forced him to take leave of Keynesianism. In an article he published in the *Journal of Finance* in 1962, Ture began to outline an economic model that would concede a specific level of governmental revenues while making variable the configuration of the tax system that yielded those revenues. He perceived that what would be found was that different levels of output, employment, and inflation emerged for every variable scenario, with revenues staying the same. Therefore, Ture reasoned, if the objective was to have good growth, employment, and inflation numbers, policy should focus on engineering a tax system that brought about these results—regardless of the overall revenue that the tax system would generate, because that would be invariable.[13]

Ture's analysis, as it developed in a series of writings in the late 1960s and early 1970s, implied that economic growth in the 1950s, indeed before 1962, had been suboptimal because business taxes, particularly depreciation allowances, had been poorly thought out. Ture strove to indicate that things like short and flexible depreciation schedules and investment tax credits make businesses invest in equipment, because then they can clearly envision profits. Since purchases of equipment necessarily incur production, not to say employment, growth results. The impact on governmental revenues is nil if not positive, in that received IRS depreciation schedules are inept in the first place.

As Ture delved into these issues, he left the JEC for the National Bureau of Economic Research (NBER) and wrote a book, *Accelerated Depreciation in the United States, 1954–1960* (1967), which remains the premier historical study of depreciation. He also began to notice that lessons apparently learned in 1962 and enunciated in his writings were being rapidly forgotten in the LBJ years, as inflation stirred and the drumbeat for tax increases began to be heard.

Ture thought, naïvely, that lessons about the benefits of low and intelligent taxes on business had been learned as a result of the incredible growth that the economy—and federal treasury—had enjoyed in the years after 1961. He was incredulous when suggestions started arising, in 1966 and 1967, that taxes be raised. He advised Congress against any such measures. Fortunately for Ture's career, if not the nation, his advice was not taken. The tax increases of 1968 and 1969 made the issue of business taxes in general, and depreciation allowances in particular, Ture's specialty. Both became hot topics in the stagflation era.[14]

Ture did some work for the Nixon White House but grew disenchanted with the president's economic initiatives. He opened his own consulting firm, Norman B. Ture, Inc. His major client was the U.S. Chamber of Commerce, an early advocate of the Mundell policy mix. Ture set to work on an econometric model of the effects of an optimal regime of business taxation. He did not like the word "optimal," actually; his term was "neutral." He wanted to see what would happen, economically, if the tax code did not treat business investment differently from other kinds of productive economic activity.[15]

When Ture finished his model, he concluded that fifteen major reforms needed to be put in place for the tax code to be neutral toward productivity. These included a repeal of virtually all of the measures of the 1969 Tax Reform Act, which introduced the minimum tax on high earners, increased the effective rate on capital gains, treated stock dividends more harshly than "ordinary income," and sought to squeeze more taxes out of businesses that seemed to be evading them, perhaps by artful depreciation. (Scoffers had quickly dubbed the measure the "Lawyers and Accountants Relief Act.") The 1969 act also included populist elements, such as increases in personal deductions that, coupled with the increases and complexities placed upon high earners and businesses, sharpened the progressivity of the code. Thus were the legislative achievements of 1962–64 undone. When high earners and businesses were soaked, investment all but disappeared. The inevitable result was less employment, higher inflation (on account of less production in tandem with Federal Reserve expansionism), and lower government revenues.[16]

By the double-dip recession year of 1974, the term "capital shortage"—that is, "investment shortage"—had become commonplace. Ture felt vindicated, and he strove to seize the initiative. "Although the phrase 'capital shortage' has become increasingly familiar in recent years," he wrote in *The Effects of Tax Policy on Capital Formation*, which reported on the model he had assembled, "its meaning today is widely misconstrued. . . . The present U.S. tax system is enormously biased against saving and in favor of consumption uses of current income, hence against capital formation."[17]

Ture went on to outline the stunning ways that the tax code bore responsibility for this state of affairs. First, he noted, sharply progressive taxation, especially regarding investment payoffs such as capital gains and dividends, made potential savers opt for consumerism instead of thrift. And this only worsened the consumerist bias introduced by inflation itself. Second, and this was Ture's main interest, there were the imponderable ways that the tax code, enhanced by Nixon by statute and by the great inflation by stealth, presented the prospect of zero if not negative returns to businesses as they contemplated investments. Ture produced astounding examples of businesses facing taxes approaching 100 percent—or more. His language was bland, but the implication was clear: taxes were choking off investment, the wellspring of production.

In one of Ture's examples, a business owner contemplated buying a piece of machinery for $1,000. Because the top bracket taxed income at 48 percent, this business, if run by a top earner who took a salary, would have to earn $1,923 to buy the machinery. Yet this was only the first step in the long gauntlet of taxation. Ture assumed, generously, that the machinery would yield 12 percent per year in profits, or $156. This $156 would itself be dunned at tax time. Ture crunched the numbers and concluded that to make a profitable investment in capital equipment of $1,000, this business owner would have to commit $2,450 of pretax income. If the owner spent the money instead, all that would be required was the original $1,923. The effective tax penalty on investment in lieu of consumption for a business owner was $500 for each $2,000 invested— an absurdity.[18]

Depreciation told an even sadder tale. With the nod given to IRS discretion by the act of 1969, depreciation schedules, far from being accelerated, as Ture had advocated in the 1960s, were extended to a standard of thirteen years—another unlucky thirteen—in the 1970s. This was brutal. Inflation averaged 9 percent in the stagflation era. After thirteen years, 9 percent inflation means that an initial price is depreciated, in the end, to 33 percent. On a depreciation schedule, this requires that businesses deduct less and less of the real purchase price of equipment every year, culminating in a deduction that is one-third of the equipment's real value.

Ture had grim fun tallying up the ways that taxes on investment could exceed impossible thresholds. Another example: A company gains income less expenses of $1,000. The corporate income tax takes 48 percent and the rest is paid out as dividends to shareholders, who must pay 70 percent tax on that type of income. The $1,000 first becomes, because of the corporate rate, $520, then $156 because of the dividend rate; $844 goes to the IRS.[19]

But was the $1,000 really income less expenses to begin with? If, say, $1,000 of expenses declared was money that had been plowed into a productive piece of equipment ten years prior and deducted according to a depreciation schedule, perhaps not. For if inflation had denuded the depreciation allowance by, say, two-thirds over that decade, the real depreciation allowance should have been $3,000. If depreciation schedules, in this case, had been indexed for inflation, the company would have not reported a profit of $1,000, but a loss of $2,000, on account of a proper depreciation allowance of $3,000. We have, in this case, a company and its owners paying $844 in taxes on a loss of $2,000. And if the loss had been greater because of inflation, the same taxes would have been paid on the greater loss. An imponderable fact, but an inevitability of the tax code all the same during the 1970s funk.

The Chamber of Commerce, the Financial Executives Research Foundation, and the American Council for Capital Formation paid people like Norman B. Ture to crunch and report the unbelievable numbers as the tax code mixed with the saltpeter of inflation to scuttle investment. But a political movement was never going to be inspired and led by accountants, sound as their case may have been in the 1970s.

Mother of Kemp-Roth

Big buyers of capital equipment stood on the sidelines as the decade unfolded. This started to worry workers. The example of U.S. Steel told a tale. In the 1970s, U.S. Steel declined to make the big capital investments that technological innovation had made necessary in the race to keep up with its competition, especially foreign competition.[20]

In particular, U.S. Steel chose not to buy the (expensive) basic oxygen process (BOP) furnaces and continuous casting machines for its plants. The storied Homestead Works near Pittsburgh went to its grave in 1987 having never replaced its Carnegie-era open-hearth furnaces with a "BOP shop," nor its ingot molds with a caster. This had easily made Homestead irrelevant in the international steel market by 1980. But by that date, U.S. Steel had found a better use for the capital it could have spent on steelmaking machines. It set aside $6 billion to acquire Marathon Oil, whose petroleum reserves increased in value with inflation. Had U.S. Steel bought capital equipment with that $6 billion, it would have been killed by taxes and inflation. Thus did the company soon to be called "USX" forsake steel for oil.

After 1982, when the transaction cleared, approximately 160,000 steelworkers lost their jobs. This was precisely the future that began to worry workers in the early 1970s in Buffalo and Lackawanna, New York, Lake Erie towns that were home to massive Bethlehem Steel plants, today as shuttered as Homestead. Their representative in Congress, Jack Kemp, realized the capital crisis was serious when he saw a help-wanted sign on a machine shop in his district that read, "Bring own lathe." He started devising legislation that would make capital investment more attractive.[21]

Kemp came to the House in 1971. He had had a stellar career in the American Football League (AFL), which after ten years in existence had merged with the NFL in 1970. Kemp was one of several players who had been with the AFL for the whole of its run, playing quarterback first for the San Diego Chargers and then for the Buffalo Bills. In a league that brought great innovations to the passing game, Kemp manned his position as well as anyone, including his peers Len Dawson, George Blanda, and Joe Namath. Kemp twice led the Bills to the AFL championship.

A Californian by birth, Kemp had thought he would hate blustery Buffalo, but he came to adore it, particularly its gritty work ethic. In the years he was quarterbacking, Kemp delved into libertarian political literature: Ayn Rand, F. A. Hayek, Barry Goldwater. He worked for Reagan during the California governor's campaign of 1966 and during his first year in Sacramento in 1967. In 1970, at the age of thirty-five, Kemp retired from football, ran for Congress in his beloved Buffalo, and won the seat.

As a freshman, Kemp began speaking on the floor in favor of investment tax credits for small as well as large businesses. He began to attract talented, indeed visionary, staff. Randal Teague, a conservative activist with credentials from the Goldwater campaign and the Nixon White House, joined Kemp's staff in 1974 at age twenty-nine. Teague worked over some of the legislation that Kemp had been proposing and concocted a new bill. At the culmination of an adventuresome seven-year career, this bill would become the Reagan tax cut law of 1981.[22]

But first, in December 1974, Kemp and a partner in the Senate introduced the bill that Teague had put together. Called the Savings and Investment Act, the bill represented an assault on the tax increases that had occurred by statute or by stealth since the late 1960s. The Savings and Investment Act more than doubled the investment tax credit, doubled the depreciation allowance, exempted more capital-gains income from tax, introduced a tax credit for savings, and strove to exempt from taxes business spending meant to keep up with new federal regulations (such as for pollution-control equipment). The populist tax increases of 1968–69 had found their response. If the federal government was going to punish businesses and high earners that were unproductive with their discretionary income, here was an opportunity for them to avoid taxes if that income was put to productive use.[23]

The bill fell flat. The opposition came from the grandees of Kemp's own party, the Republicans. The Ford White House dismissed it. There was talk that the bill was economically unsophisticated, that it had not gone through proper congressional channels, that it would fail to stimulate savings and investment as expected, that even if it did the deficits resulting from the tax cuts would gobble up the savings needed for investment. The White House had its own plan: rebate checks and a big new federal program to retrain workers laid off because of the paucity of capital investment. But 1975 then followed 1974 as a uniquely bad year in all the major economic categories.[24]

The Ford administration was not alone in its superciliousness toward the Savings and Investment Act. Bartley's editorial page at the *Wall Street Journal* also attacked the measure. The bill would increase loopholes and cause deficits, the *Journal* complained. This charge stirred from the sidelines an individual who would become the single most tenacious and canny fighter for supply-side economics that the cause ever had: Paul Craig Roberts.

Roberts, thirty-six in 1975, was an economics Ph.D., the author of a stunning exposé of the Soviet economy, and a fellow at Stanford's Hoover Institution. He had the soft Georgia voice of Jimmy Carter, but it did not take long for those who tangled with him to realize that Roberts demanded intellectual integrity from his interlocutors and opponents. Kemp had hired Roberts in the middle of 1975, and in January 1976, Bartley received a letter from him attacking the *Journal* for its criticism of the Savings and Investment Act. "We did not think it was helpful or fair," Roberts wrote to Bartley, "for your editorial to characterize those seeking . . . to reduce the existing bias against saving and investment as fighting to defend existing tax loopholes and wanting to build new ones into the system." Slowly, Bartley's page began to warm to Kemp's bill.[25]

Roberts had trouble seeing it. He became fed up with the *Journal* for its swiping at Kemp's bill and for picking on Kemp's occasional concordance with the Sierra Club. "Bob, what is the point of embarrassing a courageous and effective Republican Member of Congress?" Roberts asked Bartley in a letter. "[Kemp] has made a tremendous effort [with his bill], and the *Journal* has not so much as mentioned it. He has led the fight in Congress trying to re-orient economic policy thinking . . . , educating his colleagues [and] his Democratic, union district. . . . What is the *Journal* up to?" For its part, the *Journal* wanted sound money, low and consistent taxes, no deficits, and few regulations. The Kemp bill appeared to promise only one thing for certain, at least to those unacquainted with Norman Ture's research—namely, to complicate the tax code.[26]

As for the Ford administration, its two-pronged attack against inflation and unemployment was pathetic. Inflation would be "whipped" by moral suasion. The nation's citizens were called on to make pledges to limit their spending. You could find a pledge sheet in the local newspaper. If those who made the pledge wanted to look a little dorky, they could wear a "WIN"—for "Whip Inflation Now"—button, just as the president did. As for unemployment, the retraining bill would provide for the redundancies caused by the capital shortage. What equipment retrainees were to work with once they landed a new job was not at all apparent.[27]

All of this, it must be grasped, was taking place within the Republican camp. The Democrats seemed content to watch their opposition self-destruct. They had built a one-hundred-plus-seat majority in the House after the election of November 1974, and the Republican White House had responded with economic policies that were transparently risible. The Democrats also knew that in the recessionary environment, they could count on the help of a standard Republican proclivity: aversion to deficits. If new spending became a fait accompli, the Republicans in Congress were guaranteed to volunteer the tax increases necessary to provide the funding. Deficits were the worst of all possible worlds, in the musty Republican view, because they offended strict standards of accounting and crowded out investment. "The Democrats," as Jude Wanniski wrote in an article titled "Taxes and a Two Santa Theory," "are best suited for the role of Spending Santa Claus. The Republicans . . . should be the Santa Claus of Tax Reduction. . . . But there is something in the Republican chemistry that causes the GOP to become hypnotized by the prospect of an imbalanced budget. . . . They either argue for a tax hike to dampen inflation when the economy is in a boom or demand spending cuts to balance the budget when the economy is in recession. Either way, of course, they embrace the role of Scrooge." Wanniski proposed that the Republicans turn the tables, demanding tax cuts first and forcing Democrats either to play the spending Scrooge to pay for them or else to concede to deficits. As Kemp said at the party's convention in August 1976, "The Republican Party must move from defense to offense. The time is now."[28]

The congressional tax and spending process, however, had recently been changed to be even easier for the Democrats to play Santa and the Republicans Scrooge. This had been done in response to some Nixonian "dirty tricks." In the waning days of Watergate, Nixon had tried to punish Democrats by "impounding" certain funds that Congress had assigned for spending. Nixon would refuse to release funds if he thought the effect would be to hurt a political opponent or, indeed, if he thought the spending ill-advised. A "reform"—not the mot juste—in 1974 changed the budget process so as to make this more difficult.

Now Congress twice a year had to pass budget resolutions that outlined fully what was to be spent where and what taxes would be. Bills would be "omnibus." There was no way (such as was later created by the line-item veto) for a president to scotch this or that authorized expenditure. A professed hope of the 1974 reform was that deficit spending would become more difficult. If resolutions had to be on the complete federal budget for a fiscal year, any deficits would be apparent at the outset, instead of emerging after a long line of incremental spending increases. Congress would be shamed into restraint.

In practice, this meant that the embarrassment caused by an omnibus deficit number, if the Democrats remained unmovable on spending, would call forth the "something in the Republican chemistry that causes the GOP to become hypnotized by the prospect of an imbalanced budget." Sure enough, the deficit numbers of 1975 and 1976, the first years of the new budget process, were stratospheric. In 1975 the deficit was $53 billion, in 1976, $74 billion, blowing away the high-deficit thresholds set in the late LBJ years. The 1976 deficit was half again as big as the largest of the Vietnam era, at 4.2 percent of GDP, and had no peer in the nation's fiscal accounts since World War II.

The Ford administration played to type and insisted on revenue purity. Cheney interrupted Wanniski and Laffer at the Two Continents, as they laid out a plan for noninflationary prosperity, in order to ask about revenues. The White House dismissed Kemp's tax cuts in favor of one-time rebates that would not jeopardize revenue collections in future years. Ford even resurrected LBJ's "anti-inflation tax" idea, this time in the form of a $3 tax per barrel of imported oil. And the Ford Republicans kept silent about bracket creep, knowing that so long as inflation remained unwhipped, every year more private-sector income would be transferred to the government.[29]

In this environment, Paul Craig Roberts knew that it was time to get serious. Upon joining Kemp's staff in 1975 he hired Ture to examine rigorously the economics behind the Kemp bill and to suggest any necessary revisions. Roberts knew Ture from his academic work and had a high opinion of him. As Roberts once said of Ture, "No economist is perfect, but Norman is as close as they come."[30]

Ture dove into the project, putting the Kemp provisions into his model and following the results. Ture recommended some changes, but in all he figured that the bill's tax cuts would stimulate yearly gross national product by $150 billion, create five million new jobs over a decade, and have minimal if not positive effects on federal revenues. As Bruce Bartlett, a Kemp staffer, wrote: "The Ture analysis showed enormous supply response to the Kemp bill."[31]

Emboldened by the Ture analysis, the Kemp bill kept gathering sponsors, 136 at final count. One reason was that the bill was renamed, more winsomely, the Jobs Creation Act. Through it all, the Ford administration kept up its opposition. In particular, it dismissed Ture's econometric work. Here Ture provided another key service to the viability of the legislation. Ture had superb contacts in Washington economic circles, and he was able to learn that the administration was not really committed to the anti-stagflation policies it was pursuing on Capitol Hill, including the retraining act, the WIN program, the oil tax, etc. These were "just aesthetics" meant to "quench the thirst of the populace," Kemp was apprised in a staff memo. As for the Jobs Creation Act, the Ford administration thought it ill-informed and quixotic. Ture reported that the Ford CEA chair, Alan Greenspan, believed that "savings were irrelevant to capital formation [and] that you will never produce a growth in savings through tax reform." The only thing the administration believed in was balanced budgets, preferably achieved through spending cuts. But it was ready to go with stealth tax increases, too, even beyond bracket creep. Ture learned that the White House was proposing to "simplify" taxes by eliminating all deductions. He passed a warning on to Kemp and others on the Hill.[32]

By late 1975, the Jobs Creation Act was attracting interest among Democrats, in defiance of Wanniski's Two Santa Clauses theory. Russell Long and Lloyd Bentsen of the Senate Finance Committee were expressing interest, as indeed was Harlem's Charles Rangel. The provision the lawmakers found attractive was the tax credit for savings and investment. This spoke to the complaints they were hearing from their constituents. For public clamor against inflation was founded not merely on the fact that prices were higher at the cash register. Inflation also made it impossible to save. Bank accounts would have to earn absurd rates of interest to compete with a price index increasing by 29 percent in three years, as it did through 1973, 1974, and 1975. Regulations forbade savings account managers from dabbling in exotic investments, even though things like certificates of deposit (CDs) and money markets arose during this time as instruments that captured higher returns. Still, 29 percent over three years was never going to be cleared in a savings account, especially since interest was reported as taxable income—a standard point of Ture's. Thrifty people were left with no option but to abandon saving and buy while they could.[33]

Growth finally rebounded in 1976, at a nice rate of 5.3 percent. The consumer was buying. But then, one had no choice. Inflation and unemployment barely moderated. Inflation dropped to 5.8 percent, a historically high figure, but below the 8.4 percent average of the previous three years. Unemployment dipped all of a fraction of a point, to 7.7 percent, an unheard-of number in the 1950s and 1960s, but now a mild relief. By stagflation standards, 1976 was a passable year, but it was not nearly good enough to stem the growing interest in Kemp's tax cut, interest that was starting to take on the aspect of an avalanche.

Kemp-Roth

In 1976, Wanniski and Laffer were insinuating themselves in Washington, where they believed they could exert maximum influence. Befriending Jack Kemp, the twosome suggested some tweaking of the Jobs Creation Act. They wanted cuts on the marginal rate of the income tax, 48 percent on the highest earners in 1976. Ture was sympathetic, in that high earners make investments with after-tax income. Tax that income less, and investment will grow. Staff in Kemp's office and others on Capitol Hill started working on provisions for a reduction in the personal rate. The result came just in time to cancel Jimmy Carter's honeymoon.[34]

Carter won the presidency, barely, in November 1976, and immediately on taking office in January 1977 faced a Congress proposing an across-the-board tax cut. On the campaign trail, Carter had demonstrated no interest in tax cuts. Rather, he wanted "tax reform," specifically of those "gross inequities" which, as he wrote in a campaign manifesto, made certain that "the most surely taxed income is that which is derived from the sweat of manual labor. Carefully contrived loopholes let the total tax burden shift more and more toward the average wage earner. The largest corporations pay the lowest tax rates and some with very high profits pay no tax at all."[35]

This was certainly not Ture's analysis, which showed that corporations faced taxes on losses, as money sunk into capital investment morphed into profit on the tax return, on account of unindexed depreciation schedules. Manual labor, in the future Ture saw unfolding, was set to become ever more reduced to just that: manual labor, with no help from equipment. For as capital investment dwindled, what machines were workers to manipulate as it became uneconomical for firms to buy them? Yet Carter was a lost cause. He had his sights set on business taxes—increasing them, incredibly—and he was not going to budge. Most famously, and haplessly, he was going to go after the businessman's "three-martini lunch." The best one could say about Carter was that, on taking office in 1977, he did indicate that he would consider offsetting loophole-closing with a cut in the top personal investment rate from 70 percent to 50 percent, in order to spur capital formation.[36]

Carter, however, was destined to be a bystander to the tax and budget dramas of the years of his presidency. For the movement that Kemp had seeded with his Jobs Creation Act was poised, in early 1977, not only to introduce revisions to the tax code, but also to change the way the federal government conceived of and conducted economic policy. The leadership role would be assumed by Congress, not the executive, not even the Federal Reserve. The key development came when, in the waning days of the 1976 campaign, Paul Craig Roberts moved from Kemp's staff to that of the newly formed House Budget Committee.[37]

Roberts perceived that the new budget process instituted in 1974 could provide a platform for Congress-wide discussions of national economic policy in a way that the incremental system of the past could not. Before 1974, when individual spending bills were introduced, they were never pretexts for comprehensive discussions of the government's role in the economy. The stakes were too small. Tax bills, for their part, were rare, coming on the docket every several years, usually in a period of crisis when deliberation and discussion was not the order of the day. But with the new omnibus system, there were four times a year (twice each in the House and Senate) in which the opportunity presented itself for Congress to consider broad questions about the impact of taxes and spending on the economy.[38]

Roberts moved to the Budget Committee, where he became chief minority economist, because that committee had authority to submit amendments during the biannual events. In late 1976, he set to work with representatives sympathetic to Kemp's bill to draft a new piece of legislation that would incorporate aspects of the Jobs Creation Act as well as a 5 percent cut in the marginal income-tax rate for all brackets. In November, one of Roberts's allies on the committee, John Rousselot, Republican of California, informed the Congressional Budget Office (CBO) of the plan.[39]

The CBO moved to discredit the idea of a 5 percent reduction in rates. It issued a forecast showing that while 1978 GNP would increase by $75 billion (fully 4 percent of GDP) given the rate cut, the cost to the federal treasury would be a whopping $43 billion, or 14 percent of 1976 receipts. A 5 percent tax cut would result in a 14 percent revenue loss, in addition to economic growth of 4 percent—the numbers were bizarre, and Roberts and Rousselot were incredulous. Indeed, they had set a trap. Roberts and Rousselot knew that the economic forecasting models used by the government either were heavily biased against tax cuts with regard to government revenue (if not growth) or were being misused. The pair surmised that with CBO forecasts saying preposterous things before they introduced the legislation calling for a tax cut, opposition to the cut would be undermined.[40]

The developers of the models got worried. They charged immense fees— Otto Eckstein would sell his Data Resources Inc. model for $100 million in 1979—and could not risk public ridicule of their products. Eckstein and others wrote letters to Rousselot suggesting that the CBO had underestimated various responses to tax cuts. Still, Roberts pointed out, the Data Resources model, as well as its competitor, the Wharton model, seemed to have GNP going down on account of a corporate tax cut. Realizing that the supply-siders were in ascendancy, Eckstein spent the next two years tweaking his model in favor of their theory.[41]

The CBO, for its part, moved to put out the fire. Director Alice Rivlin informed Rousselot that she had forgotten to include "reflow" effects in her calculation of the budgetary effects of the 5 percent cut. The loss would only be $26 billion. Smelling blood, Rousselot asked her what the result would be given a 15 percent reduction in marginal rates. She answered that it would be even less, $18 billion.[42]

Perhaps, Rousselot countered, the result would actually be positive. Was the result not positive, after all, the last time marginal rates were cut, in the

1960s? He posed this question to the treasury secretary, Michael Blumenthal, and received the following response: "This increase in receipts [of $54 billion from 1962 to 1968] was the result of both changes in legislation over the period and growth in the economy. Therefore, this history shows that receipts generated by six years of growth in the economy more than compensated for any revenue losses resulting from changes in legislation." In February 1977, nobody had yet heard of the Laffer curve. But Carter's treasury secretary verified that given cuts at the margin in the 1960s, the United States had escaped the curve's "prohibitive zone" of taxation.[43]

Rousselot suggested that all of this constituted a good reason to hold hearings on the state of economic modeling. Rivlin was able to parry that request, and in time the Senate Finance Committee would commission a model respectful of supply-side effects. But in the meantime a more delicious opportunity presented itself to Rousselot. In February 1977, a month into the Carter presidency, the Democratic majority in the House authorized a third budget resolution for fiscal 1977, an unprecedented and irregular move. The first two resolutions, as provided by the 1974 reform, had already been made, with everyone acquiescing to the budget deficit that arrived of $50 billion. The third meeting was called by Democrats to provide for an additional $20 billion in "fiscal stimulus," which would swell the deficit to $70 billion.[44]

It was a case, surely, of Democrats overplaying their Santa Claus role. But it was also a move to ward off trouble. For the decent growth of 1976 had done nothing to budge unemployment. In minds in which the Great Depression was still fresh, there was no economic problem—not inflation, not the dollar, not energy—more politically portentous than unemployment. Economists had begun to warn that growth would probably not be sustained in 1977 at the high 1976 rate. Unemployment would rise, significantly. Unless something were done, the new Democratic president and Congress would be at the helm while the nation suffered the jobless levels of the 1930s.

Walter Heller advised Democrats to go with their instincts. In the first week of the new Congress, in January 1977, Heller pointed out that federal spending, despite the $50 billion 1976 deficit, had actually come in a little under the resolution target line. (This was probably because of failure to index spending to inflation.) The time had come to throw the spending gates open, in the interest of putting people to work. Heller had in mind "a new set of carefully crafted job-and-training programs." Also, "a lot of meritorious water, sewer and other public works projects are at the starting blocks and deserve early funding." Coupled with tax rebates and easy money from the Fed, Heller argued, the spending should arrest unemployment, whose ranks, he conceded, in the last six months of the recovery year of 1976 had increased by 900,000.[45]

With pedigreed authorities such as Heller pushing deficits, the majority on the House Budget Committee went ahead with the third resolution calling for the extra $20 billion in stimulus spending. Here Rousselot struck. He had thought he was going to have to wait for the first 1978 budget resolution to propose his 5 percent across-the-board cut in tax rates, but the extraordinary 1977 measure in service of stimulus was a better occasion.

Rousselot rose with difficulty (he was a polio survivor) on the floor of the House "and said in a booming voice," as Roberts recalled in his memoir: "'Mr. Chairman, I offer an amendment as a substitute for the amendment in the nature of a substitute.'" February 23, 1977, "was a historic date," Roberts wrote, "for that arcane legislative language marked the origin of the Kemp-Roth bill and the resurrection of the Republican Party." Roberts might have added that that date also marked the point where supply-side economics ceased being an intellectual parlor game and started to assume its destiny as the economic policy of a nation in renaissance.[46]

It made for a raucous day in the House. As Roberts recalled, when Rousselot rose, "many expected him to offer a balanced-budget amendment"—Scrooge—"but instead he announced that the minority was offering ... 'a simple across-the-board tax reduction for every American.'" A second Santa Claus was in the House. Rousselot made his case: "The purpose of permanent tax reduction is to reduce the tax bias against work, saving, and investment. ... The present high rate of taxation holds down production and investment, reduces employment and the incentive to work, and makes people dependent on transfer payments [from the government]." The cost to the federal treasury: $8 billion, the latest number from the CBO. A Democrat immediately responded that Rousselot's amendment would increase the deficit already on the books, an offense to strict standards of accounting. But the terms of the debate were in Rousselot's favor: the House had convened that day to consider the Democrats' proposal for a $20 billion deficit increase.

The Democrat, Jim Mattox of Texas, got the last word before Rousselot's time expired: "What the gentleman from California really is saying is that he is actually increasing the deficit." Of course he was—that was the business the House was considering—but unlike the majority's proposal, Rousselot's provided for permanent tax reductions and a *smaller* deficit increase. The only real questions were whether the majority or the minority proposal would be more stimulative and more popular. As for the latter issue, it seemed obvious that the electorate would prefer a permanent marginal tax cut as opposed to spending on sewers and a rebate. As for the prospect of stimulating the economy, common sense, if not the state of received econometric models, indicated that more people would be at work if they were taxed less.

It sounded like "trickle-down economic theory." Democrat Paul Simon from Illinois quoted that chestnut from the Herbert Hoover days as the discussion continued. The Democrats started to argue that the five-percentage-point reduction in each tax bracket would benefit the rich disproportionately. Since a percentage point of a high earner's income is greater than a percentage point of a low earner's income, the Rousselot amendment favored the rich. Roberts correctly pointed out to a Democratic aide that the minority proposal actually increased the progressivity of the code, because five points off a low bracket is a greater percentage reduction than is five points off a high bracket. Roberts's argument was dismissed and the bill was labeled as "regressive"—"a redefinition," Roberts wrote, "that destroyed the meaning of an old and honorable term."

Jack Kemp rose to the challenge. He had been plotting with Rousselot all along, and now that the amendment was out of the committee and on the floor, he could speak up. Kemp produced statistics from academic economists showing that when marginal taxes are cut, a greater share of all taxes is paid by the rich, because of incentive effects. Marginal tax cuts were not regressive, but progressive. Kemp also pointed out that the majority proposal was effectively a tax increase. Since government spending would do nothing to increase supply, inflation would result, real incomes would go down, and people would be pushed into higher brackets via bracket creep. Kemp's interlocutor, Democrat Jim Wright of Texas, Roberts would recall, "turned his back and walked off the floor. Kemp called after him: "'Mr. Wright, I'm speaking to you!'"

Rousselot's amendment lost, but it racked up 148 votes out of 406 cast. A watered-down Democratic stimulus in time became law. The economic results were mixed. Unemployment fell fractionally again in 1977, to 7.1 percent, but inflation went up by the same fraction, to 6.5 percent, giving credence to the Phillips curve and keeping the misery index at 14. Growth was 4.6 percent, a strong number. The 1977 deficit was $54 billion, though that was fudged lower by moving the term of the fiscal year. Walter Heller was roughly vindicated.

Yet it was apparent to everyone, after the effects of February 23, 1977, sank in, that the Democrats were now on their own as spending Santa Claus. There would be no more foil in the form of a Republican Scrooge. And there may even be defections from Democratic ranks to the emerging tax-cut Santa. For this Santa would need no Scrooge. This Santa was offering lower taxes, lower unemployment, more rewards for work, and lower deficits all at once.

The Republicans on Capitol Hill owed some of their inspiration to the veterans of Michael 1. The minority House report for the third budget resolution observed that Jude Wanniski's writings had influenced the members' thinking on tax cuts. Minority staff on the JEC added that "it is appropriate at this point to mention the recommendations of Professor Robert Mundell on how to break free of the Phillips curve to reach low unemployment with low inflation. A liberal fiscal policy of low taxes must be used to reduce unemployment, while a tight money policy . . . must be used to lower inflation and interest rates."[47]

Kemp continued to huddle with Roberts, Ture, Wanniski, Laffer, and new staffer Bruce Bartlett during the cold winter of 1977. In April he announced a supercharging of the Rousselot amendment. Kemp proposed a bill providing not for a five- but rather for a fifteen-percentage-point reduction in all income-tax brackets. He soon realized that any number of Republicans were about to propose the same thing. So Kemp doubled down: his would be a *thirty*-percentage-point reduction in all brackets. If the majority had trouble fending off a five-point reduction promising incentives and sounder fiscal accounts, it was sure to find six times that amount a bear of a bill. In July, Kemp found an ally in the Senate, William Roth, Republican of Delaware, who agreed to sponsor the bill in his chamber on the condition that the thirty points be phased in over three years—"10-10-10."[48]

Perhaps the bill looked crazy—a 30 percent tax cut in the face of deficits blowing through historical standards. But given bracket creep, where inflation pushes people who simply get cost-of-living raises into higher tax-rate categories, Kemp-Roth stood to return taxes to levels where they had been just a few years earlier. Inflation plus the progressivity of the tax code were removing more and more income from private earners and converting it into government revenue. The statistics were making this clear. In the absence of marginal tax cuts or increases, from 1976 to 1981 government revenues rose yearly, as a percentage of GDP, from 17.2 to 17.8 to 18 to 18.5 to 19 to 19.6. It was a steady upward line. Unless something were done, there was no end in sight, because with every passing year, even in the face of increasing revenues, deficits persisted or worsened.

Kemp-Roth promised to arrest the governmental displacement of the real economy, perhaps restoring the government revenue–real economy ratio to where it was before bracket creep set in, about 17 percent. Certainly, under Kemp-Roth people would keep more of their income, there would be more supply, and the return to working and investment would be greater. As Ture had been saying for years, find a tax policy that truly stimulates the real economy, adopt it, and then align government spending to the resulting revenues. Those revenues will be good—how could they not be, given a robust economy?

In the *Wall Street Journal* in May 1977, Irving Kristol wrote: "'We do not dance even yet to a new tune. But change is in the air. We hear but indistinctly what were once the clearest and most distinguishable voices which have ever instructed political mankind.'" Kristol was quoting Keynes, from *The End of Laissez-Faire* (1926), but he was turning the tables on him. For Keynes had envisioned, in the 1920s, the advent of governmental managers of whole economies, managers who would produce target levels of output and employment by manipulating revenues, taxes, and the money supply in aggregate. The managers would ensure an optimal outcome for all. All this came to be known as "Keynesianism" (if not "macroeconomics").

"None of this would matter much," Kristol wrote, "if [Keynes's] policy prescriptions worked. But they don't. . . . Deficits . . . cause inflation. And to the degree that the deficits give rise to heavier taxation, the economy stagnates. . . . In response to this crisis . . . , a 'new' economics is beginning to emerge. . . . This 'new' economics is sometimes described, rather cumbersomely, as 'supply-side fiscal policy.' . . . [Its] major emphasis . . . is on the need for a substantial, across-the-board cut in tax rates, because it is the high level of tax rates that is stifling incentives to growth."

These "economic ideas," Kristol went on, "[are] beginning to reshape our thinking on economic policy. . . . [This] helps explain the recent willingness of congressional Republicans to vote in favor of a permanent tax cut despite the state of the budget. They were not 'playing politics,' as some critics claimed. They were acting on an economic theory which, if only dimly understood, was nevertheless persuasive." Kristol added that the theory had its academic elaborators in Mundell and Laffer, among others. "For the first time in half a century," Kristol wrote in conclusion, "it is the economic philosophy of conservatives that is showing signs of intellectual vigor, while . . . liberalism keeps tying itself into ever more elaborate knots. As some sage once observed: You can't beat a horse with no horse. Conservatives . . . may be in the process of acquiring a horse." In 1977, they had indeed acquired a horse. In 1978, the horse bolted.[49]

7

Revolt

The Steiger amendment is not one tax provision among many, but the cutting edge of an important intellectual and financial breakthrough.

—Jude Wanniski, *Wall Street Journal* (unsigned editorial), April 26, 1978

The next of 1978's superspectacular tax revolts may pit the president against Congress. Call that one Proposition 1980.

—Louis Rukeyser, *Wall $treet Week*, August 11, 1978

When Richard Nixon began his presidency, in 1969, the Great Depression was less than three decades in the past. It was no further away in memory than the stagflation era is today. As stagflation got going with Nixon, Americans over forty clearly remembered the Depression and its greatest scourge, poverty born of unemployment.

In the 1930s, any job at all was good work, because pay held its value. If you could get a job, the pay was sure to be exchangeable for the amount of goods and services you expected, even if it was saved for spending in the future. The consumer price index moved barely a whit from 1934 to the beginning of World War II. The nationwide scramble in the Depression was not to make more money, but simply to make some money—that is, to have a job. The experience of unemployment in the Great Depression had been so frightful—there was starvation here and there throughout the decade, as John Steinbeck was correct to illustrate in *The Grapes of Wrath*—that putting people to work was the ultimate priority. The nation was decidedly more contented during World War II, when everybody was at work, either as a G.I. or on the home front, even if rationing meant that there was nothing to buy.

The memory of the Great Depression and its greatest problem, unemployment, surely affected policymakers as postwar prosperity started to wane in the late 1960s. If times were going to be tougher, unemployment had to be contained. And if inflation provided a means of attaining this objective, as the Phillips curve suggested, then inflation should be tolerated, perhaps even encouraged. When the economy sank after 1969, Nixon essentially invited this outcome by delinking gold from the dollar.

Unemployment, even when it reaches savage rates such as the 24 percent recorded in 1932, technically affects only a fractional minority of the population. In recessionary times, the threat of unemployment may stalk the populace at large, but most people in fact hold onto work, even in the worst of circumstances. Inflation, however, affects everyone. To the individual, the experience of inflation does not have the bite of losing a job, but it is a negative experience all the same. In implicitly favoring inflation over unemployment in the early 1970s, policymakers strove to exchange a horrible experience for a few—unemployment—for an unpleasant experience for all—inflation.

There was rising discontent over the historic inflation rates of 1973–75, but it was hard to gauge that discontent's intensity. Were the tremendous Democratic victories at the polls in November 1974 a verdict on Watergate or inflation? Wanniski thought the latter, but he could not convince Cheney or Rumsfeld, much less Ford, of his views. After 1975, when inflation moderated a little, the discontent over prices became a slow burn. There was grumbling and resignation, but not rage. The country-and-western tune that hit number two on the charts in 1980 captured the feeling. As Don Williams sang, "I don't believe the price of gold . . . that gasoline's in short supply [or] the rising cost of getting by." But he did believe in "babies," "Mom and Dad," and "you." Times were weird, but if one kept one's head and acted normally, everything was going to be okay.

And yet there was one factor that threatened to turn the slow burn into an explosion: the tax code. By the late 1970s, everybody had become acquainted with the main malefactor, bracket creep, which referred to the progressivity of the tax code in combination with inflation. The phenomenon was made clear to many through experience. Inflation ran at 7.5 percent per year, 45 percent total, from 1973 to 1978. If a worker making $19,000 in 1973 had cost-of-living adjustments (COLAs) equal to the rise in consumer prices, the worker was making about $27,500 after five years. In 1973, a worker making $19,000 had an income-tax rate that topped out at 25 percent. Yet in 1978, the worker would have found that every dollar of his cumulative $8,500 raise—a raise that covered only his rise in living expenses—was taxed at higher rates. The first $4,000 was taxed at 28 percent, the next $4,000 at 32 percent, and the remaining dollars at 36 percent.[1]

The COLA meant to keep the worker even with inflation, but it failed. For the COLA was additional income, and higher marginal rates applied to that additional income. To have been a real COLA, it should have been taxed at the average rate of tax for all the worker's income, in this case 17 percent. But that is not how a progressive tax system works. All new income is taxed at the highest rate an income earner is subject to. A COLA could even vault earners into a higher marginal rate bracket than that at which their last dollar of income, pre-COLA, was taxed, such as in the bitter example stylized here.[2]

The numbers were grim. For our 1973 worker to have maintained the same standard of living against inflation, the worker would have had to arrange for something like $29,400 of income in 1978. That is, a 55 percent raise (8.7 percent per year) was required to keep up with inflation as it mixed with the tax code. For most workers, this was unthinkable.[3]

In 1978, Paul Craig Roberts, working for Orrin Hatch, unearthed academic research that indicated that the effect spanned all income levels. The research showed that a person facing an average tax rate of 10 percent would need raises 11 percent above inflation in order for the raises to be real. A high earner facing marginal rates in the upper brackets would need raises 40 percent clear of inflation in order for the raise to be real.[4]

Warren Brookes, a syndicated columnist at the *Boston Herald-American*, collected stories of workers hurt by bracket creep. He found that at every income level, the people he met were getting hefty raises while their living standards withered. A factory worker named "George J." gained raises that beat inflation by 6 percent over three years, yet George J.'s real income remained unchanged on account of taxes. "William R.," an accountant who made half again as much as George J., got a 10 percent raise in 1977 and saw his real pay go down. A businessman named "Lawrence K.," who pulled in nearly double that of William R., saw his income go up by half in ten years and his after-tax purchasing power go down by a third.[5]

Even determined efforts by labor unions to overcome inflation and bracket creep yielded pittances in the 1970s. The United Steelworkers negotiated a long-term contract in 1973 that provided a nominal COLA plus 3 percent per year. The USW was duly proud of the agreement. No doubt, it was one of the most expansive contracts in the history of labor. Yet its sum accomplishment was to return little more than a real cost-of-living increase to its beneficiaries. A real 3 percent bonus was negligible in the face of inflation because of bracket creep.[6]

All this is to say that it became functionally impossible to get ahead in the 1970s. It was a trick merely to stay in place. Hence Don Williams's "rising cost of getting by." Yet if "taxflation" (as progressive taxation mixed with inflation became called) put workers in a bind, a thought can also be spared for their employers. Employers whose revenues increased in proportion to inflation could not come close to increasing their workers' wages consistent with prices. Since the 45 percent inflation of 1973–78 required a 55 percent increase in salaries, firms seeking to give real COLAs to their employees faced cash-flow problems, if not the stalking horse of bankruptcy. The only options were to cut corners and to "jawbone"—a favorite term of Ford's and Carter's—whereby employers nicely asked their workers to be satisfied with a little less, given inflation.[7]

Or one could see the light, like U.S. Steel, and get out of wage-intensive businesses entirely, instead buying access to commodities that kept up with inflation. In the late 1970s, General Electric saw the small natural-resources segment of its business portfolio yield exceptional profits. GE began to wonder if its growth plan should lie in this area, as opposed to in its core competency, manufacturing in such areas as power generation, engines, and medical devices.[8]

Taxflation through bracket creep gave the lie to the Phillips curve, disreputable as the curve may have already been in academic economics by the late 1970s. Inflation plus a progressive tax code made it impossible to have two things simultaneously: a job and pay. You could have a job, but if you militated for real pay, the employer would run out of cash and thus have to look for a less labor-intensive business to go into and make layoffs. Inflation did not cure unemployment in the 1970s; it caused it. Taxflation was the root of the misery index.

All this is merely to speak of the income tax. The tax that threatened to turn the '70s funk into the Great Depression was the property tax. In inflationary times, commodities, limited in supply by the earth, increase in price at a rate greater than inflation. This is because it is certain that their supply cannot be magically increased by an exponential order of magnitude, whereas currency may be so increased. Commodities take on the monetary function surrendered by money during inflationary times, that of the "storehouse of value." The one thing that is most limited in supply by the earth is the earth itself—land. Land values can race far ahead of the price level in inflationary times. The effect is especially acute when the land in question is generally desirable: California land, for example.

In the 1970s, California land prices spiked enormously, just as gold, oil, gas, and other commodities did, but there was a difference in owning land as opposed to a commodity. There was no excise tax on gold, tungsten, copper, and so on, even if there came to be equivalents of such things on oil. There certainly was an excise on California land, namely the local property tax, which averaged about 2.7 percent through early 1978.[9]

Ten years before, in 1968, if you had been a brave California home buyer who stretched your budget to take out a mortgage on a $50,000 home, the tax component of the monthly mortgage payment would have been about $110. But over the next ten years, as the assessors reacted to a fivefold increase in the value of the property, that component would have risen to $550 per month. Inflation had been about 100 percent, but tax inflation had been 500 percent. True, the mortgage would have been reduced in real size by inflation, but that implies that one actually keeps one's COLAs. Given bracket creep, one does not. The bottom line: by 1978, many Californians who had lived in their homes for years realized that they might soon face foreclosure.[10]

Had nothing happened, it would have made for curious history. Vast numbers of foreclosed-upon Californians would have had enough equity to buy a house, so long as it was not in California. These Californians—call them "Calies"—and many of them elderly, could have piled in the car and moved east, perhaps paralleling the old Route 66, to Oklahoma. There, helpful locals might have put them up in temporary shelters while tract housing was built. There would have been work in the oil fields. The quixotic journey might have even given rise to great literature.

But it was not to be. There would be no touching acts of compassion, no lifting of spirits, no distinctive public art—the signal achievements of the Great Depression—because activists allied with the supply-siders captured the fury of California voters and passed Proposition 13 in June 1978. Prop 13 collapsed the property tax to 1 percent and underindexed it for future inflation. Henceforth the only time the tax code would treat a house according to its market value would be upon its sale. Folks kept their homes. Prop 13 was the first indication that the nation was going to rise up against the '70s funk. Other eruptions quickly followed.

Hitting the Shelves

In early 1978, two books began to reveal that the public was getting sick of stagflation and impatient for a solution. William Simon's *Time for Truth* and Jude Wanniski's *Way the World Works* sold briskly and immediately preceded a firestorm of action on inflation and taxes. One might even say that the books touched off the firestorm. During the great tax revolts of 1978, from California to Congress, both manuals were often consulted.

An exasperated Simon, the economic wise man of the Nixon and Ford administrations, had left Washington when Ford's term expired in January 1977. With Robert Bartley, Simon had been part of the "crowding out" crowd. But also like Bartley, after so many years of stagflation he was now ready to make a break. Simon's last act as treasury secretary, in January 1977, had been to issue a report calling for unconditional tax cuts, including a cut in the top rate of almost half. A year later, *A Time for Truth* revealed that behind closed doors Simon had been fighting Nixon and Ford all along. Simon marveled that he had not been fired—and that he kept getting rehired. "I found myself compelled, in 1974," Simon wrote in the introductory chapter, "to inform President Nixon that his fiscal policies were 'insane.' ... A year later I was engaged in a verbal wrestling match with President Ford over his proposals to 'liberate' energy production in this country by intensifying and expanding state control over the energy industries."[11]

Simon had retained his opposition to budget deficits, but he made it clear that all responsibility for eliminating them lay with spending. Simon was a veteran Wall Streeter and the managing director of Salomon Brothers before he came to Washington. He knew how to analyze fiscal accounts. As he reported throughout the book, government at all levels had benefited from greatly increased revenues in the 1970s because of inflation and bracket creep. Indeed, "the share of gross national product eaten up by government has been inflating feverishly," Simon reported. "In 1930, spending ... accounted for 12 percent of the GNP. By 1976, it was 36 percent."[12]

Simon marveled that, despite the transfer of wealth from the private sector to government, government was having an ever harder time making ends meet. One of the reasons the Carter deficits were unintelligible to Simon was that they persisted, then increased, in the face of rising tax revenues as a percentage of GDP—not to mention falling military spending. When deficits go up with increasing revenues, and do so consistently, the only expectation can be for further displacement of the real economy by government. Reflecting on this "cannibalistic pattern," Simon wrote that "no economy can survive a structural war conducted against it by the state."[13]

One chapter of *A Time for Truth* detailed the fiscal crisis recently experienced by New York City. In 1975, that flagship municipality nearly went bankrupt. Simon's specialty at Salomon Brothers, a firm situated in the bowels of New York's Financial District, had been municipal finance. He scoffed at assertions that the city had missed payments because Wall Street was out to get it and Washington had been negligent. Simon recalled asking the New York mayor for the city's books when the mayor had appealed to Treasury for a lifeline in 1975. The books never arrived. "I did not realize," Simon wrote, "that the last thing on earth any New York politician desired to confront was the city's bookkeeping." No books meant no lifeline. As the *New York Daily News* headline put it: "Ford to City: Drop Dead."[14]

Simon explained how the cascade of new revenues to the city had led municipal workers' unions to keep asking for higher wages and benefits. Better benefits were preferred, because they were not subject to taxation, let alone bracket creep, but municipal workers also insisted on real COLAs. Just as in the private sector, in the 1970s this was a recipe for bankruptcy. Wall Street was the first to notice. Financiers naturally examine things like future liabilities—benefits—when deciding whether to underwrite a long-term bond. Having seen enough, they closed their windows. Simon warned that New York was a microcosm of the rest of the nation. What had happened to it would happen to the country at large if it did not reduce inflation and reverse the trend whereby the government displaced the private sector.[15]

As *A Time for Truth* settled into the best-seller lists, another book written from a similar perspective, but decidedly more optimistic, started gaining readers. This was *The Way the World Works: How Economies Fail—and Succeed*. Wanniski had spent 1977 on leave from the *Wall Street Journal* at the American Enterprise Institute. There he synthesized what he had learned from Mundell and Laffer, adding his own interpretations. When Wanniski's young son asked him what the book was about, Wanniski stumbled over an answer before saying, "It's about the way the world works." He had a title.[16]

The Way the World Works was as much an exercise in political theory as a primer in supply-side economics. For chapter after chapter, Wanniski delved into major episodes in the history of civilization and meditated on the fundamental principles of human behavior. The driving idea of *The Way the World Works* was that human beings respond to incentives. If governments permit individuals to keep more of the product of their work, they will work more, and they will cooperate more through trade. The secret of the rise and fall of empires, Wanniski argued, lay in the degree to which governments allowed their subjects or citizens to conduct themselves in their own pursuits. He had innumerable examples. One was the Nazis' expansion of bilateral trade pacts in the wake of Smoot-Hawley. German producers were allowed to trade, but American producers were not. Thus was foretold a German empire, not an American one—at least in the early 1930s.

Wanniski ascribed the economics of the book to Mundell and Laffer. Mundell was a "modern Walras" (the nineteenth-century general-equilibrium economist; in Wanniski's *Public Interest* article of 1975 Mundell had been a modern Copernicus). Laffer was a "modern Say." Their doctrine, made known to the general public for the first time in *The Way the World Works,* was the Laffer curve. Laffer had never published the curve—anywhere. He had merely scrawled it on the napkin at the Two Continents a few years before in an effort to bring Ford's lieutenants around to tax cuts. The only other time he may have used it was in the classroom. By the end of 1978, Wanniski's book had made the Laffer curve virtually a household term.[17]

The central economic lesson of *The Way the World Works,* however, did not concern the bow-shaped curve relating tax revenues and rates, but rather another doctrine of Laffer's, this one with a long pedigree in academic economics. This was the concept of the "tax wedge." The tax wedge, or simply "the wedge," is that additional product which government compels persons to make if they want to make some other product in the first place. As Wanniski described it: "If Smith and Jones each want to trade sixteen hours of their skills with each other, but in order to complete the transaction each must give the government two hours of their skills, the two must do thirty-six hours of work to transact thirty-two. The four hours 'tax' is the wedge between them." Wanniski noted that Smith and Jones may choose not to do the transaction if the work required takes thirty-six hours; what brought them together in the first place was the prospect of doing just thirty-two. The wedge could be sufficient to quash the production in question.[18]

Wanniski tallied up how wedges had been multiplying in recent years. The obvious ones were income and corporate taxes, which given inflation and bracket creep had been reaching new plateaus. There was also the Social Security tax, one of the best illustrations of the wedge, it too headed for new levels. Here Wanniski quoted Laffer, who in a 1974 memorandum to Simon had shown that since employer and employee each pay half the Social Security tax, the incentive against not contracting with each other is equal. Tariffs, regulations, "red tape and paper work," and fees for legal and accounting services to keep compliant simply piled on additional wedges to the original tax wedge. If the nation was going to tolerate so many wedges, and watch them grow with inflation and progressivity, stagnation must result.[19]

More than the Laffer curve, the concept of the tax wedge is the principal doctrine of supply-side economics. Laffer himself, in testimony before Congress in 1976, chose to elaborate on the concept of the wedge and to detail the extent and magnitude of wedges in the American economy. At the time, Congress was considering the Humphrey-Hawkins Act, which would oblige the federal government to ensure that there was full employment without inflation. Laffer informed the committee that the secret to success was increased production—Say's law, in a word. Get rid of wedges, and people will substitute work for leisure. The availability of more goods would lower the relative prices of all goods, and the objective of the act would be achieved. People would be employed and everything would be as inexpensive as possible. No heavy-handed, misguided legislation necessary. Congress rejected Laffer's advice and passed Humphrey-Hawkins in 1978. The act's main effect was not economic, but bureaucratic: it forced the Fed chairman to report to a congressional committee at regular intervals.[20]

In his memoir, Paul Craig Roberts identified the tax wedge as the idea that motivated the legislative advocates of tax cuts in the battles of 1974–81. Roberts claimed that evidence of the trade-offs implicit in tax wedges was becoming ever more apparent in American life in the 1970s. The black market expanded. Doctors combined their practices so that it would be easier to work half-time. Rich people preferred buying leisure goods (such as Rolls-Royces) to investments, since investments could be taxed at rates approaching or exceeding 100 percent. Roberts argued that it was best not to think of "tax freedom day" as that day in the spring when one stops working for the government and starts working for oneself. Rather, Roberts said, given progressive taxation, one really chooses to work through the year up to the point that government starts getting confiscatory. At that date, one starts to curtail working. An example: doctors taking more Wednesdays off to play golf. Once such professionals reached a high income level, the next dollar they earned would be dunned at rates above 50 percent. It made sense to increase one's preference for leisure over work.[21]

Wanniski informed his readers that great things were in the offing if the nation cleared wedges out of its economic system. Great things not only for the United States, but for the world, since the world loves to mimic the United States when it is successful. In an inscription he penned in Alan Reynolds's copy of the book, Wanniski wrote, "[You] will now be a partner in building an American Empire." Wanniski meant an empire gained by means of the sincerest form of flattery—imitation. If America cut taxes and stabilized money, everyone else would, too. Wanniski most certainly did not have anything militaristic in mind. (Though he was a fairly ardent Cold Warrior, his informal Marxist education seems always to have left Wanniski with a soft spot for Russia, if not Communist theory. Before his death in 2005, Wanniski spoke out ruefully against American military ventures abroad.[22])

Something must have been catching, because as the two books gained readership, things started to happen. In California, antitax activist Howard Jarvis had no problem gaining three times as many signatures as were necessary to put Proposition 13 on the ballot, and he arranged for Laffer to do a promotional tour for the initiative. In New Jersey, Michael 1 attendee Jeff Bell, with the financial backing of Simon's circle, made headway as a candidate in the Republican Senate primary on the basis of a supply-side platform. He would defeat the incumbent in the June primary.[23]

In Congress, William A. Steiger, a minority member on the Ways and Means Committee, took to heart hearings held in March about the state of venture capital. Officials from Silicon Valley, in particular, had made it clear that their sources were drying up on account of taxes. Electronics executive Edwin Zschau testified that companies founded since the capital-gains rate increase of 1969 had been only half as successful in raising venture capital as had firms founded the decade before. The consequences, Zschau said, were far-reaching. For after start-ups get off the ground and become "teenage companies," they have an "employment growth rate ... *20–40 times* [that] of mature companies." He concluded, "Actions by our government have been unwittingly killing this goose laying the golden eggs."[24]

Steiger consulted Laffer about what could be done. Laffer suggested a capital-gains rate cut. Steiger took the advice and had little difficulty signing up Democratic as well as Republican support for his amendment to Carter's tax bill. Wanniski loved the capital-gains measure so much that when it was introduced in April, he fired off an editorial in the *Journal* titled "Stupendous Steiger."[25]

Laffer: Chicago to California

By early 1978, people were starting to find the supply-siders' ideas attractive. Michael 1 was no longer the only redoubt. His newfound popularity stood Laffer in particularly good stead. Laffer had had a tough time of it, personally, since 1971. Paul Samuelson's mockery of him at the University of Chicago in that year had hurt badly. Samuelson had been "downright mean" to the young Laffer, as Martin Anderson would later recall, and the wounds took a long time to heal.

Samuelson had taken aim at Laffer on two counts. He had ridiculed Laffer's GNP forecast, and he had marveled that the young scholar, though a tenured professor at Chicago—in fact the youngest in the university's history—had still not gained the Ph.D. It was true. Laffer had not yet submitted his dissertation to the graduate committee at Stanford. One of his dissertation committee members had died, and Laffer had been dragging his feet on complying with the requests for revisions made by his replacement.

Both situations were soon remedied. Stung by Samuelson, Laffer immediately submitted his dissertation and got his Ph.D in December 1971. And every year's revision of the 1971 GNP number came closer and closer to Laffer's original OMB forecast, until it was hit on the dot in 1976.

Nevertheless, Samuelson's ridicule had made Laffer something of a pariah at Chicago. The faculty (Friedman and George Shultz excluded) shunned Laffer socially. Laffer could rely on Mundell, who was supportive as always, but in 1971 he had left for Canada. To distract himself from this unpleasantness, from 1971 to 1976 Laffer had delved into work with his intellectual confreres in Washington, particularly Simon, and with the Michael 1 group in New York. Eventually, Laffer figured he should make a clean break with Chicago. He leapt at the chance to become Thornton Professor of Business at the University of Southern California, moving to the Golden State in 1976.[26]

At USC, Laffer was friends with a university trustee named Justin Dart. Dart was an immensely successful drugstore entrepreneur (shades of Lew Lehrman) and a major force in California Republican politics. He was also an avid supporter of Ronald Reagan, who in 1976 was a year and a half removed from his two-term tenure as governor. Dart was part of Reagan's "Kitchen Cabinet," the clutch of self-made businessmen who sponsored Reagan's rise in politics, all the way to the White House in 1981. Dart brought Laffer into the Reagan fold, and soon Laffer was a frequent guest with "Ronnie and Nancy." Still, as late as early 1978, Reagan cannot have been a thoroughgoing supply-sider, because at one dinner Nancy insisted to Laffer and Simon that her husband was not supporting Jeff Bell in the New Jersey primary.[27]

Laffer loved his new life in California. He bought a nice spread south of Los Angeles, a place populated not merely with his wife and four children but also with an array of exotic plants and animals. In the Midwest, Laffer had been a closet zoologist, but in California he got to be the real thing. Everyone who came to interview him in that busy year of 1978 gawked at all the creatures, some of which perched on Laffer's shoulder as the supply-sider declaimed on wedges. Occasionally, the interviewers would leave converted. One such journalist was Robert D. Novak, whose syndicated column with Rowland Evans would do a great deal to forward the agenda of supply-side economics over the next two decades.[28]

Laffer was not new to California. He had studied at Stanford, if only sporadically, from 1964 to 1971. The Haight-Ashbury tenor of those years did not appeal to him. He wore a suit and tie to class and rolled his eyes at the counterculturalists. Indeed, Laffer was fond of the establishment and of being establishmentarian. He was forthrightly proud of being fifth-generation Yale, the son of the president of Clevite Corporation, and from a family that was once a pillar of the Cleveland WASP elite. Laffer even looked askance at the nouveau-riche Kitchen Cabinet group. He had grown up among proper Cleveland money and found the George H. W. Bush social circle more to his taste. But Bush would never cotton to supply-side economics, whereas, in Laffer's words, "for a crusty old curmudgeon, Justin Dart got it."[29]

As supply-side economics came into its own in 1980 and 1981, observers wondered if the supply-siders were not countercultural themselves, bent on "shaking up the establishment," as Ben Wattenberg said on television. Laffer believed that the establishment did not need to be torn down, à la 1960s radicalism, but rather, in his words, "reformed" and once again made functional. Laffer wanted leadership from the establishment. He longed not for a revolution, but for a perpetuation of what America had already achieved, namely the recently departed economic conditions that had resulted in so many productive livelihoods and the possibility of sustained, intergenerational wealth.

Laffer wanted to restore postwar prosperity. Reflecting on the reestablishment of the 1945–73 trend line two decades after the fact, in 2005, Laffer allowed himself this reflection: "Is this a great world or what?"[30]

Steiger

Bracket creep sowed the seeds of its own destruction. It produced outrage, and that outrage, in turn, pressured Congress to change the tax code. Before the stagflation years, congressional tax bills had been rare occurrences, coming up once a decade, twice at most. They started to become yearly in 1976. Bracket creep was too untenable to ignore. On Jack Kemp's staff in 1975, Paul Craig Roberts had striven to shoehorn tax bills into other measures, given the newly reformulated budget process. He need not have bothered. Beginning in 1976, tax bills would appear for three years straight, and in other forms after that, until stagflation was finally defeated.[31]

Bracket-expanding bills were introduced in Congress and made law in 1976 and 1977. Both were meek efforts. After the 1977 bill, brackets were moved up about $3,200 from 1975 levels. But the same rate schedule was still there, with 3 percent increases in tax rates for each $4,000 gain in income. These acts did nothing to address the issue of COLAs being taxed at the highest rate a taxpayer was subject to pre-COLA.

Jimmy Carter introduced another tax bill in early 1978. It promised a shaving of rates (though Carter wanted progressivity increased, not decreased). But the main thrust of the bill was to eliminate the pet deductions of rich people and business interests, such as expense accounts—those dreaded three-martini lunches. Since Carter's election, Congress had heard quite a bit about the inadvisability of this sort of reform, from restaurant industry lobbyists in particular. Virtually everyone was skeptical. A tax revolt was brewing, and the president was making a fetish of eliminating petty business deductions.[32]

The thirty-nine-year-old representative from Oshkosh, Wisconsin, William Steiger, introduced his amendment, which would bring capital-gains tax rates back to the 1969 level. The "Steiger amendment" roughly halved most capital-gains tax rates, from 49 percent to 25 percent. The unassuming Steiger seems to have had no idea that the amendment would instantly become a political cause célèbre.[33]

On introducing the amendment in April, Steiger found that nearly half of the Ways and Means Committee was in favor. This was surprising; Steiger was a young Republican on a committee dominated by Democrats, twenty-five to twelve. By early May, it was clear that the amendment would gain the endorsement of Ways and Means and be sent to Congress at large. Carter instructed his treasury secretary, Michael Blumenthal, to meet with congressional leaders to kill the amendment. After all, Carter's bill actually called for *increasing* the capital-gains tax by 40 percent. Blumenthal, who had been sympathetic to measures like capital-gains tax reduction in the previous year, either did not put his heart in the effort or simply failed. For it soon became clear to Washington observers that the Steiger amendment was destined for passage, with or without the rest of Carter's bill.[34]

Tax-cut fever was sweeping the land. On June 6, Proposition 13 passed in California and Jeff Bell won the New Jersey Senate primary. The June 6 events and the success of Simon's and Wanniski's books could only bode well for the Steiger amendment. Carter tried to discredit it as disproportionately benefiting the rich, but this move had no effect. In places like California, homeowners worried about foreclosure realized that they would be hit with a nearly 50 percent capital-gains tax if they sold. They were stuck. Would-be entrepreneurs, as well as small businessmen thinking about selling, perhaps to fund their retirements, also lined up in favor of the amendment. *Time* magazine quoted a lobbyist who said, "Support for Steiger is coming not from the fat cats but from middle-income people yelling 'I want a chance to make it!' The fat cat can protect his income. But the middle-income guy who still has dreams of making it wants to know he can do it big."[35]

The tax revolts of 1978 bore the earmarks of populism, to be sure. Yet the factor that was most responsible for the Steiger amendment's success was an intellectual one. In June 1978, academic economists Martin Feldstein and Joel Slemrod published a paper on the effects of the 1969 capital-gains tax increase, the increase which Steiger sought to roll back. The study, titled "Inflation and the Excess Taxation of Capital Gains on Corporate Stock," provided intellectual credibility for the Steiger amendment. It also proved to be one of the most consequential pieces of research to emerge from academic economics since the crisis of Keynesianism.[36]

The Feldstein-Slemrod study showed that everything about the 1969 capital-gains tax increase had been negative. Business investment, entrepreneurialism, the stock market, and, most interestingly, government revenues had all plummeted because of the increase. Repealing it would reverse these trends. The lead author, Feldstein, was so confident about the validity of the research that throughout the summer and fall of 1978 he dogged Congress, in committee testimony and in letters, to support the capital-gains rate cut. Feldstein's imprimatur on the Steiger amendment gave Congress the confidence it needed to pass the measure overwhelmingly, as it did in October. In 1978, tax cuts were not merely a popular enthusiasm. They were coming to be seen as logically necessary by the nation's top economists.

Martin Feldstein was Harvard University's rising star in economics. He was thirty-eight years of age in 1978 and had been tenured for nearly a decade. He had just won the John Bates Clark medal (which had inexplicably eluded Mundell) for best economist under forty and was the new president of the National Bureau of Economic Research (NBER). Feldstein would revitalize the NBER, rescuing it from its moribund status and making it the nation's premier font of economic analysis.

The most astonishing finding of Feldstein's work on capital-gains rates was that capital-gains taxes in recent years had been paid on losses. Moreover, the effect was large. As Feldstein summarized it in the *Wall Street Journal*: "We found that in 1973 individuals paid capital-gains tax on $4.6 billion of nominal capital gains on corporate stock. When the costs of these shares are adjusted for the increase in the consumer price level since they were purchased, this gain becomes a loss of nearly $1 billion. The $4.6 billion of nominal capital gains resulted in a tax liability of $1.1 billion."

Feldstein found that only about half of the $1.1 billion in capital-gains tax revenue that went to the federal government was taken from investments that had made money in real terms. The other half had been taken from investments that merely kept up with inflation, in whole or in part. "Many individuals pay a substantial capital-gains tax," Feldstein wrote, "even though, when adjustment is made for the change in the price level, they actually receive less from their sale than they had originally paid." The bad news for the Carter administration: "The mismeasurement of capital gains is most severe for taxpayers with incomes under $100,000."[37]

Feldstein was discovering in his academic research what a great many people of all stations had come to know in the stagflation era. In a period of high inflation, people often paid taxes on already accrued, as opposed to newly acquired, wealth when they paid taxes on capital gains. An example is as follows: If one buys a stock in 1975 at 100 and sells it in 1978 for 130, one's nominal gain is 30. But if inflation in that interval is 30 percent, 130 in 1978 is equivalent to 100 in 1975. The stock investor has had no real gain. But at tax time, the investor must pay capital-gains tax on the nominal increase. In 1978, this rate, for people of above-average income, was effectively 50 percent. Our stock investor has to pay $15 in taxes. A wash investment that superficially looks like a 30 percent winner suddenly becomes one in which the investor loses 11.5 percent (15 divided by 130).

The combination of high inflation and high capital-gains taxes was having a particularly deleterious effect on the stock market, where the indexes were struggling to attain 1960s levels in nominal terms. In real, inflation-adjusted terms, the indexes were losing value year after year. Hence, people stayed away. The number of investors in the stock market had declined by a fifth since 1969. A New York Stock Exchange survey of public attitudes toward investing in 1978 found that "the American public has become deeply cautious about taking the kinds of economic risks that are essential to capital raising and economic growth. . . . The concerns underlying this attitude," according to the NYSE, included "fear of continuing inflation . . . and lack of tax incentives to invest."[38]

As for assets that did appreciate, such as California homes, their ability to keep up with inflation was neutralized by a capital-gains tax that preyed on the inflationary part of the gain. There was no escape, outside of tax cuts. Small-business owners faced the same realities. On the Senate Finance Committee, Lloyd Bentsen dwelled on the effect of capital-gains tax predation on investment in such things as oil-drilling equipment. With oil production falling in his state—paradoxically in the face of high prices—he realized that the state's thousands of backyard producers were wary of buying drilling equipment if it meant paying taxes on mega-inflation when you sold the stuff.[39]

Norman Ture had been teaching such lessons in recent years, but with the Feldstein research the conclusions became inescapable. After the Steiger amendment was introduced, the major economic forecasting organizations assessed its implications. The forecasts were in line with what Feldstein had suggested. Cut the rate, and everything will boom: growth, investment, stocks, personal income—and government revenue. Ways and Means, and soon Congress at large, seemed amenable. Everything was set up for a capital-gains rate cut to become law.

Except that one last player was not going along: President Carter. Carter wanted capital-gains rates to be made equal to those applied to ordinary income. Moreover, Carter had placed a priority on "tax reform," whereby deductions that apparently benefited the rich would be curtailed. As Steiger was launched in April 1978, Carter adduced "one medical doctor, a surgeon,

[who] owns a yacht, and he took a $14,000 tax credit, a tax exemption, for entertaining other doctors on his yacht." In his tax bill, Carter wanted to deal with such inequities before any action on rates was taken. He failed to realize that in the wake of the Steiger proposal, and in the froth over Proposition 13 and Jeff Bell's campaign, there was no constituency for tax fairness. In every income level, taxpayers' savings—as well as their losses, amazingly enough—were getting soaked by the tax code, and yet the president was fixated on what the affluent were up to. Evans and Novak wrote at the time, "Tax reform lacks a constituency, provokes the business community and is not an overriding concern of either pressure groups or ordinary citizens." As Carter's resistance against Steiger stiffened that summer, the columnists added that the president failed "to appreciate that taxpayers are more interested in how much they pay rather than how little their neighbor pays—reduction, not reform."[40]

Carter remained inflexible as the excitement over prospective tax cuts exploded. Indeed, he started to refer to the Steiger amendment as a cancer. But in practice, Carter could do nothing either to derail Steiger or to promote reform. Democratic stalwarts in Congress, such as Senators Frank Church of Idaho and Daniel P. Moynihan of New York, made it known that their support of provisions akin to those in the Steiger amendment was assured. Faced with having to give in, Carter chose to pursue the only other conceivable option. He went after the forecasters.[41]

One forecast that had turned up in any number of congressional and White House offices after the Steiger launch in April 1978 was that made by Michael K. Evans of Chase Econometrics. Prompted by the Senate Finance Committee the year before, Evans was soon to declare his allegiance to the supply-side cause—in 1983, he would publish a book vindicating supply-side economics from an empirical perspective—and his forecast showed why. Evans summarized his findings on a prospective capital-gains rate cut in this fashion:

> The reduction in the maximum rate on capital-gains taxes from the current level of 49 percent to 25 percent . . . would have a positive effect on economic growth while reducing the Federal budget deficit. Under such legislation, the rate of growth . . . for the period 1980–1985 would average 3.6 percent, compared to 3.4 percent . . . otherwise. An additional 400,000 new jobs would be created by 1985. . . . In addition, the Federal budget deficit will be $16 billion *less* by 1985 than would be the case without this reduction in capital-gains taxes.[42]

The Carter administration not only remained unmoved, it sought to disprove and ridicule the Chase and similar forecasts. Treasury Secretary Blumenthal, probably against his own inclinations, sponsored a study showing that Steiger's provisions would result in a $2.2 billion revenue loss for the federal government. The lobbying group Public Citizen, allied to the White House on this issue, referred to the Evans forecast and another by Data Resources, which had come to the same conclusion, as "fundamentally flawed." In a press conference, Carter said that he would not "tolerate a plan that provides huge tax windfalls for millionaires and two bits for the average American."[43]

Lying in the wings was the Feldstein research. The administration perceived that this was sure to prove an obstacle as it tried to shore up opposition to the Steiger amendment. For the author was a Harvard professor, a John Bates Clark winner, the president of the National Bureau of Economic Research. Feldstein had a reputation as the nation's top economic statistician. Belittling Feldstein's work was not an option. The Carter people had indeed belittled the Chase and Data Resources studies, but even this had crossed the threshold of temerity. For the Data Resources study had been supervised by Feldstein's highly esteemed elder Harvard colleague, Otto Eckstein.

Treating Feldstein in a similar manner could only serve to alienate and exasperate an important quarter of the economics establishment: Harvard. The administration therefore settled on a different maneuver. It would attempt to disprove the formidable Feldstein work by putting out a critical counterstudy of its own. Feldstein not only noticed; he took umbrage. He relished going on the counterattack. A battle royale ensued, and Feldstein proved the champion.

Charles Schultze, chairman of Carter's Council on Economic Advisors, assigned an economist on his staff with the task of disproving Feldstein's work. The resulting paper came down hard on the Harvard professor's research. It argued that Feldstein and his collaborators had committed a range of unpardonable, indeed incurable, methodological errors. The CEA paper charged that the Feldstein work had overlooked important variables such as tax shelters, that it had failed to account for the decrease in dividend income that might result from a capital-gains rate cut, and that it had looked merely at one year's worth of data. The CEA paper even suggested that federal revenue from capital-gains taxes could fall, and fall dramatically, given a rate cut. The paper offered alternative research that claimed to be more comprehensive than Feldstein's. It concluded:

It is obviously important for decision-makers to obtain estimates of the revenue impact of tax provisions. In the case of capital-gains tax cuts, it is very tempting to rely on the estimates provided by Feldstein et al. . . . But it would be a mistake to rely on these estimates. In scientific terms, the study by Feldstein . . . does not rule out important alternative explanations for its results—explanations with very different policy implications—and it contains serious econometric flaws. Other research has shown that it is possible to develop formulations of investor or firm or household behavior that are not subject to these criticisms.

The language was strong—as language in economics papers often is—and Feldstein reacted in kind.[44]

One day that September, Feldstein met with Stuart Eizenstat, the White House chief domestic policy advisor. He wrote him shortly afterwards: "I learned the day after we talked that one of the young men who met with us was doing a study of capital gains for the Council of Economic Advisors. I have now read the study. It is frankly an embarrassment to the CEA. The main part of the analysis—which relates total capital gains on all assets to dividends on corporate stock—is total nonsense." This was only one of the letters that Feldstein fired off that day to various figures in Washington. To Schultze, who had commissioned the counterstudy, Feldstein wrote that he was "surprised and disappointed." The CEA paper was "utter nonsense. . . . I hope you won't try to persuade anyone to take it seriously." Turning to Congress, Feldstein addressed himself to the chairman of the Senate Finance Committee, Russell Long:

I am writing to you about a paper on capital-gains realizations that was recently circulated by the Council of Economic Advisers. . . . [It] is of such low quality that anyone who understands what [it] has done will certainly not take it at all seriously. . . . I am frankly surprised that the Council would circulate such a poor study on this important issue. . . . There is the obvious danger that a study on this subject by a CEA staff member will be incorrectly regarded as a serious piece of research and will confuse noneconomists who are seeking sound statistical information on which to base their decisions.

Feldstein went on, for three single-spaced pages, to explain to the senator the merits of his own work and the emptiness of the CEA criticisms.[45]

Feldstein had many points. First, his study was fully aware of the intricacies of the marginal tax rate, while the CEA's was not. The CEA study's purportedly more comprehensive data set was merely twenty-two annual totals of capital-gains results, as opposed to his own set of 25,000 individual tax returns. The CEA paper indulged in "a major fallacy" by analyzing, and the emphasis is in Feldstein's original, "*the meaningless ratio of total capital gains on all types of assets to dividends on corporate stock!*" In his letter to Long, Feldstein dwelled on this particular failing at length before settling on the major issue, which was that it was difficult to see how the Treasury could be affected negatively by a capital-gains tax cut. Feldstein assured the Louisiana senator that a rate cut would surely spark new sales in property and stock resulting in capital gains. By any reasonable estimate, revenue to the federal government from these sales at lower tax rates would be in excess of what had been collected in the past. At the end of one paragraph of detailed analysis, Feldstein raised the further possibility that "even the value of taxable dividends will eventually be raised by the cut in the capital-gains tax."

Feldstein was particularly amused by a section of the CEA study that implied that capital-gains realizations (not to say federal revenue) could *fall* in the event of a capital-gains tax cut, fall because a barrage of new selling aimed at taking advantage of the lower rate would depress prices. Feldstein called the CEA's realization argument "absurd" and reminded Long that his own study "calculated that reducing the capital-gains tax rates would stimulate realizations so much that the Treasury would actually gain revenue."

To put the senator at ease about supporting Steiger, Feldstein stated the case conservatively: "In short, . . . I conclude that the [CEA] paper is worthless and should not confuse your deliberations on capital gains. I remain convinced that the evidence indicates a substantial sensitivity of capital-gains realization to the tax rate and that a reduction in [that] rate will not reduce Treasury revenue." Feldstein sent similar letters to other senators on the Finance Committee and to Blumenthal as the votes in Congress neared. Russell Long loved the Feldstein research. He used folksy analogies about duck hunting as he commended it in the Senate.[46]

The intellectual battle was ending in a rout, and the political battle was nearing its conclusion, too. Steiger became a celebrity within the Republican Party, in Congress, and on Wall Street. A television commentator asked him, "Bill, tell us the truth. You're a Republican congressman in an overwhelmingly Democratic Congress. When you proposed this amendment, did you really think it was going to take off like this?" "No," Steiger replied. He noted that when the amendment was first proposed in the Senate, it picked up sixty-two cosponsors—*62 percent of the Senate as cosponsors.* Throughout 1978, Steiger kept the argument simple as to why he was proposing the measure. As he wrote in the *San Diego Union:* "Income is the incentive or reward we receive in exchange for our labor. Capital, on the other hand, is the source of the tools, the resources we require in order to utilize our labor. When we reduce our capital stock through taxation, we reduce our ability to invest in new plant and equipment, to create jobs, and to increase the welfare of everyone. In short, it does not make economic sense to levy a high tax on capital."[47]

Son of Kemp-Roth

Carter threatened a veto. "I think it's a bluff," Steiger said in August. It was. For in the fall, Carter would concede the Steiger amendment cancer in order to forestall a greater malignancy that was starting to metastasize in Steiger's wake. This was Kemp-Roth. Kemp-Roth had made a duly impressive showing in Congress the year before, prior to the nation's contraction of tax-cut fever. In 1978, it returned, and the president had a problem.[48]

Anticipating Steiger's tactics, the Republican supporters of Kemp-Roth chose to introduce their three-year income-tax cut not only as part of a budget resolution, but also as an amendment to other economic bills. In the House, Kemp-Roth came up in March as an amendment to Humphrey-Hawkins, of all things, going down now quite narrowly, 194–216. After Steiger hit in April, advocates of Kemp-Roth struck again. In the House, Marjorie Holt of Maryland added an amendment to the budget resolution providing for the Kemp-Roth tax cuts, coupled with a cap on federal spending (a generous one: it allowed for an annual 8 percent increase) that would balance the budget by 1983.[49]

It was a savvy move, and the House passed the amendment by a few votes. Once leadership realized what had happened—Kemp-Roth had just passed—a few votes were rearranged so as to defeat Holt, 203–197. Nonetheless, it was clear that momentum was going to vault Kemp-Roth into law unless its opponents took dedicated action. "The tax-cut wagon has rolled on down the road, leaving Jimmy Carter, Mike Blumenthal, and Stu Eizenstat choking in the dust," crowed Bartley's editorial page at the *Wall Street Journal* in July. On TV's *Wall $treet Week,* Louis Rukeyser said, in August, "Not in recent memory has a Democratic Congress so contemptuously dismissed the tax proposals of a Democratic president as in the legislation now moving toward the White House."[50]

For in that legislation lay the Steiger amendment, a gutting of Carter's deduction-reduction package, and, very possibly, Kemp-Roth. In August, even as it was ginning up the hopeless war against Feldstein, the White House let congressional leaders know that it would take the Steiger amendment, as well as submit to a near-complete surrender on deduction reform, so long as the nasty rumors emanating from the Senate did not come true. Those rumors were that a prominent Democrat in the body might sponsor something akin to Kemp-Roth. Russell Long, after all, seemed very much to be enjoying his indulgence of Martin Feldstein.[51]

The rumors were borne out. It was not Long, but Sam Nunn, Democrat of Georgia (the president's home state), who introduced a version of the Holt amendment, which again provided for Kemp-Roth along with spending caps. The amendment became known as "Son of Kemp-Roth." Carter's fears about what this might portend were well founded. The Nunn amendment did not squeak by in the upper chamber. It powered through, 62–28. All year long, senators had been taking testimony on the absolute necessity of tax cuts, and when Nunn gave them an opportunity to take action that was transparently fiscally responsible, that action was decisive. Impressed, the House quickly voted by a 2–1 margin to instruct its participants in conference session with their Senate counterparts to accept the Nunn amendment. For all intents and purposes, on that day—Thursday, October 12, 1978—Kemp-Roth passed both houses of Congress.[52]

That weekend, Jimmy Carter made the most fateful decision of his presidency. He sent word that he would veto the bill. Evans and Novak had marveled at the threat of a veto back in August: "It is unthinkable that the president . . . would commit the ultimate folly of vetoing an election-year tax cut. But the unthinkable is commonplace in the Carter tax policy." The unthinkable became reality that October weekend. Carter canceled a trip to Camp David, hunkered down in the executive mansion, and sent his lieutenants to Capitol Hill with strict orders to kill the Nunn amendment. Their leverage would be the presidential veto.[53]

Lobbyists came out of the woodwork to urge a compromise so that the tax bill's various preference items would not go down with the whole thing. In a House office building, the House and Senate conferees huddled and consulted with Blumenthal while Eizenstat stalked outside the door. Carter's press secretary conceded that, under the circumstances, "the president's afraid to leave town." When everyone emerged, the Nunn amendment was indeed excised,

save language that its goals should be "a matter of national policy." The Revenue
Act of 1978 was on its way to the president's desk. It barely touched the brackets, it upped standard deductions a little, and it had plenty of special-interest
provisions, thanks to the frenetic days after October 12. The act included an
equivalent of the Steiger amendment.[54]

It is interesting to speculate on what would have happened had Carter left
well enough alone, dropped the veto threat, gone to Camp David, and given his
assistants the weekend off. For ten months later, in August 1979, Carter would
appoint Paul Volcker to be chairman of the Federal Reserve. The supply-side
solution that Reagan would apply two years after that was simply the tax cut
that Carter had killed in October 1978, coupled with Paul Volcker fulfilling his
fondest wish of tightening money so as to wring inflation out of existence. The
seven-year, 4.3 percent compounded annual growth in the face of a collapsing
misery index that ensued in the 1980s, once this Mundellian policy mix was
applied, could surely have begun in the last two years of the Carter presidency.
Surely, that is to say, had Carter relaxed that Friday the Thirteenth. Would
Ronald Reagan have even thought himself necessary to American politics in
1980? After all, Carter was also contemplating a defense buildup.

But such are speculations. Carter signed the Revenue Act of 1978, with
the capital-gains cut, on November 6, 1978. This was the day before the midterm elections, in which Bell would lose the Senate race to Bill Bradley in
New Jersey. The bracket expansion in the Revenue Act of 1978 was imper-
ceptible, so the inflation that came in at 8 percent that year brought more woe
to the nation's taxpayers, especially those who had arranged for COLAs. The
small increase in common deductions was neutralized by previously scheduled hikes in the Social Security tax. The only part of the bill reflecting the
tax-revolt tenor of the year was the Steiger provision. The capital-gains tax
was just about chopped in half.[55]

In the weeks following the passage of the bill, the Carter White House
took superfluous potshots at the capital-gains rate cut that the president had
pledged to sign. The meteoric rise of the Steiger amendment—it had just been
a gleam in an obscure minority representative's eye seven months before—
had certainly stung the administration. Perhaps most galling was losing the
intellectual fight that ensued, a fight that the administration had picked, and
in which its own CEA had emerged with serious wounds.

The odd counterpunch kept coming Martin Feldstein's way. Weeks after
the Steiger amendment had passed, one CEA member, William Nordhaus,

rallied himself to defend the CEA study that Feldstein had pulverized, saying that it would be vindicated by history. Nordhaus wrote as much to Blumenthal, Senator Long, and Feldstein himself. In his letter to Long, Nordhaus made these points:

> Professor Feldstein has attempted to distract attention from [our] criticisms by obfuscation, disparagement, and provocative language. . . . The prospect that lower capital-gains taxes will lead to higher Treasury revenues is, alas, a mirage which vanishes as one looks more closely. . . . Feldstein has stated that the Council of Economic Advisers should be embarrassed by work of such low quality. Quite the contrary. [Our] review of Feldstein's paper is first-rate. I am confident that the economics profession will cast a verdict that the [CEA paper's] criticisms are sound and Feldstein's conclusions defective.

The economics profession cannot be said to have cast any clear verdict on the matter in the following decade, even if today everybody knows that when you cut capital-gains rates, revenues increase. "Contentious debate" is how one journal article of 1988 characterized a decade's worth of discussions on the effect of the Steiger rate cut.[56]

The raw numbers, for their part, are fairly arresting. Federal revenue from capital-gains taxes plunged in real terms after the rate hike of 1969, creeping back to that year's level, $9 billion, not until 1978. In 1979, capital-gains revenue went to $12 billion, and a high rate of increase was then established that brought revenue from this source steadily up to $26 billion in 1985. In 1978 dollars, this 1985 number is $16 billion, three-quarters more than the 1978 total and far above the 1969–78 average. Other metrics confirm 1978 as an inflection point. The ratio of capital gains to GDP, theoretically a stable number, leapt considerably and stayed high after 1978—just as this number had sunk with the 1969 increase in capital-gains rates.[57]

In 1978, it was the considered opinion of indisputably top economists that certain taxes can be so high as to cost the government revenue—let alone as to cost the economy growth. Martin Feldstein certainly thought so in the case of the capital-gains rates that prevailed in 1978, and he was not alone. It was the first road test of the kind of argument Mundell had been making to no avail around the world, of the theses that had made for late-night discussions at Michael 1 and, more recently, the Lehrman Institute. Bartley sensed a shift. In the wake of the Friday the Thirteenth logrolling, his *Journal* page proclaimed that "the tax bill does not leave us in a state of total pessimism. For it's possible that looking back from, say, 1984, we will see this year's tax debate as the start of a sea change."[58]

Clearly, there would have to be participation, indeed leadership, from the top. It was necessary for there to be a clued-in Fed chair, and for the president to be in favor of marginal tax cuts. As for the latter office, one candidate by virtue of his own actions had recommended himself: Bill Steiger. Toasted by Wall Street and aspiring venture capitalists across the country in the latter months of 1978, Steiger started to receive serious encouragement that he run for president, with offers of financing and organization in tow. One offer included Lew Lehrman as national campaign chair. Steiger was already close to the supply-siders in any case. In October 1978, he deflected all credit for the success of his amendment to Bartley, Wanniski, and the *Journal* editorial page.[59]

On December 4, 1978, four weeks after the capital-gains cut became law, William A. Steiger died of a heart attack. He was forty years old.

8

MALAISE

Mr. President, we're in trouble. Talk to us about blood and sweat and tears.

—Attributed to a citizen by President Jimmy Carter in the "malaise speech," July 15, 1979

I have a guilty secret
That fills me full of shame:
Another bumper sticker
Has set my heart aflame.
I'll keep his campaign buttons
Within my bedroom shrine,
But Jack Kemp is replacing
My former valentine.

—W. H. von Dreele, *National Review,* August 18, 1978

The last two years of Jimmy Carter's term were brutal ones for the president and the nation. The 8 percent inflation of 1978, which was above average even for the stagflation era, gave way to rates of 11 percent in 1979 and 14 percent in 1980. In two years, prices went up 26 percent, following the 45 percent increase from 1973 to 1978. The Phillips curve, in turn, reneged on all claims to legitimacy. Unemployment hovered at 6 percent in 1978 and 1979 and went to 7 percent in 1980. Thus did the misery index jump from 14 to 17 to 21 in the space of three years. From the advent of Bretton Woods through the LBJ presidency, the misery index touched 10 once, went as low as 4, and was usually around 7. When it hit unlucky 21 in 1980, the inevitable recession began. Growth was negative in 1980, the year of 14 percent inflation.

As for the nation's fiscal accounts, they too brought strange news. The budget deficits of the first three Carter years, 1977–79, were between $40 billion and $60 billion. The 1980 deficit arrived at $74 billion. This was 2.7 percent of GDP, two and a half times the average deficit of the Vietnam and Great Society eras. Of course, by 1980 government revenues also had risen substantially. Bracket creep ensured it. As Paul Craig Roberts noted at the time, every ten points of inflation brought in 16.5 percent more revenue to the government, a conclusion verified by Treasury. Federal revenues rose to 19 percent of GDP in 1980, steadily increasing from 17 percent in 1976. Yet the revenue gusher had no chance of keeping pace with spending. Federal spending in 1980 was 22 percent of GDP, a level never aspired to in the Vietnam–Great Society years and last seen as the nation was demilitarizing from World War II in 1946.[1]

Before 1979, bracket creep combined with inflation had encouraged vigilance on the part of wage earners. They had to get a COLA-plus in order simply to get a COLA. The inflation that came in 1979 and 1980 intensified this requirement beyond all hope. Workers from across the income spectrum were now at best breaking even against inflation and taxes. After the 26 percent inflation of 1979–80, raises had to be in the 30 percent–50 percent range in order to reach par.[2]

If an employee got such a raise, it was a brilliant coup. But it was devastating to his employer. To grant employees raises that kept up with inflation, employers had to ensure that their revenue gains outpaced inflation rates now in the double digits. As *BusinessWeek* reporter John P. Hoerr wrote of the COLA-plus arrangement in the steel industry of 1973–82, "Once this machine started operating, its generative ability was awesome. The average wage . . . industrywide . . . , including the 3 percent increases and the COLA payments, jumped from $4.27 per hour [in 1972] to $11.91 [in 1982]. . . . In that ten-year period, the steel wage rate climbed 179 percent, while inflation rose 132 percent." Unless there was supercharged productivity, raises of this order meant raids on business profits. And given the way depreciation was treated in the tax code, there was not supercharged productivity. The stock market took due note and encouraged the likes of U.S. Steel to bail out to commodities.[3]

The only certainty in this mess was that given epic inflation and bracket creep, government revenues would boom. This made it all the more puzzling that the government was running a deficit that exceeded any since World War II. The nation's fiscal and economic accounts had become disordered and unintelligible.

The financial markets reacted in kind. The bond market, for one, rushed to the brink of disaster in 1979 and 1980. Stable and boring "since the Battle of Midway," as Tom Wolfe would put it in *The Bonfire of the Vanities* (1987), the bond market had made a mean descent in the stagflation years through 1978. Bond yields roughly doubled from 1966 to 1978, meaning that prices went down by about half. In 1979 and 1980, the descent intensified. In the space of two years, yields went up by another 50 percent and prices dropped to one-third of their pre-stagflation level. "The open wounds of the bond houses have turned Wall Street into a river of red ink," wrote Bartley's editorial page in February 1980. "Traders were talking of a 'freefall' in normally glacial bond prices; they were especially stunned by a 2.5 percent one-day drop in prices [and another of] 4 percent. Nothing like it has been seen since the 1930s."[4]

Bonds were collapsing because of double-digit inflation. Bonds pay a fixed rate of interest for the life of the bond, and if that rate is less than inflation, the bond is a wasting asset and nobody wants to hold it. Before 1979, bonds naturally did not pay rates that could clear 26 percent inflation over two years, let alone whatever part of the interest payment was dunned in taxation. So prices collapsed. The stories of those left holding them ranged from the lurid to the pathetic. One bond-firm executive interrupted an interview after thirty minutes with the words, "I have to see how much money we've lost while we were talking. The way things are going, it could easily be $2 million or $3 million." Bartley knew a widow of a successful businessman who had to rely on charity by 1980. The widow's inheritance was entirely in municipal bonds. With bonds going down 65 percent between 1966 and 1980 in nominal terms—in real terms, somewhere near 80 percent—the proverbial redoubt of widows and orphans had become a path to penury.[5]

When new issues came on the market in these conditions, it was commonplace for them to promise yearly payments in the neighborhood of 15 percent for a twenty- or thirty-year term. Nobody but the most reliable of old, established companies could attract buyers for such bonds; who else could be counted on to have that kind of cash flow over the long term? If the Steiger amendment had hoped to stimulate entrepreneurialism, the inflation of 1979–80 all but killed it. Unproven ventures were in no position to promise 15 percent over the long term, so such ventures went unfinanced in the bond market.

As for the stock market, the Dow Jones Industrial Average hovered around the 850 mark through mid-1980, as it had since 1977. Theoretically given a boost by the Steiger amendment, the market could not rise because of the huge COLA requirements that threatened business balance sheets in the toxic environment of inflation and bracket creep. This is not to mention the problem of depreciation schedules providing for corporate taxes upwards of 100 percent. By treading water at 850 in 1979–80, the Dow actually lost 26 percent on account of inflation, just as it had lost value because of inflation since first hitting 1,000 in 1966. The final tally, peak to trough, for the Dow between 1966 and 1982 was about a 75 percent real loss. One writer called it "the second Great Crash" and noted that stocks lost more in the 1970s than in any other decade of the twentieth century, including the 1930s.[6]

Money fled from commerce, indeed from the financial system as a whole. It piled into safe havens as never before. Traditionally, bonds do well in recessions, because recessions are characteristically disinflationary. This changed when the negative growth of 1980 was coupled with 14 percent inflation. Now safe havens had to be storehouses of value found in the earth. Real estate became a fad. Commodities blew through the roof, with gold and oil reaching new heights. Gold, which had increased fivefold from the 1960s to 1974, and which had doubled again by 1979, doubled yet again in 1979–80 to $800 per ounce: a twentyfold increase in the fifteen years since inflation first stirred. Oil followed gold, increasing fourfold by 1974 to about $11 a barrel, doubling again by 1979, and then hitting the fourteenfold figure of $40 in 1980.[7]

Books telling the economy's tale of woe sold by the hundreds of thousands. Two of the biggest hits were the *How to Prosper During the Coming Bad Years* (1979), by Howard J. Ruff—"one of the decade's great best sellers," said the *New York Review of Books*—and *Crisis Investing: Opportunities and Profits in the Coming Great Depression* (1980), by Douglas R. Casey. Both of these "Coming" books argued that the only viable strategy for the future was to endeavor, against the odds, to feather one's own nest, preferably by buying gold. The two bestsellers found a formidable rival in Milton and Rose Friedman's *Free to Choose* (1980), a book that, along with a companion series on public television, proved immensely popular and argued for a way out of stagflation by means of minimized government, entrepreneurialism, and enlightened money creation.[8]

Pundits began to wonder if the nation was not complaining too much. On

Bartley's opinion page in the *Wall Street Journal,* Alfred Malabre Jr. and Lester Thurow laid out cases that the nation's economic anxieties were unwarranted. Since the end of the 1974–75 recession, the argument ran, the nation
had experienced nice economic growth, about 4 percent yearly. Even with
bracket creep, real incomes in 1980 were higher than they had been in 1976.
What was all the fuss about?[9]

Thurow's answer developed into another best-selling book, *The Zero-Sum
Society* (1980). Here he conceded, correctly, that under the conditions of stagflation, in order to get ahead (or even to stay in place), one had to game the system.
For example, labor and management both understood that a firm's profits would
fall to one or the other negotiator, but not both. There was no possibility of
labor's attaining a real COLA along with a firm's maintaining profitability and
paying steady dividends to shareholders. One came at the expense of another:
zero-sum. Whichever side, labor or management, was best at negotiation and
proved to have the necessary mettle in seeing through its objective would exit
the winner. There was no "free lunch" under the conditions of inflation and
bracket creep. It was an economy of winners and losers. "At the end of the
1970s," Thurow observed, "our political economy seems paralyzed."[10]

Thurow put his finger on the reason labor unions experienced an upsurge
as stagflation became more serious. Massive power blocs stood as the only
means by which labor had any hope of getting firms to do the inadvisable—
namely, to devote profits to costs. Working outside the union umbrella became
a recipe for declining living standards. As a laboring free agent, one had little
chance of obtaining a wage that kept up with prices. One had no leverage in
the zero-sum game. Minorities were particularly hard hit, because they often
found themselves subject to informal quotas, when they were not shut out of
union shops entirely. Ronald Reagan, in his radio addresses and newspaper
columns, was one of many commentators who lamented the stunning magnitude of African-American and Latino unemployment in the 1970s.[11]

But the initial point of Thurow and the others was legitimate: economic
growth is economic growth. Somebody was capturing real gains. It was not
only the government. Wage earners and businesses were capturing the 2.5
percent–3 percent gains in the real economy not displaced by the growing
government. Were people complaining while making out rather well?

Well, consumerism was rampant in the 1970s. Sales of all sorts of things,
useful goods and especially novelties such as recreational vehicles, were
robust in the Carter years. Given inflation, this was only logical. If one bought

immediately on getting paid, one exchanged money for goods. If instead one saved one's pay, that money largely evaporated. Savings could not reasonably be held in bank accounts, whose rates lagged behind inflation; nor in stocks, which were experiencing a 75 percent downturn; nor in bonds, whose future cash flow diminished with every release of the consumer price index. Savings could be put in gold, commodities, and land, and indeed they were. But as always these were tricky investments, with land having an excise tax attached to boot. Saving money became a fine art, an option foreclosed to the masses. So the masses spent. As Alice Rivlin, the head of the Congressional Budget Office, said in March 1980, economists had been surprised to find in 1979 that, "in the face of falling real incomes, consumers went on spending at such high rates, substantially cutting into saving."[12]

So the economic anxiety of the late stagflation period had a foundation after all. If real wages and profits were in fact increasing modestly, the losses on the savings side counteracted these gains and more. Workers who got real COLAs saw their savings accounts and pensions decline in value; if their houses appreciated, property taxes and loan rates surged beyond comprehension. Businesses who were good negotiators or who ran nonunion shops kept profits away from employees; yet their real share prices declined with inflation. The erosion of personal and business assets canceled the gains made in GDP. It became impossible to get ahead, it took strenuous efforts to get by, and it was imperative to spend—not save—what money one had. In any case, all of these issues became moot with the inflationary recession of 1980. There would be no getting by or even zero-sum. The scramble would be to see who lost less than everyone else.

Carter's Diminishing Options

The scuttling of the Nunn amendment in October 1978 marked the opening of a new chapter in Jimmy Carter's presidency. In the weeks after the conference that settled the Revenue Act of 1978, it became clear that inflation was increasing at a phenomenal rate. Two weeks before the November congressional elections, Carter gave a national television address on inflation policy. The address signaled that the "Great Inflation," as it was called, rather than tax fairness, would now be the focus of the administration's domestic policy. In the address, Carter outlined a program whereby increases in prices and wages in the major industries would be kept under the inflation rate. In time, Carter argued, this would result in the lowering of inflation in general.[13]

On taking office in 1977, Carter was disinclined to resurrect the wage-and-price control apparatus that had occupied so much time and energy, to no discernible effect, in the Nixon administration. But the apparatus still existed in the form of an executive-branch entity called the Council on Wage and Price Stability. Carter reinvigorated the council in 1978 and authorized it to supervise the main plank of his new program, which was to secure agreements from major producers and labor unions not to have price or wage increases above 7 percent per year. In theory, this would make it unlikely for the general inflation rate to exceed 7 percent. However, Carter introduced a fudge factor. He would give a "tip," as he called it, in the form of a tax rebate, to members of unions that obliged the 7 percent guideline.

The policy had a difficult first few months. Congress ignored the "tip" proposal. In addition, the wage-and-price guideline was voluntary, and nobody wanted to sign up. The council began to avail itself of both carrots and sticks. On the one hand, it implied that if firms and unions stepped forward voluntarily, they might get leeway on the 7 percent mark. Indeed, in early 1979, the Teamsters hammered out an agreement, with the White House's blessing, that provided for a 9 percent pay increase. On the other hand, the White House threatened noncompliant firms with getting shut out of government contracts. There was also the odd bolt of invective, such as when one administration official called firms that ignored the policy "miscreants."[14]

By spring 1979, it was clear enough that the policy was not going to produce the desired results. But it did yield Robert Bartley's Pulitzer Prize. The 1980 award for editorial writing cited Bartley's April 18, 1979, piece "Down with Big Business." The editorial had pointed out that General Motors seemed to be bullying its suppliers into accepting the price guideline, probably so that the suppliers would sell out to GM on the cheap. The Carter scheme, to Bartley, was all too easily a means by which the business establishment could keep at bay the real threat: upstarts. "A lot of little guys can make nuisances of themselves if they start resigning from giant research, inventing things, and raising money to compete with . . . GM and DuPont and GE . . . ," Bartley wrote. "If you freeze the system you will lose its thrust toward progress. But in many ways, GM's life will be easier." It was another example of the supply-siders' belief in entrepreneurialism, ratified now by the highest award in journalism.[15]

Carter's inflation-fighting policy was now essentially reduced to periodic "inflation breakfasts" with his economic advisors and whatever else the council could come up with. The council had a formidable chair in Alfred Kahn. Kahn had done yeoman's work in deregulating the airlines, which by any measure was a supply-side achievement of the Carter White House. But Kahn was at wit's end at the council, where he supervised a staff of two hundred charged with monitoring the nation's prices and wages. At one point, Kahn took seriously the suggestion of posting a sign on the White House lawn congratulating firms that did their part in keeping increases under 7 percent.[16]

As summer came, Carter was given a chance to address the inflation issue in a new way. Throughout 1979, OPEC had been raising the price of oil, the crowning move a 15 percent markup at the end of June. Carter cut short a foreign trip and called an extraordinary special meeting. He convened not only his usual advisors, but also an assortment of "deep thinkers" from across the country, summoning all to go with him to Camp David for a week. The topic would be how to diagnose and solve the problems of energy and inflation.

The result of the meeting was fated to be one of the signatures of the Carter presidency: the "malaise speech" of July 15, 1979. The speech clarified certain ideas about energy and inflation that Carter had been articulating since the 1976 campaign. Namely, the speech proposed that the energy and inflation crises, so acute in 1979, were self-inflicted by the American people. Because the nation's populace had become increasingly consumerist, firms found it easier to charge higher prices. At whatever price, people had to have their stuff. The progressive tax code punished business owners for taking advantage of this situation only to a degree, a problem Carter had tried to rectify the year before by making the code more progressive. The greatest opportunists in these circumstances were the OPEC oil exporters, who found that their American customers offered no resistance if they jacked up prices. So they did. Given that oil is a primary product, the inflationary effect was felt throughout the economy as a whole.[17]

The solution to the problem, under this diagnosis, was for the American people to show some restraint, to be less consumerist, materialistic, and self-absorbed. "Too many of us now tend to worship self-indulgence and consumption," he chided. "We believed that our nation's resources were limitless until 1973 when we had to face a growing dependence on foreign oil. . . . We are at a turning point in our history. There are two paths to choose. One is a path I've warned about tonight, the path that leads to fragmentation and self-interest. Down that road lies a mistaken idea of freedom, the right to grasp for ourselves some advantage over others." It was time, Carter said, to wake up to the reality that the root problem lay within the American people themselves. "Our excessive dependence on [oil imports] has already taken a tremendous toll on our economy and our people," Carter said. "It's a cause of the increased inflation and unemployment that we now face. This intolerable dependence on foreign oil threatens our economic independence and the very security of our nation."

Carter was not availing himself of the standard Keynesian argument about what caused the Great Inflation and thereby stagflation: the "external shock" of the OPEC increases in oil prices from 1973 to 1979. Carter did not follow, for example, Walter Heller, who after the June increase said, "OPEC has done it again.... The U.S. economy ... has been tipped into early recession by the new $20 billion 'oil tax' that OPEC is levying on American consumers." Rather, Carter held that the very need for oil imports revealed that the nation was not living within its means. It was reaching for things that it could not afford, that it did not have. The shock that hit the American economy in the 1970s did not come from an external source. The shock welled up from the nation's psychological disposition—excessive consumerism, excessive greed—and came to be accommodated by foreigners in the form of imports carrying large price tags.[18]

Carter's diagnosis was alien to supply-side views. Mundell's view was that inflation reflected speculation against the dollar given the undermining of its soundness with the end of Bretton Woods. Another mentor of Bartley's, by means of his 1977 book *The Golden Constant,* Berkeley professor Roy Jastram, noted that the gold-oil dollar-price ratio had remained in a tight band since 1965. This implied that inflation resulted from undue monetary creation and was not related to dependency on oil or any other commodity. As for Warren Brookes, he called Carter's argument about oil imports a "foolish preoccupation" and pointed out that oil imports were falling as a share of all imports and as a share of the trade deficit. Congressional candidate Phil Gramm gave supply-siders an epithet they would enjoy slinging when he mocked Carter's "moral equivalent of war" as "MEOW."[19]

In any case, Carter had a plan. It was a program of new government spending, taxes, and mandates. Carter ordered quotas on the importation of foreign oil. He set up requirements that energy producers find new sources that did not derive from oil. He spoke of "the most massive peacetime commitment of funds" for a search for alternative energy. And he urged new taxes to pay for everything, especially the "windfall profits tax" that would become law in 1980. The plan was tautological, as Carter admitted, in that, if it failed, it could always be said that the nation did not show sufficient resolve in seeing it through to success.

The malaise speech—given that name because the word "malaise" appeared in a memo prepared by a staffer working on the speech—encapsulated what had animated Carter's economic policy to date. Loopholes had to go, because they represented selfishness. Progressivity had to stay, because it prevented people from acting on selfishness. Nixonian wage and price controls were justified, because they gave management and labor the opportunity to show restraint. High oil prices were correct, for they both reflected the inordinate consumerism of Americans and gave them incentive to work toward self-sufficiency. Restraint was the key to winning the battle against inflation, for the real battle was against the demons of sloth and self-interest.[20]

The malaise speech put Carter in a weird mood. Four days after he gave it, he asked his cabinet to resign. The whole cabinet—a group of thirteen. Carter accepted the resignations of five members, itself a purging of top staff unprecedented in presidential history. Carter clearly wanted to get rid of lieutenants who were dubious about his unorthodox policies and perspectives. As one observer commented, "It wouldn't be altogether fair . . . to say that Carter lacked political skill. He had no coalition that wanted to go where he wanted to go."[21]

One of the marked men in the cabinet was Michael Blumenthal, the treasury secretary. Although he had soldiered for Carter against the congressional tax bills of 1978, it was clear enough that Blumenthal was in favor of things like rate cuts and tax reform in the traditional sense. He was also sympathetic to the exigencies of business. His experience included stints not only as a Princeton professor but also as an automotive industry CEO. Blumenthal had expressed exasperation with Carter's policies in the past and at one point had even threatened to quit. Carter was happy to accept his resignation.[22]

Volcker's Task
With Blumenthal gone, Carter needed a treasury secretary. He chose G. William Miller, the Federal Reserve chairman who had been in that office since Arthur Burns's retirement the year before. Consequently, Carter also needed to name another Fed chairman. He gave the job to the first of the regional Federal Reserve presidents, Paul Volcker of the New York bank.

Volcker was a six-foot-seven former undersecretary of the treasury (under Nixon), an alumnus of Princeton and Harvard, a Democrat, a veteran Wall

Streeter, and, as president of the New York Fed, a man who had developed a reputation of being appalled at inflation and the dollar's slide on the currency exchanges. (Laffer perceived that Volcker also found appalling Wall Street bankers who did well.) Volcker was not known to be beholden to any theory, be it monetarist or Keynesian, much less Mundellian. Rather, practical experience had taught him that a sound currency was the sine qua non of a functioning economy.[23]

Volcker's appointment by Carter in August 1979 was, by all accounts, a historic move. It marked the end of the Federal Reserve's accommodation of inflation. In the late 1960s, the Fed released money so that the Vietnam–Great Society deficits could be funded. In the 1970s, the Fed succumbed to Nixon's wishes that it gun the economy through 1973. The Fed tightened as the recession hit in 1974, was disconcerted by the severity of the downturn, and then loosened under Carter. Indeed, as recession predictions emerged in early 1979, Miller signaled that the Fed would supply money despite the raging inflation. All this was definitively over with Volcker. It would take a few years for inflation to be brought back to rational levels, but there can be no mistake that Volcker believed inflation to be unconscionable and that monetary policy bore responsibility for stopping it.[24]

Why did Carter appoint Volcker? Carter was silent about it in his presidential memoir, *Keeping Faith,* though he has said that the appointment was one of the signal moves of his presidency, which it was. The moralism that suffused Carter's economic policy perspective probably played a part in bringing him around to Volcker. Even though Carter's anti-inflation policies were ineffectual, Carter, like Volcker, found inflation disgusting and unbecoming of a great nation. In the malaise speech, Carter said that he longed for the days when the phrase "sound as a dollar" meant something. True, early in his administration Carter had leaned on the Fed to inflate more, in part because business needed more money to comply with federal regulations. But this had been out of character. Tight money from the Fed was consistent with Carter's desire that inflation be overcome by means of sacrifice and a nationwide commitment to getting by with less.[25]

Volcker faced staggering problems on gaining the chairmanship in August 1979. Chiefly, he did not have sufficient support on his board for an anti-inflation position, and he did not know the best means by which the Fed might go about being tight. In his initial moves, Volcker found himself on the winning end of 4–3 votes to raise interest rates, but 4–3 votes are a signal to Wall

Street and the exchange markets that the Fed chair is weak. By the end of the year, after months in which American policymakers got an earful from foreign leaders about the disreputable state of the dollar, Volcker was holding sway over unanimous votes.[26]

As for how to be tight, this was a knottier problem. Volcker tried two tactics, consecutively, in his first months as chairman. Initially, he raised interest rates, in particular the federal funds rate. This had no discernible effect aside from bringing nominal interest rates to places they had never been. In 1980, the prime rate climbed all the way to 21.5 percent, a level as untenable as it was unprecedented. Years later, reflecting on the episode, Volcker said that if had he known, on taking the chairmanship, that his policy would result in such a rate, he "would have crawled into a hole and cried." But Volcker did not say he would have acted differently. For he felt that austerity had to come to the nation experiencing the Great Inflation.[27]

By late 1979, Volcker was paying less attention to interest rates and more to the difficult matter of the "money supply." Milton Friedman had been teaching for years that the overall stock of money in the economy was the main determinant of recession versus growth, let alone inflation versus price stability. Getting the money supply at the right level, rather than nailing some derivative statistic such as the interest rate, was the main thing. Whether or not he had been reading Friedman, Volcker acted accordingly, for beginning in October 1979 he took a series of steps to restrict the money supply, most of which were aimed at increasing the level of reserves that banks had to keep so that they might provide less credit to customers. The hope was that less money in the system would starve inflation out.

The problem in 1979 and 1980 was that events had made obsolete this classic monetarist tactic. The usual way that the constituents of the money supply, the "monetary aggregates," were measured had little relevance by then. Bank deposits, for example, were a chief monetarist statistic. Expand or decrease such deposits, the logic went, and you expand or decrease the money supply at large. Yet by 1979 bank depositors had raided their accounts. Banked money had no hope of keeping up with inflation. Depreciating dollars had therefore migrated from accounts and into commodities, land, durables, and collectibles. Those depositors who stuck it out in banked currency were evading the places tracked by the monetary-aggregate statistics. Savings and loan associations, prohibited by a superannuated "Regulation Q" from offering savings rates that met inflation, pooled funds in certificates of deposit (CDs).

Not only were CDs immune from Reg Q, they were not counted in the usual supply categories added up by the Federal Reserve. Volcker thus had little chance of truly counting the money supply, let alone limiting it. This made inflation-fighting mightily difficult to pursue.[28]

When the Michael 1 gatherings moved to the elegant confines of Lew Lehrman's institute during the Carter years, the main topic of conversation changed. At Michael 1, the top priority had been to educate Bartley on tax cuts. Once this was accomplished, all attention turned to the economics of monetary policy. "Lehrman [was] a disciple of Jacques Rueff," wrote Bartley in his memoir, and "could and still can tilt monetary policy with anyone." The group at Lehrman's, more numerous than at Michael 1 (Alan Reynolds was now an attendee), agreed that it was necessary not only to move beyond notions of monetary policy inspired by the Phillips curve, but also to rethink the premises of monetarism.[29]

Monetarism emphasizes the supply of money. Under monetarism, if the quantity of money, particularly newly created money, is right, a free economy will hum. Milton Friedman at one point advocated a constitutional amendment mandating a 5-percent-per-year increase in the money supply. That number matched the prospective high growth rate of the economy. If money growth were guaranteed to hit that number every year, there would be no monetary barrier to maximal noninflationary growth. In contrast, supply-siders, ironically perhaps, given their name, felt that demand for money was the crucial thing. As Laffer put it in italics in November 1979: "*The omission of the demand for money from the analysis of inflation is as serious as the omission of the supply side from the analysis of output.*"[30]

To the supply-siders, banks faced an inordinate demand for their money during the Great Inflation for good reason. People wanted to take out loans because they could pay them back in depreciated dollars. The demand for credit during the 1970s had become a function of inflation. Restricting banks' ability to provide loans was to treat a symptom of a symptom of inflation. The first symptom was demand for loans. The second symptom was falling bank reserves due to the nominal demand for loans, not to mention the flight of deposits. "What is required," Laffer wrote, "are policies that lead to an excess demand for dollars relative to their supply."[31]

And that demand for dollars had to be *real*. The demand for money may be seen as a solid sphere. The real demand for money is the core; unreal demand is the volume of the sphere minus the core. Given increasing inflation and inflationary expectations, the sphere may expand just as the core shrinks. Inflation incurs speculation against the dollar, one of the forms of which is taking fixed-rate loans, the price of whose service stands to be denuded over the term of the loan. This is an expansion in *unreal* demand. Inflation also implies lesser real income (on account of progressive taxation and instability in the means of exchange) and therefore lesser returns to enterprise. *Real* demand for loans, for economic ventures as opposed to currency hedging, will fall given inflation. This is a contraction in the core of the sphere.

In order for monetary policy to remove "excess" money from the system, it would have to reduce the money supply to the core of the sphere, a core that is shrinking. Yet even heroic efforts at reducing the money supply may only cut into the unreal part of the sphere, as the sphere grows and the shrinking core gets farther out of reach. Better would be for the core to expand and the unreal volume to decline, so that the availability of dollars might be aligned with real money demand.

Elaborating how to bring about this happy result was, after all, the point of supply-side economics. It would take more than enlightened monetary policy. That much had been certain to supply-siders as far back as the 1960s. As Mundell had been arguing since 1961, when he was digesting the Tinbergen principle that he renamed "effective market classification," the most a monetary authority such as the Fed could constructively do was to target domestic price stability. And even here, Mundell came to argue, there are times when the monetary authority, however good it may be, will have insufficient power to do even that. If fiscal policy is uncooperative, the private economy will feel threatened and demand for currency to be used for economic purposes will fall, no matter the efforts of the issuer. However, if fiscal policy promotes growth, through a reduction in the government's share of the economy by means of tax cuts, demand for currency to be used for economic purposes will increase, and the monetary authority can step in to assure that prices are brought to stability. In a word, the "policy mix."

In the Princeton paper of 1971, Mundell had been at pains to show that given tax cuts, "tight" monetary policy could actually be rather expansive. "The increased momentum of the economy provided by the stimulus of a tax cut will cause a sufficient demand for credit to permit real monetary expansion at higher interest rates," he wrote. And again: "Growth of *real* output raises real money demand and thus abets the absorption of real monetary expansion into the economy without inflation." Perhaps it was an esoteric point. The record shows that the eminent listeners at Bologna did not pick up on it. But Laffer and Wanniski did, and in time so did Bartley and his editorial page. The problem facing Volcker was that *real* demand for money was impossible to discern by 1979. Did people asking for loans and credit really want the dollars, or did they just want the dollars so that they could pay for them with cheaper dollars in an inflationary future? Until the investment environment improved markedly, it would be impossible to tell.[32]

As of late 1979, the supply-siders had not only killed off the idea, inherent in the Phillips curve, that the onus of addressing recession falls on monetary policy. The supply-siders had also, contra monetarism, shown the minimal effectiveness of monetary policy in achieving price stability. In other words, for Volcker's strenuous, experimental efforts to bear fruit, there had to be an assist from fiscal policy in the form of tax cuts.

The supply-siders rallied around Volcker, the bird in hand. "You are so damned close," Wanniski wrote to Volcker that fall. "You should begin to think seriously about revising your position on fiscal policy, and begin to prepare Miller for the idea that an efficient tax cut is in order." Volcker replied by saying he was reading *The Way the World Works* on weekends. As for Bartley, his page wrote in October: "The new Federal Reserve anti-inflation package is the most hopeful economic policy development in over a decade, clearly signaling a determination to break the back of inflation." Now it was up to the political sphere to support the groping yet committed efforts on the Fed's part to stabilize the dollar. As Bartley reflected a dozen years later, "It would stretch things to say that the monetary side of Mundell's policy mix was in place, but surely [Volcker's control of the Fed] represented a major step toward it." The policy mix was a symbiotic entity, each of the two elements requiring the other to work. Thus, as the 1970s came to an end, all hope rested on the passage of Kemp-Roth.[33]

Stabilization in Flux

On January 10, 1979, Jack Kemp and Bill Roth announced that they were resubmitting their joint tax bill to Congress, reformulated to mimic the Nunn amendment that had enjoyed such popularity in both chambers the previous October. It was Roth who had given the Nunn amendment the name "Son of Kemp-Roth." As the amendment tallied its majorities, Roth passed out cigars to colleagues and staff as if he were a beaming father in a nursery. The January 1979 bill would go by the name Kemp-Roth II.[34]

"Kemp-Roth Jr." would not have quite captured it. For the bill was bigger. It included all the tax provisions of Kemp-Roth and more, including the 10–10–10 personal rate cuts and indexing, plus a regimen of spending reductions. The bill would require that spending as a percentage of GNP decrease by about a percentage point per year for four years until it got to 18. This was not meant to sound like austerity, for Kemp and Roth were predicting big growth because of the tax cut, and 18 percent of an economy made large would itself be large.

The problem for Kemp-Roth II was that the congressional environment was not propitious. On the bill's introduction, opponents moved to rejigger the amendment process to make it impossible for the measure to come up for a vote. The kin of Marjorie Holt's and Sam Nunn's amendments would face a different road in the new Congress. Now if tax and spending-cut measures were to well up in alternative venues, such as the House Budget Committee, as opposed to Appropriations and Ways and Means, they would have to name budget cuts in particular programs instead of calling for a ceiling on aggregate government expenditure. If they did not elaborate specific cuts, the measures would be ruled out of order.[35]

This was roundly against the spirit of the omnibus budget process introduced in 1974 and a death knell to the legislative strategy that the congressional supply-siders and their allies had perfected the prior year. Instead of voting to resolve to keep spending in general at a certain level, senators and representatives as of early 1979 now stood to be on the record at the outset as to what programs they were going to limit and by how much. The chance that such an amendment would attract spontaneous support was slight.

In late 1978, Paul Craig Roberts moved from his congressional jobs to a post at Bartley's editorial page, where he took the place of Jude Wanniski, who had left to start an investment business. Roberts was ideally situated to tell the newspaper's readership what was going on as Kemp-Roth II got blocked. In an editorial called "Canceling Votes with Rules," Roberts reported that it was not the prospect of tax cuts that caused Kemp-Roth II's opponents to shudder. It was the spending ceiling. The Holt amendment had wished to limit federal spending increases to 8 percent per year, and the Nunn amendment to 9 percent—both numbers comfortably above the high-trend inflation of the years prior to 1978. But to senators and congressmen addicted to the "Golden Fleece," as William Proxmire always called their pork, the prospect of these ceilings was a vision of Armageddon. "Obviously, big spenders are not going to give up without a fight," Roberts wrote. "They will have to suffer defeat at the polls more than once before they lose the power to cancel [elections] through committee assignments and rule changes."[36]

Kemp, for his part, sensed soon enough that this was the case. In 1979 and 1980, the span of the Ninety-sixth Congress, he chose not to devote himself to insinuating the bill into legislative channels. Rather, he took his case on the road, to the electorate, and he worked at burnishing the bill's intellectual credentials. In both efforts, Kemp met with success. Some supply-siders at the time thought that 1979 was a lost year. In December, Bruce Bartlett asked in *National Review*, "What Ever Happened to the Tax Revolt?" He chalked up the waning momentum to the dialectical process of history. The philosophical cast of his article was appropriate, but the resignation was misplaced. For among the achievements of the supply-side cause in 1979 was the turning of academic and theoretical economics. By 1980, advocates of tax cuts had come forth among economists across the methodological universe, and Keynesian economics was held far and wide to be in irredeemable crisis.[37]

Robert E. Lucas of the University of Chicago made his remarkable statement about the collapse of "Keynesian macroeconomics" in the summer of 1978 at a conference at the Boston Fed. The paper in which the statement appeared touched off a wave of exhalations in professional economics. It had been clear since the end of the Ford administration that classical economics, typically misidentified as the economics of the Republican Party, could no longer be blamed for the gross economic deficiencies of the 1970s. There was no Nixon, Ford, or Simon to kick around anymore. Stagflation persisted and worsened through the application of the gauntlet of Keynesian—or, if you prefer, government-interventionist—policies: suspension of currency convertibility; tax increases; tax progressivity; tax rebates; loose monetary policy; irregular monetary policy; budget deficits; a budget surplus; capital controls; industrial policy; safety and environmental regulations; welfare and unemployment compensation; jobs programs; wage and price controls; proposed "tips." What configuration of government intervention in the economy could be tried that had not already been complicit in abetting stagflation in the first place?

This was the question that Lucas's paper at the Boston Fed made inescapable. "In the present decade, the U.S. economy has undergone its first major depression since the 1930s, to the accompaniment of inflation rates in excess of 10 percent per annum.... These events.... were accompanied by ... policies which, although bearing an admitted risk of inflation, promised according to

modern Keynesian doctrine rapid real growth and low rates of unemployment,"
Lucas reminded his auditors. "That these predictions were wildly incorrect
and that the doctrine on which they were based is fundamentally flawed are
now simple matters of fact," he concluded. "The task now . . . is to sort through
the wreckage, determining which features of . . . the Keynesian Revolution can
be salvaged and put to good use and which others must be discarded." And
this task would "involve the . . . reevaluation of every aspect of the institutional framework within which monetary and fiscal policy is formulated in the
advanced countries."[38]

Such an epic effort would require care and time, not to say intellect. Economics largely obliged Lucas in his admonitions. In the late 1970s and into
the 1980s, economics narrowed its horizons, asking simple, specific questions
about particular problems. The implicit hope—à la Wittgenstein in philosophy, perhaps—was to build up enough small, logical building blocks of the
discipline that it might be created anew, and sturdier.

Lucas's own contribution, for which he would win the Nobel in 1995, was
to pioneer "rational choice" theory, by which the expectations of individual
economic actors had to be taken into account in macroeconomic considerations. His work attacked a particular Keynesian doctrine, the "money illusion," hard. The money illusion, the concept behind the Phillips curve, holds
that when currency overprinting occurs, people do not initially realize that
their real incomes are not going up. Thus, they spend the new money, and
growth and employment are goosed. Theoretically, such growth stimulus
could go on forever, an economic perpetual-motion machine.[39]

Lucas countered that people catch on rather quickly to this sort of thing,
and when they do they start to demand a premium for their money. Overprinting brings about the opposite of the effect intended. The more you overprint,
the more people doubt the value of their money, especially the new money they
get from overprinting. In overprinting environments, depositors and lenders
demand interest rates well in excess of inflation, because the monetary authority has established that it will invite inflation if it feels the urge. Since high interest rates, especially high real rates (that is, interest rates minus inflation), stifle
investment and production, stasis results. Expectations, Lucas and his rational-
choice school argued, explained a great deal of the stagflation phenomenon.

Lucas's spadework in the direction of rational expectations was a long way
from a positive policy of reform, such as Mundell was putting together for
the incipient conditions of the 1970s as early as 1958. Indeed, by 1980, it had

become rather déclassé in economics to address large policy questions. Better to do the piecework and wait for the large conclusions to emerge in time. Martin Anderson, an advisor to Ronald Reagan who was friendly to supply-side economics, found this reality exasperating as he helped to prepare the economic policies of the Reagan presidency. "If you survey the last ten years of the top scholarly economic journals in America," Anderson wrote in 1988, "you would look in vain for comprehensive economic programs. There will be dozens of sophisticated articles . . . on aspects of . . . policy. But you won't see anything that attempts to wrestle with an overall national policy." Anderson rued the fact: "When someone decides to run for president, one of the first questions . . . is, 'what is your economic policy going to be?' And the distinguished economists who have never had the audacity to write about this themselves will . . . see how this wretch of a politician will respond."[40]

It was a long way from Camelot and the days of the neoclassical synthesis and Operation Twist. Even James Tobin, the architect of the neoclassical synthesis, said in 1980, a year before he won his own Nobel Prize: "Higher inflation, higher unemployment—the relentless combination frustrated policymakers, forecasters, and theorists throughout the decade. The disarray in diagnosing stagflation and prescribing a cure makes any appraisal of the theory and practice of macroeconomic stabilization as of [today] a foolhardy venture. . . . I will just give my own observations and confess my own puzzlements." Economics was crying for help in 1980.[41]

There did remain adherents of "stabilization" theory, who held that the 1970s was the best of all possible worlds. Stabilization, in macroeconomics, refers to the ability of government to lessen the swings of economic performance. Absent big government, the logic went, booms and busts have their way with the economy. But with big government, variances, such as unemployment spikes, are smoothed out, yielding as even an economic result as possible. Arthur Okun, the "misery index" coiner and former Lyndon B. Johnson CEA chair, wrote shortly before his death in 1980: "Throughout the postwar era including the seventies, economic activity has been far more stable than [previously]. This quantum jump in stability . . . must, in my judgment, be credited to public policy. It was made in Washington. I suspect that the largest single stabilizing development stemmed from . . . the increased size of the public sector as a share of GNP."[42]

Some economists simply could not believe that Keynesian stabilization had proven faulty, even given the conditions of 1980. Okun clung to stale establishmentarianism, but economics in general firmly and humbly struck off in new directions under the guidance of lights such as Lucas.

America's Next Top Models

The matter of doing something remained. This is where Kemp hit his stride. All over the country in 1979, he spoke words such as these, delivered to an audience in New York City: "We have seen a total reversal of economic thought. . . . Conservatives are in the midst of a tremendous debate as to which way to go, whether they should go back to their austerity model or whether they should go where Bill Roth, Bill Steiger, Jack Kemp, Art Laffer, Robert Mundell, the pages of the *Wall Street Journal, Public Interest,* and some radical economists on the Street, as well as some radical young economists in academia are suggesting: toward growth, production, incentives for both labor and capital."[43]

Even Congress, despite the rules change, was coming around. The Joint Economic Committee (JEC), whose main responsibility to date had been commenting on the president's annual economic report, announced in March that for the first time in twenty years it had a unanimous report of its own. The reason for the unanimity: all were agreed on the necessity to "force the attention of the country and its economic experts on the supply side of the economy."[44]

The Democrats and Republicans on the JEC, whose chairman was Lloyd Bentsen, were not quite prepared to endorse Kemp-Roth, excluding John Rousselot. But all were ready to talk about the operative word of supply-side economics: "incentives." The report called for a business-tax cut. It stressed that economic capacity and production would increase as a result. It also offered a menu of spending programs, job-retraining initiatives, and such that the majority felt qualified as incentives in the real economy. Rousselot and other supply-side-minded members smiled at this but signed on anyway. It had become apparent that the necessity of tax cuts would become obvious soon enough.

As for why the JEC wanted to "help hold down the cost of living by increasing the goods on the shelves of the Nation's businesses"—the language of the report and a summary of the supply-side solution to stagflation—it was not because all members were distressed by the 1970s funk. Certain members, such as Bentsen, had long track records of demanding that the government let business produce more. But others, such as Edward M. Kennedy and George McGovern, belonged to the John Kenneth Galbraith school of thought, which held that the nation already produced enough. Paul Craig Roberts, in his memoir, speculated on why Kennedy in particular, along with other "big spenders" in Congress, was willing to sign the JEC report and clear the pathway for supply-side reform. "The spenders had been handing out . . . money faster than the economy could generate tax revenues and were worried about their programs running dry," he concluded. Roberts thus implied that in their secret hearts, big-government types believed that supply-side economics would succeed not only in promoting growth, but also in increasing government revenues.[45]

The JEC report marked the end of a certain kind of congressional rhetoric. In his memoir, Roberts compiled an anthology of the sophisms that supply-side advocates had had to contend with routinely in the halls of Congress through 1978. For example, there was the insistence, from an opposing staff economist, that an equal rate cut for all earners would make the tax code less progressive. And there was the contention, made by the head of the Congressional Budget Office (CBO), that cutting taxes would make people work less, not more. Based on a doctrine called the "backward-bending labor supply curve," the idea was that people have a targeted level of take-home income, and if tax cuts enable them to reach it sooner, they will take more time off from work. Roberts marveled at the logical conundrum. "It is possible for an individual taxpayer to respond in [this] way," Roberts wrote. "Yet here were economists making the mathematically impossible argument that taxpayers as a group would respond to a tax cut by working less, enjoying more leisure, and still have the same real incomes." Roberts turned the tables on the critics: "Supply-siders have been ridiculed for making excessive claims . . . , but [no one] ever claimed that tax cuts are such powerful medicine that they make it possible to produce the same amount of goods and services with less labor and no increase in capital investment. [Here] a tax cut could transform nonwork into a factor of production." "The CBO and the Keynesians," Roberts reflected, "[were] handing me a beautiful straw man to mow down."[46]

After the JEC report of early 1979, however, things had become too grave for the opponents of supply-side economics to continue in the previous vein. A new seriousness was in order. Furthermore, the public vexations of the top academic macroeconomists removed cover. Now if the opponents of supply-side economics were going to mouth Keynesian platitudes, they were on their own. There would be no assumption anymore that however mangled a formulation may be, so long as it sounded like something from the canons of Keynesianism, the necessary theoretical exactitude could be found in the academic journals.

Rousselot was correct to believe in 1979 that the JEC would come around to personal-tax cuts. The second-straight unanimous JEC report came out in March 1980. It called for doubling the business-tax cut proposed in 1979 by adding a personal rate cut of the same magnitude. The report even replaced the usual "JEC Report" title with "Plugging in the Supply Side."[47]

Upon the release of "Plugging in the Supply Side," the JEC held hearings on economic modeling and the supply-side perspective. An express point of the hearings was to call a stop to the evasions of supply-side insights in congressional debate. Alice Rivlin, who had said untenable things about supply-side economics in the past, conceded what the supply-siders had been arguing about the effects of tax and budget policy at the hearings. Rousselot savored the moment. "I remember very well just a few years ago," he said to the CBO head, "when I was on the Budget Committee writing you letters and receiving letters in return, a kind of downgrading of the whole idea. So I am delighted to see this change of approach." Rivlin responded that "we felt strongly then, as now, that the supply side was important." Rousselot had the old letters with him at the hearing, and everyone laughed.[48]

The issue before the JEC was to see how the top economic forecasters were changing their models to incorporate supply-side economics. Otto Eckstein (originator of the Data Resources model) was pleased to take part. He testified: "We are at one of those great moments where the opportunity to reverse the steady slide of our economic system exists, and where new ideas are being offered to accomplish the turnaround." He pointed out that econometric modeling to date had "made little allowance for the effects emphasized by . . . Feldstein, Laffer and others because the literature was still very limited."[49]

Eckstein outlined his new model, which took note of supply-side effects. The model verified that tax cuts would bring an end to stagflation. It also showed that nearly all preference should be given to business-tax cuts, investment tax credits, and depreciation reform—the stuff of 1962. Eckstein calculated that business-tax cuts would cause ten times the growth per unit of magnitude compared to personal cuts. Moreover, personal rate cuts, even if accompanied by tight monetary policy, would barely dent inflation. The Kemp-Roth 10–10–10 personal rate cuts, Eckstein predicted, would keep inflation above 8 percent per year through 1985.[50]

Through the election of Ronald Reagan in 1980, the principal argument made against the Kemp-Roth personal-rate cuts was that they would be inflationary. Previously, the argument had been made that they would cause "crowding out." This objection had died in the run-up to the Steiger amendment. By early 1978, it had become apparent that capital formation, as opposed to undue competition for capital in the marketplace, was what was undermining the equity and bond markets and the financing of start-ups. Before Reagan's presidency, no one thought to make an argument against Kemp-Roth on grounds that it would burden future generations with additional debt, for it was agreed that the federal government was set to run budget surpluses into the 1980s. In his JEC testimony, Eckstein predicted a $50 billion surplus for 1981. Michael Evans, at the same hearings, forecast that given no change in policy, surpluses would build to $75 billion in 1985. It is hard to imagine the forecasters saying anything else. For even though the federal government was set to run an unintelligibly high deficit of $74 billion in 1980, the momentum of federal accounts was in the other direction. With revenues poise d to increase at 165 percent of the rate of inflation, given bracket creep, the historic inflation of 1979 and early 1980 indicated to forecasters that the federal government would be hit with a surfeit of revenues so long as inflation remained untamed.[51]

Therefore, the question of whether Kemp-Roth (or Kemp-Roth II) would "pay for itself" was a double entendre. If the tax cut caused inflation, it certainly would pay for itself, because bracket creep would then bring in ever greater revenues. If the tax cut did not cause inflation, then the main way federal revenues increased would be shut off. Revenues would be less than in the heady days of 1.65 times double-digit inflation. The dealmaker was that stagflation stood to be cured in the latter but not the former case. All of these issues were clear to the testifiers at the March 1980 JEC hearing. Any prospective deficit was problematic only to the extent that it was associated with inflation.

Evans supported Kemp-Roth II at the hearings, with the caveat that everything hung on the spending cuts. The personal rate reductions alone would increase inflation, Evans testified, whereas coupled with spending cuts they would bring inflation down by at least five points per year. Both Evans and Eckstein forecast considerable revenue reductions from any sort of tax cut, reductions running over $100 billion. But given the baseline forecast of increasing surpluses into the 1980s, revenue losses on account of tax cuts had no intrinsic significance. They would matter only if the deficits that resulted caused inflation.

In his national barnstorming tour in 1979 and 1980, Kemp argued that inflation could be brought to nil even with an increased deficit on account of Kemp-Roth. It all depended on the Fed. If the Fed cared only about stable prices, it would leave any increased deficit to be financed by capital generated by the economy, as opposed to new money supplied by the central bank. Mundell had taught that this was the posture the Fed should adopt, according to "effective market classification." Kemp had absorbed this view, as was in evidence in a letter he wrote to a Buffalo newspaper reporter in May 1980:

> Even if Congress did reduce tax rates and yet refused to restrain spending, the economy would still be better off than if we allowed the tax burden to continue to increase. Were the deficit to widen for even a brief period, there would still be still more funds in the private sector, an expanded savings pool with which to finance a short-term deficit by selling bonds. So long as monetary restraint is maintained, there is no increase in inflation; indeed, insofar as the tax rate reduction increases production . . . it will contribute to reducing inflation. Conversely, an increase in taxes will increase inflation, because the quantity of money has remained unchanged while new disincentives have been imposed on the economy.

Doing nothing in a world of double-digit inflation and bracket creep would mean increased inflation and more negative growth. Tax cuts with stable money, in contrast, would solve both components of stagflation. The price might prove to be a deficit—if Congress could not screw up the resolve to cut spending—but absent inflationary effects, the deficit would lack relevance.[52]

Arthur Laffer offered his own forecast, one derived from his new "Prototype Wedge Model," which synthesized the Kemp position. The premise of Laffer's model was that there was more to tax cuts than the money put in people's pockets to save or spend. Rather, as one of Laffer's clients summarized it, "there exists a third force which influences supply and demand simultaneously and thereby drives the economy." This was the "wedge," or "the trade-off between market activities . . . and inactivity" on account of "government influences [such as] spending and the constellation of tax rates." Diminish the wedges by means of the Kemp-Roth tax cuts, Laffer showed, and the result would be a 10 percent increase in growth. The deficit, too, would increase, but only for three years, given the feedback effects of growth and modest spending reductions. This fulfilled the expectations of the American Council for Capital Formation, which on commissioning the model in 1978 had said "[it] is expected to demonstrate that carefully structured Federal tax cuts reduce Treasury revenues less than generally estimated."[53]

Laffer strove to make one point clear. There was a trade-off between the right kind of deficit increases and growth. If fiscal policy had a clear road to maximize the private economy, the preference should be for growth. As for the Laffer curve, the Prototype Wedge Model suggested that tax increases could raise revenue but reduce growth. Here the model communicated an essential supply-side point. The optimal point on the Laffer curve from the perspective of government revenue was the farthest point out. From the perspective of economic growth, however, the optimal point was somewhere beneath that point. That is to say, even if tax increases could bring in more revenue, they may be inadvisable if the effect on the real economy was stifling. This was similar to the point Ture had been driving at since 1962.

In 1980, Laffer started to depart a bit from the consensus that surpluses stood to emerge in the 1980s. He thought, along with Kemp, that in the intensified stagflationary conditions of the latter Carter years, the United States was approaching a Rubicon where continued tax increases through bracket creep and inflation would hit a wall. At some point, the reduction in growth caused by high progressive taxes would cause a march into the "prohibitive zone" of the Laffer curve.

The May 1980 JEC hearings on modeling trumpeted the point that Roberts had made for the readers of the *Public Interest* in 1978. In an article called "The Breakdown of the Keynesian Model," Roberts had showed that the 1970s exposed the flaws of Keynesian reasoning as no other period had done. Inflation plus tax progressivity must, ineluctably, cause people to make the choice for leisure over work. If the more one works, the more work will be taxed, and the less one works, the less work will be taxed, there will be less and less work—that is, less supply. Without the money stock shrinking in tandem, there would have to be more inflation in this predicament, which would only perpetuate it.[54]

The critics of the supply-side position, Roberts wrote, were stuck with making "perverse" claims. To the critics, "When tax rates go down and the relative price of leisure rises, people demand more leisure; when tax rates go up, and the relative price of leisure falls, people demand less leisure. . . . What kind of people are these?" Not the kind of people, Roberts reported, that the cutting edge of economics was studying. Roberts cited work by academic economists Gary Becker and Martin Feldstein that found that people strove to do more work the moment taxation could be avoided or lessened, such as through barter transactions where no money changes hands, or simply on the black market.[55]

The greatest Keynesian verity in the realm of taxation is that tax cuts raise "aggregate demand." This is why tax rebates, in the Keynesian mindset, are legitimate. Put money in people's pockets, and they will spend it, the logic goes, to the extent that people have a "marginal propensity to consume." As Roberts showed, the inflation and tax progressivity of the 1970s made this sort of tax cut ineffectual, if not ludicrous. Indeed, rebates would probably cause people to work less, since, given the high marginal rates, giving up extra work was virtually painless from a financial perspective. If people were simply given more money through a rebate, they might cut back on work, because the last work they were doing was barely paying anyway.

The conditions of 1980 mandated that tax cuts be marginal—as applying to the *next* dollar of income one might think to earn. As things stood, taxes were so arranged as to make one's next activity virtually unremunerative. If taxes were cut at the margin, the price of not choosing to take advantage of an economic opportunity would rise. With marginal rate cuts, there would be *incentive* for individuals to go ahead with new economic activity.

By 1980, arguments for supply-side tax cuts were in full ascendance. And yet the arguments were almost beside the point, given the disastrous economic conditions. Stagflation had reached such a depth that it had become a simple imperative that inflation abate and the rewards to work be renewed. And so the onus in that strange year passed to the political process.

PART III

IN THE ARENA

9

ERTA

What is wrong with the Kemp-Roth 30% tax cut?
To begin with, it is certain to be inflationary.

—JIM WRIGHT, Texas Democrat, House Majority Leader, in a "compendium of questions and answers" for Democratic colleagues, March 5, 1981

After the shocking death of Bill Steiger in December 1978, supply-side hopes for the presidency fell to Jack Kemp. In 1979, Kemp made it all but certain that he would make a spirited run for the presidency the following year. He rejiggered Kemp-Roth so that it approximated the vote-magnet Nunn amendment. He spoke across the country, including at places like Wall Street that were sure to provide dollars in the event of a run. And he published a book, *An American Renaissance,* that reflected on a range of issues, from economics to defense, facing the next chief executive. Furthermore, political insiders knew that Kemp had an uncommon ability to attract both blue- and white-collar support.[1]

Yet something was missing. Kemp did not want the presidency, at least in 1980, the year he was to turn forty-five. Evans and Novak recalled, after the election was over, that "Wanniski, Bell, and . . . Kristol . . . urged him to run. They had lined up pollsters, advertising experts and political technicians, ready to go at a word from Kemp. The word never came. Kemp was as cautious in plotting his personal career as he was audacious in grasping new ideological concepts."[2]

One reason Kemp may have chosen not to run in 1980, a choice he settled on late in 1979, was that the field was formidable, and not only on the Republican side. George Bush, Ronald Reagan, John Connally, and John Anderson, among Republicans, had made clear their intention to run. Among the Democrats, Ted Kennedy planned to challenge Carter in the primaries. Clearly, the incumbent was weak. The economy was deepening into the vortex created by bracket creep and the Fed's desperate attempts to control the money supply. And there were foreign shocks, including the Iranian hostage crisis that began in November 1979 and the Soviet invasion of Afghanistan that December. The prize of the presidency was likely to be won by one of the nonincumbents.

The field was strong, and to emerge victorious would require visceral ambition. Historians agree that the turning point in the primary election came in the week of the New Hampshire primary, when Ronald Reagan stood down a request to be quiet. "I am paying for this microphone!" Reagan roared. Kemp rarely said such things, rarely acted angrily or in a self-assertive way. His disposition was sunny, and not undercut by egocentrism. Kemp loved to fight, it is true, when he thought American prosperity was at stake, but not when it came to personal aggrandizement.[3]

This quality vexed the supply-siders. They wanted Kemp to be president. But they were not sure he had the ambition needed to make a successful run. So they focused on the vice presidency. Laffer developed a plan that would assure Kemp a spot as Reagan's running mate. Everything was to be tied up at a party at the Laffer home, outside Los Angeles, in October 1979. As Laffer told a Reagan biographer years later, the plan was to have Reagan, Kemp, and some friends over to dinner. On cue, Kemp would walk with Reagan to a cottage in the backyard. In the privacy of the cottage, Kemp was to say the following, according to Laffer's libretto: "'Sir, you know I adore you. I think the world of you. I've worked for you [in Sacramento in 1967], you've been my hero, my role model, all my life. What I'm going to do, sir, is I'm going to run, and every delegate I get, come convention time, I'm going to instruct all those delegates to vote for you.'"

"Jack, that's what you've got to tell him," Laffer said. The day came, and everything was going according to plan. Kemp and Reagan were alone in the cottage for half an hour while the other guests milled around the house. They "came back . . . all smiles," Laffer recalled. "'Jack, did you do it?'" Laffer rememberd asking Kemp. He said, 'Oh, no, Art, I couldn't. I told him I'd never run against him. I'd give him all the support I could.' I said, 'Jack, you just lost the vice presidency. He's not going to pick a wuss for a vice president.... Why would he take someone who doesn't run?'" In November, Bartley reported in the *Journal* that "Kemp has signed on as 'official spokesman' for the Reagan campaign, and it's no secret that Jude [Wanniski] is pushing him for the vice-presidential slot." But even Bartley had given up on that one. "A ticket with a former movie star and a former football star is just too much to imagine."[4]

As for the former movie star, in August Reagan had drawn up an economic policy plan that the supply-siders found amenable. The first plank called for the stimulation of economic growth by means of tax cuts, indexing the code for inflation, and deregulation. The second plank addressed government spending. Spending was to be cut, then controlled, through such instruments as a line-item veto. Plank three called for a balanced budget. The last plank simply insisted on sticking to the plan. Two of the planks may have reflected old-fashioned Republican concerns, spending and deficits. But primacy of place was given to growth via tax cuts. The plan was put together by Reagan advisor Martin Anderson and called "Policy Memorandum No. 1."[5]

The question that lingered was whether the tax cuts were inextricably linked to spending cuts and balanced budgets, or whether they were non-negotiable. To use James Baker's words of 2001, was Reagan a reformed drunk on tax cuts? Reagan had been making public statements in support of Kemp-Roth since its inception in 1977. By 1979, this was unremarkable, since a supermajority in Congress had recently affirmed the Son of Kemp-Roth. Still, Reagan's record was distinctive. In October 1977, for example, after the first House budget resolution battles, Reagan had given a radio address in support of Kemp-Roth that displayed clear understanding of supply-side arguments. "Twice in this century, in the 1920s and the early 1960s," Reagan said on the radio, "we cut taxes substantially and the stimulant to the economy was substantial and immediate.... Jack Kemp's bill ... would reduce the deficit which causes inflation because the tax base would be broadened by the increased prosperity."[6]

And yet there were times when Reagan could speak the old-time Republican language of "austerity" and "trade-offs"—"deep root-canal economics," as Laffer called it. Evans and Novak observed that Reagan's penchant for saying that the nation would have to suffer a "bellyache" in correcting the misguided economic policies of the '70s had to be reined in by advisors. Policy

Memorandum No. 1, for its part, included a section titled "The Myth of the Economic Bellyache," which cited evidence from Federal Reserve economists that "there appears to be *no trade-off*" between unemployment and inflation. And according to the canons of supply-side economics the implementation of the correct policy mix carried no economic costs. This had to be grasped.[7]

Keeping Kemp close to Reagan was the supply-siders' means of keeping Reagan on message concerning tax cuts. Reagan's campaign manager, John Sears, proved effective at this task. The pragmatic Sears saw wonderful electoral chemistry in Kemp. To Sears, Kemp was both a personification of the populist tax revolt of 1978 as well as an unusually good Republican vote-getter in the industrial northeast, the latter an attribute of great interest to the western-based Reagan. After Sears's campaign failed to produce a win for Reagan in the first test, the Iowa caucuses of January 1980, Sears redoubled his efforts to paint Reagan as a supply-sider. He arranged for Jeff Bell to produce television ads in which Reagan emphasized the need for tax cuts. Reagan then won the New Hampshire primary and was the front-runner for good.[8]

In campaign stops, Reagan had emphasized three things: tax cuts, domestic spending cuts, and a defense buildup. There was no sheet of numbers showing exactly how it was all to add up or a statement of what was to give in the event of difficulties. After the win in New Hampshire, this vagueness became an issue. A press release from the campaign of Reagan's main rival, George Bush, charged that Reagan was indulging in "voodoo economics." Bush himself did not use the phrase in stump speeches until the Pennsylvania primary in April, by which time Reagan had almost locked up the nomination.[9]

"Voodoo economics" was not a synonym for "supply-side economics." Rather, the epithet served to question whether Reagan's entire economic and budget package, including spending, added up correctly. Given that Reagan was promising a considerable increase in the defense budget, the domestic spending cuts plus the Laffer-curve effects of the tax cuts would have to be just as considerable, given Reagan's animus against budget deficits. "Voodoo economics" was an indictment not of supply-side economics per se, but of the Reagan economic and budget plan in toto. It expressed Bush's disbelief that taxes could be cut and aggregate spending increased (because of the defense buildup) without running a deficit.

As for his own views, George Bush was in favor of business-tax cuts but not the personal rate cuts of Kemp-Roth. He essentially staked out the position of the 1979 JEC report. Surely one reason Reagan won the nomination was that the tax revolt was still alive and well in 1980, a year in which bracket creep had become worse than ever. Soon Bush came to repent of the voodoo charge and made nice with the candidate who had bested him. In July, at the party convention in Detroit, Reagan picked Bush as his running mate. Bush had proven a tenacious fighter and a worthy opponent, just as Laffer had urged Kemp to be. Bush also appealed to Reagan because his eastern establishmentarian credentials complemented Reagan's appeal in the Sun Belt and West.[10]

At the time of the Pennsylvania primary in April 1980, an incident occurred that nearly rent the supply-siders in two and threatened to freeze them out of the Reagan economic team altogether. Jude Wanniski gave an injudicious interview to the *Village Voice,* the lowlife weekly of alternative New York. The interview was conducted by two sensationalistic journalists, Alexander Cockburn and James Ridgeway. Their main interest was in making untoward inferences about supply-side economics (such as whether the increase in income from tax cuts might bid up business for prostitutes) and seeing how their discussant dealt with it. Wanniski partially fell for it, even answering the prostitution questions in earnest. The part that got him in trouble was as follows:

AC/JR: *Does Reagan really believe in supply side economics?*
Yes. Reagan loves the stuff. John Sears kept telling Kemp that he should spend more time on the campaign trail with Reagan, because whenever he spent a day or two with Reagan, Reagan came alive. When Kemp leaves, Reagan subsides. . . .
AC/JR: *On economic policy, then, it's basically you and Kemp?*
And Laffer.
AC/JR: *Is there an opposing camp?*
The opposing camp is an official board of advisors. . . . They are more or less in a position of arguing caution.
AC/JR: *You are the wild men?*
We are the wild men.

At another point in the interview, Wanniski came close to taking credit for conceiving and writing Kemp-Roth, which came as news to people like Paul Craig Roberts and Norman Ture. Laffer was mortified. He was on good terms with Reagan and knew how to give credit where it was due. Anderson, author of Policy Memorandum No. 1, was furious and sad. Furious because the interview trivialized Reagan's economic plan; sad because the talented and heretofore indispensible Wanniski had marginalized himself. "It was too bad," Anderson wrote in his memoir, "because Wanniski had contributed to the economic part of the intellectual revolution that was beginning to sweep over the United States and the rest of the world. . . . Instead of taking great satisfaction in what he had contributed, he tried to take credit for things he had not done." Wanniski countered, "I believe [Reagan] benefits with the perception that he has a swirl of intellectual ferment around him. A man, by God, of ideas."[11]

Wanniski wrote a letter to the editor of the *Voice* in which he conceded that his remarks were ill-conceived. But with Laffer, Wanniski held his ground, insisting that they had to be careful not to let the momentum of the tax-cut revolution ebb. In particular, Wanniski said to Laffer, they had to make sure that they did not let their good relations with the Nixon and Ford holdovers in the Reagan ambit cloud their policy vision. They could not go soft on permanent and marginal tax cuts. "I will remain a maniac," Wanniski told Laffer.[12]

After the *Voice* piece, it became impossible for Wanniski to keep close to the Reagan campaign. So, keeping up the bravado, Wanniski formed a "Shadow Cabinet Committee" (after the monetarists' Shadow Open Market Committee) that was to express opinions publicly on individuals the campaign floated as potential cabinet members. The main goal was to shore up the case for Lew Lehrman as treasury secretary.[13]

Wanniski's career had been in upheaval during the two years since the publication of *The Way the World Works,* and Wanniski seemed to enjoy it. His departure from the *Journal* was the stuff of legend, an oft-told tale. One day in the summer of 1978, contrary to journalism's code of ethics, Wanniski was passing out campaign literature for Bell when he was espied by a higher-up at the *Journal.* The executive called for Wanniski's head, and Bartley obliged. Bartley maintained that he and Wanniski already had been negotiating Wanniski's departure in any case. Wanniski needed a platform to raise money for the supply-side cause and a position in which he could be politically active.[14]

Friends said that Wanniski was a genuine revolutionary in the cause of supply-side economics, even speaking in terms of the Bastille and Danton. After the *Voice* episode, Roberts cautioned him, "In your whole approach, there's too much of the nineteenth-century Romantic." Wanniski preferred Hegelian explanations: he was "putty in [the] hands [of] the forces of history." A decade later, Wanniski would identify junk-bond king Michael Milken as "the principal agent history had chosen as catalyst in [the] process" of the return to prosperity. Once, when Roberts cautioned Wanniski that his course of action might jeopardize something the supply-siders were doing in Congress, Wanniski told him, "We will sacrifice you to the revolution." All the same, Wanniski succeeded in business. His consultancy, Polyconomics, which Wanniski started in 1978 and kept in operation until his death in 2005, made money, influenced debate, and did first-order work in supply-side theory.[15]

Even without Wanniski, the Reagan campaign was stacked with economic advisors. This, indeed, was one of the reasons Anderson was put off by the *Voice* piece. He counted fully seventy-four major economic advisors to Reagan. These included the "big eight" of Friedman, Simon, Alan Greenspan, Paul McCracken (these last two former CEA chairs), Arthur Burns, George Shultz, Caspar Weinberger, and Murray Weidenbaum (the deregulation expert soon to be Reagan's CEA chair). The big eight chaired task forces on each of the major economic issues of the day, each task force itself a roster of eminent names. To Anderson, the idea that Reagan's embrace of tax cuts derived from "wild men" was infuriating.[16]

Moreover, mainstream economics was converging on the necessity of tax cuts in stagflation's most brutal year, 1980. Martin Feldstein spoke for a professional consensus when he wrote "Tax Incentives Without Deficits" for Bartley's opinion page in July. "The tax cut debate has fortunately moved from 'whether' to 'what kind,'" Feldstein wrote. "If it is done the right way, a multi-year tax cut could bring immediate increases in investment, saving, and individual effort without any increases in the government deficit now or in the future." The key was "enacting *now* a schedule of *future* tax cuts." He supported accelerating depreciation and increasing the capital-gains exclusion before reserving these words for Kemp-Roth: "Because a gradual phase-in could be financed by automatic inflation tax windfalls and by a gradual reduction in the growth of government spending, tax rates could be reduced by 30 percent over a few years without any deficits."[17]

Despite such endorsements, the supply-siders cracked up a little that summer. Wanniski was persona non grata in more circles than one. Michael Evans, in his columns in *Industry Week,* made clear that he wanted no part of tax cuts that were not matched by spending cuts. As in all objections to Kemp-Roth, Evans's fear was heightened inflation. Irving Kristol pleaded for cool heads. In a piece on Bartley's page titled "The Battle for Reagan's Soul," Kristol suggested that the scrape between supply-siders and establishmentarians was a fiction of the media. And in case he was wrong, Kristol made this observation: "By so strenuously avoiding deficits that might arise from a tax cut, [traditional] conservatism has merely assured us of deficits that arise from increased government spending." In other words, tax cuts must be nonnegotiable. Lehrman followed up a week later with a piece titled "Stop the Battle for Reagan's Soul." With a businessman's dispatch, Lehrman said, in effect, just get it done. Cut taxes, stabilize the dollar, strengthen defense, and balance the budget. Lehrman put it in italics: do it *"all."*[18]

Whatever the paroxysms of the summer of 1980, real or imagined, Kemp-Roth was never in jeopardy of falling out of favor in the Reagan campaign. At the Republican convention, the party platform endorsed Kemp-Roth. (The platform also included a plank that effectively called for a gold standard.) The only real jeopardy Kemp-Roth was in that summer came from Congress. Nunn-amendment Democrats such as Russell Long were trying to pass a tax cut that was not as serious as Kemp-Roth but would have probably forestalled Kemp-Roth for good. The majority in Congress wanted to save the election for Carter. But even in the extreme circumstances of 1980, it could not get it done. The Democrats in Congress relented. They were unable to reach agreement and unsure of presidential support. Tax cuts were to be a Republican issue.

In September, Carter again proposed bracket expansion as part of his economic package, but this old tack had run its course. By 1980, Carter's programs seemed stale, disproven, and sure to lack follow-through. Carter found more success in hurling invective at Reagan's plan and the tax cut in particular, calling Kemp-Roth inflationary. This maneuver pressured Reagan to release specific numbers. He obliged by making a speech.

This was the speech to the Chicago International Business Council of September 9, 1980, understood since by political strategists to be the point where the election tipped ineluctably in Reagan's favor. Accompanying the speech was a handout detailing Reagan's budget forecast, fed through the current Congressional Budget Office (CBO) economic forecast. The tax assumptions of the handout included Kemp-Roth's 10–10–10 personal rate cuts, subsequent indexing, and accelerated depreciation. The handout showed intensive economic growth, 60 percent in nominal terms through 1985. Domestic spending was to increase at less than two-thirds that level, by 37 percent, and defense spending at greater than the rate of growth, by 70 percent. The deficit was to become a surplus by 1983.[19]

In two ways the Reagan statement of September 9 departed from supply-side assumptions. First, it followed CBO and maintained that inflation would continue at the stagflation-era rate. The 60 percent nominal growth represented inflation at 8 percent per year, with real growth just over 4 percent. Kemp and others in the supply-side camp had been adamant that tax cuts would end inflation. In addition, the revenue reflow (or Laffer-curve) effect of the tax cuts was estimated to be lower than what the supply-siders would have claimed. Seventeen percent of revenue lost to tax cuts would be recaptured because of increased economic activity. Nevertheless, the rate cuts were treated as essential policy. Over the summer, Greenspan had been suggesting that Kemp-Roth could be phased in over three years "or more." The "or more" was off the table at Chicago. As a concession, the Ford CEA chair got what he considered realism regarding inflation and revenue reflows.[20]

Reagan's numbers were sufficient to mollify critics. By 1980, everybody thought inflation was a permanent fact of life. And tax cuts caused nominal growth—even Keynesians were on board with that. As for the deficit becoming a surplus, this was probably the least controversial aspect of the Chicago forecast. All forecasts, including Carter's, saw surpluses around the corner. With bracket creep sucking 165 percent of the increase in the price level into the federal treasury, any projection that was the slightest bit dovish on inflation had to concede a cascade of revenues that would bring the budget past balance. The 10–10–10 personal rate cut looked almost quaint next to an inflation rate at 14 percent and heading higher. What dent in federal revenues could a 10 percent tax cut make, when a COLA capturing double-digit inflation shoved a wage earner up a couple of brackets every year?[21]

Transition Wars

Reagan won in a landslide on November 4, beating Carter by ten points in the popular tally and by 440 votes in the electoral college. The winning candidate had coattails. The Republicans took the Senate and added seats in the House. For the transition, Reagan put Los Angeles headhunter E. Pendleton James in charge of recruitment. "Pen" James sent out scores of elegantly appointed letters to candidates for cabinet and other executive posts. The letters often asked for a précis of policy views. The response of Lehrman, the supply-siders' darling and a candidate for a Treasury post, was that the stock, bond, and loan markets were in a state of imminent collapse. The new president had to do all that he could, and as soon as possible, if a national financial calamity were to be avoided.[22]

Lehrman's letter reached Kemp and one of Kemp's most reliable allies in the House, Representative David A. Stockman of Michigan. Lehrman's words inspired Stockman to write a paper of his own, which would be put in the hands not of Pen James but of the members of Reagan's inner circle. Kemp made copies of Stockman's paper and headed to Los Angeles for the first meeting of Reagan's economic advisors since the election. Stockman's paper was titled "Avoiding a GOP Economic Dunkirk." Just as the British threw all that they had at the Germans in May 1940 and found that they had to beat a wholesale retreat or face disaster, so the Republicans had to defeat stagflation outright on first pass, Stockman argued. If they did not, they would find themselves overwhelmed by stagflation and run out of Washington in the next election.[23]

The central finding of the paper was that stagflation had gotten so bad that financiers were ready to bail out of the system. This is what Lehrman had clued Kemp and Stockman in on. Whereas in past stagflation-era recoveries real growth and a modicum of investment accompanied the persistence of inflation, this time the economy and the markets were displaying a complete lack of confidence about the future. Investible dollars were fleeing to commodities and collectibles, drying up resources to fund the stock and bond markets and thus the real economy. Inflation at 14 percent made even holding in these markets a dreadful course of action. As for getting loans from banks, interest rates were heading upwards of 20 percent. Lehrman's letter informed Stockman that borrowers had become so aghast at inflation, growth prospects, and interest rates that they nearly refused to contract on long-run terms. Therefore, the short-term markets were flooded with unreal demand as never before. The economic system was seizing up, and Ronald Reagan had ten weeks to idle away until he became president. "In all," Stockman wrote, "President Reagan will inherit thoroughly disordered credit and capital markets, punishingly high interest rates, and a hair-trigger market psychology poised to respond strongly to early economic policy signals."[24]

To make matters worse, federal credit demands happened just then to be soaring. The 1980 federal budget deficit was supposed to come in at $50 billion, according to the resolutions from the year's congressional budget process. As the 1980 fiscal year ended in October, it was clear that the number was going to be more like $75 billion. Fiscal 1981 was already promising to be worse. The financial market seize-up, coupled with record inflation, meant that federal expenditures stood to explode at about the time of Reagan's inauguration. Unemployment occasioned by the financial crisis would trigger layoff-compensation and job-training expenditures, and inflation would balloon indexed Social Security payments. "It is these spending growth trends . . . which are generating market expectations of a chronic and severe Reagan inflation: market participants simply will not accept . . . anti-inflation goals in light of this massive governmental domination of the credit markets," said Stockman.[25]

Kemp was the only one at Los Angeles on November 16 with a paper to pass out, and his was a humdinger. The attendees took notice and agreed: Stockman and Kemp were not exaggerating. Inflation was unmoored, interest rates were beyond the pale, stock and bond markets were losing out to alternative investments, and deficits were poised to bloat. Stockman's paper urged several policy steps. These were holding the line on the Kemp-Roth tax cuts, getting the Fed to be consistent about modest real money growth, relaxing business regulations, and cutting spending.[26]

On the last two matters, the paper descended into grim comedy:

> Unless swift, comprehensive and far-reaching regulatory policy corrections are undertaken immediately, an unprecedented, quantum scale-up of the much discussed "regulatory burden" will occur during the next 18–40 months. . . . The basic dynamic is this: During the . . . 1970s, Congress approved . . . sweeping environmental, energy, and safety enabling authorities, which . . . are devoid of policy standards and criteria for cost-benefit. . . . Subsequently, no-growth activists . . . have spent the past four years "tooling up" for implementation through a mind-boggling outpouring of rule-makings, interpretive guidelines, and major litigation—all heavily biased toward maximization of regulatory scope and burden. Thus, this decade-long process of regulatory revolution is just now reaching the stage at which it will sweep through the industrial economy with near gale force, [making for] an incredible morass of new controls and compliance procedures.

Arrest it all, Stockman said, forthwith, including: the "1981 passenger tailpipe standard . . . unproven 5 mph bumper standards . . . diesel particulate and [nitrogen oxide] standards . . . bus noise standards . . . ad infinitum." As for spending, Stockman recommended application of the meat cleaver—cut $50 billion in 1981, a fiscal year already six weeks under way.[27]

Because Kemp was the one passing out the paper, the battle for Reagan's soul seemed to have resolved itself. Here was the author of Kemp-Roth becoming a hawk on spending and regulation. Lehrman might have been on to something when he had said that the new administration must do it *all*. As for regulation, Reagan would in time install the academic doyen of deregulation, Murray Weidenbaum of Washington University in St. Louis, as CEA chair. Stockman became an obvious choice for OMB. Reagan offered Stockman the job on Thanksgiving, eleven days after the Los Angeles meeting at which his paper had made the rounds.[28]

With Stockman at the budget office, it was almost certain that a supply-sider would be installed at Treasury. Since OMB was clearly going to be hawkish on spending, there was no need to have someone at Treasury who would go slow on the tax cuts. William Simon announced that the secretary's job was his. It was not. Evans and Novak speculated that certain senators—Republican ones, and Bob Dole in particular—had told Reagan that they dreaded having Simon on the Hill once again, lecturing them and killing their favorite pork projects without offering concessions. Lehrman was passed over, too, probably because his own views were too well formed; it was questioned whether an individual of such intellectual conviction could adjust himself precisely to the Reagan agenda. Nor did the job go to the campaign's marquee Wall Streeter, Citibank chairman Walter Wriston, who had been advising Reagan from early on. Rather, Reagan gave it to a peripheral participant in his campaign, someone who had testified to Congress the previous summer that tax cuts were an essential step: Donald T. Regan, chief executive for the past ten years of the investment firm Merrill Lynch. This news worried supply-siders. Evans and Novak noted, incorrectly, that Regan had "played no part in [the] campaign and did not back [the] daring tax reduction until being named to the Cabinet." The tax cut now probably hinged, the columnists warned, on whether supply-siders were appointed as Regan's top assistants.[29]

Regan sensed that Evans and Novak's vexation expressed the supply-siders' angst that they might miss a historic opportunity. But he didn't think they needed to worry. After all, in May 1980, Regan had hosted a highly successful Reagan fund-raiser. And the next month, he had testified to Ways and Means that "we have to recognize the gross unfairness of bracket creep for individuals." Mimicking supply-siders, he had said that "tax cuts ... bolster economic growth ... by the favorable work, savings, and investment incentive effects that the tax rate cuts would produce." "Quantitative evidence [may be lacking],"

Regan had continued, "but I have faith in the common sense of individuals to save or spend their own tax savings in a better way than bureaucracy."[30]

One of the reasons supply-siders were keyed up was that the lame-duck Congress, at Dole's behest, was thinking about passing a 5 percent tax cut before the end of the 1980 calendar year. Such a move would probably have taken a major tax cut off the table for 1981. This prospect, coupled with the selection of Regan, over both Lehrman and Simon, for the Treasury post led to visions of another Nixon-Ford malaise. Those close to Reagan found all of this quite histrionic. As Martin Anderson said repeatedly, Reagan had decided long before late 1980 to cut taxes. He was going to do it no matter what, even if it meant firing people like his treasury secretary, which it would not. Allan Meltzer, brought in to do forecasting for the new administration, later said the same thing: "It didn't matter who was in which office. Reagan was going to do it. He was going to follow through with his program."[31]

Regan was chosen as treasury secretary because he had done significant work for the campaign and because he was a seasoned Wall Streeter. William J. Casey, the New York lawyer who had run Reagan's campaign after Sears's departure, knew Regan well and supported his candidacy. Moreover, after the Stockman memo, which was roundly leaked to the press, the transition team faced pressure to assure "big business" of its friendliness and competence. Some on Wall Street feared that perhaps Reagan was considering an FDR-esque "100 days" that would bring a raft of new strictures on commerce and banking. To allay such fears, Wall Street needed to see one of its own put in Treasury.[32]

To further calm fears, after Regan was announced Stockman took a tour of Wall Street, accompanied by Kemp. The tour was a big success for the OMB designate. The investment banks learned that Stockman had no interest in measures like banking holidays but instead had his eye fixed on discretionary spending reductions. An unfounded rumor got started that Stockman was going to go after the really big item, Social Security. This soon forced Reagan to declare Social Security off limits. Indeed, as president, Reagan would exempt Social Security from any budget-cutting not recommended by an independent commission. Such a recommendation was not forthcoming.[33]

Given Stockman's December tour of Wall Street and Regan's appointment, the president-elect was assured that business titans would not oppose his program. So attention turned to nuts and bolts. The program outlined at Chicago in September had to be reiterated, more formally, and in view of new conditions. Stockman assembled an economic forecasting team to crunch the data. He was successful in getting a number of supply-siders, including Alan Reynolds, to help. Stockman, Reynolds, and a few others got to work putting together an economic forecast in January 1981. As the days passed, more members were added to their team, including Lawrence Kudlow, who had left Bear Stearns to become chief economist at OMB. Kudlow was monetarist-minded but soon showed keen interest in supply-side ideas. Treasury appointees Ture, Roberts, and Stephen J. Entin (formerly of the JEC staff) also joined in to help with the forecast. The subcabinet had gotten its supply-siders. Stockman brought in someone new to anchor the nascent forecasting group: John Rutledge, thirty-two years old and founder of a southern California firm called the Claremont Economics Institute.[34]

Rutledge and Rosy Scenario

Rutledge had been teaching economics and doing consulting as a fresh Ph.D. when he caught the eye of William Simon near the end of Gerald Ford's term. Simon, looking around for things to do as a private citizen while he supervised the ghostwriting of *A Time for Truth,* brought Rutledge into his entourage with an eye to building an econometric model that would challenge the lions of the economics establishment. Rutledge worked for two years on the model, mining Simon's sterling list of contacts for advice. During this time he met Charles Parker, who told him of the Michael 1 doings. Rutledge also got to know an economist at the Northwestern Mutual Life Insurance Company by the name of Harvey Wilmeth. Over a series of conversations, Wilmeth convinced Rutledge of his own novel views of what had been going on in the economy in the 1970s. In short order, via Rutledge, Wilmeth's views were transmitted into the deposit of supply-side theory, and just in time.[35]

Wilmeth had been puzzling over the textbook explanation that the interest rate was the chief determinant of business investment and therefore of output, employment, and asset prices. He had concluded, he told Rutledge, that the key was not the interest rate at all, but the "ratio of tangible assets to securities." Wilmeth showed Rutledge a Federal Reserve publication that detailed the "balance sheet" of the nation. It showed that in the Carter years, more than 50 percent of assets in the United States were not financial assets, such as stocks and bonds, but tangible assets—hard assets such as real estate, collectibles, commodities, and consumer durables. This represented a major change. Under ordinary circumstances, financial assets can dwarf tangible assets in value. Rutledge puzzled over the data himself. One entry in particular arrested him. It showed that the value of used cars and old washing machines in the country had reached the $1 trillion mark.[36]

As Rutledge explains it today, the concept Wilmeth was getting at can be grasped by pondering comedian George Carlin's routine about "stuff." As Carlin rasped in the 1980s, "That's all your house is, a pile of stuff with a cover on it. And when you take off in an airplane, you see that everybody has their little pile of stuff." "Stuff" is what has already been produced. "Securities" or "financial assets"—stocks and bonds—are claims on what will be produced in the future. The ratio of stuff to securities is a measure, therefore, of confidence in the economic future. If the ratio is getting higher, as it was in the late 1970s, the message is that expectations are declining about the future production of stuff.[37]

Wilmeth helped turn Rutledge into a supply-sider, even though Wilmeth himself was not in the supply-side orbits of either Michael 1 or Jack Kemp. Yet Wilmeth may have been a purer supply-sider than any of them, for his main concern was future production. Wilmeth realized that the taxes and inflation of the 1970s had increased the cost of holding financial but not tangible assets. Because taxes in general were not excise but income taxes, and because inflation buoyed the value of things already produced or in the ground, the rise in income-tax rates along with inflation in the 1970s had led to a tremendous move out of stocks and bonds and into the stuff that presently existed. As for future stuff, it cannot be produced without investments in financial assets. The shift into tangibles thus prefigured a decline in production. And yet as Rutledge perceived at Wilmeth's insistence, the process stood to be reversed with tax cuts and the defeat of inflation. With the policy mix, there would be "flows" (in the Mundell-Fleming jargon) from tangible into financial assets. This kind of asset shift would initiate a great era of *new* production, not to say profits.

Rutledge soon found himself outlining these ideas to prominent clients, including General Electric executives Dale F. Frey and Reginald Jones. To men such as these, what Rutledge had to say was eye-popping. Rutledge was contending that if inflation collapsed, and if take-home returns on investments went up because of tax cuts, a great deal of money would come out of hiding to take advantage of the new conditions. The magnitudes involved were huge, in the trillions of dollars, as the Federal Reserve's national balance sheet seemed to indicate. Once the entire asset shift worked itself out, Rutledge claimed, the number might reach $11 trillion.[38]

Since the beginning of the dollar's time of troubles in the 1960s, in Rutledge's view, money around the world had been steadily and increasingly departing productive enterprises in favor of safe havens. The process had been going on for so long and had intensified so much that it had effectively created a dammed reservoir of money poised to burst if the circumstances supporting safe-haven hunting suddenly vanished. Rutledge's work was plausible as an intellectual exercise. It was a cogent inference from the Mundell-Fleming model and had echoes of the portfolio theory that would bring James Tobin the Nobel Prize in 1981.

The theoretical legitimacy of Rutledge's ideas was not, however, what caught the attention of people like Dale Frey and Reg Jones. The practical consequences were the arresting thing. What if Rutledge was right? If people like Volcker and Reagan came into power, and Rutledge's theory was viable, trillions stood to flow into enterprises, stocks, and bonds just as commodities plummeted. There would be huge money to be made if one was correctly positioned in real economic outfits or their financing instruments. Rutledge, thirty at the time, was amazed by the intense attention he was receiving from the captains of industry.

Even today, Rutledge wonders whether his own advice to Frey and Jones was not the decisive factor in GE's decision circa 1980 not to follow other behemoths out of productive enterprises and into inflation-hedging commodities. In the late 1970s, the commodity play appeared a plausible strategy. In 1978, for example, GE's natural resources business accounted for 5 percent of the total sales of the company, yet 15 percent of its profits. GE could have redoubled its efforts in this area had it been sure the conditions of the 1970s would continue. Indeed, Rutledge recalls GE executives discussing devoting considerable capital to tungsten mines in South Africa.[39]

In the 1980s, under new CEO Jack Welch, GE turned its back on all this and threw itself into manufacturing, service, and finance. However well U.S. Steel may have done as USX/Marathon Oil after 1982, General Electric became the largest, most profitable, most productive, and most admired firm in the world. Moreover, it became clear that thirty-year-old John Rutledge had correctly predicted the epic bull markets of the 1980s and 1990s.

Rutledge had caught the eye of the Reagan campaign in California in early 1980, and right after the November victory Stockman made sure to install him in Washington. Rutledge would be part of the forecasting group in service of the tax, budget, and regulatory legislation Reagan hoped to get through Congress. Rutledge, Reynolds, Kudlow, Stockman, and the others would review Reagan's policy plan, and the assumptions would be sifted through the model Rutledge had developed at Claremont Economics.

In point of fact, this took an ungodly amount of effort and patience. Rutledge had brought a dozen Claremont employees to Washington in late 1980, but the machines remained in California. Using a primordial fax machine, Rutledge took the consensus policy plan every time it was tweaked, and fed it to California, where the numbers were crunched and the results faxed back. Finally the process yielded a bottom line. Given the implementation of Kemp-Roth and the alignment of real money demand and supply, growth would be 1.1 percent in 1981, inclusive of a recession, and thereafter 4.5 percent. Inflation would drop to 4.2 percent by 1983 and to 2.6 percent by 1986.[40]

The forecast got squelched. As January turned to February 1981, an increasing number of Reagan's official policymakers did not see things Rutledge's way. "At a definitive dinner meeting dubbed the 'last supper,'" Bartley recalled in his memoir, "participants came armed with numbers . . . showing 'hellacious' deficits" based on the forecast fed through the Claremont computers. Rutledge was an economist, not a budget wonk, and what he had shown was the end of stagflation. Because bracket creep was the secret to the buoyancy of federal revenues, however, the collapse of inflation in Rutledge's model overwhelmed the effect of the growth resurgence when it came to the government's receipts. The flood of cash that had been coming the government's way in the Great Inflation years would be dammed. If spending were not held to the target level (a healthy one, 19 percent of GDP), there would be "hellacious" deficits.[41]

Given the theoretical perspective of "supply-side thermodynamics"—Rutledge's term for his model—deficits in a low-inflation, high-growth world were not catastrophic. For one thing, such deficits would not be inflationary, because the collapse of inflation was the premise of their existence. As for "crowding out," this too would evaporate. There was about to be a multitrillion-dollar asset shift into things like bonds, according to Rutledge's main insight. A "hellacious" deficit in the $100–$200 billion range would only bump aside a small percentage of the *new* money available in capital markets. "Deficits and savings rates would be rounding errors in the biggest portfolio event of the century," Rutledge believed. Whereas Mundell had originally held that tight money would be what brought in new capital flows, Rutledge was saying that tax cuts, by increasing the rate of investment return, would also bring in new flows—from old cars and washing machines.[42]

It must have sounded too free-lunchy, because the big guns in the fore-casting group criticized the scenario's irresponsibility. Even though Rutledge had been wowing the likes of Reg Jones over the past few years, at the last supper he felt like a greenhorn being put in his place by his intellectual and political superiors. "Hey, I'm thirty years old, and I thought these guys had discovered I was a genius and they were going to hand me the keys to the gov-ernment," Rutledge later told Bartley. The basic problem for Rutledge's sce-nario was that the other members of the forecasting group, which had become even larger by February, had their own pet concerns. The Treasury supply-siders wanted immediate growth, and Rutledge had offered a recession first. Stockman, as the public face of the government's fiscal accounts, wanted a small deficit if not a surplus. But Rutledge could not be made to believe, given the asset-shift avalanche he expected, that the deficit could possibly be a significant economic issue. Moreover, the deficit would be a function of the collapse of inflation, a prospect which by 1981 had to be regarded as an unqualified good.[43]

Those with the most impressive intellectual credentials among the fore-casters—monetarists Greenspan, Meltzer, and Karl Brunner—made the definitive objection. They were not prepared to say that inflation was going to vanish forthwith, certainly not to 4.2 percent in 1983 and 2.6 percent in 1986. After the long 1970s, the monetarists were not going to declare inflation over until it was over. The Great Inflation years had become too entrenched, and had befuddled and embarrassed too many top economists, for the monetarists to get on board with what seemed to be a blithe prediction of the immediate drawing and quartering of inflation. Moreover, the outside world of economic forecasters (if not the bond market) had to be persuaded. Outsiders had to find the Reagan numbers believable for the forecast to have credibility. Stockman would describe all of this colorfully in his memoir:

> "Nobody [CEA chair Weidenbaum said] is going to predict a two per-cent inflation on *my* watch. We'll be the laughingstock of the world...."
>
> Thus began a one-week march toward "realism." I pushed the group toward Weidenbaum's position.... My reason ... had to with the schedule. I needed a consensus, and I needed it fast....
>
> We now went into a white heat of pressure. The forecasting ses-sions ... degenerated into sheer numbers manipulation. The supply-siders yielded a tenth of a percentage point toward lower real growth;

the monetarists yielded a tenth of a percentage point toward higher money GNP. . . . Round after round it went. . . .

Passing the tin cup around [in this way] did not a yield high enough inflation number to satisfy Weidenbaum. So . . . we [Stockman and Weidenbaum] made . . . [a] bargain. If he'd agree to keep the real growth rate "reasonably high," I would go along with whatever inflation figure he thought he could live with as a professional economist.

Finally, before the whole group, "Weidenbum unfurled his scenario," Stockman continued. "Someone finally taunted the professor. 'What model did this come out of, Murray?'" Weidenbaum replied, "'It came right out of here.' With that he slapped his belly with both hands. 'My visceral computer.'"[44]

The Weidenbaum/Stockman scenario was now set to accompany Reagan's announcement of his economic plan, slated for February 18, 1981, four weeks after the inauguration. Given Kemp-Roth and stable, limited monetary growth, real economic growth would be 1.1 percent in 1981 and 4.3 percent per year through 1986. Inflation was to be 7 percent in 1983 and fall to 4.9 percent in 1986.[45]

The Claremont-routed forecast had put the long-term growth rate at 4.5 percent, as opposed to 4.3 percent for the administration. The difference of 0.2 percent was not significant. On inflation, however, the forecasts sharply differed, with the administration forecasting a 1983 inflation rate two-thirds higher than Rutledge's forecast, and 1986 inflation 88 percent higher. "Nobody," as Weidenbaum had said, "is going to predict a two percent inflation on *my* watch." The whole thing was a rude awakening for Rutledge, who soon fled back to California. There he would enjoy a stupendous career as the prophet of the bull market that lasted for two decades.[46]

Rutledge did revolutionary work in showing that tax cuts themselves were nearly sufficient to solve stagflation. Such cuts would initiate a rush into financial assets that would itself presage a tremendous increase in real supply, the "stuff" meant to be yielded in the future by investments in financial assets. The new stuff would represent both an increase in growth and wealth and a decrease in inflation, because the ratio of money to new stuff would necessarily be in decline.

Rutledge's pure supply-side thinking was at the cutting edge. In his original 1960s papers elaborating the open-economy macromodel, Mundell could not identify strong reasons to prefer tax cuts to increased government spending. In time, such as in the Princeton paper of 1971, Mundell would clarify his position that tax cuts can do things like "increase the demand for real money balances." And then, in his 1974 AEI paper, Mundell outlined a kind of portfolio theory whereby the price of gold and oil fall given permanent fiscal incentives on the marginal tax side. Perhaps Mundell had been something of a Keynesian in the 1960s, when in his model responsibility for stimulating the economy and employment lay with tax cuts, while investments became attractive on account of the tightening of money. After the experiences of the stagflation period, it had become clear that tax cuts, especially marginal tax cuts, could influence investment massively. By 1981, given a fifteen-year process by which money had been siphoned out of the financing instruments of the real economy in favor of inflation hedges, tax cuts stood to create a capital-flow shift of historic proportions. Asset allocation, not the interest rate or aggregate demand, was set to become the driving force of the economic future.[47]

As Rutledge prepared to slink back to California, the Stockman-Weidenbaum forecast accompanied the formal announcement of Reagan's economic plan. Reagan called for the 10–10–10 marginal income-tax cuts, liberalized depreciation, an abridgment of regulation, budget restraint (outside of defense), and consistent monetary policy. The tax cuts would reduce revenues by $162 billion by 1986. The difference would have to be made up by spending cuts, growth, the savings pool, and reflows. Soon the Washington press referred to the forecast by a pet name: "Rosy Scenario."[48]

On to ERTA

Paul Craig Roberts did not fancy "Rosy Scenario." He wondered why nobody had thought to dub the forecast "Blue Sue." The growth numbers of the Reagan forecast, after all, were skimpy compared to those proffered by the Ford and Carter administrations for the out years in their forecasts of the 1970s. Ford had been so bold in 1976 as to see three straight years of 6 percent growth in the near future; Carter, in 1979, had predicted four straight years of 4.7 percent growth. Reagan was offering 4.3 percent growth for the long term—and that following a slow start. What was more, real growth had actually averaged 5 percent from 1976 to 1978. Rosy Scenario was not even willing to commit itself to the growth standard set by the best years of the 1970s. Yet in the press, Roberts noted, "the hyperbole flew fast and loose." The *Washington Post*, leading the way, "charged that Reagan's 'scenario lies far beyond the limits of any past experience in this country or any industrial democracy.'" Roberts chuckled at this line. He knew that the administration had omitted a chart comparing its forecast to the actual performance of the American economy in the past five years, because the comparison was unfavorable.[49]

Roberts knew, of course, that the Reagan forecast had been the product of many cooks. He had taken part in the logrolling, the tin-cup passing, that had traded growth for inflation. Rosy Scenario was not particularly roseate toward either. It was the stuff of compromise. Stockman tangled this up a bit in his memoir, *The Triumph of Politics*. After recounting the story of Weidenbaum's belly slap, Stockman wrote that "the underlying architecture" of the administration forecast "was ultimately the work of a small band of ideologues. . . . Roberts, . . . Ture, and . . . Entin were in on every play. Throughout the whole process, . . . Wanniski, . . . Laffer, . . . Kemp, and . . . Lehrman were close at hand, in constant communication with their allies in the forecasting group. . . . Fittingly, then, it was the revolutionaries, myself included, who made the forecast on which their supply-side revolution was launched. Nobody else can be blamed."[50]

Not quite. Rosy Scenario was a move away from supply-side purity, as defined by Rutledge and as defended by the Treasury subcabinet. It was not a supply-side forecast in that it did not foresee the collapse of inflation given Kemp-Roth. And as a White House memo from the time put it, the "baseline scenario assumptions [were] prepared with Alan Greenspan involved for support from outside; objective is to have consistent supportable numbers for OMB, Treasury, Greenspan, and Weidenbaum." The memo ended: "Treasury Department staff and Secretary Regan have not signed off on this scenario."[51]

As for Stockman's "myself included," it was soon to become clear that Stockman was far more concerned about the budget than about the economic effects of tax cuts. As his deputy, Annelise Anderson, later recalled, initially Stockman had warmed to the idea of a collapse of inflation by virtue of Kemp-Roth. In this he was joined by Greenspan. The reason, for both Stockman and Greenspan, was budgetary. They wanted to see decreased federal outlays for massive items such as Social Security, which had built-in COLAs. Soon enough, however, they realized that the gains to government from bracket creep, in a high-inflation environment, dwarfed any COLA savings that would accrue in a low-inflation environment. In general, several points lower of inflation meant more revenue lost than a point of growth meant revenue gained.[52]

Therefore, Stockman did not want to solve the bracket-creep problem too quickly. But that was the goal of supply-side economics, and certainly of

Kemp-Roth. It was a future that Rutledge also had envisioned, but the last supper had sacrificed his ideas.[53]

After the Reagan economic agenda was put forth, the overriding objection concerned inflation. House Majority Leader Jim Wright warned that Kemp-Roth was "certain to be inflationary." He explained that deficits were innocuous if not helpful to the economy. He wanted to save deficits in the name of inflation hawkishness.

It was pretty convoluted stuff, reminiscent of the Keynesian straw men Roberts had been pleased to "mow down" in the '70s. In Wright's words: "In relation to the size of our economy [the national debt] is at its lowest point in modern times—lower even than it was in 1933. . . . In 1950, the national debt was 90 percent the size of our GNP; in 1960, it was 57 percent; today it is 31 percent." Wright cited Walter Heller, who "estimated that a $25 billion reduction in the deficit just might bring about a reduction of one-half of one percent in the inflation rate." Wright's advice was to stall the Reagan program and to maintain the status quo. Since 1961, he wrote, "more than three times as many young people are enrolled in colleges. . . . Our health is better. We are living longer; life expectancy has increased. . . . Our government must have been doing something right!"[54]

Opponents to Reagan's plan, that is to say, knew that they were opposed but were not sure why. They introduced a string of conundrums. If deficits were inflationary, they would resolve themselves, because bracket creep bred government revenues. If they were not inflationary, it would be a free lunch. If growth occurred, there must be a trade-off, such as inflation, but that led back to revenues, canceling deficits. Then again, deficits had superintended the blessed run of the New Deal–cum–Great Society stabilization since 1933. James Tobin argued that Reagan's policy was akin to two trains pulling in opposite directions. The JEC echoed Tobin, proving the consensus of 1979–80 short-lived: "The Administration's fiscal and monetary policies are working at cross purposes." And Walter Heller: "Relying on huge supply-side responses to Kemp-Roth tax cuts would be tantamount to bolting the door against inflation with a boiled carrot."[55]

As the opposition tried to settle on arguments and strategy, the administration showed that it too was not fully confident in its program. Along with scuttling Rutledge's forecast, the administration did four more things that indicated vacillation. It moved the effective date of the personal rate cuts from January 1 to July 1. It nixed eliminating the distinction between wage and investment income for high earners, a move that would have brought the top rate down from 70 percent to 50 percent right away. It tabled indexing. And it rejected the introductory essay outlining supply-side arguments that it had commissioned for the economic plan. The essay was written by George Gilder, an author who had just written a defense of capitalism from a supply-side perspective, a best-selling book called *Wealth and Poverty*.[56]

The period from February 18 until the end of March, ordinarily the time of the presidential honeymoon, were six lost weeks. The administration was not fully convincing in its advocacy of its own program and opponents were unsure what tack to take. Weidenbaum, however, and perhaps contrary to Stockman's and Treasury's expectations, proved a fighter for supply-side ideas. As he told Congress on his first appearance there as CEA chair, "We have developed . . . tax measures . . . to provide . . . the opportunity and incentive for people to increase their saving and work effort and for businesses to invest in new and productive technologies." Still, things moved slowly.[57]

Then, on March 30, 1981, a gunman shot Reagan outside the Washington Hilton hotel. Reagan recovered and did so swimmingly. Undoubtedly, the sympathy and political capital that Reagan gained from the assassination attempt helped to get his plan through Congress that spring and summer.[58]

The groundwork had been laid a few weeks earlier. On March 10, Democrats in Congress, led by Representative William Brodhead of Michigan, proposed an end to the distinction between wage and investment income— "earned and unearned income," as it was called. Effectively, this meant not only a drop in the top marginal rate from 70 percent to 50 percent, but also a reduction in the capital-gains rate from 28 percent to 20 percent. Brodhead was the point person in a Democratic consensus that had emerged since the White House had backed out of getting rid of the distinction. He was a member of the Ways and Means Committee, and its chairman, Daniel Rostenkowski, had convened hearings the previous week in which economists—including Joseph Pechman of the Brookings Institution—called for the measure to be taken. To the Ways and Means Democrats, the appeal of the tax cut derived from its growth, fairness, and revenue effects. Brodhead envisioned a "rechanneling of funds away from tax shelters toward economically sound investments." He insisted that "I am not a supply-sider," but "we have to reduce taxes on wealthy people to have more investment."[59]

The year before, in the Republican primary campaign, Bush had distinguished himself from Reagan by arguing for business- as opposed to personal-tax cuts. Bush was in favor of depreciation reform and investment credits and against reductions in income rates. Now Brodhead was holding that personal rate cuts were crucial to the recovery of investment. He even had support from liberal committee members such as Thomas Downey and James Jones. Perhaps this roster of Democrats favored the proposal because they figured it could be a substitute for the more comprehensive Reagan plan. If that was the idea, it became moot when Kemp signed on as a cosponsor of the "Brodhead amendment."[60]

In the spring months there arose a contest between competing budget and tax resolutions. On the budget side, the administration favored "Gramm-Latta," which dinged a number of domestic discretionary programs. On the tax side, the administration liked "Conable-Hance," which was soon referred to as the "bipartisan tax bill," a rhetorical boon to the administration. Rostenkowski, who had outdone the putatively supply-side administration in his preparation of the Brodhead amendment, bowed to liberal members such as Speaker Thomas P. "Tip" O'Neill and concocted an alternative tax bill. He would build a "Christmas tree" (Stockman's term) of tax breaks, for rich and poor, that would swing support away from the bipartisan bill.[61]

Gramm-Latta and the bipartisan bill had the backing of an important conservative Democratic constituency in Congress. Euphemistically, this group of southerners was known as the "Boll Weevils." The name the members preferred was the "Redneck Caucus." The Rednecks pushed a version of Gramm-Latta through to passage in June. They also told the administration that they would go along with tax cuts, but not up to the full level of Kemp-Roth. They wanted the first year of the tax cut halved, to 5 percent, and it was to become effective not on July 1 but on October 1. The Rednecks piled on tree ornaments of their own, and in doing so encouraged other members to do the same. The White House conceded to it all. Martin Anderson denied accusations that the president was weak, saying that Reagan may have overstated his goals at the outset in order to compromise back to his true position.[62]

The liberal faction in the House countered with not a three- but a four-year tax cut, the latter two years contingent on budget cutting. Gramm-Latta suggested significant budget cuts in 1983–84 but did not specify them—a "magic asterisk," wrote Stockman. Bartley's page at the *Journal* was exasperated by the obsession with out years, first with Rosy Scenario and now with the budget. "If you think any of these estimates can tell you what the deficit will be in 1984, lie down until you get over it."[63]

The administration reiterated its position on what tax cuts would do to federal revenues. A Treasury Department fact sheet in June made it plain: the tax cut would result in $152 billion less in federal revenues in 1984. This was consistent with the forecast the campaign had offered in September and that Reagan had announced on February 18. Revenue losses due to tax cuts would be great, but they were four-fifths of what the static estimates thought. As for spending, said Treasury, "the 3-year tax cut is needed to put pressure on Congress to continue to hold the line on spending." And finally, the "3-year tax cut is needed to offset the massive tax increases facing working Americans." Treasury meant the scheduled increases in Social Security taxes, along with bracket creep.[64]

Bracket creep ended up settling the debate. Donald Regan learned that there was support in the House, and particularly the Senate, for attaching an indexing provision to the bipartisan bill. The provision would prohibit income taxes from increasing with inflation after the period of 5–10–10. Here was an answer to the liberal House Democrats' four-year bill. In July, the Senate passed a version of the bipartisan bill with indexing attached, and the House followed suit. The president played a key role. On July 27, he made a televised address in which he sat in front of a big chart showing what would happen to tax rates if indexing were passed and what would happen if it were not. The first line was nice and flat, the second, representing no indexing, shot up like a rocket after 1983. After the address, there was no chance that Congress would dither on passing the bill.[65]

Steve Entin danced that night around his living room. He had designed the chart earlier in the week. He had prepared it for his boss, Regan, to use in reeling in the final congressional votes. The chart had made its way from his deputy assistant's office at Treasury to the White House, on the off chance that it might be of use to someone there. Asking around the West Wing earlier that day, Entin had been told thanks very much for the chart, and do be sure to watch the president on television tonight. The picture of Reagan with Entin's chart is one of the most famous photographs of the Reagan presidency.[66]

It was a nice moment for Entin. Another University of Chicago product, and an understudy of Ture's, he had devoted most of his energies as Roberts's deputy at Treasury to the business side of the tax cut. This too had been subject to shrinking and expansion in the strange congressional doings of that spring and summer. Wanniski had actually been telling him not to bother with business cuts. Wanniski (and Laffer) saw the personal rate cuts as the all-important ones. Since all income must at some point emerge as take-home pay, the most broadly relevant tax cuts are on the personal side. It is a debate that has remained active within supply-side economics to this day. Wanniski was dismissive of the "accelerated cost recovery system" (ACRS) and other "Entinisms" (Wanniski's term for depreciation reforms) of the tax bill, worried that they might make the personal rate cuts tradable. Back in March, Senator Roth had even written the president to say that he would vote against any tax cut backed by the White House that substituted business provisions for the personal rate cuts. In making that chart, Entin contributed to the cause of arresting the skyward march of personal income-tax rates. Today, indexing is the only code provision of the Economic Recovery and Tax Act still on the books.[67]

Such it was called, ERTA for short. It was not exactly Kemp-Roth—for it was both a little less and a good deal more. Instead of 10–10–10 marginal income rate cuts in 1981, 1982, and 1983, it was 5–10–10. This meant that the overall reduction in each bracket at the end would be 23 percent instead of 27 percent. The first cuts were not retroactive to the first of the year, as originally planned, but were instead set for October 1, the first day of fiscal 1982. The next cuts would come on July 1 of 1982 and 1983. The Christmas tree ornaments included exceptions for the Redneck districts, such as tax breaks for oil wildcatters. Balancing these concessions were an intact ACRS, the Brodhead amendment (effective January 1, 1982), and indexing beginning in 1985. One of Reagan's own CEA members would later say, "[ERTA] was better tax legislation than the president had requested."[68]

Reagan gleefully signed the bill on August 13 at his ranch in California. There was talk of a market rally. After all, the second plank of the policy mix—tax cuts—was now in place. As for the first plank, Volcker had been "so damned close," in Wanniski's words, twenty-two months earlier. How was the Fed doing now? It was a question that would torment the supply-siders for the next two years.

10

"Now, Money"

The experiment with flexible exchange rates in the 1970s started off as a disaster, from the standpoint of economic stability, but nevertheless, it set in motion a learning mechanism that would not have taken place in its absence. The lesson was that inflation, budget deficits, big debts and big government are all detrimental to public well-being and that the cost of correcting them is so high that no democratic government wants to repeat the experience.

—ROBERT MUNDELL, "A Reconsideration of the Twentieth Century"

In a sense, that is exactly what we are talking about: restoring the conditions whereby Americans from all walks of life can make whatever great success they want to make. For those conditions to exist we need a stable currency which encourages the willingness to save, to risk, to invest for the long run.

—LEWIS E. LEHRMAN, "The Case for the Gold Standard," May 1981

The day ERTA passed both houses of Congress, August 4, 1981, Jude Wanniski sent a five-page essay to Martin Anderson at the White House. "Congratulations on the splendid tax bill," Wanniski wrote in a note stapled to the essay. As for what the administration should focus on next, Wanniski's view was clear enough. "Now, Money" was the title of his paper. It began:

"On the eve of his numbing defeat on the tax bill, . . . Tip O'Neill allowed that President Reagan was a 'supersalesman.' . . . : 'He puts one ball in the air at the time, and he keeps at it. . . .' Three balls by Reagan. Three home runs. First the budget resolution, then the reconciliation bill, then the tax cut. Next, O'Neill figured, the White House would concentrate its firepower on regulation." Wanniski disagreed: "No, Tip. Now comes money."[1]

Wanniski's note asked Anderson to "please find time to read this. [It is] very important that you understand our supply-side monetary arguments." The essay touched on those arguments and made plain a goal. "The aim of the supply-siders," Wanniski asserted, "is nothing less than a commitment from the Reagan administration—and the Federal Reserve—to a path leading toward dollar convertibility. Supply-side resources are now freed to shift to currency reform, the restoration of a gold standard. The objective is to win this commitment by the end of 1981."[2]

Even before the *Village Voice* interview of April 1980, Wanniski had developed a reputation among supply-siders for making claims that stretched credulity. Wanniski's views in "Now, Money" represented the position of some supply-siders, but not all. By fall 1981, there had emerged three distinct supply-side assessments of how well the Federal Reserve was conducting monetary policy under Volcker. Wanniski's view (and more or less Mundell's and Lehrman's) was that the Fed was dithering before committing again to fixed exchange rates, if not to gold. The second view, represented by the Treasury supply-siders, was that if the Fed was pursuing a monetarist policy, it could do a better job of it. And the third view, Laffer's, was that Volcker's Fed was doing things just about right.

"Now, Money" was certainly correct in implying that supply-siders would now become greatly concerned about the theory and practice of monetary policy, and for good reason. The twelve months following the passage of ERTA would be the worst for the American economy since the Great Depression. Natural and urgent questions arose: Was monetary policy to blame? Was tax policy? Given that the supply-siders had largely gotten their tax policy made into law over the summer, monetary policy became the prime suspect. One thing was clear: 1981–82 was shaping up to be a universe away from the "no economic costs" that Mundell had predicted as the bill for his policy mix.

However brutal the dozen years of stagflation had been prior to 1981, they could not match the economic experience of late 1981 and early 1982. Real GDP rose by 2.5 percent in 1981, a decent number that was buoyed by the early quarters. In 1982, GDP fell by 1.9 percent, the worst yearly per-formance since 1946. In the last quarter of 1981 and the first of 1982, GDP dropped at a 6 percent rate, an astonishing number that easily made for the most abysmal decline since the recession of 1957–58. The six-month 1957–58 decline (of 8 percent), however, had followed a decade of good growth. The 1981–82 recession had no such wind at its back. It came on the heels of stagfla-tion and the 1980 recession.

At least inflation calmed. The consumer price index rose 3.4 percent (annualized) in the last quarter of 1981, a remarkable achievement. (The full-year 1981 figure was still 10.3 percent.) In 1982, prices in the first quarter rose at an annual rate of only 2.1 percent before yielding to a full-year rate of 6.2 percent. Thus did 1982 end a three-year run of double-digit inflation. But then there was more bad news: the Phillips curve revived. Unemployment soared to 9.7 percent in 1982, easily clearing all levels since the Depression. The misery index, at 21 in 1980 thanks to inflation at 14 and unemployment at 7, was 16 in 1982. Eight points of inflation had been traded for three of unemployment.

And what unemployment it was. Those without jobs were not "seasonal" or teenage workers. No, this is when the "Rust Belt" earned its name. Steel-workers had it the worst. Massive steel operations, including in the Lacka-wanna region that anchored Kemp's congressional district, reported layoffs mounting into the tens of thousands. And thanks to the oddities of the 1970s, layoffs in steel in the early 1980s often meant immediate poverty. Because of the guaranteed COLA-plus of the expansive union contracts of the 1970s, there had been little inducement for a worker to save money. To save money, after all, was to watch it evaporate against inflation. One spent the money one had and counted on the COLA-plus for one's future dollars. A layoff was a worst-case scenario.[3]

In 1982, eleven million members of the national workforce were out of a job. This was a number that historical experience suggested was a harbinger of revolution, or at least major political reform. The stories of the unemployed were heartbreaking. Middle-aged men in steel towns, men who had been mak-ing the Cadillac of wages in the 1970s, found themselves hanging around their parents' houses accepting tens and twenties slipped wordlessly into pockets. Women and African-American steelworkers were the first to get pink slips because of their lack of power in the union. "Government cheese" became a staple in the national parlance. Churches in mill towns from Lackawanna to

Homestead became the soup kitchens of last resort. And then, as in *The Grapes of Wrath*, people started hitting the road. Who knew where it was all going to lead, but in the Rust Belt the future seemed entirely hopeless.[4]

From "Dunkirk" into the *Atlantic*

The "economic Dunkirk" of which David Stockman and Jack Kemp had warned the year before was not exactly what was coming to pass in late 1981 and early 1982. But it was close. Stockman's "Dunkirk" paper spoke of an impending crisis in the financial markets, as opposed to the economy in general, and the financial markets were not doing well, even in the wake of ERTA. The talk of a "Reagan rally" that had surfaced in the summer of 1980 was confounded by a bond market in which interest on the highest-rated issues (triple A's) crossed 15 percent for the first time, the Dow sunk below 800 (a level first hit in 1964), and the prime rate shot up again to 21 percent. Yet the carnage in the financial markets, however severe, could not be the main economic concern. The recession was shattering lives and threatened to be the worst since the Great Depression.[5]

What was the cause? Attention focused on the Federal Reserve's chief "money stock" statistic, M1. For seven months, from March to November, the statistic was flat, at about $425 billion. Not for decades had the money stock been static for so long. In the 1970s, M1 was always making quantum leaps upward. And in the twelve months prior to April 1981, M1 had increased by 10 percent, matching the 10 percent inflation of the period. Monetarism had long taught that there must be a stable and predictable growth in the money supply. Friedman's target was an automatic 5 percent per year, an amount that would accommodate nice growth. Curiously, the 0 percent M1 growth of March–November 1981 was accompanied by interest rates that were heading upward. The inflation premium that had presumably pushed interest rates up to 22 percent the year before was now gone. Yet rates didn't drop.[6]

Days after the passage of ERTA, Stockman's OMB offered its view that rates were staying high for one reason only: the budget deficit. Though the Fed was in fact not creating more money, said Stockman, the markets worried that if deficits persisted, the Fed would call off its tightness in order to prevent crowding out. The markets were screaming to the administration to do one last thing, said OMB: close the budget gap.[7]

In response, the administration launched a "September offensive." Reagan was always enthusiastic about spending cuts, but with the September offensive he began to concede that the budget deficit itself was the primary obstacle to economic recovery. "All of us know that interest rates will only come down and stay down when government is no longer borrowing huge amounts of money to cover its deficits," Reagan said in a television address. Along with a list of new spending cuts (including $13 billion for defense), Reagan even slyly plugged for tax increases: "I will soon urge Congress to enact new proposals to eliminate abuses and obsolete incentives in the tax code." Now there *really* was going to be a battle for Reagan's soul. This was not the supply-side doctrine taught by Mundell, Rutledge, or Kemp, all of whom believed that deficits were not inflationary and that they did not produce crowding out, once tax cuts and a tight-money policy had been implemented. If Reagan was to aim at reducing the budget deficit, he would not be making supply-side arguments.[8]

On September 30, fiscal 1981's deficit came in at $79 billion, exceeding Carter's worst. The first phase of the tax cut started the next day: a 5 percent reduction across all brackets. It was a sliver of a cut and would have little impact on the economy's momentum, or lack thereof. Acrimony beset the administration. The Treasury faction perceived that in emphasizing the importance of the budget deficit Stockman somehow had gotten the president's ear. For his part, Stockman tried to prevent Treasury from lobbying Congress against tax increases. The recession deepened and became associated with "Reaganomics." A disenchanted Paul Craig Roberts wrote of the squabbles in *Fortune*. To Roberts, "Stockman seemed to decide that his success indicator was the budget deficit, not the tax cut or the inflation rate"—or even the real economy. "This would be a natural, self-protective development," Roberts continued, "because a budget director cannot take credit for tax and monetary policies." The supply-siders seemed to have lost the OMB director.[9]

It was true. Stockman foresaw an immense 1982 deficit and was not sure how it would be financed. The "Dunkirk" scenario began to look realistic. The bond markets had fully lost their appetite for debt, Stockman said, because the stuff kept losing value once bought. Government debt had become a wasting asset against inflation. Three years of double-digit increases had become too much to bear. "A $1000, 30-year T[reasury]-bond issued in February 1977 is worth $551 today. One issued in February 1980 is worth $802," Stockman wrote. How could the government possibly expect new 1982 debt (which would come in at $128 billion) to be absorbed by buyers already so burned?[10]

Superficially, it looked like a tremendous crisis. Yet the reason for the deficit, as Stockman must have understood, was precisely that this damaging inflation was already being defeated. The reason for the budget deficit in 1982 was that the Fed's flattening of M1 was killing inflation, and with it bracket creep. No bracket creep meant no federal revenue growth. No revenue growth meant deficits, in that spending continued to gallop. In fact, the scandal of the deficits of the 1970s and 1980–81 was that they existed *at all* in the face of enormous bracket creep.[11]

The Reagan deficits were different. With inflation getting close to nil in 1981–82, the revenue gusher that was bracket creep was sputtering to an end. As an October 1981 Treasury brief put it, "This is not a deficit crisis. This is a situation of too little inflation creating a deficit."[12]

As budget director, Stockman was understandably ambivalent about killing off bracket creep. At the very least, he wanted to balance the loss of revenues caused by the end of bracket creep with equivalent spending cuts. Yet he did not realize (or did not acknowledge that he realized) that in noninflationary environments, deficits are easily financed and economically benign, obviating the need for panic cuts in spending.

Stockman's convolution on all this soon came to a head. Touching off the most melodramatic sequence of the first Reagan term, William Greider wrote up his long, strange experiences he had been having with Stockman, in an extended piece for the *Atlantic*. The article, called "The Education of David Stockman," appeared in November and was accompanied with photographs by Annie Leibovitz. Without the administration's knowledge, Stockman had been leaking to Greider, a *Washington Post* reporter, at breakfast meetings continually throughout 1981.[13]

Greider's article, one of the most significant exposés ever written of an administration in power, has been cited an inordinate number of times in histories of the Reagan presidency. Typically, it is badly misread. The article concerned Stockman's frustration over cutting spending and getting legislation through the Washington mill without having to grease palms. Over twenty-seven pages, Greider described how Stockman had become exasperated with the budget process. Everyone had his hand out. Even simple acts like Kemp-Roth had to be larded with Christmas tree ornaments to be passed.[14]

But "The Education of David Stockman" owes its fame not to lines concerning spending and pork but rather to a couple of rather unrepresentative Stockman quotations regarding the Reagan tax cuts. "The hard part of the supply-side tax cut is dropping the top rate from 70 to 50 percent," Stockman explained to Greider. "In order to make this palatable as a political matter, you had to bring down all the brackets. But, I mean, Kemp-Roth was always a

Trojan horse to bring down the top rate." And: "It's kind of hard to sell 'trickle down,' . . . so the supply-side formula was the only way to get tax policy that was really 'trickle down.' Supply-side is 'trickle-down' theory."[15]

These lines were, of course, incorrect and misleading.

The Trojan horse idea is nowhere in the public record outside the *Atlantic* article; nor can it be found in the internal documentation of the advocates of Kemp-Roth. Reagan's Task Force on Tax Policy, for example, wrote in November 1980: "Priority: if supported, second order" on cutting the top rate from 70 percent to 50 percent. The highest priority was placed on such items as tax breaks for small stockholders. When the administration plan came out on February 18, 1981, it officially nixed the drop from 70 to 50, to the consternation of supply-siders. The provision was reintroduced by Ways and Means *Democrats* a few weeks later, in the form of the Brodhead amendment, on the advice of a battery of academic and professional economists, including the director of economic studies at the Brookings Institution. And Brodhead provided that this tax cut not be phased in like the others in Kemp-Roth, but done all at once. The administration had thought it would be difficult as a political matter to press for the 70-to-50 rate cut, and it was proven wrong. The cut had broad bipartisan support.[16]

In March 1981, when the administration was failing to garner significant support for its tax plan, a plan that would not emerge in legislation until that summer, the 70-to-50 amendment was the only sure thing. Stockman got it backwards. Bringing the top rate from 70 percent to 50 percent was the Trojan horse that enabled the general 5–10–10 bracket reduction. The Brodhead amendment was the bird in hand. In the wake of the *Atlantic* episode, Steve Entin reminded Donald Regan that the previous year, as ERTA was headed for passage, Democrats had bolstered their support for the Brodhead amendment in order to deter the general three-year rate cut. Brodhead had been not the secret content of a Trojan horse, but the central subject of both the tax debate and the tax compromises of spring and summer 1981.[17]

As for "trickle down," it had not been "hard to sell" at all. Capital-formation hysteria had been stock stuff since Kemp's introduction of the Savings and Investment Act in 1974. As the *Wall Street Journal* had reported in 1978, Carter's economic advisors "were left choking in the dust" while the nation rallied behind the Steiger amendment, which was manifestly a boon to the rich, as well as some small investors. The Brodhead proceedings, for their part, were marked by the same populist rhetoric that had always accompanied

Kemp-Roth. The average guy could not shelter income from bracket creep, but the rich could. Fairness, therefore, required that the rich be goaded out of shelters by means of reducing their rates on investment income. Trickle-down theory was a hot populist item.

President Reagan and Chief of Staff James Baker got steaming mad at Stockman over the Trojan horse accusation. Stockman offered an apology. A group of senior administration officials sent a mock memento to Stockman congratulating him on becoming a media darling. But Stockman did not lose his job. Indeed, he kept it for three-and-a-half more years, into the first months of Reagan's second term. Evans and Novak were surely onto something when they wrote, days after the *Atlantic* piece appeared, that Regan and other officials must have "preferred a deflated Stockman at the Office of Management and Budget to a powerful successor."[18]

With the post-*Atlantic* Stockman parked at OMB, Regan's Treasury was now in a powerful position to keep the administration holding the line on tax cuts. Other departments and agencies—and congressional fiefdoms—would also find the OMB director less effective as he tried to reduce spending and preferences. For however wobbly Stockman may have gone on tax cuts (from a supply-side perspective), he certainly remained a hawk on pork. Bill Simon was denied the post of treasury secretary the year before probably for just this reason: Capitol Hill (let alone K Street) cannot stand powerful figures who are intransigent with regard to pork. They must either be expectorated or emasculated. Stockman suffered the latter fate.

Facing 1982

As the recession hit new nadirs at the end of 1981, the administration was transfixed by the *Atlantic* controversy, a controversy nobody could even define. The administration was devolving into a shambles at a most inopportune time. Charges of "Reaganomics" and "the year of the quack" economic theory flew. The latter came from William Nordhaus, the Carter CEA member last heard predicting a falling sky from the Steiger amendment. John Rutledge was amused by the spectacle. He thought he knew what was about to happen, and he provided his thoughts in a piece that appeared on Bartley's page in December. It was called "Why Interest Rates Will Fall in 1982." The title did not capture the half of it. For the article strongly suggested that many things were going to go up, too—such as business investment, the stock market, employment, and entrepreneurial opportunity.[19]

Rutledge began by recalling a teenybopper horror movie in which Annette Funicello and her beau, Frankie Avalon, sit on the beach worrying about picnic ants while behind them an eight-hundred-pound sea monster emerges out of the foam. To Rutledge, the ants in the picture were the budget deficit, and the monster, asset shift. Rutledge said that the supply-siders themselves were wrong in insisting that the deficit would be provided for by "increases in household savings [that] will more than offset government borrowing needs." He also dismissed the "Wall Streeters" (and Keynesians) "who say . . . large government borrowing *must* push interest rates higher. . . ." "In my view," he continued, "the obsession of both Wall Streeters and supply-siders with analyzing credit *flows* has led both to forget who is the real star in the interest rate story."

That "real star" was not flows but the stock of assets, tangible and financial. Rutledge outlined the argument he had hammered out with Harvey Wilmeth. "The total stock of houses, cars, collectibles and other tangibles is worth about $7 trillion. That's more than twice the total value of the goods and services the U.S. economy will produce this year." This large number—$7 trillion—was a function of stagflation, Rutledge explained. Tangibles prove excellent hedges against inflation. When inflation soars and growth stalls, as in the long 1970s, portfolios shift from financials to tangibles.

Rutledge observed that as of late 1981, inflation had been cut in half or more. This would produce asset shift out of tangibles and into financials, such as the bonds that Wall Street was fretting could not get funded on account of crowding out. "[There] has opened a gap between paper [i.e., financial] and real asset yields that . . . looks like the Grand Canyon," he concluded. "As some households make the inevitable shift away from tangibles and back into higher-yielding paper, credit supplies will grow, and interest rates *must* fall." Rutledge predicted that "we'll see an increase in credit supplies of $400 billion to $500 billion for 1982, without counting on a nickel of increased savings. If the administration's tax cut stimulated private savings by a similar amount, the case for lower interest rates is stronger still. To my knowledge, no one has yet announced that the deficit will hit one-half trillion dollars for 1982. If it does not, interest rates *must* fall."

Rutledge's article gave the impression that Wall Street was arrayed against "Reaganomics," but this was certainly not the case. Tubby Burnham, CEO of Drexel Burnham Lambert, the iconic bond firm of the 1980s, was regularly buying full-page ads in the *Journal* urging support of the administration's original program. Goldman Sachs contended that the Reagan policy mix would work, especially on inflation, if everybody would just *think* it would. And Walter Wriston, the Citibank chair, was making his view known that (like Rutledge) he did not think interest rates were a function of domestic saving.[20]

Rutledge could not shake the idea, which had already struck some on Wall Street, that a tremendous bull market in stocks and bonds was about to occur. What was more, Rutledge perceived that it was going to be an *easy* bull market. There was going to be no secret to making money in the bonanza, no reason to fret over picking winners and losers. All an investor was going to have to do was buy and hold. The indexes were all going to go up tremendously.[21]

Nevertheless, the administration could not bring itself around to optimism. Save for inflation, the statistics—from GNP to the deficit to unemployment to interest rates—were horrendous. OMB and Treasury each predicted disaster should the other department's policies be followed. Then there was PEPAB, the Presidential Economic Policy Advisory Board. This was a panel of economic advisors drawn from the academic and financial worlds, experts and bankers of greater standing than the staff at OMB and Treasury, Regan excepted. Not only was PEPAB pessimistic. It was also rent with disagreement over how to diagnose—and solve—the problem at hand.[22]

Both Arthur Laffer and Milton Friedman were part of PEPAB in early 1982, and both argued at PEPAB meetings (which Reagan attended) that it was folly to give any ground whatsoever on tax cuts. Opposing Laffer and Friedman on PEPAB was a rump of deficit hawks. Laffer, for his part, dared to suggest that ERTA was causing the recession. He did not make the conventional argument that the tax cuts had led to crowding out or otherwise spooked the markets. To the contrary: Laffer held that the ERTA tax cuts were not coming quickly enough. Because ERTA phased in the cuts over three years, his argument went, earners were striving to defer realizations of income until all the cuts were in place. Laffer claimed to have detected all sorts of evidence that taxpayers were planning to start businesses, take on clients, and otherwise reel in revenue after 1983, not before.[23]

Laffer was onto something. Because they affected marginal income, the ERTA tax cuts produced sharp incentives *not* to produce until the cuts were fully implemented and the total amount of income that could be kept was at its peak. This would not be until 1984. In an odd way, Laffer argued, the phased-in nature of ERTA was responsible for both the image problem of Reaganomics and the awful recession.[24]

ERTA had one twist that muddied Laffer's argument. The top, 70-to-50 rate cut provided by the Brodhead amendment was fully in force as of January 1, 1982. This meant that if one could clear the top income threshold ($86,000 in 1982), all new income would be taxed at 50 percent through 1984 and beyond. There was no incentive, therefore, for high earners to defer income past January 1, 1982. Given that business owners often report income on the personal schedule, this point was of central importance to supply-side economics.

Yet this aspect of ERTA underwhelmed Laffer. He had been disappointed at PEPAB in early 1981 when the group learned how minimally the president's tax plan cut rates for top earners. Everyone had heard that Reagan was set to cut taxes on the rich, but Regan had sent letters to the members saying that this was not exactly true. ERTA, as outlined by Reagan in early 1981 and as passed into law that summer, gave no tax cut to the top earners for their top earnings. Wage (or salary) income in the top bracket was to be taxed for the duration of the law at 50 percent, the rate that prevailed when Reagan took office. What would be cut was the tax rate applied to the *investment* returns of top earners. This rate would be reduced from 70 percent to 50 percent. A law partner who cleared $500,000 in salary would get no more of a tax cut than the junior associate making $86,000. But the investment interest and dividends the partner made in addition to his salary would now be taxed at a lower rate.[25]

How Stockman missed this in his *Atlantic* wanderings is anyone's guess. Clearly, what ERTA did for the rich was to push them out of shelters and commodities and into investments in enterprises that yielded taxable returns. A Merrill Lynch memo predicted in early 1981 that "reducing [the] maximum federal tax rate on unearned income from 70 percent to 50 percent . . . would add nearly 200,000 new jobs [within eighteen months]." Some Trojan horse.[26]

Laffer was of course fine with the Brodhead amendment, but he was greatly displeased that the top "earned" income-tax rate had not been lowered. Laffer and others had thought that the actualization of Kemp-Roth under Reagan would cut the top earned rate, along with all the others, by 23 percent. In other words, Laffer had supposed that the final marginal rate for both wages and investment after ERTA would be 38 percent, with Brodhead negating the earned-unearned distinction and the top rate of 50 percent in turn reduced by 23 percent. Until 1986, Laffer remained unconvinced that Reagan had cut taxes for the rich in a substantial way because a complete across-the-board

cut had not been forthcoming, especially in light of the tax increases that followed ERTA. (When he once complained about this to Reagan, the president
responded by blowing up.)[27]

Friedman toed the Laffer line on taxes. He regarded suggestions to slow
down the tax cuts provided by ERTA as ludicrous, as he did suggestions
to introduce new taxes while keeping ERTA in place. Higher taxes would
"increase spending [and] mean higher inflation," Friedman stated. He even
referred to the Laffer curve: "No increase in tax rates can increase tax revenues. Cut[ting the] top rate to 25 percent will increase revenues." At the
very least, he pleaded, "don't stretch out [the] tax cut, Congress will spend.
Congress is under pressure."[28]

As for the recession, Friedman had an explanation: the Federal Reserve
was to blame. Friedman had been preaching for years the necessity of perfectly predictable money growth—the old 5 percent rule—and he was seeing
nothing of the sort from the Fed. In one chart, Friedman showed that the
range of money growth rates in 1981–82 was three times as great as the range
in 1978–80. The inconsistency of the Fed's policy was actually becoming
worse than it had been in the 1970s. He reasoned that the Fed was so unsure
about what was the correct anti-inflationary policy that when it adopted one,
such as in mid-1981, it was certain to overreact in the other direction when
it inevitably changed its mind. The markets, having no idea what to expect,
could only keep interest rates high. Friedman told PEPAB that "the market
is learning to live with the Fed's erratic performance, which offers hope [of
lower rates]. . . . Of course, a far better way to hasten this result would be for
the Fed to mend its ways. But that seems a forlorn hope."[29]

Laffer and Friedman were PEPAB's pessimists. Laffer urged that the
administration adopt a policy of "convertibility"—that is, gold-backed dollars, or at least gold-backed government debt. But neither his nor Friedman's
policy vision was likely to be put into practice. They were outmanned by
a group that consisted of Herb Stein, Arthur Burns, Alan Greenspan, and
Charles Walker (a former Treasury official). These advisors felt that the economy could not revive without lower deficits. No Fed policy, however tight,
they argued, could be credible if massive new deficits had to be monetized. If
tax hikes were needed to reduce the deficit, so be it.[30]

Greenspan admitted that he was bewildered by the economic conditions
of 1982. "Not seen this before—it must be interest rates. It is a budget question. Expect Fed to accommodate deficits and bring on inflation. High rates

are caused by deficits. . . . Do something on taxes," PEBAB's notes record him as saying. Stein made a curious argument. He said that ERTA had ushered in a new era in which there would have to be all sorts of ad hoc tax increases. Because ERTA solved bracket creep, Stein said, tax increases in the future would have to be statutory. If the government found itself falling short of revenue, it would have to call up a tax bill. During the 1970s, it is true, there were no statutory tax increases in the rate code—none. Bracket creep was sufficient to give the government tax increases without having to go through the bother of legislating them. Stein hailed the new honesty in government and said that a tax increase in 1982 would be perfectly within the spirit of ERTA. That spring, memos went to the president from PEPAB underscoring the Stein consensus. Friedman and Laffer began not to be invited to every meeting.[31]

OMB was also lobbying for tax increases, working the cabinet, the CEA, and the office of the chief of staff. The premise of the OMB argument, as voiced by Lawrence Kudlow, was that the nation had gotten triple the tax cut it had bargained for with ERTA. Not only had ERTA cut rates, but the deadening of inflation had slowed bracket creep. The policy mix had brought two tax cuts in one. Moreover, the drop in inflation was itself effectively a "tax cut" because it lowered consumer prices. Given the cascade of three "tax cuts" since August, it was only proper, given the deficit, to raise revenue.[32]

Treasury fought back, but it found itself outnumbered and outmaneuvered. Regan and others made the point that bracket creep was not yet dead, and coupled with Social Security tax increases, it would mean no real tax cut until 1983—let alone three of them by early 1982, as in OMB's unconventional reckoning. That argument fell on deaf ears, and Norman Ture could not get his own antitax testimony for Capitol Hill cleared by OMB. As for the CEA, smarting from the "Rosy Scenario" taunts, it was set on warding off Treasury input as it prepared a new round of "blue" forecasts.[33]

Inevitably, some supply-siders lost heart. Roberts quit his job (as assistant secretary of the treasury) shortly after New Year's 1982 and wrote a valedictory for *Fortune.* "The recession that began in the second half of 1981 is an unpleasant interlude that in the normal course of events might soon be forgotten by almost everybody except the economic record keepers," he wrote. "There is some danger, however, that it could become an event of historic importance because it is being hailed as the trial—and failure—of the economic doctrines called Reaganomics. This is a misreading of the grossest sort." Unfortunately, that "misreading" was poised to get a boost from Congress. A revenue bill that would raise taxes significantly was wending its way through both chambers. Tax-increase measures during severe recessions are exceedingly rare, unique as the Revenue Act of 1932. In the 1982 context, a tax increase would bespeak a governmental consensus that the deficit was causing high interest rates and the economic contraction.[34]

Early in 1982, lobbyists whispered that a tax increase was probably going to gain presidential approval, but that Reagan had stipulated that the key component of ERTA, the 5–10–10 tax-rate reduction schedule, was off limits. Reagan stood firm on indexing, too, an issue on which he clearly had the support of public opinion, which would soon include the *New York Times*. It was clear, therefore, that the bill would be a congeries of specific increases, punishing to whomever they happened to hit. The race was on to make sure it was the other guy.[35]

With K Street lobbyists making continual visits to Capitol Hill, it took until September for the bill to be signed into law. The final product was called the Tax Equity and Fiscal Responsibility Act, or TEFRA. The bottom line was that the phone monopoly and the airlines took whacks. Excise taxes upwards of 8 percent were put on their services, which would lead to about $33 billion more in federal revenue per year. TEFRA was soon invoked as the largest tax increase in American history. The competition was not stiff. Unlegislated bracket creep was all that had been necessary to produce TEFRA equivalents in the long 1970s.[36]

Ture had resigned from Treasury (as undersecretary) in mortification as the bill gained ground over the summer. In Congress, Kemp and Rousselot were dumbfounded. TEFRA did not touch 5–10–10, but it did compromise the accelerated cost recovery system (ACRS) and the investment-tax-credit portions of ERTA. These had been Ture's life's work since 1962, the fruits of his *Effects of Tax Policy on Capital Formation*.[37]

This left Entin and another deputy assistant secretary, Manuel Johnson, as the lone sure supply-siders at Treasury, if not in the entire administration. Senator Bob Dole wanted to complete the cleansing. He wrote the president in July, "While you . . . have worked so hard to secure passage of [TEFRA], a couple of members of . . . PEPAB have broken publicly with your program. I believe it should be a great favor to be able to advise the President [and] suggest that you consider withdrawing this honor from those who have opposed you on this important piece of fiscal legislation." Needless to say, Dole meant Laffer and Friedman. But Reagan kept them on.[38]

Gold to Williamsburg

The ACRS reversal was hard for Entin to take, as it had been for Ture. As TEFRA became law and his supervisors departed, Entin, now the acting assistant secretary of the treasury, did some theoretical work asking what might have been. In some "vacation reading" he prepared for Regan in July 1982, Entin echoed Laffer: "The phase-in of the tax cuts may have caused people to delay economic activity until later years.... We might have done better with a one- or two-year 20 percent cut retroactive to 1/1/81 followed immediately by indexing."[39]

That might have been a winning strategy, indeed. Until ERTA was secured in late July 1981, the liberal Democrats were constantly offering two-year alternatives. A 10–10 cut in January 1981 and 1982 plus indexing would have exceeded the rate cut of ERTA of 23 percent by 1984, yet it would have looked like a smaller cut. Coupled with the Brodhead amendment, it would have left no reason to defer income past January 1, 1982. Instead, early 1982 saw a tremendous contraction in economic activity.

Entin's idea would have had promise on another front, too. The tax cut would have complemented monetary policy in Mundellian fashion. In Mundell's elucidations of the policy mix, the central bank restrains the availability of money so that money has value, while tax cuts ensure that people have money. Economic transactions result, with investments and deficits financed now that dollars are sure to hold value. As it was, when the Fed brought growth in the money stock to a halt in March 1981, there was no tax cut for six months. Perhaps "no economic costs" really would have been in the offing if policy coordination could have been achieved.

Then, too, Entin wondered, what would have happened had the Fed not acted so erratically in the first year and a half of Reagan's term? In the summer of 1982, as the TEFRA battle was being lost, Entin posed a simple counterfactual about the monetary policy of the previous eighteen months and fed it into the Data Resources model. What if money creation had gone down steadily from 7 percent to 4 percent per annum over a three-year span? This, after all, had been the stated plan of the nation's central bank. Entin found that the recession would have been shorter and shallower, and growth would have been more than 2 percent greater by 1983. Interest rates and unemployment would have been fractionally better, inflation fractionally worse. The budget deficit would have been smaller because of increased receipts from the extra growth (and from bracket creep) and from reduced recession spending. There would have been no need for TEFRA, and the worst recession since the Depression would have been warded off. Alas, as Roberts wrote in his memoir, "instead of evenly spreading the reduction in money growth over a six-year period, the Federal Reserve delivered 75 percent of the reduction in the first year." The lesson was that "if monetary policy continues to fail, supply-side fiscal policies will not be enough to carry the economy to a higher real growth path."[40]

Before 1979, the Federal Reserve generally deserved its low reputation. But there can be no question that after August 1979, the Fed became serious. However poorly executed its policy may have been at times, its dropping of interest-rate targets for money-quantity targets in October of that year was intellectually legitimate. And yet by early 1981, with the prime rate at 22 percent, a misery index of 21, and a recession of major proportions, the Fed's very reputation—the sine qua non of a bank—was at stake. In 1980, exasperated with the degradation of the dollar, Senator Jesse Helms obtained passage of a law providing for a federal commission to study the possibility of returning to the gold standard. If the Fed wasn't careful, this commission might move to restrict if not eliminate it.[41]

The "Gold Commission" had a determined opposition. Certain congressional members, such as Representative Henry Reuss of Wisconsin, were manifestly anti-gold and strove to use their positions to scuttle the whole thing. By law, the commission was to report in October 1981. Opponents managed to ensure that it did not meet for the first time until just two months before that date. Lew Lehrman was named to the commission and with others worked to get the deadline extended into 1982.[42]

Since the Dunkirk memo, Lehrman had been devoting his energies to the cause of gold. When the Reagan administration assumed power, he was confident that it would succeed in cutting taxes and regulation, even if it was not as successful in slashing spending. But he worried that the monetary component of doing it "all" was in jeopardy. Even though the administration had called for slow and stable money growth, the responsibility for achieving this lay outside the administration, with the Federal Reserve, and Lehrman had no confidence in the Fed. After all, in early 1981 the Fed, purportedly governed by strict quantity targets, was pumping up the money stock by 10 percent, many times in excess of the rate of economic growth. Lehrman stopped short of saying that the Fed had to go. But he did say that it had to become "self-denying."

In a widely read interview of May 1981 with the investment bank Morgan Stanley, Lehrman said that the time had come for the Fed to abide by a strict rule: it must pursue one target and one target only. "Instead of trying, as it now does," said Lehrman, "to influence the level of interest rates, the foreign exchange value of the dollar, the quantity of money in circulation, or the level of employment, the Federal Reserve must realize that, in general, [it] barely [is] within its power to attain a single policy goal." And that goal was not among the four he had just mentioned. Rather, "the goal of the Federal Reserve System should be the stability of the purchasing power of the dollar or, saying it another way, . . . an end to inflation. In the absence of success on this point, what use is the Fed?"[43]

Twenty years earlier, Mundell had argued that the nation's central bank should strive, to the exclusion of all other goals, to ensure a balance-of-payments equilibrium. In practice, given the anchor status of the dollar under Bretton Woods, this meant that the goal of the Federal Reserve should be to ensure that no one had reason to think that gold might rise above $35 per ounce. Lehrman sought something similar in 1981. For inflation to be brought under control the Fed had to orient its policy toward a forecast of future inflation. This could not be the consumer price index, for this was a measurement of past inflation. Commodities were the market's index of superfluous money creation, and the classic commodity was gold. Therefore, Lehrman argued, the only viable policy for the Fed was to prepare the way for the creation of a new gold standard.

Mundell, along with Bartley, Wanniski, Reynolds, and others in the supply-side demimonde, had been to Lehrman's East Side institute many times since the Michael 1 days. As the Morgan Stanley interview made plain, Lehrman was in perfect agreement with the supply-siders that the Fed's monetarist emphasis on quantity targets after October 1979 was incomplete. Quantity policy could not, of its nature, align itself with real monetary demand. Only an inflation-oriented policy from the Fed could address both sides of the money supply–money demand equation. And the only inflation-oriented policy worthy of the name was one that eyed future inflation, or at least inflation expectations. Providing for a stable price of gold, Lehrman argued, was the inescapable future of a functioning Federal Reserve.

During the debates at his institute, Lehrman had held out as the Jacques Rueffian. That is, he was concerned that the Bretton Woods–era policy of maintaining the price of gold in the open markets was insufficient. After all, all sorts of expedients had been devised to ensure the $35 price in the face of excessive dollar production. Chief among these was restricting the right to redeem dollars for gold with the U.S. government to national monetary authorities, authorities who could be enjoined to "cooperate." Before 1933, this right had accrued to all holders of dollars.[44]

This was the regime to which Lehrman urged a return. If the United States made the dollar convertible to gold (at the right price), gold would become flatly stable and thus a viable anchor for all the world's currencies. In Lehrman's vision, the Fed would not simply *target* the price of gold—that is, issue and retract dollars so that gold did not fluctuate in the markets. Rather, the Fed would operate within a regime in which the dollar was *redeemable* into gold. Any Fed mistakes would immediately be exposed not simply by price movements in gold, as in the 1960s, but by something much more forceful: redemptions (or demands for dollars), as in 1914–33. Fort Knox would be put under pressure.

Lehrman called for a gold-convertible dollar by 1984. The Fed could pursue whatever policies it wanted until then, but on January 1, 1984, Fort Knox should be prepared for redemption claims at some prearranged, fixed dollar-to-gold ratio. Lehrman conceded that this would probably have to be somewhere in the neighborhood of $500 per ounce, the current price. He felt that if this policy were announced by the president (presumably in conjunction with a congressional endorsement of a Gold Commission report in this vein), "all market participants would realize that, with the resumption of convertibility, the fluctuation in the value of paper dollars, and therefore of gold prices expressed in paper dollars, would end."[45]

It made for a curious coincidence that just as the Gold Commision was coming into existence and gaining its most forceful gold advocate in Lehrman, the Federal Reserve brought the growth of the money stock to a halt. To be sure, the Fed had other reasons to be dissatisfied with its previous policy, and zero growth for seven months represented an innovative move. But the confluence of events is inescapable. In the form of the Gold Commission, a vehicle for removing all discretionary policy from the Fed was set into motion. If the Fed did not quickly regain credibility for its ability to maintain the soundness of the dollar, there was reason to believe that its days were numbered. If in fact the great recession of 1981–82 was a function of the lack of growth in the money supply, this itself may have resulted from the Fed's concerns about its own impending demise.

As the Gold Commission convened in fall 1981, Mundell, Wanniski, and confreres wrote pro-gold pieces in the *Washington Post*, Bartley's *Journal*, and other outlets. Alan Reynolds testified before the commission. These efforts were met with an outpouring of anti-gold rhetoric, including an anti-gold piece from Greenspan on Bartley's page as well as a chorus of editorials (such as Nordhaus's) saying that the gold standard was economic quackery. In a *National Journal* essay, Robert J. Samuelson managed to refer to the advocates of gold as "emotional," as "romantic," and as "acting like a few soldiers impersonating a division." The gold standard was a "crackpot idea," a *"cause célèbre,"* a "religion." "At heart, it reflects a basic mistrust of democracy."[46]

Monetarists were in charge of the commission. Its CEA representatives were monetarists, as was its executive, Anna J. Schwartz. The monetarist belief was that the Friedman formula—slow, steady, preannounced monetary growth—had yet to be tried, so a punt to gold was not yet in order. The commission reported at the end of March 1982 and indeed did not advocate a return to gold. Rather, it looked sternly at the Fed and asked for better. The report was in essence a history of the gold standard in the United States. Schwartz's contribution was clear. The report of the Gold Commission may be thought of as a supplement, if not a sequel, to Friedman and Schwartz's *Monetary History of the United States.*[47]

Laffer had provided the original economic study for the Gold Commission. In a 1980 report solicited by Helms called "Reinstatement of the Dollar: The Blueprint," Laffer had outlined a way to return to gold. His plan was to make the dollar convertible into gold for all holders at a specified rate, with adjustment periods, or "holidays," in case things got dicey. This was an arrangement akin to that which Bretton Woods had provided for currencies. Under Bretton Woods, currencies were fixed to the dollar at rates that the supervising authority could change if things got weird. Laffer made sure in his "blueprint" to drop Paul Volcker's name. "This paper makes extensive use of Federal Reserve Chairman Paul Volcker's ideas as found in the 1972 U.S. proposals to the [IMF]," said page one. True enough, Volcker had argued throughout the 1970s the necessity of restoring soundness to the currency. Laffer was determined to wrest the issue from the realm of the crackpot.[48]

After the commission's March 1982 report, Laffer found himself once again in concordance with Volcker. He was meeting with the chairman and other Fed officials regularly in 1982, and he noticed that something was happening. The easing and tightening of monetary policy in the summer of 1982 seemed to vary directly with the price of commodities, particularly gold. Tightening came shortly after price spikes in commodities, easing after drops. Laffer wondered whether the Fed was indeed targeting commodity prices, not quantity aggregates. For the moment, he could not tell, because the Fed movements still fell within the official quantity ranges.[49]

Then, in the fall, the Fed took action consistent with commodity-price targeting that went outside the quantity guidelines. Laffer had his evidence: the Fed had put itself on a price rule, perhaps a gold-price rule. He reported his surmise on Bartley's page. "Evidence for this change has been mounting since early June," Laffer wrote. "But it was not until Oct. 4 that the Fed had to choose between stabilizing commodity prices and keeping within its target range for money supply growth." Specifically, in September and October commodity prices had been falling. The Fed had had to inject more money into the banking system, above its quantity targets, if it wanted to arrest the drop. And that is exactly what it did. Laffer wrote, "A price rule for monetary policy—the final precondition for the roaring '80s—is being put into place."[50]

As the supply-siders had contended since October 1979, by targeting prices—especially the price of gold—in its monetary policy, the Federal Reserve could align real money demand with real money supply. Monetarism's quantity targets were not enough. They were too difficult to measure, they were not intrinsically linked to the legitimate appetite for money, and they prevented an economy from expanding if it wanted to grow past 5 percent. Falling gold prices indicate a shortage of money, as investors realize that money demand from real economic enterprises is drying up the sources of capital. The markets were yearning for more money in the fall of 1982, and Volcker was supplying it, in defiance of prearranged quantity ceilings.[51]

It was no illusion that dollars were facing increased demand as a means for investment in the real economy. The Dow had risen from 770 in August 1982 past the mythical 1,000 mark in October, a 30 percent increase in just two months. This time it stuck. The Dow stayed above 1,000 for the rest of the year. And whatever else the TEFRA episode may have been, it was a clear signal that the marginal rate cuts of ERTA were going to keep on coming. The next effective tax cut came on January 1, 1983, when new income would be subject to half of the final 10 percent rate cut. If the phase-in of the rate cuts was leading to a postponement of economic activity, the markets seemed to be betting that business was going to be big in the near future. Stocks are vehicles for capturing the forthcoming profits of real assets. If the economy was in a brutal recession in 1982, the policy mix indicated that soon it was going to be in a rather different state.

As for that policy mix, the two elements leaned hard on each other. The tax cuts both increased the marginal product of work effort and provided for a burst of new economic activity. The Fed followed suit by increasing the monetary float as economic decisions flowing from the tax-cut schedule created increased demand for new money. Had TEFRA reversed the marginal rate cuts or indexing of ERTA, the new economic activity would have lost its raison d'être. The Fed would have been forced to cut money or face inflation. Yet given the rate-cut provisions of ERTA, had the Fed stuck to its mid-1981 and early 1982 decisions and impassively stopped money creation—in the name of inflation-fighting if not the institution's own credibility—the boom that the tax cuts had made possible would have gone unfinanced. Mundell had said it in the 1971 Princeton paper: "The correct policy mix . . . is based on *fiscal ease* to get more production out of the economy, in combination with *monetary restraint* to stop inflation. The increased momentum of the economy provided by the stimulus of a tax cut will cause sufficient demand to permit real monetary expansion at higher rates."[52]

The definitive indication that the supply-side revolution was under way was that inflation came to a full stop as the Fed expanded the money supply from June on. In the latter half of 1982, as the Fed topped its quantity ceilings while commodities stayed stable and the markets swelled, inflation was flat—less than half a percent yearly. The long 1970s were coming to an end.

What of the deficit? In the fall of 1982, as monetary expansion coexisted with an exactly stable price level and an asset boom, the federal deficit for the fiscal year ending September 30 came in at $128 billion. This was two-thirds higher than the record 1981 deficit, with 1983 promising even greater heights. The 1982 deficit occurred in tandem with the cessation of inflation and with markets raking in cash. The argument perennially made against Kemp-Roth was in dire jeopardy. This had been that the tax cut would cause deficits and hence inflation and/or crowding out.

Even OMB came around. Its memos from September and October recorded the developments with precision. "The inflation rate has declined by an order of magnitude that has been much greater than virtually any forecaster in or out of government predicted," Kudlow wrote to the subcabinet. (Rutledge was the reason for the "virtually.") And as Kudlow told the White House press office: "Investors want to switch from the high inflation commodity play (gold, silver, oil and gas, real estate, etc.) to the low inflation financial asset play (stocks, bonds, money market funds, IRA's . . .)." Kudlow promptly quit his job and became a supply-sider for life.[53]

Realizing what was going on, Mundell, Laffer, and Kemp joined forces to bring about a final reform. Now that the United States had its fiscal and monetary policy right and the economy was going to cruise, it was time for the nations of the world to fix their currencies to the dollar again. As Mundell had been saying since the 1960s in response to the charges of "exorbitant privilege," what the world wants and needs is for the superpower to hum. If it does, all currency uncertainty can be ended by a fix to the great and good dollar.

The three conspired to hold a shadow conference to the economic summit of the heads of state of the major industrial nations (the "G-7") set to be held in Williamsburg, Virginia, in early 1983. The supply-side event, to be held in Washington a few weeks before the G-7, would introduce precise intellectual content that the photo-op real event could consider ratifying. The hope was to get an agreement on the necessity of fixed exchange rates. It was a little dreamy, but why not try? Some pretty big names even showed up, including Henry Kissinger.[54]

At the conference, Mundell was at pains to argue that unless the currencies of the world—especially those of smaller, marginal countries—could fix to the dollar, they had no real hope of becoming robust intermediaries of economic transactions. Prosperity was a function of the ability of the world to deliver a sound currency system. And an opportunity had arisen to get just that. After fifteen years in the wilderness, the dollar was now stable and an engine of investment. Join the "convoy," Mundell said, because now the leader was going in the right direction. Fix to the dollar, and all would be right.[55]

Now, Mundell was not so naïve as to suppose that dollar stability was anything but evanescent. Indeed, he called the new monetary policy wisdom in the United States the "Volcker standard." That is, if Paul Volcker were suddenly taken from this vale of tears, or if he were to prove capricious, the standard would vanish. Mundell knew that for the sake of the world, let alone the United States, the dollar needed an anchor more permanent than the technique that had caught Paul Volcker's fancy. As for convertibility to gold, Mundell had seen too much fluctuation in the price of gold in the 1970s to believe that the yellow metal was truly an island of stability. He knew that gold had become overwhelmed by the awesome power of the Federal Reserve Bank of the United States to dictate the terms of the world price level, commodities included. Gold was not a sure thing anymore. It was merely a hedge against the dollar. It yo-yoed inversely with the greenback. If the dollar were redeemable in gold, the dollar would be self-referential. "Gold had become a passenger in the system," Mundell said in 1999.[56]

That is to say, gold was the photo negative of the policy probity of the Fed. To the extent that that probity was variable, so was gold. For this reason, Mundell was not willing to support along with Lehrman and his coauthor of the minority Gold Commission report, Representative Ron Paul, a gold-convertible dollar. In Mundell's view, the dollar should be anchored to something stable; indeed, it should be convertible to something stable. But the 1970s had proven gold unstable. What could take its place? Perhaps units of gold plus units of other major world currencies as formidable as the dollar and independent of the Federal Reserve—the yen and the euro, the latter incipient in 1983.

These ideas were fated not to take hold, at least not right away. The gold/commodity price rule for the dollar, as adhered to by Paul Volcker, was the most the United States could guarantee. If other countries wanted to fix to the dollar in these circumstances, they would benefit as long as the United States stayed consistent. As it happened, the United States basically did stay consistent. The tax and monetary revolution represented by Reagan and Volcker was sustained for a quarter century. But Mundell had made a valid point. Why not develop a mechanism, other than personality or precedent, that could keep this good thing going? There was no formal reform of the international monetary system in 1983. The Volcker standard would have to do.[57]

What did bring the Fed to develop this standard in 1982 and to adhere to it for some two decades? This question has occupied economic commentators for twenty-five years. Was it "genius"? After all, Volcker and his successor, Greenspan, are generally regarded uncritically as folk heroes, "elevated in prestige beyond all reason." During his chairmanship, Greenspan led the "committee to save the world," according to *Time*.[58]

In fact, the Gold Commission probably had something to do with it. It was the lever that produced the Fed's self-transformation. Prior to the convening of the commission in the summer of 1981, the Fed was accommodating double-digit inflation, whatever lip service it may have given to quantity targets. After nine months of the commission's paroxysms, the Fed emerged targeting gold. The practical result was sufficient to constitute a monetary policy that was becoming of the world's leading nation.

Leadership on tax policy had already been established through ERTA. TEFRA served to show that the nucleus of the 1981 law—marginal tax cuts and indexing—was untouchable. Tension was building. The incredible recession of 1981–82 could not hold. Unlike in 1930–31, too many opportunities were emerging to justify holding out in a safe haven. With inflation nil and returns to work and investment getting ever better with the tax cuts, people were eager to jump into the real economy. John Rutledge had spoken the year before of a monster in abeyance, an asset-shift eminence out there in the sea. It was biding time until real nourishment appeared on land. As 1982 became 1983, this thing, this asset-shift beast, had moved onto shore, inhaling budget-deficit ants and more than a few further financial assets. It was about to roam into open territory, still hungry, meaning that the nation's economy was about to roar as almost never before.

11

BELLE ÉPOQUE

To put it as modestly as possible, surely something went right in the 1980s.

—ROBERT L. BARTLEY, *The Seven Fat Years*

Reagan was elected and the musk of profit once again scented the air.

—LUC SANTE, *New York Review of Books,* November 6, 2003

From the peak of spring 1973 until the trough of winter 1982, the GDP of the United States improved at the rate of 1.8 percent yearly. Over the same period, population increased 1 percent per year. Economic growth per capita, the signal measure of a nation's prosperity, was thus almost stagnant. Not that the nation's inhabitants had decided to take a permanent break, trading work for leisure. Far from it. From 1973 to 1982, the size of the labor force increased from 85 million to 100 million. People strove to work ever more, just as the returns to more labor leveled to zero. Feminism's encouragement of women to enter the workforce, the maturation of the last tranche of the baby boomers, and immigration (of exceptional entrepreneurial quality) from Indochina and Cuba ensured a large increase in the number of those seeking jobs. Yet it was all a mad dash. GDP growth controlled for labor-force and population growth from 1973 to 1982 approximated just one period in American history: 1929–40, the Great Depression.

The winter quarter of 1982 would prove to be the hinge on which the GDP march of the United States would swing back to the historical norm, the trend memorialized by the phrase "postwar prosperity." The quarter century beginning in winter 1982 would see growth at 3.3 percent per year, precisely the rate that had held for the quarter century following World War II. Reversion to trend, the most venerable of all phenomena in statistics, was honored in the economic accounts of the United States in the last fifth of the twentieth century and the early years of the twenty-first.

Growth at 3 or 4 percent per annum has been standard since Alexander Hamilton's hitch as first secretary of the treasury. Until World War I, variation in economic performance was confined to periods of "panic," such as in 1837, 1857, 1873, 1893, and 1907. Panics characteristically involved bank failures and business collapses as well as runs on money and pushes into gold. Many people found themselves out of work while the panic held, but such periods usually lasted only for a few months; at the most, as in 1873–75 and 1893–95, they lasted for two years. Furthermore, both of these busts presaged eras of enormous growth. One reason that the "robber barons" became so wealthy in the "Gilded Age" is that those who aspired to that mantle bought heavily during times of panic and emerged on the other side as the employers of choice. As for prices, they held at par for the century prior to the creation of the Fed, the one exception being the "greenback" inflation spawned by the Civil War, which was resolved by 1879.[1]

After the creation of the Fed in 1913, variation in economic performance became far more expansive. Indeed, a novel branch of economics, macroeconomics, had to be formulated in order to deal with it. The first example of the new order came in the seven years after 1913, when inflation was 102 percent. The Commerce Department (also founded in 1913) had difficulty tracking it, and Treasury denied that it was even taking place, a fact about which Mundell chuckled during his Nobel address. Since the gold price was fixed at $20.67, the doubling of consumer prices must have been some kind of mirage, in the Treasury view. Americans whose pay packets were no longer heavy enough to pay for the groceries saw it differently.[2]

Warren Harding and Calvin Coolidge led the nation out of the 1913–21 economic crisis, but the new variation was only getting started. To look in the annals of developed economies for an analog to the Great Depression is an exercise in futility. The Great Depression was sui generis. To compare the most extreme instances of unemployment (and privation) of the nineteenth century with the Great Depression is an impossibility. In what other depression was there unemployment at 17 percent for eleven years, only to be followed by five years of wartime employment in which wages were given back in bond purchases to the employer (the government), which eventually returned the so-called wages in degraded currency? A casual look at the account statistics of other nations from the dawn of the industrial revolution reveals any comparison to be an absurdity.

John Maynard Keynes stopped what he was doing in the early 1930s (including working out his analysis of the need for a viable international currency system) to address the problem of the new variation. What emerged was the *General Theory*. The lesson to be drawn from the *General Theory*, according to postwar "Keynesianism," was that priority must be placed on ending the new, wild flux. Even if it meant slower growth, stabilize the economy. Get unemployment and inflation (or deflation) back to sane levels. "Stabilization," the holy grail of Keynesianism, indeed of macroeconomics, became the goal of economic planners whose minds were formed after 1913. Invariably, the operational procedures of stabilization involved manipulating the new tools invented in that year. Unfortunately, what almost no one understood was that the very creation of these tools—the central bank and the federal income tax—was the origin of the variation problem to begin with.

At Bretton Woods, it was clear enough that Keynes had forgotten about the *General Theory* and was once again preoccupied with restoring the pre-1914 currency system in a way that respected current geostrategic realities. As World War II was ending, Keynes was reorienting himself toward the issues he had introduced not in 1936, but in 1923 in his *Tract on Monetary Reform*. In a fateful development, the economics profession did not follow his lead and stayed with the *General Theory*. Shortly after Bretton Woods, after a meeting in Washington with American economists, Keynes quipped, "I found myself the only non-Keynesian present."[3]

Among postwar Keynesians, there were some "neo-Keynesians," including those of the Yale school and the neoclassical synthesis, who argued that growth had to be given wider berth than that afforded by an overwrought commitment to stabilization. As for the *General Theory*, it actually would be a source of inspiration not only to establishmentarian liberal economists, but also to incipient supply-siders John Rutledge and Harvey Wilmeth as they pondered the meaning of the stock of assets, the subject of the great work's sixteenth chapter.[4]

Twenty-five years into postwar prosperity, in the early Nixon years, stabilization policy (call it Keynesianism) was in full flower. What with the Fed and all its branches; the CEA (whose chairmen appeared on the cover of *Time*); the tax code; the regulatory apparatus; the many government economists at the various agencies and on the congressional bureaus and staffs; the business economists and financial journalists and forecasters; and the thousands of university economists, there was not a sporting chance for the new variation to pop its head out of the ground again. And yet when the fight came, the new variation won.[5]

Indeed, by 1980, if not by 1970, the university economics establishment knew that stabilization theory had long been rotting, that it had been supplanted by more innovative approaches. Monetarism was twenty years old by the election of 1972, when the Fed defied it. The price revolution in economic theory, which began in the early 1960s at Chicago, had made a profound case that prices are the most imperative datum in the economy. Anything that distorts them—regulation, taxes, monetary policy—will cause confusion and entrepreneurial hesitation among economic actors. Nobel Prize after Nobel Prize was awarded to economists arguing that government has to interfere with the economy as little as possible.

And yet the economics discipline's free-market revolution found it difficult to penetrate the realm of policy. Friedman's case was instructive. He not only dominated academic economics in the 1960s and 1970s; with an assist from his wife, he also became one of the nation's preeminent public intellectuals. And yet, although he had the ear of nearly everyone in power, sold books in huge numbers, had a nationwide readership in *Newsweek,* and became a television star, his ideas affected policy only when Arthur Laffer was by his side at PEPAB and they both insisted on maintaining the marginal rate cuts of ERTA. Keynesianism had certain advantages that made it hard to defeat.

The supply-siders would in time win their Nobel (by 1981 they already had their Pulitzer), and they came to enjoy a prime place in the firmament of free-market intellectuals. But the decisive difference separating the supply-siders from their confreres in the free-market movement was that they were dedicated to, and good at, getting things done in practice. Perhaps by himself Mundell could not prompt policymakers to action, but his ideas, combined with the ground game of a Paul Craig Roberts, made for an irresistible force. As for Bartley, had he not retained an acute interest in developing his economic and philosophical understanding (and in solving the nation's problems), it is unlikely that the establishmentarian *Wall Street Journal* would have had the patience or foresight to serve as a platform for the Mundell-Laffer hypothesis. The triumph of supply-side economics issued from a most unusual combination of intellectual profundity, journalistic acumen, and political strategy. There is no amalgam like it in the distinguished history of the free-market revolution.

What Were the 1980s?

The permanent recovery began in the last quarter of 1982. In 1983, GDP growth was 4.5 percent; in 1984, it was 7.2 percent. An "overheated" economy by any conventional reckoning was one that grew by 12 percent in two years. Yet 1985 reacted by delivering growth of 4.1 percent. The average rate of growth for these three years was 5.1 percent. This was a repetition of 1976–78, which Rosy Scenario had shied away from predicting in the event of a Reagan Revolution. It came anyway.

That 1976–78 record had been bounded, fore and aft, by ugly conditions. The 1973–75 stagflation-recession was an atrocious one, and yet it was outdone by what emerged in 1979–82. So what followed 1985? Growth of 3.5 percent in 1986, 3.4 percent in 1987, 4.1 percent in 1988, and 3.5 percent in 1989. The three-year run of 5.1 percent growth that marked the escape from stagflation moderated to 3.6 percent for the next four years, both numbers significantly above the trend of postwar prosperity. Indeed, the 4.3-percent-per-annum run of growth for the seven years beginning with 1983 was reminiscent of the salad years of postwar prosperity—the years that followed the de facto implementation of the policy mix in 1962. Recalling Genesis, Bartley called 1983–89 "the seven fat years."[6]

Trade-offs? In the 1980s, the misery index dropped continually from ledge to ledge. By 1983, the 21 level had cooled to 13; from there the index lost a point per year for three years before settling between 9 and 10 for the duration. The heroic 6–8 level of the post-1913 era was within striking distance.

Disinflation led the way. The 1982 drop in the consumer price index to 6.2 percent after three years of double-digit rates was a harbinger of things to come. In 1983, inflation was down to 3.2 percent. It inched up to 4 percent the next two years before sinking to 1.9 percent in 1986, fulfilling the prophecy that had gotten Rutledge run out of town five years before. In the last three years of the decade, inflation hovered around 4 percent. As for unemployment, it drifted steadily downward. From a high level of 9.6 percent in 1983,

it fell into the seven-point range for the next three years, the six-point range
in 1987, and the five-point range for the latter two years. The Phillips curve
was finished.

In the canons of macroeconomics, a nation's "success indicators" are considered to be GDP growth and the inflation and unemployment statistics.
Thus, the seven fat years took their place with 1922–29 and 1962–68 as con-
stituting one of the great runs in post-1913 economic history. The common
policy thread running through each episode was the coordination of money
supply with money demand and the institution of marginal tax cuts, including at the top rate. As Robert Lucas said in the *Wall Street Journal* in 2007, this
represents no less than the greatest macroeconomic lesson of modern times.[7]

To the individual, aside from having a job whose pay holds value, a prime
success indicator is how well his bank account and IRA are doing. Surely one
of the reasons the textbooks have omitted to mention that there was a reversion to trend in growth, unemployment, and inflation in the 1980s is that other
economic successes were even more obvious. For example, the stock market.

Following the 75 percent real collapse in the Dow from 1966 to 1982, a
record which again apes what happened in 1929–40, the stock market started
the greatest and longest run in its history. The 30 percent jump in the Dow in
late 1982 was the opening act. The Dow rose 20 percent the next year, gave
back 4 percent in 1984, then went up 28 percent, 23 percent, and 2 percent
in 1985, 1986, and 1987, respectively. Investors may recall that there was a
"crash" in 1987, in the traditional month of October, just as in 1929. On October 19, 1987, "Black Monday," the Dow lost 23 percent. And just as in 1929, the
market's performance for the calendar year was flat. However, after 1929, the
market went to nil over the next three years, dropping from 250 to 40. After
1987? There was another bull run of 42 percent growth in 1988 and 1989, col-
lectively. Over the next decade, a further 400 percent would be added.

Bonds did the same thing. Triple A's appreciated by 85 percent from the
1981 trough to the 1987 peak, settled a little lower, then resumed the march
so that the 1987 high was exceeded by 69 percent in 2005—all this exclusive
of interest. The U.S. government's main financing instrument, the thirty-year
"long" bond, followed suit. In 1981, Stockman blanched at the idea of funding
historic deficits at an interest rate of 15 percent a year, then the going rate.
With bracket creep gone, how on earth could the government remain solvent?
The answer was to halve the long-bond rate to 7.1 percent, as was achieved
by 1986. Deficits financed at ever-cheaper rates coincided with an asset boom

breaking all precedents, destroying the "crowding out" canard. Commodities fell, with oil sinking to $12 per barrel by 1986. Gold fell to $300 per ounce and stayed there, perhaps because of Volcker's Fed.[8]

With the 1980s boom, Mundell's Nobel Prize was a foregone conclusion. He was still a little young—fifty in 1982. The Swedish committee made Mundell wait, and the delay cost him. The Tax Reform Act of 1986 made prizes taxable. When Mundell got his million bucks in 1999, he had to give half of it to the government. The rest went into repairs at leaky Santa Colomba, but even that was not enough. "We have to leave something for the next generation to do," he quipped.[9]

John Rutledge smiled over what he had wrought. Smiling even more were those who had seen things his way, such as General Electric. GE forgot about the tungsten mines and other commodity plays and under new CEO Jack Welch entered manufacturing and finance in a big way. So big that GE became the world's greatest company. GE acquired or developed a finance company, a television network (NBC, which dominated the ratings), and manufacturing units in areas ranging from engines to MRI machines. Welch became known as "Neutron Jack," because he laid off so many workers while leaving the businesses standing, just as an N-bomb kills people but does not blast buildings. "In lieu of a gift, a GE employee has been laid off in your name," Johnny Carson read in his Christmas card from corporate.[10]

GE's main competitor, Westinghouse, had undertaken exactly the opposite strategy. It had decided to get out of real enterprises in favor of commodity plays. In the 1980s, Westinghouse decided to wind down its core competency, nuclear power, and gobble up land out west, as if it were a time for survivalism. The company, long one of the crown jewels of world industry, its stock a member of the Dow 30, edged to the brink of bankruptcy in the late 1980s and 1990s and was forced to reverse-merge into a shell. After a few years, the Japanese took the nuclear business off the company's hands on the cheap. (Today that business is a world-beater, producing electricity for the Chinese for the foreseeable future. It is also a jobs machine in America. Now, after a twenty-five-year holiday, GE has to start looking over its shoulder again.)[11]

Although it was committed to being lean, GE continued to employ hundreds of thousands as it surged into the twenty-first century. And having a job at GE was remunerative. With regard to pensions and stock options and employee stock ownership plans (ESOPs), GE's issue went up eighty times under Jack Welch. Rank-and-file workers made out like bandits. Compared to a line job in the auto industry, where you had to loaf in a job bank so as to spread around the little work there was while the big bosses lobbied Washington for bailouts, there was singular pride in doing things like making the first MRI devices at GE's Milwaukee plants.[12]

Still, industrial layoffs were a regular occurrence during the years of Reaganomics. This is why Jesse Jackson announced his bid for the presidency in Pittsburgh in 1987. But as the democratic socialist John P. Hoerr's *And the Wolf Finally Came: The Decline of the American Steel Industry* (1988) amply documented, it was the combination of 1970s stagflation and strong unions that could negotiate a COLA-plus that had eviscerated the nation's heavy industries like steel, along with management decisions to get into commodities at precisely the wrong time. The industrial difficulties of the 1980s were a residual effect of the 1970s.[13]

Smokestack industries turned around only when management and labor recognized two things. First, in a booming economy it might be best for business owners to keep an open mind about investing capital outside the company—U.S. Steel's and Westinghouse's oil and land plays notwithstanding. As Michael C. Jensen of Harvard Business School has written, the companies that did best in the 1980s were those disinclined to reinvest profits in their own businesses and keen to invest in any enterprise that promised a nice return. This forced businesses to compete for capital, even their own, and hence was a path to becoming more efficient, indeed more profitable. If there had not been a general boom in the 1980s, according to Jensen, there would have been little reason for business owners to consider opportunities for their capital other than reinvestment. Jensen's virtuous circle would not have been brought into action.[14]

The second truth was likewise a sheep in wolf's clothing. If heavy industries buy the latest capital equipment, the result will be supercharged productivity and thus fewer jobs. As a USX executive said repeatedly in the 1980s, "There are not enough seats in the steel lifeboat," and he was right. Approximately 265,000 steelworkers lost their jobs in the 1980s as equipment became cheaper because of tax changes. Indeed, today the nation's steelmakers make prodigious quantities of steel, having finally modernized all their plants.[15]

The happy result for workers is that when there are jobs in steel, they pay handsomely. The United Steelworkers now make steel of far better quality than what was produced in the 1970s, using gleaming new BOP furnaces and casters (in Pittsburgh no less). They sell it to hungry customers the globe over, and get contracts that in the words of USW officials "provide . . . very significant wage, substantial bonus and pension increases."[16]

Did the nation become one of haves and have-nots as a result of the 1980s? Today steel employs only one-tenth the number of workers it did a generation ago; that tenth is doing exceptionally well, but what about the large majority that was let go? Here it is crucial to grasp that the *central* economic event of the 1980s was the small-business revolution. John Kenneth Galbraith had predicted in 1967 that in a few decades all work in the United States would be done under the aegis of a handful of mega-employers. Thanks in part to the supply-side revolution, he was wrong.[17]

The number of enterprises in the United States began to mushroom in the 1980s, a process that has proceeded unabated. Just as mega-employers such as U.S. Steel slashed their workforces, small businesses expanded theirs. As Ed Zschau had told Congress in 1978, in testimony that launched the Steiger amendment, in boom times small-business hiring can outpace that of large firms by a factor of twenty to one. In the 1980s, large employers engaged in mass layoffs while the unemployment rate steadily fell, proving Zschau's point.[18]

A mega-employer that emerged in the 1980s, Wal-Mart, is itself often blamed for destroying small businesses by the thousands, the "mom and pop" stores of once-thriving Main Streets. Supply-siders generally discount this criticism. Former JEC staffer Richard Vedder has argued that Wal-Mart has been an unqualified boon to the American economy. And to be sure, Wal-Mart, along with another corporate icon that emerged in the 1980s, Federal Express, serves as wholesaler and distribution network for America's many new small businesses.[19]

And yet it is plainly obvious that small towns have struggled mightily since the 1980s, just as jobs at Wal-Mart pay less (although they are cleaner and safer) than did those in heavy industry in the 1970s. Supply-siders might consider changing their tack on Wal-Mart. They could learn from the work that won Robert Bartley the Pulitzer. Bartley argued that large governmental intrusions in the economy, such as price controls, benefit large businesses at the expense of small ones. Bigness confers power to gain exemptions from controls, and thus an advantage over smaller competitors. "Down with Big Business," Bartley thundered in 1979, in the editorial that won him the prize.

Though federal tax rates have decreased markedly since 1980, local tax rates, particularly for schools, have gone up. (This is not because of smaller federal outlays to states and localities; since the founding of the Department of Education in 1980, such outlays have been consistently large.) The primary reason is the unique power of teachers' unions, today by any measure the strongest labor organizations in the country.

Wal-Mart's modus operandi is to demand exemptions from taxes and regulations in whatever locality in which it wishes to do business. Typically, local governing boards cave in to the demand because of the prospect of Wal-Mart jobs. The effect is to place a greater share of the tax burden on the remaining businesses in town, which further worsens their competitive position. In other words, one of the secrets to Wal-Mart's success is its ability to leverage its bigness to gain favors against competition. The solution to restoring balance would be to cut local taxes. If local taxes were low, it would not matter as much to area businesses if Wal-Mart were exempt. Arguments along these lines constituted Bartley's distinctive contribution not only to the popularization of supply-side economics, but to supply-side theory itself.

A neologism entered the dictionary in 1986: "McJobs." Men used to work at the mill, and now they flip hamburgers, the term implied. Supply-siders were stupefied at how one particular statistic was adduced in the 1980s (by Lester Thurow, for example) to prove the McJobs point. This was the rise in the trade deficit, which swelled into the hundreds of billions of dollars in the 1980s. A trade deficit is the difference between a nation's imports and exports. In the McJobs view, a trade deficit is a bad thing, in that it indicates that good jobs are flowing to foreign countries. In the supply-side view, given high growth and a strong currency a trade deficit is a wonderful thing. For a trade deficit, as the supply-siders explained, means that a country gains material goods equal to the deficit *in addition* to what the country produces on its own.[20]

In the 1980s, the United States kept its nice growth in goods and services for itself, and then got a tip in the form of the $100 billion–plus trade deficit. In exchange, the United States supplied the world with currency. In economics, currency producers who get goods and services without having to supply the same things in exchange are known as having "seigniorial privilege." The world desired this arrangement in the 1980s because the dollar once again held value and using it as an investment medium was a good idea. The trade deficit of the 1980s was akin to a "maraschino cherry on top," wrote Bartley, of the policy mix's success.[21]

It is certainly inconceivable that the small-business revolution would have occurred had marginal tax rates not been cut. Typically, small-business people report income on a personal return. Additionally, small-business profits often vary wildly from year to year. Thus, under a regime of steeply progressive tax rates, a good year is punished by the government, and nothing is left over to help through a bad year. In this regard, the 1986 law that eliminated brackets and brought the top rate down to 28 percent was probably more important than ERTA.

Killing Time in Washington

Once the boom got going, the administration turned its attention elsewhere. In various agencies there was devotion to deregulation, which Reagan CEA chair Murray Weidenbaum (who resigned in 1982) and Laffer argued was equivalent to a supply-side tax cut. Reagan strove to cut spending on discretionary items, succeeding only in one area, the civil service. Defense costs increased substantially, as did those associated with Medicare and Social Security. As for Social Security tax rates, they continued to balloon under Reagan, as they had been doing since 1957. The last increase came in 1990. It took the rate at which low and moderate wages were dunned (in addition to income taxes) to the punishing level of 15.3 percent.[22]

The deficit became the overriding political issue in Washington, virtually preventing action on any other front. By any measure, the budget deficits of the Reagan years were the highest in the country's peacetime history. The jocular characterization of the Reagan years attributed to Daniel Patrick Moynihan gets the basic metrics right: "That's when we borrowed a trillion dollars from the Japanese and threw a party." From 1982 to 1989, U.S. federal budget deficits accumulated to a total of $1.4 trillion, or an average of $175 billion per year. In nominal terms, this was almost three times higher than the average deficit of the Carter years, which was $60 billion. And the Carter deficits themselves had been historically large.

What caused the deficits? During the Reagan years, revenues, controlled for population growth and inflation, never fell below the twenty-year moving average, so it was not a lack of receipts. It was spending. In the latter half of the stagflation years, federal spending as a percentage of GDP was in the 20–22 percent range. From the end of World War II to 1975, the 20 percent threshold had been breached only twice, at the peak of both the Korean and Vietnam wars. It was then breached every year from 1975 to 1996. In the Reagan years, federal spending accounted for 22–24 percent of GDP. Defense accounted for part of the increase in this percentage, but the major reason was the collapse of inflation, which in two ways led to a balloon in spending.

First, it ensured that existing debt had to be serviced with nondepreciated currency. The deficits of the double-digit inflation years of 1979–81, for example, deficits that totaled $194 billion, had average interest payments in the neighborhood of 11 percent. People who bought this debt expected the 11 percent to do little but clear inflation. Yet with inflation down to 3 percent for the long term after 1982, the real interest-payment obligations of the federal government increased markedly. In the 1980s, the government had to pay upwards of a real 8 percent on debt issued in the double-digit inflation years. Those payments drained the treasury.[23]

This strange interlude represented a sort of honesty in government, as well as a windfall to bondholders. Less sublime was the impact of the collapse of inflation on the congressional budget process. By the late 1970s and into the 1980s, when resolutions were proposed for the coming year's spending, the standard assumption was that inflation would continue at a high rate. In order for spending to hold at a real level, given this assumption, high spending ceilings consistent with high inflation had to be set. Yet after 1981, the anticipated inflation levels never came. Needless to say, no authorized outlays were ever canceled ex post facto on the news that disinflation had materialized.[24]

In the Holt and Nunn amendments of 1978, the spending ceilings that were set were 8 percent and 9 percent per year, respectively. In the prevailing conditions, this would have provided for no real growth in spending, because the ceilings were roughly equal to the inflation rate plus the population-growth rate. But once inflation fell in 1982, and then hit low levels for the long term in 1983, in order for spending to stay at par it became necessary for the budget process to anticipate this disinflation. This refiguring never occurred. Spending increases continued to be scheduled at rates worthy of inflationary times. From 1981 to 1989, federal outlays soared from $678 billion to $1,145 billion, an increase of 69 percent, or 6.6 percent per year. Inflation in that span was 36 percent, or 3.9 percent per year. Population increased about 0.9 percent per year, meaning that spending growth exceeded real parity by about 1.8 percent per year, or 15 percent total over the two Reagan terms.[25]

Revenues in 1982 and 1983 were just over par when accounting for inflation and population (compared to the twenty-year moving average), then increased. By the late '80s, the revenue growth rate surpassed the high growth rate of spending maintained throughout the decade. Thus, the Reagan deficits peaked in 1986 and then shrunk in the president's second term. Reagan blamed the deficit on imprudent spending increases and said that economic growth and budgetary vigilance would eventually solve the problem. The momentum of his second term gave credence to his argument. The deficit declined from an average of $200 billion in 1983–86 to an average of $150 billion in 1987–89, even as the top tax rate was cut in steps from 50 percent to 28 percent with the Tax Reform Act of 1986.[26]

Nonetheless, Reagan's own administration initially had given Congress the opportunity to act as if inflation would not soon vanish. That is, Rosy Scenario predicted that prices would rise 5 percent per year after 1982. Five percent plus a typical 1 percent increase in population gives nearly the number by which spending increased in the Reagan era. Conceivably, had the administration produced a supply-side forecast in lieu of Rosy Scenario in 1981, such as was urged by Rutledge and the supply-siders' allies in Treasury, in which the long-term price deflator was predicted to rise 3 percent annually, it would have been more difficult for Congress to deny the evidence of disinflation that came with each passing year.

Rosy Scenario was not the only timid economic forecast in the early 1980s. Few were the brave who insisted that inflation was over and done with. After the long 1970s, such a posture risked making one a "laughingstock," as Weidenbaum feared. In banking, real interest rates stayed high, indeed in some cases grew, making the gap between the nominal rate and the inflation cover yawn. To lend on long terms in anticipation of permanently low inflation was to take a major risk. The prime rate graph for 1982–2005 is a steady regression line downward, with a clear slope. Inflation essentially stayed at the same 3 percent level during this period, yet the prime lending rate did not decline all at once but only steadily. This reflects the long process by which expectations came to acknowledge the new era of low inflation. In business, you either figured it out quickly or got burned, as the opposite fates of GE and Westinghouse showed.[27]

As for the CEA, in forecasts subsequent to Rosy Scenario it issued mea culpas for the 1981–82 recession and predicted slow growth. Then again, CEA forecasts after 1982 were hardly relevant, in that there was no legislative proposal of any consequence to buttress, and business was off to the races of its own accord. Martin Feldstein, the new CEA chair, gently insisted to Reagan that he consider a modest tax increase here and there. Reagan parried the suggestions with Lafferian arguments that tax hikes had never resulted in revenue increases. Feldstein patiently tried to show the president that this was not the case, but by that time Reagan had changed the subject. As it was, small tax-increase measures passed in 1983 and 1984.[28]

Feldstein implicitly endorsed the Herb Stein view that, after the defeat of bracket creep, it was necessary for there to be ad hoc tax increases when the budget fell into deficit. But even so, Feldstein was a full-throated supporter of ERTA, and in 1980 he had endorsed Kemp-Roth. Feldstein had an immense reputation in academic economics. Since his torching of the Carter CEA on behalf of the Steiger amendment in 1978, his eminence had only grown. It was clear that Reagan had brought in Feldstein in order to provide assurances that the best economics scholarship was represented in the White House, what with the reputation of supply-siders for being renegades.[29]

On staff at CEA, Feldstein nurtured the premier second-generation supply-sider in Larry Lindsey, as well as an economist who in future years would become supply-side economics' sharpest critic: Paul Krugman, the 2008 Nobelist. Despite his prominence in the field, Krugman's record with predictions is mixed. Consider a memo Krugman and a colleague wrote to Feldstein in September 1982, which surfaced in 1999 at the *Wall Street Journal.* "We believe that it is reasonable to expect a significant reacceleration of inflation in the near future," the memo ran. "Much of the apparent progress against inflation has resulted from temporary side effects of tight money and high real interest rates. These side effects must be expected to reverse themselves." The memo went on to note that dollar strength at the time "was well above reasonable estimates of a long-run equilibrium level." It also said that the "very low commodity prices . . . are . . . a result of unsustainably high real exchange rates and real interest rates. As real interest rates decline and the economy recovers, we can expect the real exchange rate and real commodity prices to return to approximately their historical levels. Our very rough guess is that the correction of these distorted relative prices will add five percentage points to future increases in consumer prices." Furthermore, "This estimate is conservative."[30]

From the perspective of 1999, of course, the memo was a laugher. In Bartley's newsroom, some wag created a chart plotting the memo's position against actual events, which was passed around to Bartley and colleagues and showed just how terribly and completely wrong Krugman had been about the dollar, inflation, and commodity prices.[31]

Krugman had not been alone in his faulty reckoning of the future of inflation in the early 1980s. The administration forecasting group that produced Rosy Scenario had gotten it wrong too, if not to so great a degree. And one more thing can now be settled: the Reagan plan of September 1980 was coherent. If all other spending had stayed at par in the 1980s, the tax cut and defense increase would have yielded a budget in balance. That is to say, had the rise in nondefense spending held at inflation plus population growth, outlays would have eventually met the level of receipts.[32]

Stockman finally resigned from the OMB in August 1985. Five months later his memoir, *The Triumph of Politics,* appeared. The book, which sold immensely, did more than anything else to mislead people about the origins of the Reagan deficits. Its four hundred pages were almost exclusively devoted to detailing how the spending bill of 1981 had been larded with goodies. But a few passages effectively blamed the budget deficits on ERTA. An appendix titled "The Fiscal Facts" claimed that the reason Reagan presided over hellacious deficits was that there had been a "$660 billion mistake" and a "$2 trillion error." The "mistake" was the difference between what Rosy Scenario had predicted for 1986 and what 1986 nominal GNP actually was. The "error" was the difference between the Rosy Scenario prediction for cumulative nominal GNP for the years 1982–86 and the true cumulative nominal GNP for those years. Because nominal GNP had failed to live up to the predictions of Rosy Scenario, federal receipts came in low. The deficits were the result.[33]

Stockman's appendix badly misstated the actual nominal GNP history of the United States in the 1980s. The *Statistical Abstract of the United States* of December 1985, which reprinted data that had been made publicly available the previous year, had nominal 1982–84 GNP $173 billion higher than reported in Stockman's chart. *Triumph* did not give a citation for its numbers, and an inaccuracy of this kind with the former OMB director's name on the cover is simply inexcusable. What seems likely to have happened was that Stockman's editors and ghostwriters failed to catch their *own* error about the previous three years of GNP; as the acknowledgments pointed out, literary types were brought in by publisher Harper & Row to manage the composition of the book, with much of Stockman's writing meeting its "deserved demise on the cutting-room floor."[34]

GNP numbers are subject to revision, and as the 1982–86 run was revised over the next few years, the numbers aligned ever more closely with Rosy Scenario, thereby undermining the entire premise of *The Triumph of Politics.* As the official national account statistics of the United States now show, nominal GNP in the United States in 1986 was (in $billion) 4,481. Stockman put it at 4,152 in *Triumph.* The "$660 billion mistake" overstated matters by 50 percent. As for cumulative 1982–86 nominal GNP, the official number is 19,562. *Triumph* figured on 17,855. The "$2 trillion error" was itself a fivefold error.[35]

Nevertheless, since 1986, *The Triumph of Politics* has continued to mislead pundits and historians. As a statistical representation of Reaganomics, the book is worthless. Its value lay (as Martin Anderson noted at the time) in its description of the machinations surrounding passage of the spending bill, Gramm-Latta, in 1981. William Greider's original article in the *Atlantic* had gleaned all that was useful from Stockman.[36]

Bond Bores No More

"That's when we borrowed a trillion dollars from the Japanese and threw a party," Daniel Patrick Moynihan reportedly once said of the Reagan era. What was in it for the Japanese and the others who were financing the U.S. budget deficit? What could *their* rationale have been? Unlocking the secret to this question necessarily brings us back to Mundell and the great preoccupation of his career since the implementation of supply-side economics in the early 1980s: how to deal with a world in which a stable dollar, yet a dollar not backed in gold, is the dominant currency.

Debt was popular in the 1980s. It was not only a fancy of the federal government. Corporate debt also entered an entirely new era, with the most famous—or notorious—business innovation of the 1980s the leveraged buyout, or LBO. In an LBO, an investor with little or no cash or assets buys an established company by issuing bonds (that is, debt), and then uses the receipts to purchase the company. The trick is to convince stockholders to redeem their shares for the new bonds. LBOs defined the big-business landscape for the duration of the Reagan years.

Total federal debt for the decade was $1.5 trillion; the corporate tally was half again as much, about $2.3 trillion. As with government debt, the new corporate debt of the 1980s easily exceeded the new corporate debt of the 1970s, perhaps by a factor of five to one. All of which is to say that in the 1980s there emerged a superabundance of promissory notes indicating fixed future payments in dollars, and these promissory notes found their way to every corner of the world's economy. Many of the notes initiated then sit even today in investment accounts around the globe.[37]

Here it is necessary to make a technical distinction between the rate (or "coupon") of a bond and the rate (or "dividend") of a stock. A stock dividend is declared quarterly by the governing corporate board and can be raised or lowered at any time. In inflationary times, this is an important power. The board may find that as the real value of share prices is undermined by inflation, it is prudent to counteract this trend by raising the dividend above the inflation rate. This sort of thing happened frequently in the 1970s, as corporations became desperate to persuade investors to buy shares in the context of a grim capital-gains environment. Bonds have no such flexibility. They are issued with yearly or quarterly coupons that are permanently fixed. Thus, in inflationary times, one is loath to be a bondholder. For as soon as the inflation rate exceeds that of the coupon, the bond becomes a wasting asset.

In the 1970s, therefore, bonds got killed. Those unlucky enough to hold them for the entire decade saw their investments diminished by a trebling of the price level (not to mention by taxes on the coupon). As for issuers of bonds, once inflation sets in, they have to offer supercompensatory rates, just in case inflation goes even higher. A perusal of newspaper financial pages from 1980 will reveal corporate bond offerings with annual coupons moving into the neighborhood of 20 percent.

At that time, almost no corporation could afford to promise a 20 percent annual payout for a fifteen- or twenty-year term. Only firms with the soundest balance sheets, clearest prospects, and best reputations could think in this direction. This made the business of getting good ratings from bond agencies exceedingly difficult. How is such an agency to issue a positive rating if a bond promises a 20 percent coupon for decades? The financial statements, not to mention the business model, of a qualifying firm would have to be something worthy of a Standard Oil or Morgan Guaranty Trust. All other enterprises would have to be satisfied with their issues rating as "junk."

All this changed with the collapse of inflation in the 1980s. With inflation down to 3 percent, and seemingly permanently so, corporations found that people were willing to buy bonds once again. The bond market exploded. The volume of trade in new issues, secondary issues, preexisting issues—everything in the bond universe—far exceeded anything that had ever been seen before. Much of this trade centered around the unfortunately named junk bonds. For the label of "junk" that attached to so many corporate offerings in the 1980s merely reflected the slowness of the bond-rating agencies to recognize that a new, healthier reality had dawned.

Very few people fully understood what was going on at the time. The iconic novel of the 1980s, Tom Wolfe's *Bonfire of the Vanities,* has as its protagonist a bond trader, a "top producer" by the name of Sherman McCoy, who works for the mythical Wall Street house of Pierce & Pierce. McCoy makes a million dollars a year selling bonds. He recalls how his boss, Gene Lopwitz, had once explained why, just now, there was so much money in this line of work:

> In the Lopwitz analysis, they had Lyndon Johnson to thank. Ever so quietly, the U.S. had started printing money to finance the war in Vietnam. Before anyone, even Johnson, knew what was happening, a worldwide inflation had begun. Everyone woke up to it when the Arabs suddenly jacked up oil prices in the early 1970s. In no time, markets of all sorts became heaving crapshoots: gold, silver, copper, currencies, bank certificates, corporate notes—even bonds. For decades the bond business had been the bedridden giant of Wall Street. At firms such as Salomon Brothers, Morgan Stanley, Goldman Sachs, and Pierce & Pierce, twice as much money had always changed hands on the bond market as on the stock market. But prices had budged by only pennies at a time, and mostly they went down. . . . The Pierce & Pierce bond department had consisted of only twenty souls, twenty rather dull souls known as the Bond Bores. The less promising members of the firm were steered into bonds, where they could do less harm.

And then the 1980s hit:

> Well, there was no more talk about the Bond Bores these days. . . . The bond market had caught fire, and experienced salesmen such as himself were all at once much in demand. . . . Bonds now represented four-fifths of Pierce & Pierce's business, and the young hotshots, the Yalies, the Harvards, the Stanfords, were desperate to get to the bond trading room.[38]

McCoy's analysis, by way of his boss, was passable. But the bond traders really had Richard Nixon and Paul Volcker to thank for the boom in their profession. Nixon had delinked the dollar from gold and hence had ensured that dollar-denominated assets had to have a feature—a coupon, perhaps—that could compensate for inflation. Volcker had brought the money supply under control and initiated a stable dollar. This guaranteed that even a small coupon was sufficient to cover or even exceed inflation. A small coupon means a high price, and bonds boomed.

All of this is essential information in assaying why there were maximally high federal budget deficits in the 1980s. For the reason there was so much debt in the 1980s, federal and corporate, is that an inordinate number of investors wanted to buy it. This was only natural: if debt can reliably keep up with, or modestly exceed, inflation, money invested in debt will not be lost. One might ask, then, why there was not a debt boom in previous eras of low inflation, such as the 1950s. The short answer is: because there was a reliable gold standard. In the 1950s, an investor could simply hold cash—that is, dollars—and expect the holding to retain its real value. After all, dollars were linked to the greatest market indicator of the real value of currencies, gold. So long as the market price of gold did not exceed $35 an ounce, investors could be confident that for dollars to retain their value, they needed only to be held. No coupon was necessary. Furthermore, cash is safer than bonds, which after all are promissory notes to pay cash in the future.

In the 1970s, after the U.S. had reneged on its pledge to keep dollars at $35 per ounce of gold, no holding was guaranteed to be low risk. Cash badly devalued under high inflation, as did bonds with low coupons. Stocks could theoretically compensate for inflation by means of future dividends indexed for inflation, but that was a big "if." The only reliable storehouse of value was commodities. In Wanniski's phrase, the growth rate in the supply of commodities is a function of "the limitations of the planet's resources." Not so with currencies, whose natural limitation is the earth's supply of small pieces of paper—not much of a limit. Hence, in inflationary environments, commodities naturally rise in price, at a minimum, at the same level as inflation. Yet inflation was conquered in the early 1980s. This enabled the buying of bonds en masse.[39]

There was an alternative scenario. Had the United States also, in the 1980s, returned to a gold standard, there may well not have been the boom in debt. Because a gold-backed dollar would have been a sure bet not to lose value, cash would have competed with bonds for the risk-averse portion of investors' portfolios. But because there remained the possibility of inflation in the absence of a dollar link to gold, a modest coupon on cash was necessary. Hence the bond boom.

The supply-side insistence on gold in the wake of the August 1981 tax cut is important to remember when apportioning "blame"—and that is surely not the right word—for the stratospheric federal deficits of the two Reagan terms. Had there been a return to a reliable gold standard in 1982, there would have been dramatically lower demand for debt instruments in world markets in upcoming years. Investors would have been willing to hold cash in the ballast portions of their portfolios. But in the absence of a gold-backed dollar, some premium had to be paid on cash to hedge the small-inflation scenarios of the Volcker era. The instrument of the bond fitted this role perfectly. Soon investors were baying for debt as never before. The federal government (as well as corporate America) proved perfectly willing to supply it. Thus did the deficits meet not resistance from the markets, but enthusiasm.

The fundamental apparatus of economics is the nexus of supply and demand. For some indeterminable reason, virtually all analysis of the 1980s deficits has focused on the supply component of this nexus, indeed on just one contributing factor to that supply—federal marginal tax rates after the passage of ERTA. Tax rates are not revenues, and revenues are not deficits. Revenues are one component, along with expenditures, of one aspect of deficits, their supply. The supply of deficits, not deficits tout court, is the difference between revenues and expenditures.

The real revolution as regards the federal deficit—toward debt broadly—was on the demand side. The markets wanted deficits and debt in the 1980s. They had not in the 1970s. Both proclivities are intelligible. In the 1970s, inflation ate up the real value of debt. In the 1980s, it did not. The great demand for debt in the 1980s is the reason interest rates started the march downward and the value of underlying debt soared. In supply-demand curve language, in the 1980s the demand curve gained elasticity once the U.S. government signaled that it was serious about keeping inflation at bay. Thereafter, if the United States (or corporations) were going to issue debt, the markets would buy it. For the graphically inclined, it was all deducible from the Mundell-Fleming model.

Bipartisanship

Jimmy Carter had pledged during his 1976 campaign to dedicate his tax policy to reform. He would seek not to cut rates but to close loopholes. Classically, "tax reform" involves "neutrality," in that any loophole-closing in favor of the government is balanced by rate cuts in favor of payers. Carter stumped for the loophole-closing but not for the rate reductions, so that "reform" would be a one-way street in government's favor. This was all the more incredible given that Carter easily could have packaged his crackdown on the three-martini-lunch deductions with reductions in marginal rates. Instead, he determined to kill the Son of Kemp-Roth bill, even if it meant no progress on loopholes. It probably cost Carter the presidency.

By 1985, after the personal ERTA cuts were fully implemented, supply-siders were planning their next move. At a conference of the faithful called by Kemp in 1983, an attractive idea was raised. Why not seek a cut in the top rate down to a very low level, along with elimination of virtually all progressivity in the code, in exchange for concessions on exemptions and loopholes? Democrats in both chambers were thinking along these lines, and it piqued the supply-siders' interest.[40]

Senator Bill Bradley was the driving force. In a stellar example of rapprochement, in the mid-1980s Jeff Bell had agreed to work with Bradley, the man who had defeated him for the New Jersey Senate seat in 1978, to see through a tax-reform bill. Bell kept Bradley in touch with the supply-siders as the senator built up support for reform among congressional Democrats. The election of 1984 came and went, Reagan winning reelection in a landslide. Shortly afterward, the president indicated that he would enthusiastically receive any sound reform bill that might emerge from Congress.

At the same time, Arthur Laffer was himself planning a 1986 senatorial run against Alan Cranston in California (a run that would prove unsuccessful). Laffer was encouraged by the tax-reform talk and figured he could be a deal-sealer in Congress. Here was an opportunity to complete ERTA, he thought, by bringing the top rate down as well as by flattening the code.[41]

Other supply-siders were not so sure. Entin and Ture had already seen ACRS canceled by TEFRA and wondered whether "loophole-closing" would mean more negative developments on the business-tax side. Perhaps investment credits and write-offs stood to be sacrificed to "uniformity" in the tax code. Furthermore, uniformity might also mean bringing the rate for capital gains up to the level of the marginal personal rate.

A think tank started by Ture and joined by Entin, the Institute for Research on the Economics of Taxation (IRET)—which remains to this day the premier supply-side policy-research outfit—churned out papers warning against erasing phantom loopholes in the code. Even so, Entin and Ture knew that with inflation low for the long term, if preferments for capital gains and investment in plant and equipment were lifted, the effect would not be so severe as in the 1970s.[42]

The reform wave had built up too much momentum for IRET's concerns to carry much weight. As Alan S. Murray and Jeffrey L. Birnbaum relate in *Showdown at Gucci Gulch* (1988), almost miraculously, both lobbyists (their hangout in the Capitol was called Gucci Gulch) and members of Congress came to see that complexities in the tax code, which typically represented political favors, were worth setting aside for lower rates. The provisions of the Tax Reform Act as it moved through both chambers in 1986 were stunning. IRET's worries aside, it was a near-perfect example of supply-side purity. Loopholes were closed en masse as the number of income-tax brackets on the personal side was cut to four. In the 1970s, there had been twenty-five brackets; under ERTA, fifteen. As for rates, the new law sent the top personal rate down from 50 percent (as under ERTA) to 39 percent in 1987 and 28 percent thereafter. The bottom rate was 15 percent. After the law was phased in, the code would be the flattest it had been since 1913, and rates were low.

Laffer finally got the reduction in the top rate for both wage and investment income that he had desired in 1981. Indeed, the Tax Reform Act of 1986 outdid Kemp-Roth. The lowest level to which Kemp-Roth had striven to bring the top rate was 36 percent. The major concession was that the individual capital-gains tax rate, as Entin and Ture had feared, was allowed to rise from a maximum of 20 percent (as under ERTA) to 28 percent.

Capital-gains rates ordinarily are set below the marginal rate for income because capital gains reflect inflationary as well as real gains. In the 1970s, inflation made virtually all capital gains unreal. Therefore investment had dried up, as representatives from Silicon Valley had had to tell Congress in 1978 in anticipation of the Steiger amendment, and as Feldstein had verified in his academic research. With the collapse of inflation after 1981, however, the inflation component of capital gains was far lower in the 1980s than it had been for years. It is possible, therefore, that the effective capital-gains rate was lower after 1986 at 28 percent than it was in 1982 at 20 percent, when inflation was still hovering near 10 percent.

Bartley was pleased with the Tax Reform Act of 1986, but he also sought to remind his readers of what had been achieved with the capital-gains reductions of 1978 and 1981. He wrote in *The Seven Fat Years*: "Capital gains were especially important to the young entrepreneurial company; this was the pot at the end of the rainbow that moves breakaway engineers to take out mortgages on their houses to start a business." One review doubted that Apple Computer cofounder Steve Jobs "was motivated by dreams of 'bountiful capital gains.'" But Bartley countered that they may well "have motivated venture capitalist Arthur Rock, who did indeed finance [Jobs]." Bartley's research files for *The Seven Fat Years* are stocked with sheets of historical data on venture-capital commitments in the United States. The big inflection point upward is invariably 1978.[43]

As for loopholes, Bartley asserted that the Tax Reform Act of 1986 had treated business well. "If you cut the [marginal personal] rate to 28 percent, you don't have to launch a search-and-destroy mission for loopholes; they will dry up in any event," he wrote. In other words, it would be uneconomical for business to divert money into the hands of K Street lobbyists if the marginal rate of taxation was as low as 28 percent. Indeed, as Murray and Birnbaum showed in *Gucci Gulch*, some of the nation's largest employers, such as IBM, Procter & Gamble, and General Motors, were determined advocates of the Tax Reform Act of 1986.[44]

Another *Belle Époque*?

As the 1980s came to a close, Bartley swelled with pride over the accomplishments of supply-side economics, of the policy mix of his boon companion Mundell. "To put it as modestly as possible, surely something went right in the 1980s," Bartley wrote at the end of *The Seven Fat Years*. He had been as coy in his Iowa State University commencement address of 1981, in which he said (surely with Michael 1 in mind), "Since about 1974, the recuperative powers of this great nation have been at work."

Yet Bartley also wondered whether the nation was handling the new prosperity as well as it could. He marveled at all the shoppers at the mall, with their prodigious disposable incomes and $100 Reebok sneakers. He conceded that many individuals would go home from the mall not to their parents or families, but to their own places, which they could now afford and where it was easier to indulge in the fruits of the sexual revolution. The great prosperity of the 1980s had brought about not only lots of new "stuff," but also the conditions whereby morality became a more private and relative affair. "In one sense, it's a symptom of social pathology," Bartley wrote.[45]

Supply-siders typically waved off charges that the 1980s were the "decade of greed." Or else they maintained that greed was good, to the extent that start-ups, LBOs, and visionary outfits like GE enabled people to make good on their talents for work and to obtain remuneration that held its value. Yet it remains a fair point that the 1980s, while prosperous, did not in any recognizable way make America better from a moral point of view—the sharp increase in philanthropic giving notwithstanding. Abortions continued in their yearly millions, race relations settled into an uneasy truce, and both high and popular culture remained debased and degraded.

The greatest challenge for any successful economic theory is to make the leap to "normative economics"—the science of not merely what is, but what ought to be. It cannot be said that supply-side economics made this heady transition, though there are stirrings in the writings of Bartley, Mundell, and Ture. Now, this is to criticize supply-side economics from a lofty vantage point indeed. Perhaps the only rigorous economic theories to achieve normative heights are those of Aristotle, the School of Salamanca, Hume, Smith, Marx, Mill, Mises, and Hayek. Keynes was out of his depth as a moralist.[46]

And yet twentieth-century liberalism, which professed to adopt the economics of the *General Theory* wholesale, made a valiant if flawed effort to marry normative with economic concerns. Liberalism strove to capture the excess in prosperity and redistribute it to the poor and disenfranchised. Under FDR, this meant declaring that there already was enough aggregate wealth in existence and using the power of the federal government to play Robin Hood. Under JFK, this meant striving to increase the size of the pie.

JFK's strategy was superior. Above all, it was more honest. Growth was objectively necessary during the Great Depression, and yet FDR preferred to consider growth a characteristic of the Roaring '20s and hence undesirable as he pursued the New Deal. JFK, in contrast, conceded that growth was a paramount goal and prefatory to all other goals. To be sure, from the perspective of politics, it was easier for JFK to push for growth than for FDR. JFK inherited the unprecedented Eisenhower sluggishness, three recessions in a two-term presidency. FDR, though he followed the disastrous Republican Hoover, knew that had he plumped for growth, he would have been seen as in league with Hoover's Republican predecessors, Coolidge and Harding.

The problem with JFK's plan was one of tactics. The policy mix of the neoclassical synthesis—loose money and high taxes—got it backward. After JFK realized this, about a year and a half into his presidency, the policy mix was reversed and the boom started. Then the great liberal project of skimming off excess wealth in order to make a better society became plausible. Alas, LBJ did not skim but rather lopped off. His spending exceeded the huge 5 percent real increases in federal revenue in the six years after 1962. Thereafter, "big-government liberalism" would have a bad name. If LBJ's spending had been more constrained, or if JFK had lived, the whole thing would have worked. Thus, for example, the 1963 economic report outlined small-scale redistributionist spending programs that, had they fully constituted the Great Society, would have made it a success.

In the 1980s, it was typical of Reaganites to dismiss complaints that America was not good enough. Such charges reminded them of the tiresome moral hectoring of the 1960s. George Bush, who succeeded Reagan as president in 1989, recognized that something was deficient nonetheless, as evidenced in his "thousand points of light" speech in which he called for a rebirth of volunteerism.

The deeper issue is one that perhaps America has never fully faced. The United States is the most fabulously prosperous civilization in world history. To live virtuously in such an atmosphere will take effort, thinking, and reflection. Marx was surely wrong when he speculated that when the condition of perfect abundance is attained (under communism), it will not be necessary to learn morality, because it will be obvious: since there will be plenty to go around, simply be nice to people, and all will be okay. A more serious view was that pioneered by the early avant-garde artists, including such figures as Matisse and Cézanne, whose paintings sought to indicate that the newly prosperous bourgeois needs to learn how to live well in two important ways. First, he must learn how to enjoy prosperity without being embarrassed by it. Second, he must see to it that his conscience is well-formed despite the distractions of getting and spending. In the 1950s and 1960s, it was one of the signal achievements of the first "neoconservative" critics to recognize and write about this wholesome and relevant trend in early avant-garde art.[47]

Has America ever owned up to its obligation to learn how to live well under prosperity? Do Americans realize they even have this obligation? If not, perhaps the reason is the frequency of recessions. Aside from the economic discomfort they bring, recessions interrupt any momentum that may be building toward a serious effort to live virtuously in prosperity. Bartley suggested that recessions provided a sort of moral cop-out. When it is hard to make a living, a compensation is that one is relieved of the duties of prosperity. From the moralist's point of view, poverty, too, has its temptations.

12

The World Over

Desiderantes meliorem patriam
"They desire a better country"
—Hebrews 11:16, and motto of the Order of Canada

The United States slipped back into recession in 1990. The efficient cause was twofold. First, the federal government forced part of the banking system to close. This was the savings and loan (S&L) portion of the system. Created by Depression-era regulation, S&Ls offered customers savings accounts on which they could not write checks, which in theory meant higher rates of interest. In the 1970s, it became difficult for the S&Ls to attract and hold depositors, because the dollar was weak and taxes punished income from bank interest with rates that rose to 70 percent. As depositors left the S&Ls, the institutions were forced to make riskier loans in order to stay in business. Then, in the 1980s, the boom in stocks and bonds made S&L deposits even less attractive. So these institutions' search for higher returns intensified.[1]

When some of the banks inevitably started to fail in the late 1980s, the United States forbade S&Ls from holding junk bonds. The junk market was going through a decline at the time, and this decision only accelerated it. Suddenly, S&Ls had to divest themselves of performing holdings, "mark-to-market" (the beast of 2008 played a role in 1989), and sell at fire-sale prices. Capital positions deteriorated and regulators moved in to close doors. Even formerly well-run S&Ls were forced to shut down because of the new regulatory regime.

Bartley was aghast at the spectacle. He had watched Michael Milken's junk bonds fund such enterprises as TCI Communications, McCaw Cellular, and Turner Broadcasting in the 1980s. Obviously, these bonds had not truly been junk. They had only appeared so to a bond-rating profession nurtured on the long 1970s. Furthermore, Bartley marveled, bond raters seemed to be biased toward public over private issues, making them miss "spectacular defaults like . . . the Washington Public Power Supply System, or WHOOPS."

A restriction in the credit market on the order of some three thousand closed banks would mean leaner business times in any context. But then, in 1990, President Bush suggested a tax increase, and Congress obliged. The top rate was taken up three points to 31 percent in 1991. The 28 percent marginal rate, the high achievement of the Tax Reform Act, had been in effect all of three years: 1988, 1989, and 1990. In the face of a partially closed banking system and increased taxes, the economy shrunk at a 3 percent rate in the last quarter of 1990 and a 2 percent rate in the first quarter of 1991. From 1982 through 2007, a span of a quarter century, this would be the only episode of two consecutive quarters of negative economic growth.

The old rule of thumb is that a "recession" is two quarters in a row of GDP contraction. Officially, recessions are now counted by the National Bureau of Economic Research (NBER). The NBER has a formula, based on many things in addition to GDP growth, that determines periods of recession. By the NBER formula, there was also a recession in 2001. In this period, however, as indeed in all periods from the end of 1982 through 2007, exclusive of the 1990–91 turn, there was not one stretch of two consecutive quarters of negative economic growth.[2]

A twenty-five-year run of growth at the rate of postwar prosperity interrupted by one mild contraction: this is surely one of the greatest examples of sustained prosperity in the history of the world since the industrial revolution.

Stabilization was the goal of Keynesianism. Governmental management of the economy would smooth out the cycle of booms and busts. There would have to be trade-offs (the essence of the Phillips curve), such as slow growth in exchange for smoothness and inflation in exchange for unemployment. But there would be no repeat of the Great Depression. And yet, ironically, the greatest stabilization occurred under the auspices of Keynesianism's relentless adversary, supply-side economics. Twenty-five years of noninflationary growth at a fabled rate, with one recession blip, is a result that Keynesians could have aspired to only in their dreams. Keynesians, for their part, had a hard time acknowledging what was happening as the new stabilization unfolded. A Brookings publication said in 1985: "America's inflationary symptoms may well have been suppressed for a time. Nonetheless, inflation and stagflation formed a part of the wider challenge that still grips Western societies. . . . Growth may not become so spectacularly rapid again." And: "The remainder of the decade [of the 1980s] will test whether [the new] approach can continue to command enough enduring support to prevail. When it no longer does, Americans must think seriously about the reconstruction of political economy on a more open and democratic basis."[3]

Robert Lucas at last called on academic economics to acknowledge what was taking place. In a widely read journal article of 1990 called "Supply-Side Economics: An Analytic Review," Lucas applied econometric analysis to the supply-side record and found the results impressive. He told the profession that supply-side economics had produced significantly more growth, with fewer trade-offs, than previous models would have expected. "I have called this paper an analytical review of 'supply-side economics,'" Lucas wrote, "a term associated in the United States with extravagant claims about the effects of changes in the tax structure on capital accumulation. . . . The supply-side economists . . . have delivered the largest genuinely free lunch I have seen in 25 years in the business, and I believe we would have a better society if we followed their advice." In 1995, Lucas devoted his own Nobel address to recollecting his part in lancing the theory of the Phillips curve, the death of which in practice supply-side economics had secured in the 1980s.[4]

By the twenty-fifth year of the great run, Lucas called for general recognition of what the policy mix had wrought. He wrote in the *Wall Street Journal* in 2007:

In the past 50 years, there have been two macroeconomic policy changes in the United States that have really mattered. One of these was the supply-side reduction in marginal tax rates, initiated after Ronald Reagan was elected president in 1980. . . . The other was the advent of "inflation targeting," which is the term I prefer for a monetary policy focused on inflation control to the exclusion of other objectives. As a result of these changes, steady GDP growth, low unemployment rates, and low inflation rates—once thought to be an impossible combination—have been a reality in the U.S. for more than 20 years.

"Once thought to be an impossible combination"—the words apply not least to Lucas himself. In 1981, in two *New York Times* articles, Lucas had written that Reagan was doing it the same old wrong way. Reagan was initiating a budget deficit that would have to be paid for with fiat money. It was time for everyone in the profession who had dismissed the supply-side policy mix, Lucas himself included, to concede that it had met with success.[5]

What Were the 1990s?

When George Bush raised taxes in 1990, the supply-siders deserted him. This was a strange move. The Bush increase took the top rate up a mere three percentage points, to 31 percent. This rate was fully nineteen points lower than the marginal rate of ERTA. Surely, during the wrangling over tax reform in 1986, if the supply-siders had been offered a final top rate of 31 percent they would have taken it.[6]

Perhaps success had spoiled the supply-siders. In any case, Laffer opted to support Bush's opponent, Bill Clinton, in the 1992 election, while Wanniski threw in with third-party candidate Ross Perot. When Clinton won, he immediately pushed the top rate up to 39.6 percent. He also proposed major spending initiatives, including a plan to nationalize health care. The push for higher taxes and spending ended with the midterm elections of 1994, when the Republicans took Congress.

Under Clinton, economic growth inverted the pattern of the Reagan years. For the three years 1993–95, annual growth was 3 percent. For the following five years, 1996–2000, the figure was 4 percent per year. In the three years after the Mundellian policy mix was implemented in 1982, growth had surged at 5.1 percent before moderating for the following four years to 3.6 percent. This had become the pattern: fast growth after a recession followed by moderate growth as the economy got into a groove. In the Clinton years, the period of moderate growth came first, and fast growth second. As for the stock and bond markets, they hit their floor on election day, November 1994.

The great boom of the latter 1990s forced the supply-siders to ask whether tax cuts are necessary to spur growth. The argument they settled on was a plausible one. The tax policy pioneered by Reagan in the 1980s had actually been maintained in the 1990s. As Alan Reynolds pointed out, under ERTA, the top rate was 50 percent, giving way after a few years to 39 percent, then 28 percent, and the capital-gains rate was 20 percent (upped to 28 percent in 1986); under Clinton, the top rate was 40 percent and the capital-gains rate 28 percent, lowered to 20 percent in 1997. The differences were a wash.

Reynolds also observed that federal revenue from the income tax as a percentage of GDP was not only constant from Reagan through Clinton; it had been constant in the postwar era generally. It was almost always in the neighborhood of 8–9 percent. In other words, in terms of revenues, according to "Reynolds's Law" it does not matter whether tax rates are high or low. The take from the income tax will be the same relative to output. So why not have low rates?[7]

What changed in the 1990s was spending. After the Republicans took Congress, Clinton became the greatest spending hawk in the modern history of the presidency. His major domestic spending proposal (AmeriCorps) did not even reach the $1 billion mark in yearly appropriations. As for foreign aid, he asked for amounts in the low millions. Futhermore, in the late 1990s the great expenditure categories of the previous fifteen years were scaled down or vanished. The victory in the Cold War reduced defense spending by $100 billion per year, and the S&L bailout, which had been costing $30 billion per year, was completed in 1996.[8]

Therefore, the budget tallied to balance in 1997 and to surplus in 1998. In 2000, when the surplus peaked at more than $200 billion, federal spending was 18.4 percent of GDP. In 1987 and 1989, tax receipts had been 18.4 percent of GDP. The Clinton years proved that given the perpetuation of Reaganite tax policy, all that was necessary to balance the budget was spending vigilance.

The achievement of budget balance in the late 1990s, given tax rates identical to (if not a little lower than) those under ERTA, affords an opportunity to assess the Laffer curve. It is important to grasp that the caricature view of the Laffer curve—that deficits after tax cuts must be smaller than before—was never correct. It was never correct because this was not the interpretation offered by the supply-siders themselves when the curve was introduced, as evidenced by a range of key sources, from Wanniski's "It's Time to Cut Taxes" article of 1974 to the announcement in 1978 and publication in 1979 of Laffer's Prototype Wedge Model. Moreover, it was never correct because it begged questions, including whether the supply-siders had really wanted federal revenues to displace upwards of 24 percent of the economy in 1983, which was the level of federal spending that year.

The supply-side record on what would happen to revenues given tax cuts was clear. Kemp-Roth II projected revenues dipping yearly, to 18 percent of GDP. The Prototype Wedge Model had income-tax revenues sinking between 5 percent and 14 percent percent per annum for five years, given Kemp-Roth. Ture, from 1962 on, insisted that government set up the tax system with one goal in mind: achievement of the highest possible growth in the real economy. His model assumed unchanging receipts.[9]

The supply-siders had long said that revenues would be good, even above average, given low marginal tax rates, because the economy would be booming. But by no means were revenues to increase as a percentage of GDP. That would mean that the government was displacing the real economy, as Mundell explained in his Nobel address. It was an article of faith among the supply-siders that revenues must *decrease* as a percentage of GDP.

The supply-siders wanted to make a deal with government. Revenues would be large by absolute measurements (that is, as compared to population growth and inflation, a standard metric), but they would shrink as a fraction of the real economy. The real economy was to grow at a faster rate than government receipts. If there was to be budget balance, spending too had to grow at a slower rate than GDP. The former had been occurring since 1982, and the latter finally occurred in the second half of the 1990s. Hence, in 1998 the budget went into surplus.[10]

The consensus on tax policy in the United States influenced the rest of the world. In economics, the "demonstration effect" occurs when successful policies on the part of one actor are adopted by others. The American successes of the 1980s and 1990s engendered just such a demonstration effect. In the 1990s and early 2000s (in some cases because of the express advice of supply-side proponents), virtually all of Eastern Europe, Ireland, and various countries in Africa, Latin America, and Asia set up tax regimes that mimicked those of the United States: top rates well below 50 percent, code progressivity kept to a minimum. High growth rates ensued.

Nonetheless, Western Europe—"old Europe," in Wanniski friend Donald Rumsfeld's phrase—stuck with high tax rates and progressivity. Another economist with a supply-side perspective, Nobel-winner Edward Prescott, asked in the title of a 2004 journal article, "Why Do Americans Work So Much More Than Europeans?" The abstract gave the answer: "Americans now work 50 percent more than do the Germans, French, and Italians. . . . The surprising finding [of this article] is that [the] marginal rate accounts for the predominance of differences at points in time and the large change in relative labor supply over time." This is the point Paul Craig Roberts had made three decades before. If trading further work for leisure is encouraged by high marginal rates, people will trade further work for leisure. To Prescott, this is the reason Western Europe has grown at such a slow pace—60 percent slower—compared to the United States since 1982.[11]

Reynolds said in Lithuania in 1997: "It is useful to examine the experience of many countries that emerged from serious economic trouble and began sustained periods of prosperity. These are called 'economic miracles.' *Every* economic 'miracle' . . . has included a large reduction in the highest marginal tax rates. Some of the most famous miracles . . . also included a huge reduction of taxes on imports. . . . Some of the most durable reforms . . . also included a currency board or similar firm commitment to preserve the value of money."[12]

Openness to trade had also been demonstrated brilliantly by the United States in the 1990s. Here Clinton completed the work of Reagan's supply-side revolution. Free trade may have been one of the "pillars of Reaganomics," as Laffer has often said, but in fact Reagan's record on free trade was ambiguous, especially in his first term. One of Reagan's second-term initiatives, however, was the North American Free Trade Agreement (NAFTA). NAFTA died in Congress in the 1980s and early 1990s, but Clinton embraced it with gusto. In one of the greatest feats of presidential determination since the passage of ERTA, in 1993 Clinton willed NAFTA into law against stern opposition from the Democrats in Congress, then still in a healthy majority. After NAFTA, Clinton consistently toured the globe striving to make further free-trade agreements for the United States wherever possible. Often, the local humiliations the American team would have to endure were sharp, but Clinton was persistent.[13]

As for monetary policy, the United States demonstrated to the rest of the world that a premium must be placed on price stability. It is unlikely that Alan Greenspan (who replaced Volcker as Fed chair in 1987) followed a gold-price rule, but it is highly likely that he did follow a similar regimen, probably the "Taylor rule," named after supply-side ally John B. Taylor of Stanford University. The Taylor rule is a simple equation showing what Fed policy should be given various levels of inflation, unemployment, and output, with the primary emphasis on inflation. An advantage accrues to the economy if the Fed even *seems* to be following it or any inflation-targeting rule: monetary policy is predictable. Business therefore feels free to run. Throughout the 1990s, as in the Reagan years, inflation stayed low, averaging about 3 percent. In 1998, the misery index hit 6, its lowest level since 1965.

Shanghai 2010

Lithuania, other nations in post-Communist Europe, Ireland, and all the other countries moved by the demonstration effect could control their own tax policies. As for trade, smaller countries could cut duties and quotas, and they could set up bilateral or multilateral agreements with partners. But monetary policy was a different matter entirely. To have a stable currency in the pre-1913 days meant to fix to gold. But now gold swung wildly, from $35 per ounce through the 1960s, to $800 in the following period, down to $300 in the era of the policy mix, to $1,000 in 2008. To fix to gold was to fix to a yo-yo, a yo-yo unconsciously controlled by the United States Federal Reserve.

Certain countries, in exasperation, had tried to fix to gold despite this variation. Jacques Rueff's prompting of France to hoard gold in the 1960s led to an experiment that the nation would like to forget. In the 1970s, France issued bonds backed in gold. This meant that if the gold price shot upward, so would France's debt-service obligations. As gold blew through the roof in the 1970s, when the United States Federal Reserve printed more money, France's debts went up accordingly. (The "Giscard," as this instrument was called, became a plot device in Tom Wolfe's *Bonfire of the Vanities*.)[14]

Fixing either to international money or to gold became impossible for smaller countries after 1913, or at least after 1929, because there *was* no stable international money. There was Bretton Woods, but what was a nonsuperpower to do after 1971? Follow the convoy of currencies being led by a sound dollar, Mundell said at Williamsburg in 1983. But that strategy still left one at the mercy of the helmsman, the Fed. Could there not be a better way?

In the 1990s, a country with rapid economic growth on its mind invited Mundell to be the first Westerner granted full rights of residence within its capital city. This country was China. China knew, as it contemplated growth, that no one would accept its currency in any volume on the international markets. If China wanted to engage in trade, it either had to dollarize its economy or make an ironclad fix to a major currency. Thus, China adopted a policy whereby it fixed its currency unit, the yuan, to the dollar at a rate of about 7–1. China also gained the means by which it could guarantee the fix by running huge trade surpluses with the rest of the world, and particularly with the United States.

This allowed it to amass a fund of reserves, mainly dollars. In the event that the yuan sold below the 7–1 ratio, the Chinese could use their dollars to buy yuan on the international foreign-exchange markets and thus raise its price. If the Chinese currency appreciated, it could be sold for more dollars.[15]

The Chinese were not so naïve to as to keep upwards of $1 trillion in reserves in a single currency; the dollar, after all, had lost four-fifths of its value as recently as the 1970s. The Chinese diversified their holdings into other major currencies (and assets) and gold. This made their huge stash of currency reserves better positioned to stay at about par. If the dollar went up in value, gold would sink, and vice versa.

This Chinese strategy bears the marks of Mundellian theory. It has been Mundell's view since the triumph of supply-side economics in the 1980s that the next essential reform is to complete the work of Bretton Woods. In his Nobel address, he argued that there must be a restoration of something like the classical gold standard. Currently, gold has become merely a "passenger in the system," in Mundell's view, because of the "awesome power" of the Federal Reserve to determine its price. If, however, there were other currencies as stable as the dollar, as indeed there were in the generation before 1914, the price of gold would no longer be beholden to the Fed's whim. A safe haven out of dollars could be the yen—or the euro.[16]

The other area of work for which Mundell won the Nobel concerned "optimum currency areas." This scholarship has earned him the label of "godfather of the euro," because he argued that if a zone of the world with a transactions area as large and as prosperous as that of the United States had one currency, that currency would be a genuine alternative to the dollar as the unit of account in asset sheets around the world. In particular, national stashes of currency reserves, which have a special need to maintain their value, would be keen on stockpiling not only dollars but also this viable rival.[17]

Mundell was gleeful when the euro was created in the 1990s. Here at last was a one-currency transactions area as large as the United States and nearly as prosperous. The "nearly" was the rub. From 1982 to 2007, the United States left the Eurozone economy in the dust. The United States grew at a 60 percent premium to the big Eurozone countries in this period. Mundell knew that the euro could not pressure the dollar into being stable if investments in euros were linked to a perpetually slow-growth zone. Thus, he came to believe that it is Europe's great obligation to the world to grow faster by means of tax, regulatory, and labor-market reform. In other words, Europe must subject itself to a supply-side revolution. As Mundell said of the United States in 1969, "There is no more socially useful service a very large country like the U.S. can perform for the entire world than to preserve price stability and full employment for itself."[18]

Mundell has seen potential rivals to the dollar come and go. In the 1980s, it appeared that the yen might displace the dollar as the world's major reserve currency. After all, Japan had half the population of the United States and the same per-capita GDP. But then in the 1990s Japan went into a bizarre funk, one spawned by regulation and taxation, that left its economy static for a decade and a half.

Today, however—as growth rates converge and major new economies, such as India and China, yearn for stable money in international transactions—is a good moment, Mundell believes, to complete the work of Bretton Woods. The first step is to restore fixed exchange rates. This could be done de facto if the major central banks committed to price stability as their sole objective. As Mundell wrote in 2000, "Let us imagine for a moment that we had a smoothly working fixed exchange rate system among the [major countries] and that the agreed-upon inflation target was jointly pursued. Under these circumstances, what would be the function of exchange rate volatility? Apart from keeping hedge funds in business, there is none! There is no function for volatile exchange rates between areas that have a high degree of price stability." Next, Mundell thinks that currencies should once again become convertible—not "pegged," whereby currency reserves are brought to bear when exchange rates move out of bands, but convertible to something else. What would that something else be? Gold?[19]

Not quite. Mundell would like to see an arrangement whereby the dollar, and all major currencies, would be convertible to a new unit. This unit might be a fraction of a euro, a fraction of a yen, and a fraction of a dollar. Perhaps, in the future, you could go to the Treasury and for $100 get, say, 30 euros, 300 yen, and 30 dollars. Conversion would be "automatic"—as it was in the nineteenth century. The Fed would have to maintain reserves in yen and euros in the event of conversion requests. The same would apply to the other central banks. Alternatively, and Mundell believes that this is more plausible, the entire system could be managed by the IMF. Indeed, managing requests for the "DEY" (dollar-euro-yen) could be the IMF's raison d'être, something the fund now lacks.[20]

The advantage of such a system would be that the overprinting of currency by any of the major countries would result in redemption requests and thus the drawdown of reserves. Overprinting would have to stop in order for the offender's convertibility to be maintained. This would mimic the methods of the classical gold standard. As for gold itself, in this new arrangement it would be the vehicle of choice for central banks' inflation targeting. An increase in the market price of gold in dollars, for example, would signal to the Fed that it is printing too many dollars. Under the DEY agreement, the Fed would then curtail dollar production.

In sum, Mundell wants the major central banks to target inflation by watching the private price of gold in their respective currencies, as well as to maintain convertibility to a unit that is the sum of their currencies. This would be Bretton Woods with several key currencies, the currencies themselves functioning in gold's role as the reserve asset. There would be fixed rates and stable prices to the extent that the private price of gold stayed stable. And anyone who held a potentially depreciating currency could demand that it be redeemed for others at a set rate.

As for smaller countries, Mundell would prefer that their currencies fix to the major currency in their area: Latin America to the dollar, North Africa to the euro, Asia to the yen. Geopolitical concerns and nationalistic rivalries would appear to make such a proposal rather unrealistic. China accepting leadership of the yen? The Middle East that of—whom, a dazzling Iraq? Perhaps the currencies of India and China will in time become candidates for inclusion in this scheme. But that date remains decades away, particularly for China, which must overcome the world's memory of Mao in order to be taken seriously as a currency issuer.

Mundell is now pressing for another international monetary conference on the order of Bretton Woods. No such conference has been held since 1944. It should be held, he believes, in some newfangled place, such as Shanghai, perhaps in 2010, coincident with the World's Fair. The economic fate of the world truly hung in the balance in 1944. Given the current financial crisis, the world today just as badly needs a worthy successor to Bretton Woods.[21]

Crackup

Supply-side economics experienced a small and ambiguous reprise in the first term of President George W. Bush. Bush chose to meet the slowdown of 2000–2001 with a tax cut. However, the marginal rate was brought down only 0.5 percent and rebate checks were mailed out. Bartley was exasperated. He wrote in the *Journal*:

Fiscal policy can stimulate the economy . . . by changing the incentives taxpayers face. . . . The principal measure of incentives is the *marginal* tax rate—the tax you will pay on your *next* dollar of income. A reduction in marginal rates increases the reward for working, saving and risk taking; and higher rewards produce more effort and more economic activity. So to get growth you cut marginal rates.

Ongoing incentives, also, are not changed by backward-looking windfalls. Tax rebates can't be expected to stimulate, and temporary tax changes will at most move activity around from one period to another. For stimulus, you need to change future incentives, so the tax cut has to be permanent.

Finally, phased-in tax cuts have ambiguous effects. They may improve incentives over past rates, but they also create incentives to postpone activity pending lower future rates. The Reagan boom didn't start until 1983, when the last tranche of the 1981 tax cuts became effective. For stimulus, a tax cut should be immediate.

Growth was small in the face of the Bush tax action. In 2001 and 2002, GDP went up 1 percent per annum, and there were several negative quarters (though not two consecutively). Then, in early 2003, Bush signed another tax cut, one that brought the top rate down to 35 percent (from 39.1 percent) and the capital-gains rate to 15 percent (from 20 percent). A nice boom ensued of 3.1-percent-per-annum growth through late 2007. Inflation and unemployment, as had become the norm, remained low. The deficit exploded, but responsibility lay on the spending side. Receipts again exceeded 18.4 percent of GDP in 2006 and 2007.[22]

As for the other half of the policy mix, stable money, with tightness coordinated with tax cuts—it never came. In the late 1990s, the Fed started to wobble from its rule-like behavior. In 1999, it created a great deal of new money so that the banking system could fix computers that might be bedeviled by the "Y2K" glitch at the turn of the millennium. The Fed then withdrew this money in 2000, sparking the recession called by the NBER. This episode reprised the weird Fed thinking of the 1970s, when money to comply with federal regulations was to be supplied by the Fed instead of coming out of firms' capital budgets.

Stranger things were to come. Throughout the 2000s, the Fed was never convinced that the slowdown of 2000–2002 had really ended. Therefore, in response to the significant Bush tax cuts of 2003, the Fed kept money loose, violating the Taylor rule (and Mundell's policy mix) egregiously. Perhaps the Fed feared that since the 2001 tax cut had not sparked the economy, the 2003 one was sure to fail as well. Whatever the reason, incredibly low interest rates—in real terms, the federal funds rate was negative from late 2001 to late 2005—led to shocking increases in commodity prices. Gold topped $1,000, oil went to $140, and house prices zoomed upwards. Yet since home loans could be had at near-negative interest rates, people took out mortgages anyway. Banks provided many questionable loans. This was bad decision-making on their part, but it was supported by the loose money as well as guarantees from the government's mortgage warehouses, Fannie Mae and Freddie Mac, and it was encouraged by federal community-reinvestment regulations.

In 2006 and 2007, the Fed started to jack up interest rates again, but it was too little, too late. The expiration date of the 2003 tax cuts (2010) was creeping ever closer, meaning that the policy mix stood to be tight money and high taxes: a recipe for economic stoppage. The stoppage came in 2008.

Unrevised GDP numbers show 2008 growth at about 1 percent, with two negative quarters happening in succession in the second half of the year. The stock market and the banking system—being indications of, respectively, future corporate profitability and future individual and firm solvency—experienced near collapse. The Dow fell by about half, and a number of large financial institutions either closed their doors or had hasty takeovers arranged for them by regulators.

John Rutledge would surely draw a lesson or two regarding the present crisis from the experience of a generation ago. Financial assets—stocks, bonds, mortgages—are bets on people being productive *in the future*. They have nothing to do with the past. The prospect facing the economy in late 2008 and early 2009 was of a Federal Reserve that was acting erratically, a tax system that was poised to displace more of the real economy, and a banking system that had to consider the possibility of nationalization. For the market for financial assets to improve, there must be a clear reason for businesses and individuals to believe that there will be stable money, low taxes, and beneficial but spare regulation as *new* economic initiatives are undertaken.[23]

As of early 2009, the government had adopted a three-pronged approach to this crisis. First, the Fed would keep money as loose as ever. Second, the federal government would strive to collect all the bad mortgages for itself so as to ensure the solvency of the banks, which would in turn have to play by new rules, as yet unclear. Third, the government would provide some $1 trillion in spending and nonmarginal tax cuts so as to initiate economic activity.

Here perhaps we finally saw the real-world consequence of the historical negligence perpetrated against supply-side economics. Economic crises caused by loose money and high taxes were cured by the Mundellian policy mix in 1922, 1962, and 1981. Likewise, similarly caused crises that did not call forth the Mundellian response—the recessions of 1969–70 and 1974–75—festered until the proper cure came. There is not one word of historical scholarship on any of this. Sean Wilentz, one of the deans of American history, wrote in his 2008 book *The Age of Reagan*: "There is, as might be expected, a lengthy and argumentative literature on Reagan's supply-side economic policies." Technically, this is not true. In academic history, the secondary literature on supply-side economics is nil. Many things have been written about supply-side economics, but none of them falls in the category of "literature" as the term is used by historians.[24]

It therefore should come as no surprise that as the economic crisis deepened in 2008 and 2009, public officials were quick to compare it with the 1930s. It was as if the Great Depression were the only economic crisis, and the New Deal the only solution, they had ever heard of. How could it have been otherwise? What serious books could be read, what courses taken, on the new vehicles of economic stabilization that had been pioneered since JFK's time? Economists tracked this history to some degree, but their specialty is statistics and models. Documenting what policymakers did in the past, and why, is a job for historians.

What might history teach President Obama and the favorably inclined Congress he enjoys? First, it is time to understand what great Democrats achieved in the past. It is difficult to believe that had FDR honored George Washington's precedent and not sought a third term, he would be regarded today as anything short of a grand failure. The recession that started right after FDR's reelection in 1936 canceled all gains made by the New Deal and perpetuated the Great Depression until the clouds of war came. For all the make-work programs of the Works Progress Administration and the crusades against big business, the New Deal in its classic period—1933–39—did nothing to restore prosperity.

JFK, in contrast, took all the right advice and knew when and how to defy it. His ambition was such that he was going to have spectacular growth on his watch, no matter whom he had to cut deals with—even if that meant the

Chamber of Commerce and Ford Motor, as opposed to the supporters of the neoclassical synthesis who made up his Council of Economic Advisors. JFK was clever enough to assign credit for his policy mix to his assistants, but the documentary record is clear that his CEA got mugged by reality and over-ruled by its president.

JFK's is the result Obama should aspire to, not FDR's. His plan of action should include pursuing the following policy set:

1. Endorsing the stable price/low tax consensus endorsed by Robert Lucas and so many others. In practice, this would mean perpetuating the 2003 tax cuts beyond 2010.

2. Allowing the Federal Reserve to restore confidence in the dollar (and thus raise interest rates and reestablish the discipline of the Taylor rule) by cutting taxes, perhaps the corporate rate.

3. Curtailing the unfunded liabilities of Social Security and Medicare, which imply huge *future* increases in taxation. This is easier than it sounds, in that any individual who is part of Generation X or younger would gladly take sixty-seven cents on the dollar of promised Social Security benefits.

4. Spending on pet programs as a new president might wish, but achieving balance by means of cutting spending from the pet Bush or Republican earmark programs, of which there is hundreds of billions of dollars' worth.

5. Making a serious effort toward an international concord on fixed exchange rates and free trade.

As for the banking system, it would right itself on account of the real lending opportunities that would be unleashed by the above reforms.

The president should also be careful not to give too much ear to the assertion that income inequality has dramatically increased since the supply-side revolution, thereby justifying public-policy correctives—such as tax increases. Income inequality *has* grown since 1982—and the phenomenon is largely a positive one.

Income gains of the rich boomed as the top tax rates were cut a generation ago and savvy investors moved out of commodities (whose appreciation does not regularly register as income) into financial assets (whose appreciation largely does)—a process that, as John Rutledge calculated, pulled upwards of

$11 trillion out of hiding and put it to work in the economy. In turn, the economic opportunities made possible by this immense shift attracted millions of poor immigrants (such as Mexicans) into the country. Realized income grew at the top, and the ranks of the poor expanded, on account of a surfeit of opportunity. It is a shame that the income-inequality studies by economists Thomas Piketty and Emmanuel Saez, studies that seem to drive so much of the 2010 administration budget message and urge tax increases, do not strive to take into account the epic portfolio effects of tax cuts and stable money.[25]

Supply-siders offered advice as the crisis hit in 2008 and 2009. Alan Reynolds was a regular in the press, offering injunctions to remember the lessons of the past quarter century. Laffer told Larry Kudlow that he was "ready to dust off his armor and do battle again" in the service of the supply-side revolution. And Mundell pushed for a reduction in the corporate tax rate to 15 percent. This is a Machiavellian suggestion. Mundell knows that in this era of innumerable small businesses, taxpayers have a choice between reporting income on a personal or a corporate return. Taking the corporate rate to 15 percent would effectively eliminate all personal rates above that number. Something akin to a low, flat income tax would thereby be achieved.[26]

For all the petulance the supply-siders have met in the blogosphere, their ideas have traction in professional economics. Bruce Bartlett electrified discussion in the field with his April 2007 *New York Times* article called "How Supply-Side Economics Trickled Down." Therein Bartlett reported that many of the fundamental ideas of supply-side economics are received truths in economics today, including supply-side notions about incentives, marginal taxation, progressive taxation, stable money, free trade, and regulations. And indeed, the supply-siders have not been deprived of honors. There was Mundell's Nobel (not to mention Prescott's), Bartley's Pulitzer, a Palm of the Legion of Honor from France for Roberts, and a Presidential Medal of Freedom for Bartley. In 2003, there was also Mundell's investiture into the Order of Canada, the highest honor of the country in which young Robert had grown up. Mundell joins Joni Mitchell, Gordon Lightfoot, Céline Dion, and other Canadian greats in having "C.C."—"Companion of the Order of Canada"—attached to his name.[27]

Ture died in 1997, just as he was beginning a series of normative reflections on the economics of low taxation. Bartley died within days of getting his Medal of Freedom in 2003, President Bush having rushed to give Bartley the award on news that he had an inoperable tumor. Wanniski died in 2005, and

Kemp in 2009. Today, the *Wall Street Journal* opinion page retains its supply-side orientation, occasionally running columns by Stephen Moore under the byline "Supply-Side." Moore represents a second generation of supply-siders, which also includes such figures as investment advisors and commentators Brian Wesbury, Michael Darda, and John Tamny. And Laffer's consultancy, located in Nashville, brims with ebullient young supply-siders. Laffer tires out his young hotshots with days and nights of conversation, analysis, and deals.[28]

It was unusual that in the 1970s a cadre of ambitious young people should have arrogated to itself the responsibility of navigating the nation out of an unprecedented economic funk. It would have surprised anyone from the pre-1913 world. Theodore Roosevelt had charged those with keen abilities in macroeconomic affairs (a term not around yet for him to use), those with "the money touch," with the responsibility of making sure that the nation's economy was kept on the keel of stability and growth. TR assumed that such people would invariably hail from the settled rich and that their motivation would stem from the obligations of patriotism, if not from the obligations of nobility.

With respect to the advent of supply-side economics, TR was wrong about the settled rich, but right about the motivation of patriotism. In the 1970s, as an older generation talked of diminished expectations, it was an improbable clutch of youth, full of sharp desire, fierce necessity, and love of country, who set hope above despair. America has always been a land of expansive entrepreneurial opportunity. Indeed, that has been one of its defining characteristics. The avid young supply-siders of the 1970s believed that and felt it in their bones. They were not going to tolerate an American economy that no longer served as a proving ground for big doings.[29]

As our current economic crisis demonstrates, there remains unfinished business on the supply-side agenda. Indeed, in many ways the supply-siders' arguments will need to be made all over again. For the most part, that will be the work of new minds in a new context, as the supply-side innovators of a generation ago exit the global stage. This new generation will do well in reminding its auditors that the international success of the supply-side revolution testifies, in the end, to its enduring affinities with basic human qualities and desires—especially fairness, optimism, and the yen to put one's talents to good use.

NOTES

The following abbreviations are used in the notes:

For archives:

DTR	Donald T. Regan papers
JCL	Jimmy Carter Library
JKCP	Jack Kemp congressional papers
JRP	John Rousselot papers
JTP	James Tobin papers (JFK Library)
JWP	Jude Wanniski papers
LVM	Ludwig von Mises papers
RLB	Robert L. Bartley papers
RRL	Ronald Reagan Presidential Library
WAS	William A. Steiger papers

For newspapers:

NYT	*New York Times*
WP	*Washington Post* (n.b., all Evans and Novak, and Robert D. Novak, articles are WP)
WSJ	*Wall Street Journal*

Chapter 1: That '70s Funk

1. www.universalexports.net/scripts/goldfinger.shtml, Reel 9.

2. Measuring the Dow Jones Industrial Average from peak to trough, 1968–82. Peak (Dec. 3, 1968),

985.21; trough (Aug. 12, 1982), 776.92, down 21.85 percent. This result is reduced by the consumer price index (CPI) deflator, the quotient between the Aug. 1982 CPI, 97.7, and the Dec. 1968 CPI, 35.5. The result is a 71 percent real loss in the level of the index. Going back to 1966, when the Dow had hit a higher peak (994.2), reveals a real loss in the index Jan. 1966–Aug. 1982 of 75 percent. As for the moderating impact of dividends on this real loss, dividends were taxable, usually at marginal rates (as opposed to unrealized capital gains, which were untaxed), and subject to tax rates upwards of 70 percent as well as alternative taxes. It is therefore difficult to assess how much dividends may have moderated this real loss, though it is reasonable to conjecture that the effect was minimal. As Burton G. Malkiel has noted, even after the 1980s run-up in prices, stocks after inflation were flat in the period 1967–87 (Malkiel, "Irrational Complacency?" WSJ, Apr. 30, 2007). In 1980, the unemployment rate was 7.1 percent (rounds to 7) and inflation 13.5 percent (rounds to 14): 7 + 14 = 21 for the misery index.

3. A point made by supply-side friend William E. Simon (the former treasury secretary) in a book that paved the way for the popular reception of supply-side economics, *A Time for Truth* (New York: Berkley, 1978), 29–33.

4. See Bruce W. Jentleson, *Pipeline Politics: The Complex Political Economy of East-West Energy Trade* (Ithaca, NY: Cornell University Press, 1986), ch. 5, and Thomas L. Friedman, *Hot, Flat, and Crowded: Why We Need a Green Revolution—and How It Can Renew America* (New York: Farrar, Straus & Giroux, 2008), 108–10.

5. See Nicholas Lemann, "How the Seventies Changed America," *American Heritage* 42, no. 4 (Jul.–Aug. 1991), 39–49.

6. The line from the movie is slightly different, adapted in the fashion here by Howard Jarvis, the leader of the California tax revolt of 1978. Andy Klein, "Jiveass Jarvis: The Origin of the Mantra, 'I'm Mad as Hell,'" *LA City Beat,* Jan. 23, 2008.

7. Throughout this work, real growth rates are calculated by the following method, which is standard in econometrics. The end figure is divided by the beginning figure, and the natural logarithm (ln) is taken of the quotient, this new figure then divided by the number of units of the interval (such as years). In this case (in constant 2000 $billion, as throughout this work), 1945 GDP was 1,786.3 and 1973 GDP 4,341.5, giving a yearly growth rate of 3.17 percent, or 3.2 percent; 1982 GDP was 5,189.8 at quarter (Q) 4 and 2007 GDP was 11,625.7 at Q3, giving a yearly rate of 3.26 percent, or 3.3 percent. It is appropriate to suppose that measuring from the 1945 quarterly trough to the 1973 quarterly peak the 1945–73 figure would rise to 3.3 percent. We have the quarterly data for 1973 (the peak was 4,355.1 at Q2) but not for 1945. In any case, growth may have been marginally higher in 1982–2007 than in 1945–73. Economic growth in Japan and the large Western European countries has averaged about 2.2 percent yearly since 1982, about 1.8 percent since 1990. These statistics break down as follows. Japan's growth in 1982–2007 was 2.3 percent, and since 1990 1.4 percent; Britain's, 2.8 percent and 2.5 percent; Germany's, 2.1 percent and 1.7 percent; France's, 2.1 percent and 1.9 percent; Italy's, 1.8 percent and 1.4 percent. The United States' growth rate in these intervals was 3.3 percent and 2.8 percent, a 50 percent premium on the developed world. And 1982 was a trough year for the American economy, 1990 a peak year. As of 2007, these were the world's six largest national economies, exclusive of China.

8. U.S. GDP at Q4 of 1982 was 5,189.8, at Q2 of 1973 4,355.1. The growth rate was 1.8 percent. This is to measure GDP from peak to trough. Robert L. Bartley, in his memoir of supply-side economics, *The Seven Fat Years,* argued for measuring growth in segments peak-trough-peak. Bartley, *The Seven Fat Years: And How to Do It Again* (New York: Free Press, 1995), 6.

9. As David Frum points out, Paul Ehrlich was invited on the *Tonight Show Starring Johnny Carson* twenty-five times. Frum, *How We Got Here: The 70s, the Decade That Brought You Modern Life—for Better or Worse* (New York: Basic Books, 2000), 160.

10. Bartley, *The Seven Fat Years*, 43.

11. The details and sources of the Michael 1 episode are given here in chapter 5.

12. Robert D. Novak, *The Prince of Darkness: 50 Years Reporting in Washington* (New York: Crown Forum, 2007), 321; Peggy Noonan, *What I Saw at the Revolution: A Political Life in the Reagan Era* (New York: Random House, 1990), 57.

13. Jude Wanniski, "The Mundell-Laffer Hypothesis—A New View of the World Economy," *Public Interest* 39 (Spring 1975), 31–52.

14. Robert A. Mundell, "The Dollar and the Policy Mix: 1971," *Essays in International Finance* 85 (May 1971), 3–28.

15. Martin Anderson, *Revolution: The Reagan Legacy* (Stanford, CA: Hoover Institution, 1988), 147–48.

16. Webcast of Mundell's Nobel Prize Lecture, at nobelprize.org.

17. Robert D. Novak, "The Imperial Federal Reserve," Aug. 30, 1999.

18. Federal Reserve historian Allan H. Meltzer observed that the leaders of the Federal Reserve were decidedly opposed to the passage of the Humphrey-Hawkins Act. Interview with Meltzer.

19. A portrait of one congressional figure who attempted to impose order on the tax code is Julian E. Zelizer, *Taxing America: Wilbur D. Mills, Congress, and the State, 1945–1975* (Cambridge: Cambridge University Press, 1998).

20. Robert A. Mundell, "A Reconsideration of the Twentieth Century," *American Economic Review* 90, no. 3 (Jun. 2000), 335.

21. The origin of the term is discussed here in chapter 6.

22. Allen J. Matusow, *Nixon's Economy: Booms, Busts, Dollars, and Votes* (Lawrence, KS: University Press of Kansas, 1998), 91.

23. Arthur B. Laffer, "The Bitter Fruits of Devaluation," WSJ, Jan. 10, 1974; Nixon-Ford-Carter policy in the face of stagflation is discussed here, chapters 4–8, and in Matusow, *Nixon's Economy,* and W. Carl Biven, *Jimmy Carter's Economy: Policy in an Age of Limits* (Chapel Hill, NC: University of North Carolina Press, 2002).

24. Paraphrased from "Keynes, John Maynard," Economics A-Z, www.economist.com.

25. Monetarism's founder and main star, Milton Friedman, had already hurt monetarism's credibility as a force against stagflation by means of his advice to President Richard Nixon, a point stressed in Matusow, *Nixon's Economy.*

26. Robert E. Lucas Jr. and Thomas J. Sargent, "After Keynesian Macroeconomics," given in 1978 at a conference sponsored by the Federal Reserve Bank of Boston, www.minneapolisfed.org/research/QR/QR321.pdf, 1.

27. Richard K. Vedder and Lowell E. Gallaway, *Out of Work: Unemployment and Government in Twentieth-Century America* (New York: Holmes & Meier, 1993), 141–42; for the paradox of FDR's problem-solving reputation despite the persistence of historic unemployment, see David M. Kennedy's definitive treatment in *Freedom from Fear: The American People in Depression and War, 1929–1945* (New York: Oxford, 1999).

28. "The Growth of Growth Theory," *The Economist,* May 18, 2006.

29. Bruce Bartlett, "How Supply-Side Economics Trickled Down," NYT, Apr. 6, 2007.

30. Paul Krugman, "Supply-Side Virus Strikes Again," slate.com, Aug. 16, 1996, at www.slate.com/ id/1910/; Jonathan Chait, "Get Lucky," *The New Republic,* Dec. 17, 2002, at www.tnr.com/doc.mhtml? i=20021223&s=diarist122302; Michael Kinsley, "Abracadabra Economics," slate.com, Feb. 24, 2006, at www.slate.com/id/2136886?nav=wp; Dailykos.com, Jan. 3, 2006, www.dailykos.com/tag/Supply-Side%20Economics; Chris Farrell, "The 'Straight Story' with Chris Farrell," *Marketplace* radio show, Jun. 17, 2005; delong.typepad.com/sdj/2006/05/daniel_gross_is.html; angrybear.blogspot. com/2007/01/social-security-reform-two-options-or.html; delong.typepad.com/sdj/2005/12/dan_ gross_is_un.html. Chait is the author of *The Big Con: The True Story of How Washington Got Hoodwinked and Hijacked by Crackpot Economics* (Boston: Houghton Mifflin, 2007), half of which is a history of supply-side economics. Laffer's response is Arthur B. Laffer, "The Onslaught from the Left, Part 1: Fact vs. Fiction," *Laffer Associates: Supply-Side Investment Research,* Oct. 31, 2007.

31. *The United States since 1945: Historical Interpretations,* eds. Doug Rossinow and Rebecca Lowen (Upper Saddle River, NJ: Pearson Prentice Hall, 2007), 251.

32. Some candidates are as follows. W. Elliot Brownlee called on archival sources from the Reagan Library for two book chapters, "The 'Reagan Revolution,' 1980–1986," in his *Federal Taxation in America: A Short History* (Washington, DC: Woodrow Wilson Center Press, 2004), and (with C. Eugene Steuerle) "Taxation," in *The Reagan Presidency: Pragmatic Conservatism and Its Legacies* (Lawrence, KS: University Press of Kansas, 2003). Yet archival sources in these (valuable) short works are few in number and do not carry the narrative. It is exceedingly difficult to find one work of scholarship, done by a holder of a Ph.D. in history and an occupant of an academic position, who has investigated at least a substantial subtopic of supply-side economics by means of striving to command a source base.

33. These works are often illuminating and provide guidance to those doing source-intensive secondary work. Examples in this case are the relevant portions of two volumes by Robert M. Collins, *More: The Politics of Economic Growth in Postwar America* (New York: Oxford University Press, 2000) and *Transforming America: Politics and Culture in the Reagan Years* (New York: Columbia University Press, 2006); and John W. Sloan, *The Reagan Effect: Economics and Presidential Leadership* (Lawrence, KS: University Press of Kansas, 1999).

34. This state of affairs is being recognized. As a reviewer recently noted, "The literature on Reagan's foreign policy is more or less complete—until additional classified documents are released or new Soviet sources are revealed. By contrast, the story of Reagan's domestic policy remains clouded and obscure, in part because we are still wrestling with many of the same issues today—tax cuts, trade and budget deficits, [etc.]. The domestic story is harder to tell because it is less amenable to the direct personal and moral dimensions of the Cold War and because of the wider range of complicated issues." Steven F. Hayward, "Reagan and the Historians," *Claremont Review of Books,* Fall 2007, at www. claremont.org/publications/crb/id.1485/article_detail.asp.

35. Quoted in John Lukacs, *A Student's Guide to the Study of History* (Wilmington, DE: ISI Books, 2000), 26–27.

Chapter 2: 1913

1. The official Nobel record of the event is nobelprize.org/nobel_prizes/economics/laureates/1999/ mundell-speech.html. See also Laura Wallace's interview of Mundell, "Ahead of His Time," *F&D: A Quarterly Magazine of the IMF* 43, no. 3 (Sept. 2006).

2. Wallace, "Ahead of His Time," and Robert L. Bartley, "World Money at the Palazzo Mundell: Does the Global Economy Need a Global Currency?" Jun. 30, 2003, www.opinionjournal.com.

3. Mundell, "The Dollar and the Policy Mix"; see also Mundell's c.v. on www.robertmundell.net and Rudiger Dornbusch, "Robert A. Mundell's Nobel Memorial Prize," *Scandinavian Journal of Economics* 102, no. 2 (Jun. 2000), 208.

4. Mundell, "A Reconsideration of the Twentieth Century," 327, 331.

5. Mundell, "A Reconsideration of the Twentieth Century," 328.

6. Louis D. Johnston and Samuel H. Williamson, "What Was the U.S. GDP Then?" Measuring Worth, 2008, at www.measuringworth.org/usgdp/.

7. A transcript of the speech may be found at www.theodoreroosevelt.org.

8. See Robert Stanley, *Dimensions of Law in the Service of Order: Origins of the Federal Income Tax, 1861–1913* (New York: Oxford University Press, 1993).

9. The description here of the 1907 event and the inspiration given to the creation of the Federal Reserve is taken from Ron Chernow, *The House of Morgan: An American Banking Dynasty and the Rise of Modern Finance* (New York: Atlantic Monthly Press, 1990), ch. 7.

10. See the discussion further on in this chapter, under the heading "The Faulty Return to Gold," for Mundell's views on Keynes's statement.

11. Allan H. Meltzer argues that the Federal Reserve Act did not set up a central bank for the United States, in that power was diffuse over the twelve regional banks. He argues that the Federal Reserve only became effectively a central bank over a period of decades. Meltzer, *A History of the Federal Reserve, Vol. 1: 1913–1951* (Chicago: University of Chicago Press, 2004), ch. 1. Furthermore, as Barry Eichengreen, Niall Ferguson, and others have shown, central banking had largely arisen in Europe during the period 1870–1913 because European governments increasingly needed a reliable arm of government to finance deficit spending for defense purposes. Yet the U.S. federal budget, especially its defense component, remained minimal in this period. The United States was "late" in creating a central bank because its government did not need a reliable partner to finance deficits. The United States was not running deficits because it was not preparing for war. Indeed, as Meltzer shows, domestic concerns about spreading lending around the country and tempering the plutocracy were at the forefront in the creation of the Fed. See Michael D. Bordo and Barry Eichengreen, "The Rise and Fall of a Barbarous Relic: The Role of Gold in the International Monetary System," in *Money, Capital Mobility, and Trade: Essays in Honor of Robert A. Mundell,* ed. Guillermo A. Calvo et al. (Cambridge, MA: The MIT Press, 2001); and Niall Ferguson, *The Pity of War: Explaining World War I* (New York: Basic Books, 1999). The following section of text relies on Meltzer, *A History of the Federal Reserve,* as well as on Milton Friedman and Anna Jacobson Schwartz, *A Monetary History of the United States, 1867–1960* (Princeton, NJ: Princeton University Press, 1963).

12. Tables of the World Gold Council, at www.gold.org/assets/file/value/stats/statistics/pdf/Pages%20from%20tim-green.pdf. Britain and France were able to maintain passable stocks of gold through the war, though not enough to cover increased currency floats. Germany's and Italy's gold positions were roughly at 1913 par after the war, with much more currency outstanding. The Ottoman, Russian, and Austrian stocks all went to nil after 1913. American stocks increased 125 percent from 1910 to 1920, an increase on the low end of the neutrals made up by Argentina, Spain, Sweden, Japan, Holland, and Switzerland.

13. Friedman and Schwartz, *A Monetary History of the United States,* 239. As these authors note (on the same page), "In its first years, the Federal Reserve System was powerless to offset the inflows of gold. During the active participation of the United States in the war, it could not be a free agent. Its poor

performance in that trial is understandable. There was no strictly comparable American experience on which to base policy or judge the effect of actions designed to stimulate or retard monetary expansion. . . . The contemporaneous gold reserve ratio was a simple, easy guide; economic stability, a complex, subtle will-o'-the-wisp."

14. Mundell, "A Reconsideration of the Twentieth Century," 328–29.

15. "U.S. Index of the General Price Level, 01/1860–11/1939," www.nber.org. There was also little yearly variation in the essentially nil inflation trend of the period.

16. Mundell, "A Reconsideration of the Twentieth Century," 328; Friedman and Schwartz, *A Monetary History of the United States,* 214; Vedder and Gallaway, *Out of Work,* 55. See also Christina Romer, "Spurious Volatility in Historical Unemployment Data," *Journal of Political Economy* 94, no. 1 (1986).

17. Friedman and Schwartz, *A Monetary History of the United States,* 239. The authors also state that for thirteen months beginning December 1919, the enlightened Benjamin Strong of the New York bank was absent from the Fed for reasons of health (231).

18. A theme of David Cannadine's *Mellon* is that contrary to all legend, Mellon as a banker was a soft touch. It was hard for an entrepreneur to get money from Mellon's bank, but once secured, the entrepreneur was assured that Mellon would not let things like repayment schedules foil a going business. As treasury secretary, Mellon was a determined advocate of rescheduling European World War I debt. Cannadine, *Mellon: An American Life* (New York: Knopf, 2006), 318–23.

19. Robert Bartley used this term to characterize the Reagan years as a reprise of the Mellon years in his memoir of supply-side economics, *The Seven Fat Years.* For the remarkable story of the new Federal Reserve discipline of the 1920s, see both Friedman and Schwartz, *A Monetary History of the United States,* 240–98, and Meltzer, *A History of the Federal Reserve,* 127–235. As these authors show, the Federal Reserve was prepared of its own accord to follow a policy of price stability after late 1920.

20. Vedder and Gallaway, *Out of Work,* 68–69.

21. The inspiration that supply-siders took from the Mellon actions of the 1920s is apparent in these sources: Jack Kemp, Trent Lott, and Bob Michel, *Less Is More: The Classical Economic Case for Cutting Marginal Income Tax Rates* (Bailey's Crossroads, VA: The National Conservative Foundation, 1981), 56–61; Arthur B. Laffer, "The Laffer Curve: Past, Present and Future," in *Laffer Associates: Supply-Side Investment Research,* Jan. 6, 2004, 3–5; Michael K. Evans, "Taxes, Inflation and the Rich," WSJ, Aug. 7, 1978. Martin Feldstein validated the supply-side interpretation of Mellon's actions in "Structuring the Personal Tax Cut," WSJ, Mar. 17, 1981.

22. After the 1926 tax cut, the last Mellon was able to get, which aside from cutting top rates eliminated low ones, he wrote, "The income tax in this country has become a class rather than a national tax"—after the fashion of TR's Sorbonne speech. Quoted in Cannadine, *Mellon,* 318.

23. Andrew W. Mellon, *Taxation: The People's Business* (New York: Arno, 1973), 13.

24. See Ferguson, *The Pity of War,* and Richard Pipes, *Russia under the Bolshevik Regime* (New York: Knopf, 1994), esp. 370–419.

25. "NBER Macrohistory: I. Production of Commodities," www.nber.org.

26. Robert Mundell and Milton Friedman, "One World, One Money?" *Options Politiques* (May 2001), 28; Mundell, "A Reconsideration of the Twentieth Century," 328.

27. Mundell, "A Reconsideration of the Twentieth Century," 328.

28. Robert Mundell, "Should the Euro-Dollar Exchange Rate Be Managed?: Revised version of the lecture presented in Luxembourg on March 8, 2000, on the occasion of the publication of *The Euro*

as a Stabilizer in the International Economic System, Robert Mundell and Armand Clesse, eds., Boston/
Dordrecht/London: Kluwer Academic Publishers," at www.ieis.lu/lectures/Mundell.pdf, 5–6.

29. See Meltzer, *A History of the Federal Reserve,* ch. 4.

30. Robert A. Mundell, "The Sixth Lord Robbins Memorial Lecture: Reform of the International
Monetary System," in *Monetary Stability and Economic Growth: A Dialog between Leading Economists,* eds.
Robert A. Mundell and Paul J. Zak (Cheltenham, UK: Edward Elgar, 2002), 4.

31. For Europe and gold in the 1920s, see Jacques Rueff, *The Monetary Sin of the West,* trans. Roger
Glémet (New York: Macmillan, 1972), and Barry Eichengreen, *Golden Fetters: The Gold Standard and
the Great Depression, 1919–1939* (New York: Oxford, 1992), chs. 4–6. France strove to reestablish the
prewar parity but did not fix the franc to gold until it was 80 percent depreciated from 1914 par in
1926. To Eichengreen, this "lateness" was the secret to the *high* French growth in the period. *Golden
Fetters,* 182–83.

32. "The British were applying pressure to preserve sterling balances in London, and, in 1928, as
[Jacques] Rueff tells us, Sir Austen Chamberlain wrote to President Poincaré: 'We know that you
are entitled to ask gold for our sterling, but in the frame of the close friendship between Britain and
France we ask you, so as to avoid trouble for the City of London, not to do that.'" Robert A. Mundell,
"The Monetary Consequences of Jacques Rueff," *Journal of Business* 46, no. 3 (Jul. 1973), 387.

33. Mundell's "Monetary Consequences of Jacques Rueff" differentiates Mundell's position.

34. The classic work strongly implicating the crash among causes of the Great Depression is John
Kenneth Galbraith, *The Great Crash, 1929* (Boston: Houghton Mifflin, 1955). Galbraith argued that the
poor corporate structure of American business and banking, along with inequities of wealth distribution brought on by this structure, necessitated the crash and the Depression.

35. Interpretations of the origins of the Great Depression from supply-siders include the following: A
Friedmanite perspective in Lawrence M. Stratton and Paul Craig Roberts, "The Fed's 'Depression'
and the Birth of the New Deal," *Policy Review* 108 (Aug.–Sept. 2001). Bartley's views concerning multiple governmental policy mistakes are outlined in "Prolonging the Great Depression: The New Deal:
Time for a New Look," Oct. 20, 2003, www.opinionjournal.com. Wanniski emphasized the onset of
the Smoot-Hawley Tariff in *The Way the World Works: Why Economies Fail—and Succeed* (New York:
Basic, 1978), ch. 7. His view was supported by Alan Reynolds in "What Do We Know about the Great
Crash?" *National Review,* Nov. 9, 1979, 1416–21. Jonathan Chait, in *The Big Con,* mistakenly characterized the supply-siders as monolithic on this issue: "What caused the Great Depression? ... Supply-siders insist that the single cause was the 1930 Smoot-Hawley Tariff" (19). Mundell, "A Reconsideration
of the Twentieth Century," 329–30.

36. The literature on the causes of the Great Depression is the largest in the field of macroeconomic history. It may be taxonomized as follows. The Galbraith school (*The Great Crash,* 1955), now
defunct, argued that the collusive tendencies of big business and big banking were at fault. This
school was largely displaced, in the 1960s, by the now regnant monetarist school, which broadly
held, after Friedman and Schwartz, that a judicious infusion of bank reserve credit would have
averted the whole crisis and could have been applied at many points during 1930–32 by the Fed.
Allan H. Meltzer (*A History of the Federal Reserve*) is a representative of this view. A third powerful
school is that represented by Barry Eichengreen (*Golden Fetters*), who with justice may be called a
New Keynesian. Eichengreen argues that flexible exchange rates were the key to escaping the Great
Depression. Flexible exchange rates were endorsed in Friedman's monetarism, though Eichengreen

departs from the monetarist consensus by emphasizing not the lack of monetary infusion from the central banks during the Depression but simply the adherence to gold. The fourth major school is that represented by Mundell. Mundell differs from Eichengreen in that Mundell holds that flexible exchange rates would have required vastly more foreign exchange reserves (in particular gold) than any country was capable of amassing or managing correctly. Eichengreen differentiates his view from Mundell's in Bordo and Eichengreen, "The Rise and Fall of a Barbarous Relic: The Role of Gold in the International Monetary System."

37. Mundell in 1973: "In retrospect, a resounding increase in the price of gold by Britain, which would have forced the gold bloc to follow, would probably have been a better total strategy and kept alive Britain's world position. Britain opted out of international monetary interdependence in 1931 and reduced the pressure on her to find a correct world solution. The flagship deserted the convoy. . . . Given the total social crisis, a large devaluation of sterling quite possibly could have saved the gold standard and the accompanying elements of the European political order." Mundell, "The Monetary Consequences of Jacques Rueff," 387–88.

38. Eichengreen, *Golden Fetters,* 246–57.

39. Mundell, "A Reconsideration of the Twentieth Century," 328.

40. A narrative of these events may again be found in Rueff, *The Monetary Sin of the West* and Eichengreen, *Golden Fetters.* Mundell's remark is in the webcast of the Nobel address.

41. Friedman and Schwartz, writing in 1963: in 1930, there came "the sharpest rise [in interest rates] within so brief a period in the whole history of the System, before or since." *A Monetary History of the United States,* 317.

42. Here is where the difference between Mundell and Eichengreen on the role of gold in the onset of the Great Depression may be discerned. For Mundell, the flight to gold was flight out of a kind of money that was primarily a means of exchange into a kind of money that was primarily a storehouse of value. For Eichengreen, gold was a constraint that disenabled the production of more money at times when more was needed. Mundell holds that there was plenty of "money" already in the world after 1929. The problem was that this money (currency) was abandoned for gold, gold which was not fungible or investible every day in the real economy as currency was. Currency would not have been abandoned had the price of gold been correctly adjusted. Eichengreen, in contrast, sees the abandonment of the gold standard tout court into a system of flexible currency exchange rates as necessary for escape from the crisis. An example of Mundell's many musings on the difference between money as storehouse of value and means of exchange may be found in Robert A. Mundell, *Man and Economics* (New York: McGraw-Hill, 1968), ch. 6.

43. Mundell, "A Reconsideration of the Twentieth Century," 330.

44. Mundell, "A Reconsideration of the Twentieth Century," 330.

45. GDP growth 1929–39 was 1.0 percent per annum, with population growth 1930–40 0.7 percent per annum.

Chapter 3: A Hotel in New Hampshire

1. Ludwig von Mises, "Autarkie—der Weg ins Elend," *Der Europäer* 3, no. 3 (Mar. 1937).

2. If there were any lingering arguments that Europe was mainly autarkic in the Middle Ages, perhaps in the "Dark Ages," they were undermined by Michael McCormick, *Origins of the European Economy: Communications and Commerce A.D. 300–900* (New York: Cambridge University Press, 2001).

3. Jörg Guido Hülsmann, *Mises: The Last Knight of Liberalism* (Auburn, AL: Ludwig von Mises Institute, 2007), 723–39.

4. For unemployment rates through the Great Depression, see Vedder and Gallaway, *Out of Work*, 142; for examples of Great Depression starvation, see Kennedy, *Freedom from Fear*, 169–70. For the Soviets, see Robert Conquest, *The Harvest of Sorrow: Soviet Collectivization and the Terror-Famine* (New York: Oxford University Press, 1986) and *The Great Terror: A Reassessment* (New York: Oxford University Press, 1991).

5. Ludwig von Mises, "Economic Nationalism and Peaceful Economic Cooperation," in *Money, Method, and the Market Process*, ed. Richard M. Ebeling (Norwell, MA: Klewer, 1990). See this source for the quotations in the following paragraph as well.

6. See Hülsmann, *Mises*, 787–98. Mises was confused by the offer. It probably was meant merely to facilitate his entrance into the United States and thus his exit out of German-controlled Europe. This is indicated in part by the stilted language of the Berkeley offer (in the Grove City archive), which Hülsmann discusses. "Mises knew that it would be hard for him to find a suitable position in the United States—fortunately he had no idea just how hard" (789).

7. Ludwig von Mises, "The Republican Platform," 8, B34, S471, F1, LVM.

8. "Carthaginian peace" was the epithet that Keynes used to discredit the Treaty of Versailles in *The Economic Consequences of the Peace* (New York: Penguin, 1971), 36.

9. Andrew Phillips and Maria Ullsten, "Mundell Wins Nobel Economics Prize," *Macleans* (Oct. 25, 1999). In another interview, Mundell said that the devaluation of the pound in 1949 started his interest in economics. See "Dr. Mundell, what do you think are the major factors that contributed to your success today?" N.A., N.D., Box 104, F "Supply-Side Nobel," RLB.

10. Kennedy, *Freedom from Fear*, 803–4.

11. The following account of Bretton Woods is derived from Judy Shelton, *Money Meltdown: Restoring Order to the Global Currency System* (New York: Free Press, 1994), ch. 1; and Harold James, *International Monetary Cooperation since Bretton Woods* (New York and Washington: Oxford University Press and the IMF, 1996), chs. 2–3.

12. See the extensive citations of White in Sam Tanenhaus, *Whittaker Chambers: A Biography* (New York: Random House, 1997) and M. Stanton Evans, *Blacklisted by History: The Untold Story of Senator Joe McCarthy and His Fight Against America's Enemies* (New York: Crown Forum, 2007).

13. An assistant of White's in the drafting of the Bretton Woods protocol, a State Department economist by the name of John Parke Young, had this reflection on White and his philia for the Russians: "Well, Harry White was a difficult person, a very rude person, and rather slippery. . . . He was a very competent person, extremely competent and very good to his own people in the Treasury. So, my work on the committee with Harry White was interesting. Put it that way. . . . In these meetings at the Treasury preparing plans for the IMF and the World Bank, we were inviting foreign countries to send representatives to discuss the plans with the United States. Harry kept talking about the Russians; he hoped that they would send somebody; he didn't know whether they would or not. But it was quite obvious that he was urging, wanting the Russians to come. Finally he announced that the Russians were sending a delegation to discuss the plans with us. He was elated. He was like a child with a new toy. And when the Russians finally came he was extremely close to the Russians." In the Nobel address, Mundell noted that Young was one of the few who, in the 1920s, understood why the gold standard was a barbarous relic. "Oral History Interview of Dr. John Parke Young," Feb. 21, 1974,

Harry S. Truman Library, www.trumanlibrary.org; Mundell, "A Reconsideration of the Twentieth Century," 328n4.

14. For enthusiasm for Bretton Woods from the Michael 1 era, see Jude Wanniski, "The Mundell-Laffer Hypothesis," 37–47. For Bartley's Bretton Woodsish musings in the 1990s, see *The Seven Fat Years*, ch. 13.

15. Mundell, "A Reconsideration of the Twentieth Century," 331–32.

16. Author's correspondence with Mundell; see Mundell's observation about Canadian reluctance to fix to the dollar in Mundell, "Toward a Better International Monetary System," *Journal of Money, Credit, and Banking* 1, no. 3 (Aug. 1969), 641n.

17. Though as Mundell pointed out in 1971, Keynes conceded that an increase in the money supply generally results in a commensurate decrease in wages. Mundell, "The Dollar and the Policy Mix," 12.

18. Overprinting occurred by the transitive property. Monetary growth in terms of new dollars from the Federal Reserve was actually rather small in 1945–48. But the massive governmental surpluses that resulted in debt retirements in these years dramatically raised the reserves of American banks. Under the rules established by the Federal Reserve, this rise in the cash balances of the banks enabled the banks to increase loans by a commensurate degree. This was the source of the monetary growth that caused the inflation. Conceivably, a tax cut in 1945, coupled with less debt retirement on the part of the Treasury, would have resulted in a noninflationary boom. See Friedman and Schwartz, *A Monetary History of the United States,* 574–85, and Meltzer, *A History of the Federal Reserve,* 629–31.

19. The serious inflation occurred through 1947, then stopped, then recurred briefly again in the early 1950s; for domestic bond purchases during the war, see Friedman and Schwartz, *A Monetary History of the United States,* 571–74.

20. Mundell, "A Reconsideration of the Twentieth Century," 332.

21. In this and the following chapters, details of the history of the Bretton Woods system are drawn from Shelton, *Money Meltdown,* and James, *International Monetary Cooperation since Bretton Woods.*

22. Mundell emphasized the following about the Marshall Plan: it was not possible to be a recipient of both Marshall aid and IMF stabilization funds. Therefore, the acceptance of Marshall capital itself was sufficient to compel countries to maintain stable currencies. If they did not do so, they would be cut off from the dollar-link system forthwith. Mundell, "The European Monetary System 50 Years after Bretton Woods: A Comparison Between Two Systems," paper presented at Project Europe 1985–95, the tenth edition of the "Incontri di Rocca Salimbeni" meetings, Siena, Nov. 25, 1994, www.robertmundell.net, 2–3. For a current discussion of the motors of European growth since 1945, see Barry Eichengreen, *The European Economy since 1945: Coordinated Capitalism and Beyond* (Princeton, NJ: Princeton University Press, 2007).

23. "Dr. Mundell, what do you think are the major factors that contributed to your success today?"

24. Robert A. Mundell, "On the History of the Mundell-Fleming Model," *IMF Staff Papers* 47, Special Issue (2001), 216; "Dr. Mundell, what do you think are the major factors that contributed to your success today?"

25. Mundell, "On the History of the Mundell-Fleming Model," 216; "It is generally understood that Mundell is a master in [the] construction and deployment [of graphs]," write Russell S. Boyer and Warren Young in "Mundell's *International Economics*: Adaptations and Debates," *IMF Staff Papers* 52, Special Issue (2005), 169; Mundell, "A Theory of Optimum Currency Areas," *American Economic Review* 51, no. 4 (Sept. 1961), 657–65.

26. See D. E. Moggridge, *Harry Johnson: A Life in Economics* (Cambridge: Cambridge University Press, 2008), for various episodes in Mundell's career as well as an incomparable portrait of life in the University of Chicago economics department.

27. This and subsequent paragraphs follow Herbert Stein, *The Fiscal Revolution in America* (Washington, DC: AEI, 1996).

28. As recalled by James Tobin and Robert Solow, Introduction to the Kennedy Economic Reports, in *Two Revolutions in Economic Policy: The First Economic Reports of Presidents Kennedy and Reagan*, eds. James Tobin and Murray Weidenbaum (Cambridge, MA: The MIT Press, 1988), 4, 7.

29. Samuelson recalled the history of his and Tobin's "neoclassical synthesis" as follows, and his account is in accord with Mundell's in the Nobel address. Samuelson wrote in 1997: "From 1950 on, ... both Tobin and I were nagging Democratic leaders ... toward a high-employment mix, weighted toward capital formation and away from current consumption. . . . In my case it was precisely the tools of the 'neoclassical synthesis' . . . that were employed to deduce how austere budget surpluses cum expansionary Fed mode could augment a low-saving nation's productivity growth rate without occasioning structural unemployment." In this article, Samuelson provides references for his views dating from the 1950s and indicates that the term "neoclassical synthesis" describing his economics first appeared in a private-placement textbook in 1955. Paul Samuelson, "Credo of a Lucky Textbook Author," *Journal of Economic Perspectives* 11, no. 2 (Spring 1997), 156. On "fiscal drag," see Paul Craig Roberts, *The Supply-Side Revolution: An Insider's Account of Policymaking in Washington* (Cambridge, MA: Harvard University Press, 1984), 17–18.

30. See Tobin's reflections at cowles.econ.yale.edu/archive/reprints/tobin_86_laureate.html, sections "Developing Keynesian Macroeconomics and Synthesizing it with the Neoclassical Tradition" and "Policy and Public Service."

31. Mundell, "A Reconsideration of the Twentieth Century," 333.

32. Mundell had in mind "The Monetary Dynamics of International Adjustment Under Fixed and Flexible Exchange Rates," *Quarterly Journal of Economics* 74, no. 2 (May 1960), 227–57, and "The International Disequilibrium System," *Kyklos* 14, no. 2 (1961), 154–72. "Interview with Dr. Robert A. Mundell, December 1999," www.robertmundell.net; Mundell, "On the History of the Mundell-Fleming Model," 222.

33. Mundell, "On the History of the Mundell-Fleming Model," 222; Boyer and Young, "Mundell's *International Economics*," 163–64.

34. The IMF DM was seven pages; the *Staff Papers* piece was eight and had a slightly different title. On the footnote change turned the supply-side revolution. The *Staff Papers* piece included a footnote absent in the DM explaining that the author preferred tax cuts to government expenditures as a means to move down the "budget surplus" line. This matter is discussed here in subsequent chapters. As for when Mundell definitively realized that tax cuts are preferable in this model, Mundell has said, "This is a difficult question to answer, but the issue was not finally resolved until the early 1970s. In the early 1960s in my models I stressed the tax cuts and fiscal stimulus without distinction between supply-side effects and budgetary effects. The economics world at that time was almost universally Keynesian and that is why my policy mix ideas were so readily accepted. But I was aware of the supply-side effects of tax rates from my earliest writings, which were entirely in a classical international framework." (Correspondence with the author.) Robert A. Mundell, "The Use of Monetary and Fiscal Policy for Internal and External Stability," International Monetary Fund Departmental Memorandum

61/27, Nov. 8, 1961, IMF archives; "The Appropriate Use of Monetary and Fiscal Policy for Internal and External Stability," *IMF Staff Papers* 9 (Mar. 1962), 70–79.

35. Mundell, "On the History of the Mundell-Fleming Model," 221.

36. Mundell, "The Appropriate Use of Monetary and Fiscal Policy for Internal and External Stability," 70, 77.

37. Mundell, "On the History of the Mundell-Fleming Model," 222.

38. J. Herbert Furth, "The New 'Mix' and the Adjustment Process," Jan. 6, 1964, Series 5 (typescripts of speeches and position papers), Box 4, No. 107, J. Herbert Furth papers.

39. Mundell, "On the History of the Mundell-Fleming Model," 222–23.

40. *Two Revolutions in Economic Policy,* 51, 55.

41. *Two Revolutions in Economic Policy,* 40–43.

42. *Two Revolutions in Economic Policy,* 42; Mundell, "The Dollar and the Policy Mix," 23.

43. JFK's Press Conference 39, Jul. 23, 1962, at www.jfklibrary.org; Wallace Carroll, "Steel: A 72-Hour Drama with an All-Star Cast," NYT, Apr. 23, 1962; Kennedy's rendition of the quotation is in Benjamin C. Bradlee, *Conversations with Kennedy* (New York: Norton: 1984), 81–82; Robert L. Bartley, "What's a 'Bubble,' Anyway?" Aug. 5, 2002, www.opinionjournal.com.

44. Bartley, "What's a 'Bubble,' Anyway?"

45. *Two Revolutions in Economic Policy,* 104, 160. As Bruce Bartlett has noted, advisors of Kennedy's outside the CEA and the purview of the neoclassical synthesis had been recommending investment tax cuts and across-the-board reductions in rates since 1960. Bartlett, "Kennedy's Tax Cuts," Jan. 27, 2004, www.ncpa.org; the CEA memo is in the following citation.

46. CEA "Memorandum to the Staff," Jul. 3, 1962, Box 1, F "Tax Cut? Summer '62," JTP.

47. Walter Heller, "Memorandum for the President," re "Economic situation for your meeting today with businessmen," Jul. 12, 1962, Box 1, F "Tax Cut? Summer '62," JTP.

48. "Comments on the Attached Materials" and encl., Jul. 9–12, 1962; "Memorandum for the President," Jul. 12, 1962, re "Business Economists on the Economic Outlook and Tax Policy"; CEA, "Public Statements on the Need for a Tax Cut," Jul. 12, 1962, Box 1, F "Tax Cut? Summer '62," JTP. For Congress's, particularly Ways and Means's, tax activities in the period (beginning with Eisenhower), see Zelizer, *Taxing America.* For Heller's recounting of the episode, see Walter Heller, "Kennedy's Supply-Side Economics," in *Viewpoints on Supply-Side Economics,* ed. Thomas J. Hailstones (Richmond, VA: Robert F. Dame, 1982). This piece includes these words from Heller: "Alas, the Cambridge–New Haven [i.e., neoclassical synthesis] hope for full employment surpluses had to go by the boards" (44). The literature on the rise of the JFK-LBJ tax cut after the sunset of the neoclassical synthesis in the summer of 1962 is considerable. A place to start is Herbert Stein, *The Fiscal Revolution in America.* The advisor Arthur Okun played a key role in the JFK-LBJ proceedings, prompting one source to call him "one of the original supply-siders." "Arthur M. Okun," Library of Economics and Liberty, www.econlib.org. Fixing the top rate at 70 percent instead of 65 percent also meant that Kennedy did not fully fulfill the recommendation of his original Taxation Task Force.

49. Entin and Robbins have entertained this view in seminars at the Heritage Foundation. Interview with Stephen J. Entin and conversation with Gary Robbins.

50. Mundell, "On the History of the Mundell-Fleming Model"; James M. Boughton, "On the Origins of the Fleming-Mundell Model," *IMF Staff Papers* 50, no. 1 (2003), 1–9. Mundell has begged off the common summary of the Mundell-Fleming model as expressing an "impossible trinity" of mone-

tary policy, fixed exchange rates, and capital controls. See Robert A. Mundell, "Reflections on the International Monetary System," Asia Society Hong Kong Center Spring Gala Dinner, May 3, 2007, www.asiasociety.org/speeches/07hk_mundell.html.

51. "Robert A. Mundell: Distinguished Fellow," *American Economic Review* 87, no. 4 (Sept. 1997), U1. A discussion of the import of the Mundell-Fleming model in the history of macroeconomic thought is Maurice Obstfeld, "International Macroeconomics: Beyond the Mundell-Fleming Model," *IMF Staff Papers* 47, Special Issue (2001), 1–39. This article is adapted from an IMF "Mundell-Fleming Lecture" (of 2000), itself a testament to the "workhorse" nature of the model decades after its elaboration.

52. "Wanniski-ism, RIP," at www.economicprincipals.com/issues/2005.09.04/164.html. It is easy to see that Mundell was a not dropout by 1978. The view of Rudiger Dornbusch will suffice: "There was no international monetary issue of the 1960s and 1970s in which he was not prominently and decisively involved." Dornbusch, "Robert A. Mundell's Nobel Prize," 200. As for Mundell's Nobel work "done in the 1950s," Warsh takes all too literally Mundell's recollection that at Stanford in 1958 he had had the "aha!" moment. Jacques Polak at the IMF in 1961, for one, was of the mind that Mundell had more "work" to do on the model that he and Fleming would make a centerpiece of economics. Furthermore, the graphs that Mundell drew up in the *Staff Papers* piece of 1962 were new and were responsible for carrying the momentum of his argument. The Nobel press release speaks of the 1960s. Robert J. Barro, "Mundell," *BusinessWeek*, Nov. 1, 1999, 28. The comments of Warsh and Barro may be contrasted to those of Maurice Obstfeld: "The contributions of Mundell and of J. Marcus Fleming ... exemplify the most successful interactions of method and subject. No wonder this body of work has now been honored through the award to Mundell of the 1999 Nobel Prize in Economic Sciences." Obstfeld, "International Macroeconomics," 2.

53. Mundell, "On the History of the Mundell-Fleming Model," 222.

Chapter 4: Bitter Fruits

1. Mundell, "On the History of the Mundell-Fleming Model," 222.

2. Zelizer, *Taxing America,* chs. 8–9.

3. For the Martin saga, see Robert P. Bremner, *Chairman of the Fed: William McChesney Martin Jr. and the Creation of the Modern American Financial System* (New Haven, CT: Yale University Press, 2004).

4. Allan H. Meltzer, "From Inflation to More Inflation, Disinflation and Low Inflation," Keynote Address, Conference on Price Stability, Federal Reserve Bank of Chicago, Nov. 3, 2005, at www2. tepper.cmu.edu/afs/andrew/gsia/meltzer/FR_of_Chicago.doc, 5.

5. Mills has found his historian in Zelizer, *Taxing America.*

6. Federal Reserve behavior in the face of the Johnson spending is reviewed in Allan H. Meltzer, "The Origins of the Great Inflation," *Federal Reserve Bank of St. Louis Review* 87, no. 2, part 2 (Mar./Apr. 2005), 152–68.

7. Matthew Connelly, *A Diplomatic Revolution: Algeria's Fight for Independence and the Origins of the Post–Cold War Era* (New York: Oxford, 2002), 155–56.

8. For details of the French perspective and French activities in the 1960s gold-exchange predicament (and the de Gaulle quotation), see James, *International Monetary Cooperation since Bretton Woods,* 168–70, and Rueff, *The Monetary Sin of the West.*

9. The 1965 endorsement of the Twist may be found in the *Economic Report of the President for 1965,* 66–67, as discussed in Myron H. Ross, "Operation Twist: A Mistaken Policy?" *Journal of Political Economy* 74, no. 22 (Apr. 1966), 195–99.

10. Discussions of the pressures the United States placed on (particularly European) allies to limit dollar redemptions in gold may be found in Francis J. Gavin, *Gold, Dollars, and Power: The Politics of International Monetary Relations, 1958–1971* (Chapel Hill, NC: University of North Carolina Press, 2004), and Hubert Zimmermann, *Money and Security: Troops, Monetary Policy, and West Germany's Relations with the United States and Britain, 1950–1971* (New York: Cambridge University Press, 2002). For the "Roosa bonds" that hedged against devaluation, see C. Fred Bergsten, *Dilemmas of the Dollar: The Economics and Politics of United States International Monetary Policy* (Armonk, NY: M. E. Sharpe, 1996), 411. The other measures are contained in LBJ's statement of Jan. 1, 1968, at John T. Woolley and Gerhard Peters, *The American Presidency Project* [online], Santa Barbara, CA: University of California (hosted), Gerhard Peters (database), at http://www.presidency.ucsb.edu/ws/?pid=28804.

11. Rueff, *The Monetary Sin of the West,* 23, 89.

12. Rueff, *The Monetary Sin of the West,* 79.

13. Rueff, *The Monetary Sin of the West,* 8; for the French pressure on the dollar in this period, see Michael D. Bordo, Dominique Simard, and Eugene N. White, "France and the Bretton Woods International Monetary System: 1960–1968" (May 1996), NBER Working Paper No. W4642.

14. There was a significant degree of public academic support for Johnson's policy. Early examples (from 1966) are canvassed in Eileen Shanahan, "Tax Experts Split on Details of Rise," NYT, Mar. 18, 1966.

15. LBJ's New Year's statement, 1968.

16. LBJ's New Year's statement, 1968.

17. Robert L. Bartley, "Time for a Tax Cut," www.opinionjournal.com, Oct. 16, 2000. For the following section of text, an account of the Kennedy administration's position on tax cuts during the summer of 1962, further documentation may be found throughout the James Tobin, Walter Heller, and C. Douglas Dillon (the treasury secretary) papers at the JFK Presidential Library. The key moment was Jun. 29, 1962, when the Chamber of Commerce made a public call for a permanent reduction in the top rate to 65 percent exclusive of any loophole-closing or otherwise counterbalancing tax reform. In a memo to the president of that day, Heller quoted the chamber's press release: "The assertions of tax experts that our tax structure placed its burdens on the wrong part of the enterprise system—the productive end—was acknowledged in theory and ignored in practice." The previous CEA reports included such "assertions," and after Jun. 29, the administration realized that it had to consider the 65 percent mark the basis of any future negotiations, with business or Congress, on the matter of getting the economy moving again. For a short while, Heller and others in the administration continued to suggest that "non-temporary" tax cuts would expire after a year or two and that a 4 or 10 percent cut (as opposed to the chamber's 26 percent cut) was consistent with the chamber's suggestion. By the fall, the administration was in full accord that its policy was the cut to 65 percent without any attendant reform—that is to say, that its policy was precisely that which had been outlined by the Chamber of Commerce in June. As for cause and effect, it is actually reasonable to conclude that the chamber itself controlled events. Once its June 29 bombshell—and Heller treated it as such in his all-capital-letter memo to the president that day—hit, a cut to near 65 percent became inevitable. Heller–The President, "White House Outgoing Message," Jun. 29, 1961, Box 22, F "Tax Cut, 6/62–7/62," Walter W. Heller papers, JFK Library.

18. Mundell, "Toward a Better International Monetary System," 642, 644. The "socially useful" remark is one (as the article indicates) that Mundell had first made in 1964 at the conference of the American Economic Association.

19. Alan Waters, "Milton Friedman," in *The New Palgrave: A Dictionary of Economics,* vol. 2, ed. John Eatwell et al. (London: Macmillan, 1987); for Chicago, also see Moggridge, *Harry Johnson.*

20. Monetarism held that having the correct supply of money was the main determinant of an economy's success. The question monetarism begged was, what amount is the correct amount? There were many answers. Some monetarists held that steady, moderate, permanent increases in the quantity of money (as measured conventionally), perhaps 5 percent per year, would yield an optimal money supply. Others argued that the money masters must simply have a "feel" for the economy; Alan Greenspan would be the high representative of this sort of monetarism. All monetarists felt that the Fed must act in a crisis, but they worried about providing so much liquidity that the Fed would become impotent—that it would be "pushing on a string." Allan Meltzer's Shadow Open Market Committee in the 1970s (discussed later) did a great deal to clarify what real-world monetarist policy might actually look like. Meltzer's *History of the Federal Reserve* is a meditation on monetarist principles in view of the policy actions of the past. See also Alan Waters, "Friedman, Milton," in *The New Palgrave.*

21. Mundell once made this remarkable statement about Friedman's success in lobbying for flexible exchange rates: "James Meade, in London, had been an early advocate of flexible exchange rates, and Milton Friedman, at Chicago, was an avid proponent of floating rates. These two fine economists provided the main intellectual inspiration for breaking up the international monetary system in the 1970s into a 'system' of national currency areas connected by flexible exchange rates. But think about it for a minute! It was an alliance made in Hell! Meade was a liberal socialist, Friedman a conservative libertarian. Meade wanted flexible exchange rates so that the Labour Party in Britain could manage domestic industry without having to worry about the balance of payments; and he wanted flexible exchange rates among the Common Market countries. By contrast, Friedman wanted flexible exchange rates to get rid of exchange controls and fixed quantities of money to move toward his version of a free society." "Dr Mundell, what do you think are the major factors . . .'"

22. Rudi Dornbusch, "The Chicago School in the 1960s," in "One World, One Money?"

23. Dornbusch, "The Chicago School in the 1960s"; Dornbusch, "Robert A. Mundell's Nobel Memorial Prize," 208.

24. For various uses of the concept of the "leaky bucket," see Arthur Okun, *Equality and Efficiency: The Big Tradeoff* (Washington, DC: Brookings Institution, 1975).

25. John Rutledge, "Supply-Side Thermodynamics," *American Spectator,* Jul./Aug. 2002, 48–53.

26. Interviews with Meltzer and Entin.

27. Matusow, *Nixon's Economy,* 17. For Nixon's relationship with the Federal Reserve under Burns, see Meltzer, "Origins of the Great Inflation," 166–72.

28. Louiza Chwialkowska, "The Global Economist at Home," *Ottawa Citizen,* Jul. 25, 1998.

29. The proceedings are *Inflation as a Global Problem,* ed. Randall Hinshaw (Baltimore: Johns Hopkins University Press, 1972). For "St. Sebastian," see 119.

30. *Inflation as a Global Problem,* 116, 123.

31. *Inflation as a Global Problem,* 114, 118.

32. Mundell, "The Dollar and the Policy Mix."

33. James, *International Monetary Cooperation since Bretton Woods,* 205–19. Nixon's treasury secretary, John Connally, on the dollar drama of 1971: "Foreigners are out to screw us. Our job is to screw them first" (210).

34. As Richard Pipes has observed, "Aristotle, who in all matters preached moderation, said that there were situations in which 'inirascibility' was unacceptable: 'For those who are not angry at things they should be angry at are deemed fools.'" Pipes, *Russia Under the Bolshevik Regime*, 509–10.

35. Mundell, "The Dollar and the Policy Mix," 12–14.

36. Paul A. Samuelson and Robert M. Solow, "Analytical Aspects of Anti-Inflation Policy," *American Economic Review* 50, no. 2 (May 1960), 177–94.

37. The fate of the Phillips curve at the hand of academic economics at the time is illustrated in the Nobel Prize citations for Milton Friedman, Robert E. Lucas, and Edmund S. Phelps, nobelprize.org; the Treasury Department recognized "overheating" as a cliché. See "Fact Sheet: Taxes: History of the U.S. Tax System," heading "The Reagan Tax Cut," at www.treas.gov/education/fact-sheets/taxes/ustax. shtml; Robert E. Lucas Jr., "Monetary Neutrality," Prize Lecture, Dec. 7, 1995, nobelprize.org, 251.

38. Mundell, "The Dollar and the Policy Mix," 15.

39. Mundell, "The Dollar and the Policy Mix," 17–23.

40. Mundell, "The Dollar and the Policy Mix," 16–18.

41. Mundell, "The Dollar and the Policy Mix," 24.

42. Mundell, "The Dollar and the Policy Mix," 24–25.

43. A review of this historic episode is given in Shelton, *Money Meltdown*, 79–84. As Shelton notes, Nixon's Aug. 15 announcement also included a 10 percent surcharge on imports. Nixon seemed to be oblivious to the magnitude of what he was doing. In a briefing with his economic advisors the week before, his main concern was, not atypically, press leaks. Nixon Tapes, Conversation 560–1, Aug. 10, 1971, National Archives.

44. The Labor Department and a Cost of Living Council were also involved, along with other aspects of the federal bureaucracy. See Matusow, *Nixon's Economy*, 158–61. Also included was the IRS: as Nixon said on Jun. 13, 1973: "I have ordered the Internal Revenue Service to begin immediately a thoroughgoing audit of the books of companies which have raised their prices more than 1½ percent above the January ceiling. The purpose of the audit will be to find out whether these increases were justified. . . . If they were not, the prices will be rolled back." *The American Presidency Project.*

45. As Dow Jones Newswires described Bartley's 1980 prize in editorial writing: "Bartley's Pulitzer was awarded for a wide-ranging set of editorials. One, titled 'Down with Big Business,' argued that General Motors' support for Jimmy Carter's wage-price guidelines was a means to squeeze small competitors, such as 'XYZ Bumperlight Lens Co.' The editorial concluded: 'Historically, capitalist economies have prospered through competition, innovation and particularly a sensitive price mechanism transmitting unimaginably efficient signals for less production here and more investment there. If you freeze the system, you will lose its thrust toward progress. But in many ways, GM's life will be easier. So don't look to big business for unequivocal defenses of capitalism. We guess that's up to the folks at XYZ Bumperlight Lens.'" "Robert L. Bartley, the *Wall Street Journal*'s Editor Emeritus, Dies at 66," Dec. 10, 2003, www.opinionjournal.com.

46. On the easy money of 1972, see Matusow, *Nixon's Economy*, 190–92, and for a monetarist's exasperation with Federal Reserve accommodation of presidential year electioneering, see Allan H. Meltzer, "Commentary," *The Phenomenon of Worldwide Inflation*, ed. David I. Meiselman et al. (Washington, DC: AEI, 1975), 54.

47. "1065 and All That," *Time*, Feb. 22, 1971; Arthur B. Laffer and R. David Ranson, "1065 and All That!" *Financial Analysts Journal* 27, no. 3 (May–Jun. 1971).

48. For Laffer's collaboration with Ranson, see RG 56, Subject Files of R. David Ranson, National Archives.

49. "Keeping Up: Shed a Tear for the G.N.P.," *Fortune,* Dec. 1976, 69. Robert Bartley noted the *Fortune* vindication in *The Seven Fat Years,* 43.

50. Laffer, "The Bitter Fruits of Devaluation."

51. Mundell, "The Dollar and the Policy Mix," 11; the opening free-lunch salvo was Walter W. Heller, "The Kemp-Roth-Laffer Free Lunch," WSJ, Jul. 12, 1978.

Chapter 5: Michael 1

1. Edward E. Sharff, *Worldly Power: The Making of the* Wall Street Journal (New York: Beaufort, 1986), 252.

2. OILPRICE, research.stlouisfed.org.

3. For inflation component data in this and subsequent paragraphs, see *A Guide to Consumer Markets 1974/1975,* ed. Helen Axel (New York: The Conference Board, 1974), 241–49.

4. For the food price saga of 1973, in this and subsequent paragraphs, see Matusow, *Nixon's Economy,* 219–40.

5. Matusow, *Nixon's Economy,* 225.

6. For early public interest in the economic discomfort index, see Richard F. Janssen, "The Outlook: Appraisal of Current Trends in Business and Finance," WSJ, Jan. 4, 1971; Okun, then popularizing the term, in 1975: "I have specialized throughout my career on the trade-off between inflation and unemployment. To put it mildly, the search for a satisfactory way of managing it has not been successfully completed. I, for one, have not given up; indeed, I plan to spend the rest of my professional life on that problem." Okun, *Equality and Efficiency,* 2; Samuelson borrowed "stagflation" from British users, as in Edward Nelson and Kalin Nikolov, "Monetary Policy and Stagflation in the U.K.," working paper, 2002, www.bankofengland.co.uk, 9n2.

7. Bartley, *The Seven Fat Years,* 44; Scharff, *Worldly Power,* 250.

8. Details of Jude Wanniski's biography in this and following paragraphs are from Scharff, *Worldly Power;* John Brooks, "Annals of Finance: The Supply-Side," *The New Yorker,* Apr. 19, 1982; and "Jude Wanniski Biography," www.polyconomics.com.

9. The 1980 episode is discussed here in chapter 9.

10. Jude Wanniski, *The Way the World Works,* 20th anniversary edition (Washington, DC: Regnery, 1998), xvi.

11. Sidney Blumenthal, *The Rise of the Counter-Establishment: The Conservative Ascent to Political Power* (New York: Union Square, 2008). The conference was cosponsored by the Hoover Institution.

12. Allan H. Meltzer, "The Shadow Open Market Committee: Origins and Operations," at www.somc.rochester.edu/SOMCOriginsApr00.pdf.

13. The proceedings are *The Phenomenon of Worldwide Inflation.* Meiselman (the editor) is the one to whom Mundell had quoted Bizet in 1961. Mundell, "On the History of the Mundell-Fleming Model," 222. In 1974, Haberler was Harvard professor emeritus and a resident scholar at AEI.

14. Mundell, "Inflation from an International Viewpoint," in *The Phenomenon of Worldwide Inflation,* 144.

15. Mundell, "Inflation from an International Viewpoint," 148, 149.

16. Mundell, "Inflation from an International Viewpoint," 147.

17. Mundell, "Inflation from an International Viewpoint," 148–49.

18. Mundell alluded to the fact that OPEC deposits in Western banks functioned as "high-powered money" that compromised the Federal Reserve's ability to limit the world dollar supply. This was a major issue in monetarist debates in the 1970s. Within the United States, bank reserves had to be at a certain ratio before loans could be made. But given the massive presence of dollars in foreign banks, dollarized loans were available from non-American sources that were beyond the reach of Fed rules. So even if the Fed increased the reserve ratio in an effort to limit the money supply, dollar credit could be easily obtained from the world or "Eurodollar" market. Mundell, "Inflation from an International Viewpoint," 147–48.

19. Scharff, *Worldly Power*, 258; interview with Laffer; Jude Wanniski, "The Case for Fixed Exchange Rates," WSJ, Jun. 14, 1974; Wanniski, "Fixed or Floating," Nov. 6, 2004, www.polyconomics.com.

20. Jude Wanniski, "It's Time to Cut Taxes," WSJ, Dec. 11, 1974; Jude Wanniski, "Early Days of Supply-Side," Jun. 23, 2000; "It's Time to Cut Taxes," Mar. 7, 2003, www.polyconomics.com.

21. Sources include Scharff, *Worldly Power*, 259–60; Arthur B. Laffer, "The Laffer Curve"; Wanniski, "It's Time to Cut Taxes," www.polyconomics.com; extensive Wanniski-Cheney-Rumsfeld correspondence is to be found in the JWP. Most sources indicate the meeting to have been held in December, possibly December 4. The photo of the napkin to be found on the Internet (at times on Wikipedia and at www.polyconomics.com) and dated Sept. 13, 1974, is most certainly an ex post facto creation. Wanniski, "The Early Days of Supply-Side"; Sen. Lloyd Bentsen (D-TX), a future supply-side friend, had made the same point about the elections a year earlier. "Economy Issue Seen by Senator," *Dallas Morning News,* Sept. 27, 1973.

22. Scharff, *Worldly Power,* 259.

23. Robert L. Bartley and Amity Shlaes, "The Supply-Side Revolution," in *Turning Intellect into Influence: The Manhattan Institute at 25,* ed. Brian C. Anderson (New York: Reed, 2004), 34.

24. Laffer, "The Laffer Curve."

25. Corr. Wanniski-Cheney/Rumsfeld and Bartley-Cheney, 1975, Box 110, NF, RLB; letter, Cheney-Wanniski, Sept. 19, 1978, Box 25, F "Mail," JWP.

26. Memoranda, Laffer-Simon, with encl., Nov. 25, 1974, and May 17, 1974, Drawer 10, "Internal Memoranda: J-R," F 11, "Laffer, Arthur B. (Consultant to the Secretary): 1973–1975," William E. Simon papers.

27. Bartley, *The Seven Fat Years,* 59.

28. Wanniski, "The Mundell-Laffer Hypothesis," 31–32. Rumsfeld told Wanniski that he had given a copy of the article to President Ford. Letter, Rumsfeld-Wanniski, Jan. 17, 1975, Box 32, NF, JWP. For the influence of this article on Ronald Reagan's 1976 presidential campaign, see Scharff, *Worldly Power,* 261.

29. Scharff, *Worldly Power,* 255.

30. Scharff, *Worldly Power,* 255.

31. For Bartley's biography and demeanor, see Scharff, *Worldly Power,* 240ff; Peggy Noonan, "Freedom's Best Friend," Dec. 11, 2003, www.opinionjournal.com; and Brooks, "Annals of Finance."

32. A flavor of Bartley's opinion about establishments is given in Robert L. Bartley, "The Press: Time for a New Era?" Jul. 28, 2003, www.opinionjournal.com; and in his C-SPAN *Booknotes* interview, May 17, 1992, www.booknotes.org.

33. Robert L. Bartley, "Thirty Years of Progress—Mostly," Nov. 20, 2002, www.opinionjournal.com.

34. Robert L. Bartley, "A Few Final Words as Editor," Dec. 30, 2002, www.opinionjournal.com.

35. Bartley, *Seven Fat Years*, 277; Robert Bartley–Charles Maier correspondence, Jan.–Feb. 1976, Box 64, F "RLB Business Correspondence—M," RLB. In economics jargon, the debate was over "Pareto effects."

36. This is discussed here in chapter 8.

37. See the discussion of Bartley's Pulitzer Prize in chapter 8.

38. Society column quoted in letter, Bartley–Erwin Glikes, Box 94, F "RLB's Book Outline and Correspondence," RLB; Bartley, *The Seven Fat Years*, 141.

39. To date the meetings, see Bartley and Shlaes, "The Supply-Side Revolution," and Robert Bartley's datebooks, Box 68, RLB. The datebooks indicate that dinner at Lew Lehrman's (replacing Michael 1) continued through the 1970s.

40. Details of the Michael 1 gatherings are drawn from Bartley, *The Seven Fat Years*, ch. 3, and from an interview with Laffer.

41. Novak, *The Prince of Darkness*, 140–41.

42. Brooks, "Annals of Finance"; Wanniski, "The Mundell-Laffer Hypothesis," 32n1; Laffer, *Private Short-term Capital Flows* (New York: Dekker, 1975); Laffer's paper "The Phenomenon of Worldwide Inflation: A Study in International Market Integration," in *The Phenomenon of Worldwide Inflation*.

43. E-mail, Mundell-Bartley, re "bubbles," Jul. 30, 2002, Box 104, F "Mundell-Addresses—etc.," RLB.

44. Bartley, *The Seven Fat Years*, 59.

45. Bartley, *Seven Fat Years*, 49; the definitive modern exposition is Thomas Sowell, *Say's Law: An Historical Analysis* (Princeton, NJ: Princeton University Press, 1972). The price level would stay the same in that an increase in the overall stock of goods would increase the value of existing money and thus call forth new money commensurate with the increase in goods.

46. Bartley, *Seven Fat Years*, 54–55.

47. Scharff, *Worldly Power*, 261–63.

48. The run of the correspondence is Box 41, NF and Box 42, F "Corr. with friends—W"; Bartley-Reynolds, Apr. 15, 1976, Box 41, NF, RLB.

49. Reynolds-Bartley, Apr. 1, 1975, Box 42, F "Corr. With Friends—W"; Apr. 21, 1975, Box 41, NF, RLB.

50. James A. Baker III, "A 'Reformed Drunk' on Tax Relief," Apr. 18, 2003, www.opinionjournal.com; "Keynes Is Dead," WSJ, Jan. 31, 1977.

Chapter 6: The Hill

1. Alan Reynolds, "Supply-Side Economics after 30 Years," lecture, Vanderbilt University, Jan. 29, 2003, transcript in personal collection of Alan Reynolds. See James M. Buchanan and Dwight R. Lee, "Tax Rates and Tax Revenues in Political Equilibrium: Some Simple Analytics," *Innovative Applications of the Laffer Curve* (Chattanooga, TN: Probasco Chair, 1998).

2. Reynolds, "Supply-Side Economics after 30 Years"; interview with Laffer.

3. Interview with Reynolds; Bartley, *The Seven Fat Years*, 44. At a Brookings Institution conference in 1975, Marina v. N. Whitman, a former member of the Nixon CEA, had suggested another name for the Mundell-Laffer view: "global monetarism," a name that would have traction into the 1980s as a substitute for "supply-side economics." Whitman, "Global Monetarism and the Monetary Approach

to the Balance of Payments," *Brookings Papers on Economic Activity* 1975, no. 3, 491–555; by early 1978, the term "supply-side economics" was current.

4. Bartley, *The Seven Fat Years,* 27.

5. Herbert Stein, "Economics at the *New Yorker*," WSJ, Nov. 12, 1979; Stein, *On the Other Hand: Essays on Economics, Economists, and Politics* (Washington, DC: AEI, 1995).

6. Letter, Reynolds-Bartley, Apr. 6, 1976, Box 41, NF, RLB. Niskanen elaborated his call for marginal tax cuts in William A. Niskanen, "The Long-Run Effects of Federal Tax Reduction," Tax Foundation 28th National Conference, Dec. 1, 1976, W305–6, "JK's Economics-Back Up Material, ca. 1975–77," F 1, JKCP.

7. "Rep. Kemp's Position," WSJ, Mar. 15, 1976. On Mar. 26, it was 107 sponsors. Memorandum, Randal Teague–Kemp staff, re "Jobs Creation Act," Mar. 26, 1976, W305–6, "Jobs Creation Act, 1974–75," F 5, JKCP.

8. The fifteen ways are enumerated in Ch. III, Norman B. Ture and B. Kenneth Sanden, *The Effects of Tax Policy on Capital Formation* (New York: Financial Executives Research Foundation, 1977).

9. Brooks, "Annals of Finance: The Supply-Side"; Ture's bibliography: "Norman B. Ture, Books, Papers, Speeches, Conference Presentations, and Congressional Testimony," www.iret.org.

10. See Zelizer, *Taxing America.*

11. Bruce Bartlett, a congressional staffer in the supply-side years, pointed out that the White House tapes illustrate Ture's role, via Mills, in the Kennedy tax cuts. Bartlett, "Kennedy's Tax Cuts."

12. Daniel M. Holland, "Business Tax Provisions of the 1962 and 1964 Acts," *Journal of Finance* 20, no. 2 (May 1965), 273–91.

13. Ture, "Growth Aspects of Federal Tax Policy," *Journal of Finance* 17, no. 2 (May 1962), 271.

14. Norman B. Ture, "Statement on the August 3, 1967 Tax Proposals of the President," to the Committee on Ways and Means, U.S. House of Representatives, Sept. 12, 1967, and "Tax Changes for Shortrun Stabilization," statement to the Joint Economic Committee's Subcommittee on Fiscal Policy, 89th U.S. Congress, 2nd Session, 1966. A blogger called Ture a "supply-side goofball" for his testimony thirty years after the fact. "George W. Bush = LBJ on Fiscal Policy," May 12, 2006, at angrybear.blogspot.com/2006/05/george-w-bush-lbj-on-fiscal-policy.html.

15. For Ture's final views on taxation and neutrality, as they matured over his lifetime, see "The Inflow Outflow Tax—A Saving-Deferred Neutral Tax System," www.iret.org.

16. For the depreciation provisions, see "Corporation Income Tax Brackets and Rates, 1909–2002," 290n14, at www.irs.gov/pub/irs-soi/02corate.pdf; Laurence N. Woodworth, "Tax Simplification and the Tax Reform Act of 1969," *Law and Contemporary Problems* 34, no. 4 (Autumn 1969), 711–12.

17. William E. Simon, "Watering the Money Tree," *National Review,* Mar. 5, 1976; Ture and Sanden, *The Effects of Tax Policy on Capital Formation,* 13, 58.

18. Ture and Sanden, *The Effects of Tax Policy on Capital Formation,* 62–63.

19. Ture and Sanden, *The Effects of Tax Policy on Capital Formation,* 98.

20. The details of steel industry history are drawn from John P. Hoerr, *And the Wolf Finally Came: The Decline of the American Steel Industry* (Pittsburgh: University of Pittsburgh Press, 1988).

21. Today, a few hundred people work in industry on the Lackawanna site, as do a few hundred on the Homestead site. Bethlehem Steel (once the nation's third largest company) went bankrupt in 2001 and was dissolved in 2003. Bruce Bartlett, "Revolution of 1978," *National Review,* Oct. 27, 1978, 1333.

22. Roberts, *The Supply-Side Revolution,* 33.

23. Bartlett, *Reaganomics: Supply-Side Economics in Action* (Westport, CT: Arlington House, 1981), 125–26.

24. Letter, James T. Lynn (OMB director)–Jack Kemp, May 27, 1975, W305–6, "Jobs Creation Act, 1974–75," F 3, JKCP.

25. Paul Craig Roberts, *Alienation and the Soviet Economy: Toward a General Theory of Marxian Alienation, Organizational Principles, and the Soviet Economy* (Albuquerque, NM: University of New Mexico Press, 1971); letter, Roberts–Bartley, Jan. 6, 1976, Box 41, NF, RLB.

26. Letter, Roberts–Bartley, Feb. 12, 1976, Box 41, NF, RLB.

27. Frum, *How We Got Here*, 300–301.

28. Jude Wanniski, "Taxes and a Two Santa Theory," *National Observer,* Mar. 6, 1976; Bartlett, *Reaganomics,* 218.

29. Yanek Mieczkowski, *Gerald Ford and the Challenges of the 1970s* (Lexington, KY: University Press of Kentucky, 2005), 225–26.

30. "A Tenth Anniversary Celebration of the Kemp-Roth Tax Cuts: The Importance of America's Victory Over Washington," Heritage Lecture #344, Oct. 20, 1991, www.heritage.org.

31. Norman B. Ture, "Economic and Federal Revenue Effects of the Jobs Creation Act of 1975," Oct. 20, 1975, personal collection of Stephen J. Entin/Institute for Research on the Economics of Taxation (IRET); Bartlett, *Reaganomics,* 126.

32. Memorandum, Roberts-Kemp, re "Treasury Critique of Ture Study," Mar. 15, 1976, W305–6, "Jobs Creation Act, 1974–75," F 4; Roberts, *The Supply-Side Revolution,* 30; memorandum, Randal Teague–Jack Kemp/Craig Roberts, re "The 'Seidman position,'" n.d. (ca. Feb. 1976), W305–6, "Jobs Creation Act, 1974–75," F 5, JKCP; Ford relented of the stealth tax increases as a lame duck in early 1977. "Remember the Ford Tax Plan," WSJ, Jan. 24, 1977.

33. Memo to Kemp, "Jobs Creation Act," ca. Mar. 1976, W305–6, "Jobs Creation Act 1974–75", F5, JKCP.

34. Interview with Laffer.

35. Jimmy Carter, *Why Not the Best?* (New York: Bantam, 1976), 174–75.

36. See the discussion in Barnaby Conrad III, *The Martini: An Illustrated History of an American Classic* (San Francisco: Chronicle Books, 1995), 79–81. The rumor of a Carter proposal to cut the 70 percent rate is discussed in memorandum, Entin–JEC minority, re "Greenspan breakfast," Mar. 24, 1977, Box 29, F "Tax Cut," JRP. In view of later accusations (of David Stockman) that Kemp-Roth was "always" a "Trojan horse" to bring the top rate down to 50 percent, the documentary record suggests the reverse. That is, when the 70–50 rate cut first surfaced as something that might get done, in early 1977, Kemp and his allies immediately countered with a general cut in lieu of the 70–50 cut. This is discussed further in chapter 10.

37. Roberts, *The Supply-Side Revolution,* 30–33.

38. An example of Roberts's work with further Republicans on the Budget Committee is "Report Prepared for Representative Del Latta and the Minority Members of the House Budget Committee," Jan. 1977, W305–6, "JK's Economics-Back Up Material, ca. 1975–77," F 1, JKCP.

39. Letter, Alice Rivlin–Rousselot, Jan. 18, 1977, Box 29, F "CBO Letters," JRP.

40. Letter, Rivlin–Rousselot, Jan. 18, 1977.

41. Box 29, F "Budget Testimony Letters"; Paul Craig Roberts, "Economic Models, Eco-nomic Policy and Politics," Box 29, F "Tax Cut," JRP.

42. Memorandum, Kent-Rousselot, re "Revised Budget Loss Figures from CBO," Feb. 2, 1977; letters, Rivlin-Rousselot, Feb. 3 and 22, 1977, Box 29, F "CBO Letters," JRP.

43. Letter, Blumenthal-Rousselot, Feb. 28, 1977, Box 29, F "Budget Testimony Letters," JRP. Blumenthal went on to argue that revenues would have been greater in the 1960s had measures other than tax cuts produced the growth. He did not indicate what those other measures might have been.

44. The quest to hold model hearings is a theme of ch. 2 of Roberts, *The Supply-Side Revolution*. See also Bartlett, *Reaganomics,* 131, and letter, Delbert Latta and Rousselot to Rivlin, Feb. 25, 1977, Box 29, F "CBO Letters," JRP.

45. Walter W. Heller, "Economic Recovery Is Still Flabby," WSJ, Jan. 7, 1977.

46. The account of Feb. 23, 1977, is drawn from Roberts, *The Supply-Side Revolution,* 7–33. The event may be followed in the *Congressional Record,* but as Roberts notes, the *Record* sanitizes raucous moments.

47. *Third Concurrent Resolution on the Budget—Fiscal Year 1977,* Feb. 8, 1977 (GPO), 90; *The 1977 Joint Economic Report* (GPO), 79.

48. Roberts, *The Supply-Side Revolution,* 31–32. After the success of Feb. 22, Republicans in Congress worked on tax-cut bills. The major proposals are summarized in memorandum, John Meagher–Republican Tax Group, re "Republican Proposal for Permanent Tax Reduction," Apr. 25, 1977, W304, "The Model; Binder on Economics; 1975–1980," JKCP.

49. Irving Kristol, "Toward a 'New' Economics?" WSJ, May 9, 1977.

Chapter 7: Revolt

1. In this stylized example, $19,000 implies $16,000 (actually $15,999) of taxable income—that is, income after deductions, which in this case is $3,001. The standard deduction (including exemptions) for married couples was $2,800 in 1973. There were other common deductions (and credits) that make the $3,001 in this case an understatement. In 1973, $19,000 was about 1.57 times median family income. This worker could be a skilled manufacturing employee, or the example could refer to a middle-class working couple. The return is married filing jointly. Median family income data, Census Bureau, www.census.gov/hhes/www/income/histinc/f07ar.html. For historical deduction figures, see the tables at the Tax Policy Center site, www.taxpolicycenter.org/taxfacts. There was a bracket expansion in 1977 that would have moderated this effect in all the brackets in 1977 and early 1978. But the original thresholds would have been in effect for raises gained by this worker from 1974 through early 1977. Moreover, there were Social Security tax increases perhaps not offset by deduction increases, an effect that increased the rate at which all income was taxed. See the tables at the Tax Policy Center site referring to Social Security taxes.

2. The average tax rate in this example is the amount of income tax paid if $16,000 of the $19,000 is adjusted gross income. This surely overstates the average tax experienced by most filers in the period, and hence understates the difference between the average tax and marginal rate. The larger that difference, the more the COLA falls short of being real. For workers making $15,000 in this period, average tax rates were around 9 percent, with marginal rates at 19 percent. "Tax Sense and Nonsense," *National Review,* Sept. 1, 1978, 1064.

3. Earned income was taxed to 50 percent, investment income to 70 percent. But because of an IRS procedure known as "stacking," high earned income was often effectively taxed up to 70 percent. By this point, however, taxpayers typically fled to shelters and the alternative minimum tax.

4. Paul Craig Roberts, "Some Tax Myths: Who Pays What?" *National Review,* Apr. 28, 1978, 524.

5. Warren T. Brookes, "The Case for the Kemp-Roth Tax Cut Bill," *Human Events,* Oct. 14, 1978.

6. Hoerr, *And the Wolf Finally Came,* 109–15. If a USW member was the one making the $19,000 in 1973, the 3 percent bonus would have been about 2 percent, with the remaining 1 percent covering for the inadequacy of the COLA before the progressive code and the bonus itself facing the code.

7. In "The Mundell-Laffer Hypothesis," Wanniski observed that in the presidential economics of rent years, "a jawbone was brandished." See also Biven, *Jimmy Carter's Economy.*

8. In this regard, GE is discussed here in chapter 9.

9. The official estimate prepared for the Prop 13 vote was 2.7 percent, March Fong Eu and William G. Hamm, *California Voters Pamphlet: Primary Election,* Jun. 6, 1978, 56. Also see this source for the provisions of Prop 13.

10. Bartlett, *Reaganomics,* 140–43. In these pages, Bartlett adduced an example of a family making $18,000 a year in 1973. In "The Great Tax Revolt," Feb. 10, 1978, Evans and Novak cited examples of California homes bought in 1968 for $50,000 costing $5,000 a year in property taxes by 1978.

11. Department of the Treasury, "Blueprints for Basic Tax Reform," Jan. 17, 1977 (GPO). Simon, *A Time for Truth,* 3–4.

12. Simon, *A Time for Truth,* 98.

13. Simon, *A Time for Truth,* 106.

14. Simon, *A Time for Truth,* 139; *Daily News,* Oct. 30, 1975.

15. The chapter "New York: Disaster in Microcosm" is followed by "U.S.A.: The Macrocosm," 137–227.

16. Beginnning Jul. 2, 1978, *A Time for Truth* was a regular presence among the fifteen top nonfiction sellers on the *New York Times* list for the rest of the year. For Wanniski's book, see Bartley and Shlaes, "The Supply-Side Revolution"; interview with Reynolds.

17. Wanniski, *The Way the World Works,* x; "The Mundell-Laffer Hypothesis," 32.

18. Wanniski, *The Way the World Works,* 84.

19. Wanniski, *The Way the World Works,* 85.

20. Arthur B. Laffer, "Unemployment and Taxes," *National Review,* Feb. 4, 1977.

21. Roberts, *The Supply-Side Revolution,* ch. 2; even though salary income-tax rates topped at 50 percent, an earner in this category had investment tax rates upwards of 70 percent. By the property of income "stacking," this made the effective salary top rate 70 percent.

22. Personal collection of Alan Reynolds.

23. Bartlett, *Reaganomics,* 140–41; interview with Laffer.

24. "Statement of Edwin V. W. Zschau," *The President's 1978 Tax Reduction and Reform Proposals,* Mar. 7, 1978 (GPO), 1307,1313.

25. Interview with Laffer.

26. The details in these paragraphs are drawn from an interview with Laffer.

27. Bob Colacello, *Ronnie & Nancy: Their Path to the White House—1911 to 1980* (New York: Warner Books, 2004), 471.

28. Novak, *The Prince of Darkness,* 321–22.

29. Quoted in Colacello, *Ronnie & Nancy,* 471.

30. "Wealth and Poverty: A Discussion of Supply-Side Economics," television program, U.S. Information Agency, 1981, RG 306, National Archives; Bill Steigerwald, "Is This a Great World or What?" *Pittsburgh Tribune-Review,* Feb. 5, 2005, the title suggested by Laffer (interview with Laffer).

31. There were express revenue acts in 1976–78. Roberts found that all sorts of devices were used in 1979–80 both to introduce tax measures and to prevent them from being introduced. *The Supply-Side Revolution*, 87–88.

32. Bartlett, *Reaganomics*, 171–73; see Evans and Novak, "How Much Has Carter Learned?" Apr. 20, 1978, and "Tax Reform: Foe of Tax Reduction," Dec. 26, 1977.

33. The effective maximum rate of capital-gains taxes was 49 percent on account of both statutory capital-gains rates and the minimum tax.

34. "Stupendous Steiger," WSJ, Apr. 26, 1978; Evans and Novak, "Losing Credibility Over Capital Gains," May 25, 1978; Bartlett, *Reaganomics*, 172–73.

35. Quoted in "About-Face on Capital Gains," *Time*, Jun. 12, 1978.

36. Feldstein and Slemrod, "Inflation and the Excess Taxation of Capital Gains on Corporate Stock," *National Tax Journal* 31, no. 2, (Jun. 1978), 107–18; see also Feldstein and Shlomo Yitzhaki, "The Effect of the Capital Gains Tax on the Selling and Switching of Common Stock," *Journal of Public Economics* IX (Feb. 1978), 17–36.

37. Martin Feldstein, "Inflation and Capital Formation," WSJ, Jul. 27, 1978. The NYSE study cited below found the effect acute for people with incomes above $10,000 (56 percent of median family income).

38. Letter, William A. Batten, CEO, NYSE, to Steiger, Jun. 5, 1978, Box 32A, F4, WAS.

39. Lloyd Bentsen, "1978 Intangible Drilling Cost Tax Amendment," *Oil Daily*, Nov. 1, 1978.

40. President's news conference of Apr. 25, 1978, *The American Presidency Project*; Evans and Novak, "Once Again the Authentic Jimmy Carter," May 5, 1978 (as this article observed, Carter misrepresented the tax code in this case), "How Much Has Carter Learned?" and "Will They Talk Carter into a Tax Counterrevolt?" Jun. 23, 1978.

41. Evans and Novak, "Will They Talk Carter into a Tax Counterrevolt?" and "Losing Credibility Over Capital Gains."

42. "Executive Summary," Michael K. Evans, Chase Econometrics, Inc., "The Economic Effects of Reducing Capital Gains Taxes," Apr. 17, 1978, F "Capital Gains, Steiger Amendment (2)," Charles Schultze files (all JCL files hereafter are from these files), JCL; Evans, *The Truth about Supply-Side Economics* (New York: Basic Books, 1983).

43. Treasury's analysis is summarized in "STEIGER AMENDMENT, WS 6/5/78"; Public Citizen's remark in "Facts about the Steiger Amendment and the Taxation of Capital Gains," Jun. 8, 1978, both F "Capital Gains: Steiger Amendment [2]," JCL; Carter's remark, the president's news conference of Jun. 26, 1978, *The American Presidency Project*.

44. Schultze's introduction to and summary of the study, letter of Schultze–Sen. Russell Long, Sept. 28, 1978; the CEA study, "Feldstein on Capital Gains Realizations," F "Capital Gains: Steiger Amendment [1]," JCL; the block quotation, 13.

45. Letters, Feldstein-Eizenstat, Oct. 2, 1978; Feldstein–Schultze, Oct. 2, 1978; Feldstein-Long, Oct. 2, 1978, F "Capital Gains: Steiger Amendment [1]," JCL. Quotations in the following paragraphs come from the last document.

46. Various Feldstein letters, F "Capital Gains: Steiger Amendment [1]," JCL. Evans and Novak, "Tax Solution: Aim Ahead of the Flying Ducks," Aug. 23, 1978.

47. *Wall Street Week with Louis Rukeyser* #806 (Baltimore: Maryland Center for Public Broadcasting), Aug. 11, 1978, 13; William A. Steiger, "The Consumptive Society," Box 1, F14, WAS.

48. *Wall $treet Week*, Aug. 11, 1978, 16.

49. Bartlett, *The Reagan Revolution*, 133.

50. Roberts, *The Supply-Side Revolution*, 81–84; "Off the Wagon," WSJ, Jul. 31, 1978; *Wall $treet Week*, Aug. 11, 1978, 1.

51. Evans and Novak, "How Carter Muffed a Tax-Relief Compromise," Aug. 14, 1978, and "Tax Solution."

52. Roberts, *The Supply-Side Revolution*, 85–87; "Congress Gets the Antitax Message," *Time*, Oct. 23, 1978.

53. Evans and Novak, "How Carter Muffed a Tax-Relief Compromise."

54. "Congress Gets the Antitax Message"; Roberts, *The Supply-Side Revolution*, 86–87.

55. See the summary at www.thomas.gov, Public Law 95–600. Also included in the bill was relaxed capital-gains treatment for home sales.

56. Letter, William D. Nordhaus to Russell Long, Oct. 31, 1978, F "Capital Gains: Steiger Amendment [1]," JCL; Alan J. Auerbach, "Capital Gains Taxation in the United States: Realizations, Revenue, and Rhetoric," *Brookings Papers on Economic Activity* (1988), 596.

57. "Capital Gains and Taxes Paid on Capital Gains," www.taxpolicycenter.org.

58. "The 1979 Tax Increase," WSJ, Oct. 17, 1978.

59. Letter, Fred M. Alger–Steiger (includes the Lehrman offer), Aug. 15, 1978, and the correspondence from such firms as Drexel Burnham Lambert, Box 46, F 36; letters Steiger–Bartley-Steiger, Oct. 1978, Box 32A, F 4, WAS. As for the credit Steiger gave to Laffer, see letter, Steiger-Laffer, Jun. 21, 1978, Box 86, F "LA-LAP," WAS.

Chapter 8: Malaise

1. Roberts, "Some Tax Myths," 524; the Treasury conclusion, letter, Spencer S. Reibman (staff of Rep. John Rousselot) to Peter Davis, Joint Committee on Taxation, Jan. 19, 1978, W303, F "Jul. 14, '78 Record Testimony," JKCP.

2. The effect of bracket creep as of tax day in April 1979, including the effect of state and local taxes, is laid out in Andrew Stein, "Government Plays the Tax Game with Loaded Dice," WSJ, Apr. 13, 1979.

3. Hoerr, *And the Wolf Finally Came*, 113–14.

4. For bond interest rates (price is 1/[interest rate]), see the historical data on corporate issues at research.stlouisfed.org; "Bloodbath at Home," WSJ, Feb. 22, 1980, 20.

5. Biven, *Jimmy Carter's Economy*, 7.

6. James H. Lorie, "The Second Great Crash," WSJ, Jun. 2, 1980.

7. OILPRICE, research.stlouisfed.org.

8. Jason Epstein, "Help!" *New York Review of Books*, Feb. 21, 1980.

9. Alfred L. Malabre Jr., "Why Worry About Inflation?" WSJ, Jun. 7, 1979; Lester C. Thurow, "The Real Sources of Economic Pain," WSJ, Jul. 6, 1978.

10. Lester C. Thurow, *The Zero-Sum Society: Distribution and Possibilities for Economic Change* (New York: Basic Books, 1980), 24.

11. See "Youth Employment," in *Reagan: In His Own Hand: The Writings of Ronald Reagan That Reveal His Revolutionary Vision for America*, eds. Kiron K. Skinner and Annelise and Martin Anderson (New York: Free Press, 2001), 303. Another example of pointing out minority unemployment is Jack Kemp, "The People Aren't Fooled," WP, Jun. 5, 1979.

12. "Forecasting the Supply-Side of the Economy: Hearing before the JEC, May 21, 1980" (GPO), 17.

13. For a narrative of Carter's economic policies at the time, see Biven, *Jimmy Carter's Economy.*

14. "White House Endorses Teamsters' Pact as Gain in Anti-Inflation Effort," Apr. 12, 1979, and for Kahn's concession that the rules had been bent, "Having It Both Ways on the Economy," Apr. 15, 1979, NYT; Walter B. Wriston, "Repressing Economic News," WSJ, May 4, 1979.

15. "Down with Big Business," WSJ, Apr. 18, 1979. See Bartley's discussion of the article in *The Seven Fat Years,* 40–41. On the Pulitzer, see "Robert L. Bartley, the *Wall Street Journal*'s Editor Emeritus, Dies at 66."

16. "Ways and Means?" WSJ, Feb. 2, 1979. About Kahn, including his great successes as a deregulator, see Thomas K. McCraw, *Prophets of Regulation* (Cambridge, MA: Harvard University Press, 1984).

17. "Address to the Nation on Energy and National Goals," Jul. 15, 1979, *The American Presidency Project.*

18. Walter W. Heller, "Recession, Oil and Tax Policy," WSJ, Jun. 27, 1979.

19. Mundell's view at the time was aptly summarized by Wanniski, "The Politics of Gold," Polyconomics, Sept. 1980, 56; Roy W. Jastram, "A Picture of Inflation," WSJ, Dec. 12, 1979; Bartley, *The Seven Fat Years,* 39, 108–9. Kemp put Warren Brookes's article, "The Trade Deficit: Exploding the Carter Myths," in the *Congressional Record,* Mar. 1, 1979.

20. Jeremy Beer, "On Christopher Lasch," *Modern Age* 47, no. 4 (Fall 2005), 336–37.

21. Quoted in Biven, *Jimmy Carter's Economy,* 259–60.

22. On Blumenthal's threat to quit, Bartley, *The Seven Fat Years,* 83.

23. Interview with Laffer.

24. Heller, "Recession, Oil and Tax Policy."

25. Biven, *Jimmy Carter's Economy,* 239.

26. For a review of Volcker's first several months, see "Support Mr. Volcker," WSJ, Oct. 8, 1979, and Bartley, *The Seven Fat Years,* 84–86.

27. "Commanding Heights" interview with Paul Volcker, at http://www.tc.pbs.org/wgbh/commandingheights/shared/pdf/int_paulvolcker.pdf, 9.

28. For the Fed's scramble to include all the banking innovations of the 1970s in the monetary aggregates, see Kenneth Kavajecz, "The Evolution of the Federal Reserve's Monetary Aggregates: A Timeline," research.stlouisfed.org.

29. Bartley, *The Seven Fat Years,* 44; interview with Alan Reynolds.

30. Arthur B. Laffer and Charles Kadlec, "The Monetary Crisis: A Classical Perspective," *Economic Study,* A. B. Laffer Associates, Nov. 12, 1979, 1.

31. Laffer and Kadlec, "The Monetary Crisis," 1.

32. Mundell, "The Dollar and the Policy Mix," 24.

33. Letters, Wanniski-Volcker, Aug. 23, Sept. 24, Oct. 9, 1979, Box 18, F "Washington Correspondence," JWP; "Support Mr. Volcker"; Bartley, *The Seven Fat Years,* 86.

34. News Release, Senator Bill Roth, Jan. 10, 1979, W304, F "Senate Bill," JKCP. See this source for the provisions of the bill in the following paragraph; "Congress Gets the Antitax Message."

35. "Canceling Votes with Rules," WSJ, Jan. 31, 1979.

36. "Canceling Votes with Rules."

37. Bruce Bartlett, "What Ever Happened to the Tax Revolt?" *National Review,* Dec. 7, 1979.

38. Lucas and Sargent, "After Keynesian Macroeconomics." Rudiger Dornbusch later spoke of "when

the new classical revolution cleaned house in the 1980s." Dornbusch, "Robert A. Mundell's Nobel Memorial Prize," 209.

39. See the various materials at the Nobel site on the work that brought Lucas the 1995 prize.

40. Martin Anderson, *Revolution,* 112.

41. James Tobin, "Stabilization Policy Ten Years After," *Brookings Papers on Economic Activity* (1980), no. 1, 19. Tobin reiterated these concerns as he won the Nobel. See his banquet speech, Dec. 10, 1981, nobelprize.org.

42. Arthur M. Okun, "Postwar Macroeconomic Performance," *The American Economy in Transition,* ed. Martin Feldstein (Chicago: University of Chicago, 1980), 162–63.

43. Jack F. Kemp, "Case for Economic Growth" G. Tsai & Co., Jun. 1, 1979, 4.

44. *The 1979 Joint Economic Report* (GPO), 3.

45. *1979 JEC Report,* 3; Roberts, *The Supply-Side Revolution,* 46–47.

46. Roberts, *The Supply-Side Revolution,* 41–42; Letter, Roberts-Wanniski, Apr. 8, 1980, Box 25, F "General Correspondence Received—1980," JWP.

47. *The 1980 JEC Report* (GPO).

48. "Forecasting the Supply-Side of the Economy," 15.

49. "Forecasting the Supply-Side of the Economy," 26, 31.

50. Eckstein's prepared statement considered the various permutations of tax cuts and spending and monetary policy scenarios, and under the best of them, given Kemp-Roth, long-term inflation was 8 percent (37).

51. "Forecasting the Supply-Side of the Economy," 24, 49.

52. Letter, Kemp to Ray Herman, *Buffalo Courier-Express,* May 5, 1980, W304, Black Binder tab "inflation-general," JKCP.

53. "The 'Prototype Wedge Model': A Tool for Supply-Side Economics," H. C. Wainwright & Co. Economics, Sept. 14, 1979, esp. 33ff.; "'The Prototype Wedge Model': A Tool for Supply-Side Economics," American Council for Capital Formation, W304, Black Binder, tab "econometrics," JKCP; "Walker Announces New Econometric Model in Speech Before Economic Club of Detroit," American Council for Capital Formation, Jan. 9, 1978, Box 75, F "American Council for Capital Formation on: Laffer Model," JRP. As the press release (which included a letter of support from Senator Russell Long) went on to say, certain kinds of tax cuts could increase government revenue, particularly those directed at business and capital formation, presumably the capital-gains tax among others. This projection was largely vindicated given the effects of the Steiger amendment in law after 1978.

54. Paul Craig Roberts, "The Breakdown of the Keynesian Model," in *The Supply-Side Solution,* eds. Bruce Bartlett and Timothy P. Roth (Chatham, NJ: Chatham House, 1983).

55. Roberts, "The Breakdown of the Keynesian Model," 83. As the New Growth Theory would indicate, what changed in the supply-side 1980s was not so much aggregate hours worked as dedication to their effectiveness.

Chapter 9: ERTA

1. Jack Kemp, *An American Renaissance: A Strategy for the 1980s* (New York: Harper & Row, 1979).

2. Rowland Evans and Robert Novak, *The Reagan Revolution* (New York: Dutton, 1981), 65–66.

3. Lou Cannon, *President Reagan: The Role of a Lifetime* (New York: Public Affairs, 2000), 47. For Kemp's margins, see the various *Almanacs of American Politics* (Washington, DC: National Journal).

4. Colacello, *Ronnie & Nancy,* 479–80; interview with Laffer; Bartley, "Jack Kemp's Intellectual Blitz," WSJ, Nov. 29, 1979, 24. Bartley was wrong about Wanniski's support of Kemp. Wanniski was pumping Donald Rumsfeld, his friend and constant correspondent since 1974, for vice president. See various letters by Wanniski, ca. Dec. 1979, Box 1, F "Correspondence Sent, Jun.–Dec. 19," JWP.

5. Anderson, *Revolution,* 114–21.

6. "Taxes," in *Reagan: In His Own Hand,* 274–77. The diction of Reagan's transcript is regularized here.

7. Evans and Novak, *The Reagan Revolution,* 69; Anderson, *Revolution,* 115–16.

8. John Mueller, "Supply-Side Economics: A Case Study in the Making of American Economic Policy," 12–15, W303, F "1984 Speeches for Me," JKCP; Evans and Novak, *The Reagan Revolution,* 62–76.

9. "Interview with Annelise Anderson," Ronald Reagan Oral History Project, Final Edited Transcript, Miller Center for Public Affairs, 20.

10. "An Interview with George Bush," WSJ, Feb. 19, 1980; "Interview with Annelise Anderson," 21; letter, George Bush–Wanniski, Apr. 17, 1981, Box 28, F "Washington Correspondence Received 1981," JWP. This letter says: "Now about the 'voo-doo,' that witch doctor left when our program contained spending cuts, regulatory relief and a sound monetary policy."

11. Alexander Cockburn and James Ridgeway, "Worlds in Collision: The Battle for Reagan's Mind," *Village Voice,* Apr. 7, 1980; Roberts, *The Supply-Side Revolution,* 31n15; interview with Laffer; Anderson, *Revolution,* 157–61; letter, Wanniski-Anderson, Aug. 13, 1980, Box 15, F "1980–1996," JWP.

12. Letter to the editor, *The Village Voice,* Apr. 28, 1980; letter, Wanniki-Laffer, Apr. 9, 1980, Box 1, F "JW, General Correspondence Sent," JWP.

13. Letter, Wanniski-Anderson, Aug. 13, 1980.

14. Bartley, *The Seven Fat Years,* 149–50. Warren Phillips (the Dow Jones CEO) concurred that Wanniski was leaving to pursue his own political objectives. Letter, Phillips-Wanniski, n.d. (ca. Aug. 1980), Box 25, F "Mail," JWP.

15. Letter, Roberts-Wanniski, Apr. 8, 1980; letter, Wanniski-Anderson, Aug. 13, 1980; letter, Wanniski–Kimba M. Wood, Box 15, F "1997–1979," JWP; Roberts, *The Supply-Side Revolution,* 30; Brooks, "Annals of Finance: The Supply-Side."

16. Anderson, *Revolution,* 170–74; members of the economic task forces may be found throughout DTR.

17. Feldstein, "Tax Incentives without Deficits," WSJ, Jul. 25, 1980; Roberts dissented from this article several weeks later on the same page in "Dawdling with Incentives," Aug. 7, 1980; Bruce Bartlett noted a raft of economists in support of Kemp-Roth, naming them in *Reaganomics,* 132.

18. Michael K. Evans, "The Reagan-Kemp Inflation Plan," Apr. 28, 1980, *Industry Week,* and "Balanced Budget? Don't Believe It: How Deficit Will Deepen," Jun. 23, 1980, *Industry Week;* Irving Kristol, "The Battle for Reagan's Soul," WSJ, May 16, 1980; Lewis Lehrman, "Stop the Battle for Reagan's Soul," WSJ, Jun. 16, 1980.

19. "Fact Sheet on . . . Ronald Reagan's Economic Program, released . . . Sept. 9, 1980," contained in "Report of the Task Force on Tax Policy," Box 185, F 2, "Transition Task Force on Tax Policy," DTR; Anderson, *Revolution,* 122–39.

20. Evans and Novak, "Platform Quarterback," Jul. 14, 1980.

21. *Budget of the United States Government: 1980,* 579.

22. Evans and Novak, *The Reagan Revolution,* 118–19.

23. Evans and Novak, *The Reagan Revolution,* 119–21; "Avoiding a GOP Economic Dunkirk," W404, F "Kudlow, Lawrence A., Economist/The New Economic Review," JKCP.

24. "Avoiding a GOP Economic Dunkirk," 2.

25. "Avoiding a GOP Economic Dunkirk," 7–8.

26. Evans and Novak, *The Reagan Revolution*, 112–13; "Avoiding a GOP Economic Dunkirk," 13–23.

27. "Avoiding a GOP Economic Dunkirk," 9–10, 18–19.

28. Evans and Novak, *The Reagan Revolution*, 122.

29. Evans and Novak, "Cabinet Choices—or Echoes?" Nov. 7; "What Simon Says," Nov. 14; "Transition Wars," Nov. 21; "An Old Gray Cabinet?" Nov. 24; "What Happened to Simon?" Dec. 1; and "The Sub-Cabinet May Be the Key," Dec. 15, 1980; interview with Martin Anderson.

30. "Statement of Mr. Donald T. Regan," Jul. 25, 1980, Box 241, F 7, p. 3; Bert Cox to John Kelly, "DTR on 'Supply Side Economics,'" Merrill Lynch Economics Inc., Interoffice, Dec. 17, 1980, Box 241, F 6, DTR.

31. Evans and Novak, "Whose Tax Cut and When?" Nov. 12, 1980; interviews with Martin Anderson and Allan H. Meltzer.

32. Evans and Novak, "The Sub-Cabinet May Be the Key" and *The Reagan Revolution*, 126; interview with Martin Anderson.

33. Evans and Novak, "Stockman's Wall Street Tour," Dec. 26, 1980, and *The Reagan Revolution*, 126–31.

34. Interviews with Alan Reynolds and Martin Anderson; see Roberts, *The Supply-Side Revolution*, for information about himself, Ture, and Entin in the administration.

35. Information in this and following paragraphs from interview with John Rutledge.

36. As an NBER study found, as late as 1975, financial assets were 10 percent greater than tangibles, down from a peak in 1967, with the growth trend strongly favoring tangibles. By 1980, tangibles had crossed the 50 percent mark, and among financials securities were the laggard and loans the leader. Raymond W. Goldsmith, *The National Balance Sheet of the United States, 1953–1980* (Chicago: University of Chicago, 1982), 23, 26, 200, 201.

37. George Carlin, *A Place for My Stuff!* (sound recording; Atlantic, 2001 [1981]).

38. The $11 trillion was the asset shift Rutledge identified within the United States alone. Global flows were additional. Rutledge, "Supply-Side Thermodynamics."

39. *GE 1978 Annual Report*, 18.

40. Interview with Rutledge; Alan Reynolds, "What Really Happened in 1981," *Independent Review* 5, no. 2 (Fall 2000), 277–78.

41. Bartley, *The Seven Fat Years*, 98–99.

42. Rutledge, "Supply-Side Thermodynamics," 51.

43. Bartley, *The Seven Fat Years*, 98.

44. Interviews with Annelise Anderson, Meltzer, and Rutledge; Stockman, *The Triumph of Politics: Why the Reagan Revolution Failed* (New York: Harper & Row, 1986), 96.

45. *Two Revolutions in Economic Policy*, 316. The inflation figures in this forecast, as in the Claremont-routed one, refer to the GNP deflator, not the CPI.

46. Interview with Rutledge.

47. Mundell, *International Economics* (New York: Macmillan, 1968), 236n4.

48. *Two Revolutions in Economic Policy*, 304–14.

49. Roberts, *The Supply-Side Revolution*, 110–12; *Economic Report of the President, 1980*, 94.

50. Stockman, *The Triumph of Politics*, 98–99.

51. Stockman, *The Triumph of Politics*, x; "Economic Program Working Lunch—Baseline Economic

NOTES

Scenario" (Feb. 13, 1981), Box 138, F 1, "Economic Recovery Program, Nov. 16, 1980–Feb. 17, 1981";
further documentation of Treasury's unsuccessful holding out for a supply-side forecast: letter,
Roberts-Regan, Jan. 2, 1981, Box 160, F 4, "Roberts, Craig 1981–1984"; "Memo to the Secretary from
Paul Craig Roberts," Jun. 3, 1981, and Steve Entin, "Memorandum for the Secretary: Who Made the
Scenario Rosy?" Oct. 5, 1982, Box 47, F 5 "Entin, Stephen Jul.–Oct. 1982," all DTR.

52. Interview with Annelise Anderson.

53. Roberts speculated on Stockman's motives in "'The Stockman Recession': A Reaganite's Account,"
Fortune, Feb. 22, 1982, 56–70.

54. Attachment to letter-to-colleagues, Jim Wright, Mar. 5, 1981, p. 4, Box CFOA83, F "Economic
Recovery Package [1 of 7]," Martin Anderson Files, RRL.

55. James Tobin, letter to the editor, WSJ, Jan. 20, 1981; JEC Staff Study, "A Simulation of the
Economic Effects of the President Reagan's Fiscal and Monetary Proposals, 1981–1984," 5, Box 138,
F 6, "Economic Recovery Program, Jun.–Sept. 1981," DTR; Heller, "Can We Afford the Costs of
Kemp-Roth?" WSJ, Feb. 10, 1981.

56. Roberts's account of the paralysis of those days is in "The Keynesian Attack on Mr. Reagan's Plan,"
WSJ, Mar. 19, 1981, and *The Supply-Side Revolution,* 106–10, 119–24. See also William A. Niskanen,
Reaganomics: An Insider's Account of the Policies and the People (New York: Oxford University Press, 1988),
73–74; and Evans and Novak, "Sidestepping the Supply-Siders," Feb. 20, 1981. George Gilder, *Wealth
and Poverty* (New York: Basic Books, 1981).

57. Murray L. Weidenbaum, "Ten Questions and Answers on the President's Economic Program,"
Statement Before the House Ways and Means Committee, Feb. 24, 1981, Box CFOA83, F "Economic
Recovery Package [1 of 7]," Martin Anderson Files, RRL.

58. Mundell has made the not entirely tasteful observation that *Taxi Driver* (1976) was the most significant movie in recent history, in that it motivated the gunman to shoot Reagan and thus spurred
support for the president's legislative program. Robert Mundell, "Acceptance of an Honorary Degree
from the University of Bologna," Sept. 2, 2006, www.robertmundell.net/pdf/AcceptanceSpeech_
BolognaUniversity.pdf.

59. Evans and Novak, "Supply-Side Breakthrough," including quotations, Mar. 18, 1981; "The Brown-
Rousselot-Roth Bill," in "Report of the Task Force on Tax Policy"; *Tax Aspects of the President's Economic
Program,* Part 1 (GPO, 1981), 452.

60. Evans and Novak, "Supply-Side Breakthrough."

61. Evans and Novak, "Triumph of the Tax Cut," Apr. 29, 1981, "Cutting Taxes Another Day," May 18,
1981, and "Tax Cuts: Will There Be a Compromise?" May 29, 1981. "Christmas tree" and "ornaments"
are the terms Stockman would apply to all the bills of that season, including the bipartisan tax bill.
The Triumph of Politics, 239–50.

62. Evans and Novak, "Triumph of the Tax Cut" and "Cutting Taxes Another Day"; Anderson, *Revolution,*
284–85. Reagan's philosophy of negotiation has become one of the keenest questions in Reagan scholarship. An essential entry is Thomas W. Evans, *The Education of Ronald Reagan: The General Electric Years and
the Untold Story of His Conversion to Conservatism* (New York: Columbia University Press, 2006).

63. Evans and Novak, "Taxes and Counterattacks," Jul. 3, 1981; Stockman, *The Triumph of Politics,*
124ff.; "John Maynard Domenici," WSJ, Apr. 16, 1981.

64. "The Bipartisan Tax Reduction Program Fact Sheet," Department of the Treasury News, Jun. 5,
1981, 2.

65. Evans and Novak, "Goodies—with a Message," Jul. 29, 1981, and "How the Bill Was Won," Jul. 31, 1981; Presidential Address to the Nation, Jul. 27, 1981, *The Public Papers of Ronald W. Reagan* (RRL).

66. Interview with Entin, for information in this and the following paragraphs; Roberts, *The Supply-Side Revolution,* 164; the photograph, C3241–20, "President Reagan Addresses the Nation from the Oval Office on Tax Reduction Legislation," 7/27/81, RRL.

67. Letter, William V. Roth–The President, Mar. 24, 1981, Box 138, F 4, DTR.

68. Evans and Novak, "Goodies—with a Message"; Ernest D. Fiore, *Analysis of the Economic Recovery Tax Act of 1981, Enacted August 13, 1981* (New York: Matthew Bender, 1981); Niskanen, *Reaganomics,* 74.

Chapter 10: "Now, Money"

1. Note, Wanniski-Anderson, Aug. 4, 1981, and encl., "Now, Money," Polyconomics, Inc., Aug. 5, 1981, Box CFOA 84, F "Gold Commission," Martin Anderson Files, RRL.

2. Wanniski, "Now, Money," 1.

3. For details of the industrial recession, see Hoerr, *And the Wolf Finally Came.*

4. See the oral histories of the Pittsburgh Steel Valley that compose the Papers of Steffi Domike 1946–94, University of Pittsburgh Archives Service Center, excerpted in Domike's *Crashin' Out: Hard Times in McKeesport* (self-published, 1983).

5. "Moody's Seasoned AAA Corporate Bond Yield," research.stlouisfed.org.

6. From Mar. 30 to Nov. 2, M1 was in the 420s at every interval. "M1 Money Stock," research.stlouisfed.org.

7. Details of the "September" or "Fall Offensive," Stockman, *The Triumph of Politics,* ch. 10, "The Morning After."

8. "Address to the Nation on the Program for Economic Recovery Sept. 24, 1981," *The Public Papers of Ronald W. Reagan.*

9. Letter, Regan-Stockman, Aug. 21, 1981, and encl., Box 160, F 1, "Office of Management and Budget, 1981," DTR; Roberts, "'The Stockman Recession,'" 58.

10. "Stockman's Comments," n.d. (ca. Oct. 1981), Box 10523, F "Economic Policy [Feb. 81–Dec. 81]," David Gergen Files, RRL.

11. Stein, "Government Plays the Tax Game with Loaded Dice."

12. "Secretary's Briefing Book: Budget Strategy Session," Oct. 29, 1981, tab C, Box 114, F2, "Budget Strategy Briefing Book 1981," DTR.

13. William Greider, "The Education of David Stockman," *Atlantic,* Dec. 1981, 27–53.

14. Greider, "The Education of David Stockman," 51.

15. Greider, "The Education of David Stockman," 48–49.

16. "Report of the Task Force on Tax Policy," 3.-1.

17. Entin to Regan: "The Brodhead Amendment to lower the top rate from 70 percent to 50 percent in one year was offered during the debate over ERTA by the . . . Democratic leadership in hopes of dissuading the bipartisan coalition from pressing for the third year and indexing." Memo, "Tax Cuts at Various Income Levels," Apr. 27, 1982, 4, Box 47, F 4, "Entin, Stephen, Feb.–Jun. 1982," DTR. One Democratic version from summer 1981 had the Brodhead provision phased in over two years. See "An Analysis of the Reagan Tax Cuts and the Democratic Alternative," Heritage Foundation Issue Bulletin, Jul. 13, 1981. *The Triumph of Politics,* chs. 1–9, details Stockman's chief concerns and activities, almost exclusively budgetary, through the passage of ERTA. The book is nearly silent about the 70–50

cut. When it does speak of it, it is in positive terms and at variance with the *Atlantic* statement: "The deal with the Boll Weevils hadn't seemed that expensive, and much of it consisted of surprisingly sound tax policy. One element of it called for reducing the top rate on investment income from 70 to 50 percent—immediately. That was even more supply side than Kemp-Roth" (248).

18. Stockman, *The Triumph of Politics*, Prologue, photograph 32; Evans and Novak, ". . . Chiding in the Capital," Nov. 18, 1981.

19. William Nordhaus, "Economic Affairs: Gold in the Year of the Quack," NYT, Oct. 4, 1981; John Rutledge, "Why Interest Rates Will Fall in 1982," WSJ, Dec. 14, 1981.

20. A compendium of Drexel's ads appeared in the WSJ, Sept. 15, 1982; Goldman Sachs Economic Research, "Financial Market Perspectives," Oct. 1981; Wriston's remarks, "Economic Advisory Board—Notes—Dec. 10, 1981," Box 162, F 9, "President's Economic Policy Advisory Board, Sept.–Dec. 1981," DTR.

21. Rutledge, "Supply-Side Thermodynamics."

22. PEPAB's roster, "White House Announcement on the Formation of the President's Economic Policy Advisory Board," Feb. 10, 1981, *The Public Papers of President Ronald W. Reagan.*

23. Laffer's remarks, notes, "PEPAB Meeting 3/18/82," 1, Box 162 F 10, "PEPAB 1982," DTR; PEPAB notes, Dec. 10, 1981, 3. The "secretary" was Regan. The typescript notes are from his own manuscript hand, possibly with help from an assistant; on evidence for deferrals, interview with Laffer.

24. Larry Lindsey explained the legal fiction of the completion of the 5–10–10 rate cuts in 1983 (as opposed to 1984) to CEA chair Martin Feldstein, memo (n.d., ca. Jan. 1983) re "Tax change due to 'third year of the tax cut' in 1983," Box OA 9810, F 6, "Memos to CEA Chairman From Larry Lindsey, Staffer," Martin S. Feldstein Files, RRL. See also "Federal Individual Income Tax Rates History," taxfoundation.org.

25. Regan's letters and attachments, Feb. 11, 1981, Box 162, F 8, "PEPAB Feb.–Jun. 1981," DTR. As it was, the 70 percent rate rarely applied because of the (lower) alternative minimum tax incurred by shelters, also explained to Feldstein by Lindsey in the "Tax change" memo.

26. "Interoffice memorandum, Bert Cox–Don Regan," Jan. 1, 1981, Box 173, F 11, "Tax General Jan.–Aug. 1981," DTR.

27. Interview with Laffer.

28. Friedman, Dec. 10, 1981, and Mar. 18, 1982, PEPAB notes.

29. Memo, Friedman to PEPAB, re "Interest rates and the budget," May 17, 1982, Box 162, F 10, DTR.

30. Laffer was deemed "most pessimistic," PEPAB notes, Mar. 18, 1982; on the consensus, see various documents in the same folder from Mar. 18 and May 20 (Box 162, F 10, DTR). In Reagan's diary after one of the PEPAB meetings: "Art Laffer dropped a grenade on his colleagues when he said we weren't going to solve the fiscal program until we returned to the convertibility of money for gold. I would like to have heard the discussion among those economists after I left" (Jun. 11, 1981). *The Reagan Diaries,* ed. Douglas Brinkley (New York: HarperCollins, 2007), 25.

31. PEPAB notes and memos, Dec. 10, 1981, and Mar. 18, 1982; memorandum, Stein–Martin Anderson, Aug. 18, 1981, Box 162, F 9, DTR; Evans and Novak, "Return of Dr. Pain," Mar. 12, 1982.

32. Lawrence A. Kudlow, "Memorandum for the Cabinet Council on Economic Advisors," May 17, 1982, re "Economic and Financial Update," ID #124734, BE004, WHORM: Subject File, RRL. This same document can be found across the files of the Washington players of 1982.

33. "Secretary's Briefing Book," tab D; Evans and Novak, "The Tax Grabbers," Dec. 14, 1981; memo, Roger B. Porter–Regan, re "The Cabinet Council on Economic Affairs and Macroeconomic Policy,"

Nov. 23, 1981, Box 161, F 7, "Personal Miscellany 1981–1984," DTR; Roberts, *The Supply-Side Revolution,* 197–212.

34. Roberts, "'The Stockman Recession,'" 56.

35. See the run of Evans and Novak columns from spring and summer 1982. "Truth in Taxing," NYT, Mar. 10, 1983.

36. The provisions of the bill are in the Matthew Bender Tax Staff, *The Tax Equity and Fiscal Responsibility Act of 1982* (New York: Matthew Bender, 1982); Bruce Bartlett, "A Taxing Experience: The Stars Are Aligning for a Tax Increase," *National Review Online,* Oct. 29, 2003.

37. The White House understood that Ture's resignation would strengthen the idea that Reagan was backing off his economic program, in violation of the priority his administration and campaign had placed on it dating back to Policy Memorandum No. 1. See letter, Regan–James A. Baker III, Jun. 17, 1982, amid other enclosures in ID #065407ff, FG012, WHORM: Subject File, RRL; Roberts's recounting of the congressional doings over TEFRA is given in ch. 7 of *The Supply-Side Revolution.* Niskanen noted that some of Kemp-Roth's staunchest supporters, such as Marjorie Holt, voted for TEFRA, which was of course signed by the president. *Reaganomics,* 79.

38. Letter, Bob Dole–the President, Jul. 28, 1982, Box 162 F 10, DTR. For Regan's defense of supply-side economics that summer, see untitled digest of Regan's congressional testimony, 17 (see the whole document for further examples of Regan's response to the TEFRA push), Box 161, F 7, DTR.

39. Author's interview with Entin; Niskanen, *Reaganomics,* 78; memorandum, Entin–Regan, re "Vacation Reading," section "Taxes—Was the Timing or the Structure Wrong?" Jul. 2, 1982, Box 47, F 5, DTR.

40. Entin, "Memorandum for the Secretary," re "Monetary Volatility . . ." and attachments, Jul. 2, 1982, Box 47, F 5, DTR; M1 went to $440 billion the first week of January 1982, 4 percent higher than the $425 billion average through early November. M1 did not subsequently leave the 440s until the third week in August, when it went higher. "M1 Money Stock," research.stlouisfed.org; Entin, "Memorandum for the Secretary," re "Computer Simulation of Original Policy vs. Actual" and attachments, Jul. 2, 1982, Box 47, F 5, DTR; Roberts, *The Supply-Side Revolution,* 116, 223, 292. Roberts also notes (116) that another monetary aggregate, M1B, was negative through November 1981.

41. The history of the commission was detailed shortly afterward by its executive director, Anna J. Schwartz, "Reflections on the Gold Commission Report," *Journal of Money, Credit, and Banking* 14, no. 4, part 1 (Nov. 1982), 538–51.

42. Evans and Novak, "Enemies of Gold," Aug. 5, 1981.

43. Lewis E. Lehrman, "The Case for the Gold Standard: Reflections on the Struggle for Financial Order," Morgan Stanley Investment Research, May 1981, 6–7.

44. Lehrman, "The Case for the Gold Standard," 1.

45. Lehrman, "The Case for the Gold Standard," 28.

46. Robert A. Mundell, "Gold Would Serve into the 21st Century," WSJ, Sept. 30, 1981; see also Mundell, "Gold at $10,000," NYT, Oct. 19, 1980; Jude Wanniski, "To Lower Interest Rates, Go Back to Gold," WP, Nov. 10, 1981; Reynolds's testimony occurred at public hearings, Nov. 13, 1981; Robert J. Samuelson, "Good as Gold," *National Journal,* Sept. 26, 1981, 1734.

47. *Report to the Congress of the Commission of the Role of Gold in the Domestic and International Monetary Systems* (Mar. 1982). The report included a dissenting minority report of Lehrman and Rep. Ron Paul.

48. Arthur B. Laffer Associates Economic Study, "Reinstatement of the Dollar: The Blueprint," Feb. 29, 1980.

49. Interview with Laffer.

50. Arthur Laffer and Charles W. Kadlec, "Has the Fed Already Put Itself on a Price Rule?" WSJ, Oct. 28, 1982.

51. Arthur B. Laffer and Charles W. Kadlec, "The Point of Linking the Dollar to Gold," WSJ, Oct. 13, 1981.

52. Mundell, "The Dollar and the Policy Mix," 24.

53. Lawrence A. Kudlow, "Memorandum for T-2/T-3," re "Disinflation and Economic Growth," Oct. 1, 1982, Box 10523, F "Economy [Jun. 1982–Oct. 1982] [1 of 2]," David Gergen Files, RRL. See also (about Mundell and Kudlow at the time) Larry Kudlow, "Reagan + Friedman + Keynes: We Need All the Help We Can Get," Oct. 24, 2008, www.nationalreview.com.

54. "A 'Pre-Williamsburg' International Monetary Conference," May 17, 1983, W304, F "The Republican Study Committee; Binder with the proceedings of 'A Pre-Williamsburg,'" JKCP.

55. "A 'Pre-Williamsburg,'" 31.

56. "A 'Pre-Williamsburg,'" 34. One thing the supply-siders never got was one of their own appointed as Fed chairman. There were some possibilities when Volcker's term elapsed. See Evans and Novak, "1 Monetarist, 1 Supply-Sider," Aug. 21, 1985, and "Backstage at the Fed," Mar. 17, 1986; Mundell, "A Reconsideration of the Twentieth Century," 332.

57. Mundell, "A Reconsideration of the Twentieth Century," 332.

58. Novak, "The Imperial Federal Reserve"; *Time*, Feb. 15, 1999.

Chapter 11: *Belle Époque*

1. Sustained depressions such as those following 1873 and 1893 sponsored nice growth. Measuring peak-to-trough, 1864–75, industrial production increased 3.1 percent yearly, a level the twentieth century aspired to trough-to-peak. After 1875, this statistic leapt prodigiously for seventeen years, 6.5 percent per annum through 1892. The 1893 panic peak-to-trough (1894) saw a decline of 15 percent; peak-to-peak, 1892–1913, the yearly increase was 4.0 percent. In contrast, the twentieth century had recessions at roughly the same periodicity, but they could be far worse. During 1929–45, there were two contractions, but they were so much greater, and the recoveries so much milder, that a technically rather variable period such as 1873–93 (or for that matter the Roaring '20s) saw far higher growth. "U.S. Industrial Production Index (1790–1915)," "Business Cycle Expansions and Contractions," www.nber. org. Some research has found acute unemployment in the 1890s (*Historical Statistics of the United States: Millennial Edition* [New York: Cambridge, 2008], 2–82). This represents an odd combination of both growth and unemployment at exceptionally high levels—or a productivity feat unique in history.

2. Mundell's chuckle may be seen in the Nobel address webcast.

3. The quotation is an attribution from its auditor, Austin Robinson, "John Maynard Keynes: Economist, Author, Statesman," *Economic Journal* 82, no. 326 (Jun. 1972), 541–42.

4. Interview with John Rutledge.

5. About Keynesianism, Lucas said in 1979: "I suppose that I, along with many others, was in on the kill in an intellectual sense, but I don't say this as any kind of boast, or even with much pleasure. It's just a fact." Although there was pleasure. Two pages later: "What happens now? In academic circles: total chaos. Everyone has his own theories, and since orthodoxy has no way of discriminating, all get a fair hearing. It's a great time to be a macroeconomist." Robert E. Lucas, "The Death of Keynes," in *Viewpoints on Supply-Side Economics*, 3, 5.

6. Bartley, *The Seven Fat Years*, 21.

7. Robert E. Lucas Jr., "Mortgages and Monetary Policy," WSJ, Sept. 9, 2007.

8. research.stlouisfed.org, AAA and DGS30.

9. As Mundell would note in the Nobel address, technically the 1980s policy mix was an adoption of a similar paper he had written in the early 1960s concerning fiscal and monetary policy in the context of flexible exchange rates. The control in the 1961 paper was, naturally, fixed rates; in the webcast, Mundell lamented the taxing of the prize; the Santa Colomba remark quoted in Wallace, "Ahead of His Time."

10. See the run of GE annual reports from the time; Carson quoted in the NYT obituary, Jan. 24, 2005.

11. *Westinghouse Electric Corporation 1993 Annual Report*. See this and other annual reports from the time for the faulty real estate plays undertaken by the company in the 1980s. For the Toshiba sale, see "Toshiba Completes Westinghouse Acquisition," Oct. 17, 2006, www.toshiba.co.jp/about/ir/en/news/20061017_2.htm.

12. See the *GE 1985 Annual Report* for the status of the company at mid-decade.

13. Michael Oreskes, "Jesse Jackson Enters Race for the Presidency," NYT, Sept. 8, 1987.

14. Michael C. Jensen, *A Theory of the Firm: Governance, Residual Claims, and Organizational Forms* (Cambridge, MA: Harvard University Press, 2003).

15. "Steelworkers Are Told Jobs May Be in Jeopardy," NYT, Aug. 6, 1986; 265,000 is the figure of Hoerr, *And the Wolf Finally Came*, 416, for 1975–86, surely most of it in the 1980s.

16. Len Boselovic, "U.S. Steel, USW Reach 'Historic Agreement'; 4-year Pact Has 'No Steps Back' as Industry Prospers," *Pittsburgh Post-Gazette*, Aug. 13, 2008.

17. Parker, *John Kenneth Galbraith: His Life, His Politics, His Economics* (New York: Farrar, Straus & Giroux, 2005), 436. Supply-siders discount criticism that inequality widens in the wake of tax cuts. They argue that the income of the rich and the number of poor swell after tax cuts for benign reasons. The income of the rich increases because of lesser penalties on realization (a point first made by Mellon); and poor immigrants numbering in the millions are attracted to the country when GDP growth surges. Alan Reynolds's response to the inequality criticism is provided in his *Income and Wealth* (Westport, CT: Greenwood, 2006).

18. The number of business establishments in the U.S. went static in the mid-1970s and increased only 10 percent between 1974 and 1982. With the seven fat years, this statistic went up by 35 percent. U.S. Bureau of the Census, *Statistical Abstract of the United States* 1985 (518) and 1994 (546).

19. Richard Vedder and Wendell Cox, *The Wal-Mart Revolution: How Big Box Stores Benefit Consumers, Workers, and the Economy* (Washington, DC: AEI, 2007); Roger Frock, *Changing How the World Does Business: FedEx's Incredible Journey to Success—The Inside Story* (San Francisco: Berrett-Kohler, 2006).

20. The Merriam-Webster dictionary dates "McJobs" from 1986.

21. Letter, Bartley–Michael Evans, Sept. 3, 1991, Box 74, F "Feldstein/Hauser/Etc.," RLB; Gary Robbins, Heritage Foundation, formerly of the Reagan Treasury Department, expressed a standard supply-side view in telling the author that he worries when the trade deficit declines, because that also means that the nation's capital imports decline. See also Ed Rubenstein, "More than McJobs," *National Review*, Aug. 31, 1992, 31.

22. An account of deregulation is Niskanen, *Reaganomics*, ch. 4; Weidenbaum, "Ten Questions and Answers on the President's Economic Program," 6; Laffer, "The Four Pillars of Reaganomics," Jan. 16,

2007, www.heritage.org, web memo #1311; defense increased by 8 percent per year 1980–90, with a nominal difference of $165 billion between fiscal 1990 and 1980; "off-budget" items (for Social Security) increased 1980–90 at 7.4 percent per year, increasing in nominal terms by $130 billion by 1990 compared to 1980; health expenditures increased by 8.5 percent per year, 1981–90, farm expenditures by the same rate 1980–88, and general government declined over the decade in nominal as well as real terms (historical tables, *Budget of the United States Government, 2009* [hereafter all historical budget figures are from this source]); "Historical Social Security Tax Rates [1]" at www.taxpolicycenter.org.

23. To the extent Treasury funded the double-digit era debt with coupon bonds (such as the long bond), it was relieved of having to pay the average 11 percent on accrued interest. If an investor wanted to devote the long-bond coupon to treasuries, the treasuries would have to be bought anew in the 1980s at higher prices. To the extent that Treasury issued zero-coupon debt, however, it had to pay the average 11 percent on both principal and accrued interest. William Niskanen (of the Reagan CEA) has argued that spending did slow 1979–89, exclusive of defense, and that the collapse of inflation that made real interest payments higher may have sufficed to cause the record deficits. See Niskanen, "A New Deal: The Reaganomics Record," Jun. 10, 2004, www.nationalreview.com.

24. This interpretation is outlined in Paul Craig Roberts, "Debt, Lies, and Inflation," *National Review,* Aug. 31, 1992, 31–35.

25. The Holt and Nunn amendments envisioned capping spending at 1 percent over inflation. The assumption was that spending caps of this variety plus tax cuts would certainly not be capable of accompanying yet higher inflation, such as that experienced in the three years after these amendments failed in Congress.

26. Twenty-year moving average database prepared by author from budget, CPI, and census tables; "Address to the Nation on the Federal Budget and Deficit Reduction," Apr. 24, 1985, *The Public Papers of Ronald W. Reagan.*

27. Series associated with PRIME, research.stlouisfed.org; the relationship between rates and inflationary expectations, interview with Meltzer.

28. *Economic Report of the President: 1983,* 17–28, 142–45; in this report, the Reagan CEA posted a real GDP growth goal for 1983–84 at 5 percent, whereas it came in at 12 percent; Martin Feldstein, Memorandum for the President, re "Tax Rates and Tax Revenue," Jan. 10, 1984, Box OA9815, F "Memos to the President (Eyes Only), Oct. 18, 1982–Jul. 15, 1984 [2 of 8]," Martin S. Feldstein Files, RRL; Niskanen, *Reaganomics,* 79–84.

29. Martin Feldstein, Memorandum for the President, re "Standby Tax," Aug. 3, 1983, Box OA9815, F "Memos to the President . . . [5 of 8]"; Memorandum for the President [on indexing], Mar. 1, 1983, F "Memos to the President . . . [6 of 8]," Martin S. Feldstein Files, RRL; Feldstein, "Tax Incentives without Deficits"; Donald T. Regan, Memorandum for Edwin L. Harper et al., re "Treasury Recommendations for CEA Chairman," Jul. 29, 1982, Box 161, F 9, "Personnel Miscellaneous Materials, 1981–1984," DTR.

30. See Larry Lindsey, *The Growth Experiment: How the New Tax Policy Is Transforming the U.S. Economy* (New York: Basic Books, 1990), as well as the Lindsey and Krugman files within the Martin S. Feldstein Files at the RRL; the citation for the Krugman memo is given below. One entry in the Krugman criticism: "Supply-side economics was a political doctrine from Day 1; it emerged in the pages of political magazines, not professional economics journals" (Paul Krugman, "The Tax-Cut Con," NYT, Sept. 14, 2003). This is untrue. From "Day 1," it emerged on the pages of the *IMF Staff*

Papers. To be more precise, it emerged with Mundell's presentation of a paper in 1958 to a Stanford faculty seminar, the attendees of which were a list of important scholars, including the editor of the *American Economic Review.* These scholars suggested specific revisions that resulted in the early academic versions of Mundell's theory of the policy mix as published in the *Quarterly Journal of Economics* and *Kyklos,* articles that antedated the *Staff Papers* piece. These articles were the ones that prompted Polak at the IMF to get Mundell to reiterate his views. This is not to mention the intensive scholarly discussion of Mundell's theory of the policy mix from 1961 to 1971, from Herbert Furth at the Fed to the Chicago seminars to the Bologna conference to the Princeton paper. Mundell, "Updating the Agenda for Monetary Reform," Dec. 5, 1997, www.robertmundell.net, and "On the History of the Mundell-Fleming Model."

31. Memorandum, Paul Krugman and Larry Summers, re "Inflation During the 1983 Recovery," Sept. 9, 1982, and attachment, Box 104, F "Supply-Side Nobel," RLB.

32. Nondefense spending increased 61.4 percent in 1981–89, whereas the GDP deflator plus population increased by 41.4 percent. Nondefense spending totaled $521 billion in 1981 and $840 billion in 1989. Had the 1981 figure increased by 41.4 percent, it would have been $736 billion in 1989, a difference of $104 billion. The deficit in 1989 was $153 billion. The $49 billion gap between these two numbers conceivably could have been closed by higher economic growth in 1981–89 on account of lower spending (an argument suggestive of Friedman and Barro) and would certainly have been closed by the early years of the peace dividend.

33. Stockman, *The Triumph of Politics,* 395–411.

34. *Statistical Abstract* 1986 (431); Stockman, *The Triumph of Politics,* ix–x.

35. GNPA, research.stlouisfed.org. Oddly, Stockman understated Rosy Scenario's reckoning of 1982–86 GNP by $500 billion.

36. Anderson, *Revolution,* 237.

37. Various *Statistical Abstracts;* the "decade" is the Reagan era, 1981–89.

38. Tom Wolfe, *The Bonfire of the Vanities* (New York: Farrar, Straus & Giroux, 1987), 59–60.

39. Wanniski, "The Mundell-Laffer Hypothesis," 51.

40. The chronicle of events leading up to the 1986 law is drawn from Jeffrey H. Birnbaum and Alan S. Murray, *Showdown at Gucci Gulch: Lawmakers, Lobbyists, and the Unlikely Triumph of Tax Reform* (New York: Vintage, 1988).

41. Evans and Novak, "Laffer's Political Curve," Dec. 17, 1985.

42. Interview with Entin; for Ture's view on the law that emerged see Norman B. Ture, "The Tax Reform Act of 1986: Revolution or Counterrevolution?" in *Assessing the Reagan Years,* ed. David Boaz (Washington, DC: Cato Institute, 1988); and "The Economic Fallout of the Tax Reform Act of 1986," Economic Policy Bulletin, IRET, Apr. 8, 1987.

43. Bartley, *The Seven Fat Years,* 157, xiv; Box 94, F "Charts/Statistical Background," RLB.

44. Bartley, *The Seven Fat Years,* 154.

45. Bartley, *The Seven Fat Years,* 276. The last chapter of Bartley's book is called "Another Belle Époque?"

46. An impressive attempt by a supply-side fellow traveler to speak to normative concerns is Irving Kristol, *Neoconservatism: The Autobiography of an Idea* (New York: Free Press, 1994).

47. See "The Age of the Avant-Garde," in Hilton Kramer, *The Age of the Avant-Garde* (New York: Farrar, Straus & Giroux, 1973).

Chapter 12: The World Over

1. Bartley's two chapters on the S&Ls, replete with "Reg Q" implications, are the source for the following chronicle of the S&L episode (*The Seven Fat Years*, 219–34, 257–70).

2. "The NBER's Recession Dating Procedure," www.nber.org/cycles/recessions_faq.html.

3. Charles S. Maier and Leon N. Lindberg, "Alternatives for Future Crises," in *The Politics of Inflation and Economic Stagnation*, eds. Lindberg and Maier (Washington, DC: Brookings, 1985), 587–88.

4. The article was originally a lecture in 1989. Robert E. Lucas, "Supply-Side Economics: An Analytical Review," *Oxford Economic Papers* 42, no. 2 (1990), 314.

5. Robert E. Lucas Jr., "Mortgages and Monetary Policy"; "Economic Scene; Deficit Finance and Inflation," Aug. 26, 1981, and "Economic Scene; Inconsistency in Fiscal Aims," Aug. 28, 1981, NYT.

6. Bush's CEA chair, Michael Boskin, was sympathetic to supply-side economics. See his *Reagan and the Economy: The Successes, Failures, and Unfinished Agenda* (San Francisco: Institute for Contemporary Studies, 1987).

7. Reynolds, "Supply-Side Economics after 30 Years."

8. The principal economic memoir of the Clinton presidency is Gene Sperling, *The Pro-Growth Progressive: An Economic Strategy for Shared Prosperity* (New York: Simon & Schuster, 2005).

9. "The 'Prototype Wedge Model,'" 33. Ture's views as of the first Reagan term are outlined in Norman B. Ture, "Supply-Side Economics and Public Policy," *Essays in Supply-Side Economics*, ed. David G. Raboy (Washington, DC: IRET, 1982); Roberts, *The Supply-Side Revolution*, 16. Laffer wrote of Kemp-Roth in 1981, "It is reasonable to conclude that each of the proposed reductions would, in terms of overall tax revenues, be self-financing in less than two years. . . . By the third year . . . it is likely that the net revenue gains from the plan's first installment would offset completely the revenue reductions attributable to the final 10 percent rate cut." Laffer went on to say that by overall revenues, he included those that accrued to state and local governments. In practice, of course, this vision was never put to the test. The first two tax cuts of the simulacrum of Kemp-Roth, ERTA, were not 10–10 but 5–10, and they were delayed until fiscal 1982. Moreover, the third 10 percent installment (as well as indexing) was under constant threat until the TEFRA fight was finally settled in September 1982. Laffer, "Government Exactions and Revenue Deficiencies," in *The Supply-Side Solution*, 137.

10. Tax receipts were 20 percent of GDP or higher, 1998–2000.

11. Edward C. Prescott, "Why Do Americans Work So Much More Than Europeans?" *Federal Reserve Bank of Minneapolis Quarterly Review* 28, no. 1 (Jul. 2004), 2–13. The supply-side verity drawn from these experiences is that people will work more if they can. They will not if they cannot. If people can, by working, keep a significant portion of their earnings, they will keep on working. This is the supply-side counterargument to those who argue that Western Europeans do not work because they are satisfied with their current standard of living. Supply-siders will be convinced only when Western European tax rates at the margin are low. In this case, nonwork will represent a real preference for leisure.

12. Alan Reynolds, "Tax Reform in Lithuania and Around the World," Dec. 5, 1997, www.freema.org.

13. David Smick, *The World Is Curved: Hidden Dangers to the Global Economy* (New York: Portfolio, 2008), 218. Also see Sperling, *The Pro-Growth Progressive*.

14. Paul Lewis, "Gold-Indexed Bond Is Costly for France," NYT, Jun. 30, 1980.

15. Wallace, "Ahead of His Time"; this section on Mundell's views regarding China derive from Mundell, "Reflections on the International Monetary System." A university in China is named in

Mundell's honor, the Mundell International University of Entrepreneurship, www.miue.edu.cn/
enAbout.asp?articleid=18.

16. These terms occurred in "A Reconsideration of the Twentieth Century."

17. Chiefly, "A Theory of Optimum Currency Areas," the ideas of which, as Mundell has noted, originally derived from his work on the incipient Mundell-Fleming model. Mundell, "On the History
of the Mundell-Fleming Model." On Mundell's responsibility for the euro, see Ronald McKinnon,
"Mundell, the Euro, and Optimum Currency Areas," May 22, 2000, www-econ.stanford.edu/faculty/
workp/swp00009.pdf.

18. Mundell's views on the creation of the euro may be sampled in "Should the Euro-Dollar Exchange
Rate Be Managed?"; for the 1969 comment, see ch. 4.

19. Mundell, "Should the Euro-Dollar Exchange Rate Be Managed?" 14.

20. Mundell's views regarding the DEY and the new role for gold may be sampled in the Nobel
address, "One World, One Money?" and "The International Monetary System in the 21st Century:
Could Gold Make a Comeback?" Mar. 12, 1997, www.robertmundell.net; and Wallace, "Ahead of His
Time."

21. Kyle Wingfield, "An Economist Who Matters," WSJ, Jun. 21, 2008.

22. Robert L. Bartley, "Permanent, Marginal, Immediate," Nov. 25, 2002, www.opinionjournal.com.

23. For Rutledge's current reflections, see www.rutledgeblog.com.

24. Sean Wilentz, *The Age of Reagan: A History, 1974–2008* (New York: HarperCollins, 2008), 525.
Professor Wilentz's colleague at Princeton, Daniel T. Rodgers, is preparing a history of social thought
in the 1980s that will give considerable treatment to supply-side economics. In his Mellon biography,
David Cannadine, in a comment cited earlier, indicated that the Roaring '20s foreshadowed supply-
side economics.

25. *A New Era of Responsibility: Renewing America's Promise* (OMB, 2010); the original Piketty-Saez paper,
since followed up with further research, is "Income Inequality in the United States, 1913–1998," *Quarterly
Journal of Economics* CXVIII, no. 1 (Feb. 2003), 1–39. Piketty and Saez found that income inequality rises
with tax cuts and falls with hikes, and argued that tax policy should be set so as to prefer equality.
The two economists picked low-hanging fruit. Of course the income gains of the rich inversely track
the marginal tax rate. The founding idea of modern accounting, as variously stated by such figures as
Mellon, Frank Knight, and Peter Drucker, is that profit is that portion of cash flow that one is satisfied
to submit to taxation. In high-tax and high-inflation times, the rich do things such as buy gold (whose
appreciation before sale is not subject to taxation), stake the gold as collateral for loans as it appreciates,
and take the interest deduction on the tax return. Thus the rich get richer but look poorer in such times.
In low-tax and low-inflation eras, these strategies are dropped in favor of purchasing financial assets (not
to say starting businesses) that inherently are more beneficial than tangibles to other members of the
economy, the point driven home by Ed Zschau in 1978. The extent to which Piketty and Saez note these
large effects is small, confined to examining whether income is bunched (or "kinked") near thresholds in
the rate code. They find that it is not kinked as goes the personal schedule. Yet as abundant research has
shown, it most certainly is kinked on the capital-gains side. At any rate, regarding inequality—not the
flawed concept of "income inequality"—Piketty and Saez have to construct a far more expansive database, one that fully accounts for the trillions in portfolio shifts (and the new immigration). Once this formidable task is accomplished, then proper conclusions can be drawn about the degree and malignancy
of inequality. As it is, the Piketty-Saez database includes fascinating elements, such as that the average

individual tax rate across income groups flattens with the progressivity of the rate code. They found that in 1960, when the average individual tax rate of the richest notionally would have been well north of 50 percent (the statutory rate was 91 percent), their average tax rate was 31 percent. Piketty and Saez, "How Progressive Is the U.S. Federal Tax System? A Historical and International Perspective," *Journal of Economic Perspectives* 21, no. 1 (Winter 2007), 11–12.

26. Kudlow, "Reagan+Friedman+Keynes."

27. Governor General of Canada, www.gg.ca/honours/search-recherche/honours-desc.asp?lang=e &TypeID=orc&id=6874.

28. www.medaloffreedom.com/RobertBartley.htm. An example of next-generation supply-side thinking concerning current affairs is John Tamny, "Henry Paulson to Supply-Side Economics: Drop Dead," Nov. 18, 2008, www.realclearmarkets.com.

29. Mellon: "Any man of energy and initiative in this country can get what he wants out of life. But when that initiative is crippled by legislation or by a tax system which denies him the right to receive a reasonable share of his earnings, then he will no longer exert himself and the country will be deprived of the energy on which its continued greatness depends." *Taxation,* 12.

SELECT BIBLIOGRAPHY

Bibliographical information for all published sources may be found in the notes. Primary sources are identified as follows:

Archives

Robert L. Bartley papers (Hoover Institution, Stanford University)
Lloyd M. Bentsen papers (Center for American History, University of Texas)
Steffi Domike papers (University of Pittsburgh)
J. Herbert Furth papers (University at Albany)
Jack Kemp congressional papers (University at Buffalo)
Ludwig von Mises papers (Grove City College)
Donald T. Regan papers (Library of Congress)
John Rousselot papers (University of Southern California)
William E. Simon papers (Lafayette College)
William A. Steiger papers (Wisconsin Historical Society)
Jude Wanniski papers (Hoover Institution)
Various collections in:
International Monetary Fund archives, Washington, DC
National Archives I and II
George Bush Presidential Library
Jimmy Carter Presidential Library
John F. Kennedy Presidential Library
Ronald Reagan Presidential Library

Interviews, Correspondence, and Conversations with the Author
Annelise Anderson
Martin Anderson
Edith Lillie Bartley
Jeffrey Bell
Stephen J. Entin
Arthur B. Laffer
Allan H. Meltzer
Robert A. Mundell
Robert D. Novak
Alan Reynolds
Gary Robbins
Paul Craig Roberts
John Rutledge
Michael Schuyler

Datasets
References in the text to these data categories are to the following sets:

GDP: "Current and 'real' GDP" and "Percent change from preceding period" tables, www. bea.gov
Aggregate yearly federal budgets: "Summary of Receipts, Outlays, and Surpluses or Deficits," raw data and as percentage of GDP, www.gpoaccess.gov
Labor force and unemployment: "Employment status of the civilian noninstitutional population, 1940 to date," www.bls.gov
Inflation: "Table Containing History of CPI-U.S. All Items Indexes and Annual Percent Changes from 1913 to Present," www.bls.gov
Population: "Historical National Population Estimates: July 1, 1900 to July 1, 1999," www. census.gov
Gold price: www.kitco.com/charts/historicalgold.html
Stocks: Yahoo! Finance and *The Dow Jones Averages,* 1885–1991 (Business One Urwin, 1991)
Income tax rates: www.taxfoundation.org/files/federalindividualratehistory-20080107.pdf
National accounts of countries other than the United States: National Accounts Statistics Portal, www.oecd.org
Various sets in the FRED database of the Federal Reserve: Dataset call numbers are given in the notes with "research.stlouisfed.org"

ACKNOWLEDGMENTS

Fikst, a word of appreciation for my graduate advisor, the late Donald Fleming, who was a prism through which one could see the true colors of intellectual history. Also from Harvard days, note should be made of Michael McCormick, the historian par excellence of our day; James Hankins; the late William E. Gienapp; and from the economics department, David S. Landes, Jeffrey G. Williamson, and Murray Milgate. This book truly began life in high school, during the first Reagan term, at Central Catholic in Pittsburgh, where on the forensics team I had to give speeches on supply-side economics. I should like to thank my excellent coaches, in particular Brother Robert Wilsbach, the dedicatee of this book.

I researched and wrote this book while a faculty member at Sam Houston State. This institution enabled the book in many ways, not least financially. As for individuals, I owe thanks to Tom Cox, Don Freeman, Nancy Zey, David Mayes, Delia Gallinaro, Jim Olson, and Jason Morgan.

Those who helped me plot the book, its findings, arguments, and strategy, are George H. Nash, Mark Molesky, John J. Miller, Alan Levy, John Rocha, Richard Gosselin, Michael Coulter, Paul Kengor, Gerald Russello, Brian Hooper, Ivan and Ron Domitrovic, and Tom Spence. I would like to express my appreciation.

Thanks are owed for the hospitality of Lynette and Bill Perkins and Anne and Max Lomax (in-laws all), Valerie Domitrovic, Manuel Figallo, and Anya Schmemann and Eric Lohr; and of sources Stephen J. Entin, Michael Schuyler, Alan Reynolds, and Arthur B. Laffer. I should like to thank all sources who gave of their time, memory, and personal collections. I should also point out that Bill Perkins helped me with statistical tasks and Lynette Perkins with congressional research.

Among the archivists, librarians, and associated staff who provided assistance, I wish to make special mention of Kelly Barton of the Reagan Library; Cassy Ammen of the Library of Congress; Robbie Moses of the Federal Reserve Bank of Dallas, Houston Branch; Premelia Isaac of the IMF; and Trinie Thai-Parker of the Harvard Law Library. I must also thank Kathleen Connolly and Robert Holzweiss for helping me gain access to sources. Grateful acknowledgment is made to Mrs. Robert L. Bartley, Martin Feldstein, and Mrs. Jude Wanniski for permission to reprint certain letters that appear in this book.

This book benefited from grants from the Earhart Foundation. I also wish to acknowledge the Faculty Research Council at Sam Houston State, Winston Elliott of the Center for the American Idea, Michael Gleba, and various peer reviewers, as well as the staff at ISI Books, including Jed Donahue, Jeremy Beer, Jennifer Connolly, and Rich Brake.

My wife, Jessica, helped with the book from start to finish. Many thanks to her. And to the little ones, a pat on the head.

Brian Domitrovic
The Woodlands, Texas

INDEX

T

"take a businessman to lunch" campaign, 71

Tamny, John, 295

taxation: academic economics and, 13; balanced budgets and, 82; bracket creep and, 37; Bush, George H. W., and, 280; business, 129–33; capital formation and, 10; capital-gains, 13, 158–59, 161–69; Congress and, 13; deficits and, 146; economic crisis of 2008–9 and, 24; fairness and, 12, 165, 180, 214, 225, 236; government spending and, 78; growth and, 36–37; inflation and, 37; investment and, 132; Keynesianism and, 15; loopholes and, 140, 184; neoclassical synthesis and, 128; progressive, 61, 94, 109, 132, 144, 145, 157, 184; property, 152–54; savings and, 138; Social Security, 157, 171; windfall profits, 183. *See also* tax code; tax cuts

Taxation: The People's Business (Mellon), 38

tax code, 13; bracket creep and, 13, 16, 150–52; indexing, 109, 124; inflation and, 13; loophole-closing and, 272, 273, 275; nominal vs. real income and, 4, 37; progressivity of, 150–52, 195. *See also* taxation; tax cuts

tax cuts: Bush, George H. W., and, 206–7, 225–26; Bush, George W., and, 289–91; Carter and, 14, 139–40; deficits and, 112–13, 122, 210; demand and, 126, 200, 222; Eisenhower and, 65; Ford and, 111; government revenue and, 112, 123, 129, 130, 227, 283–84; growth and, 95–96, 282–83; incentives and, 112, 123, 126; inflation and, 96; JEC and, 14, 194–97; Johnson, Lyndon B., and, 71, 78; Kennedy and, 13, 71, 93, 128–29; Keynesianism and, 96, 199–200; postwar prosperity and, 61; Reagan and, 14, 22, 205, 206–7, 209, 222, 224–28, 234–35, 236–42, 265, 272–75; Roaring '20s and, 36–38; sluggishness and, 88, 126; stagflation decade (1973–82) and, 10, 12–14, 15, 123–24, 209; supply-side economics and, 6, 15, 26, 36–37; unemployment and, 112; work and, 195. *See also* taxation; tax code

Tax Equity and Fiscal Responsibility Act (TEFRA), 242, 243–44, 248–49, 251, 273

"Taxes and a Two Santa Theory" (Wanniski), 136–37

taxflation, 152

"Tax Incentives without Deficits" (Feldstein), 209

tax rebates, 124, 143, 181, 191, 200, 289–90

Tax Reform Act of 1969, 131, 132

Tax Reform Act of 1986, 259, 265, 274–75, 280

tax shelters, 166

tax wedge, 156–58, 198

Taylor, John B., 285

TCI Communications, 280

Teague, Randal, 134–35

TEFRA. *See* Tax Equity and Fiscal Responsiblity Act

Tennessee Coal & Iron, 30

That '70s Show, 7

theoretical economics, 191

Theory of Justice, A (Rawls), 117

"Theory of Optimum Currency Areas, A" (Mundell), 64

three-martini lunches, 140, 161

Thurow, Lester, 7–8, 179

Time for Truth, A (Simon), 154, 158, 162, 216

Time magazine, 162

Tinbergen, Jan, 121

Tobin, James, 65, 67, 70, 75, 193, 218, 224

trade, 52, 285

trade deficit, 32, 262

Treasury, U.S., 19

"trickle-down economic theory," 144, 235–36

Triffin dilemma, 84, 86

Triumph of Politics, The (Stockman), 223, 267–68

Truman, Harry S., 61, 65, 67

Ture, Norman B., 127–33, 199, 223, 227, 241, 243, 294; business-tax cuts and, 129–33; econometric model of, 131, 138; JEC and, 13, 128; Kemp-Roth and, 145; Keynesianism and, 128, 130; Reagan monetary policy and, 242; Rosy Scenario and, 216; Savings and Investment Act (1974) and, 136, 138; Steiger amendment and, 164; supply-side economics, birth of, and, 13–14; Wanniski *Village Voice* interview and, 207

Turner Broadcasting, 280